Over Ruled

ALSO BY NEIL GORSUCH

A Republic, If You Can Keep It
The Future of Assisted Suicide and Euthanasia
The Law of Judicial Precedent (coauthor)

Over Ruled

THE HUMAN TOLL OF
TOO MUCH LAW

NEIL
GORSUCH

and *Janie Nitze*

HARPER

An Imprint of HarperCollins*Publishers*

HarperCollins books may be purchased for educational, business, or sales promotional use. For information, please email the Special Markets Department at SPsales@harpercollins.com.

FIRST EDITION

Library of Congress Cataloging-in-Publication Data

Names: Gorsuch, Neil M. (Neil McGill), 1967– author.
| Nitze, Janie, author.
Title: Over ruled: the human toll of too much law
/ Neil Gorsuch and Janie Nitze.
Description: New York: HarperCollins Publishers, 2024.
| Includes index.
Identifiers: LCCN 2024001360 (print) | LCCN 2024001361
(ebook) | ISBN 9780063238473 (hardcover) | ISBN
9780063238480 (ebook)
Subjects: LCSH: Effectiveness and validity of law. | Ignorance
(Law) | Jurisprudence.
Classification: LCC K260 .G69 2024 (print) | LCC K260 (ebook)
| DDC 340/.1150973—dc23/eng/20240209
LC record available at https://lccn.loc.gov/2024001360
LC ebook record available at https://lccn.loc.gov/2024001361

24 25 26 27 28 LBC 5 4 3 2 1

For the men and women whose experiences
are recounted in these pages

Those who won our independence by revolution were not cowards. . . . They did not exalt order at the cost of liberty.

—JUSTICE LOUIS BRANDEIS[1]

CONTENTS

PROLOGUE 1

CHAPTER 1   An Introduction to Law's Empire. 9

CHAPTER 2   Far from Home 33

CHAPTER 3   Bureaucracy Unbound 66

CHAPTER 4   The Sword of Damocles 101

CHAPTER 5   The Forgotten Americans. 132

CHAPTER 6   Three Freedoms 158

CHAPTER 7   The Spirit of Liberty. 185

EPILOGUE. 215

Acknowledgments 217

Notes and Sources 221

Information on Images 283

Index 285

Over Ruled

PROLOGUE

"But the plans were on display . . ."

"On display? I eventually had to go down to the cellar to find them."

"That's the display department."

"With a flashlight."

"Ah, well, the lights had probably gone."

"So had the stairs."

"But look, you found the notice, didn't you?"

"Yes," said Arthur, "yes I did. It was on display in the bottom of a locked filing cabinet stuck in a disused lavatory with a sign on the door saying 'Beware of the Leopard.'"

—DOUGLAS ADAMS,

THE HITCHHIKER'S GUIDE TO THE GALAXY[1]

ABOUT A YEAR BEFORE IT MOVED ACROSS THE STREET INTO ITS own building, the Supreme Court gathered, as it had for more than seven decades, to hear argument in the Old Senate Chamber in the Capitol.[2] There, the Justices confronted a curious problem.

"Is there any official or general publication of these executive orders?" Justice Louis Brandeis asked the government lawyer at the podium.

"Not that I know of," the attorney replied.

The hearing that day concerned charges against two firms.[3] Government officials alleged that the companies were busy producing more oil from fields in East Texas than a federal quota allowed.[4] The only trouble was, no one could seem to lay hands on the executive order containing the production quota that the companies had supposedly flouted.

"Well, is there any way by which one can find out what is in these executive orders when they are issued?" Justice Brandeis pressed.

"I think it would be rather difficult," the government's lawyer answered.

When his turn at the podium came, one of the companies' lawyers— a "portly, red-haired man with a frontier manner of speech"—told the Court that the only set of rules he had ever seen had come from "the hip pocket of an agent sent down to Texas from Washington." Newspapers reported that even the normally staid Chief Justice, Charles Evans Hughes, couldn't help but crack a smile. Other Justices enjoyed a "good-natured chuckle[]."[5]

Later, the government's lawyer told Congress that his staff had looked everywhere. They had found plenty of rules governing the companies' activities. But they "never did get to see . . . the original" of the executive order at issue. The best anyone could muster was a copy—and it turned out to contain no production quota at all.[6] As the Court wrote in its judgment, it appeared that the case against the two companies had proceeded through the entire judicial system "upon a false premise," a government mandate "which did not exist."[7]

I used to think the Hip Pocket Incident a quirk of history. For some time, federal officials had resisted publishing their regulations for the public, arguing that the government wasn't in the "newspaper business."[8] But Justice Brandeis had long urged more transparency, and some say his questions at oral argument sealed the deal. Soon afterward, the government agreed to create the Federal Register and publish there every new regulation it produced.[9]

Fast-forward about eighty years. I was sitting as a judge on the federal court of appeals in Denver. The federal government had accused a Kansas home health care company called Caring Hearts of fraud. Never a light matter, a charge like that threatened the firm's future. For six years, the dispute had dragged through layers of administrative and judicial appeals. By the time it made its way to my court, Caring Hearts had lost at just about every turn.

But as my colleagues and I dug into the case, we could hardly believe what we found. Yes, Caring Hearts' conduct defied *current* published regulations. But the company had followed the rules in place *at the time* it had acted. Quite simply, Caring Hearts stood accused of breaking rules that hadn't (yet) existed.[10] How could a case like that carry on so long and make it so far? It turned out that the government produces such a large number of rules, at such a furious clip and with such complexity, that even the agency officials responsible for them had become confused.

I think it was then that the idea for this book began to take hold in my mind. It wasn't just that I had experienced my own version of the Hip Pocket Incident. The episode led me to reflect on my years as a judge and realize that I had seen many—so many—cases where the sheer volume and complexity of our laws had swallowed up ordinary people.

The pattern repeated itself in the years that followed: the man who is told he can't see the evidence officials are relying on to reject his application for Social Security benefits; the veteran who is denied disability benefits because he fails to apply quickly enough for the taste of the Department of Veterans Affairs—even when Congress has instructed the agency to accept applications like his as timely; the immigrant who follows the law and is still refused a place in this country because the government changes the rules of the game on him retroactively.[11] I could go on.

As cases like these passed through my courtroom, I found myself thinking back to a speech that Václav Havel, the first democratically elected president of Czechoslovakia, gave as a dissident in 1965. More than two decades before the fall of the Berlin Wall, the country was in the grip of communist rule. At the time, Havel observed that Prague was experiencing a rash of peculiar events: window ledges from old buildings kept falling on people's heads. Often, after those episodes, some official or media personality would publish an article observing that, while *of course* no one wants plaster plummeting on people, readers should focus on the larger questions facing "mankind" and marvel at the "progress" of their society "as a whole." Articles like these, Havel remarked, were the product of the "purest of intentions." But they also contained a false logic, one that "separated thought" from any "contact with [the] reality" of ordinary people and their lived experiences.[12]

Prague's window ledges struck me as a kind of metaphor for what is happening in our law. Often enough, men and women going about their lives with no intention of harming anyone are getting thwacked, unexpectedly and at times haphazardly, by our multitude of statutes, rules, regulations, orders, edicts, and decrees. Almost always, one authority or another replies that, while the impact on the individual at hand is most regrettable, we should really focus on the greater good our laws and regulations seek to achieve and the collective social progress they promise. But what do events and responses like these tell us about the health of our legal edifice?

Before putting pen to paper, I wanted to spend some time studying in more depth the trends in our law that I saw playing out in individual cases. By the end of that process, I came to appreciate that—during just my lifetime—our laws and regulations have exploded in number and have come to reach much more deeply into our daily lives. None of our institutions is immune from this development. Law has proliferated at the local, state, and federal levels alike. Much of it now comes from administrative sources largely unresponsive to democratic elections. But plenty also comes directly from our elected representatives.

Others have written about the economic costs that come with so much law. But my thoughts ran in a different direction. Those who can afford sophisticated lawyers may be able to muddle through. Those armed with influential lobbyists may even find ways to make a profusion of laws work to their advantage. But what about everyday Americans and the rights promised to them in our Declaration of Independence, Constitution, and Bill of Rights? What happens to those people and their foundational freedoms—like the right to speak, pray, and gather freely—when our laws increasingly restrict what we may say, monitor what we do, and tell us how we may live? What does it mean for our nation's promise of equal treatment when our laws become so numerous and so complex that only an affluent or connected few can navigate their way? And what happens to our respect for law itself when the law no longer just reflects commonsense norms but includes unpredictable traps for the unwary?

Those are the questions I wanted to explore and invite you to consider as this book unfolds.

This isn't an academic work or a legal brief. It is a book of stories—stories about real people, their struggles to make their way in a world awash with law, and the toll on their lives and families. You will not meet lawyers in these pages but fishermen and foster parents, an Amish community, hair braiders and monks, even a magician and the polydactyl descendants of Ernest Hemingway's cat.

Why stories? Throughout history, we have understood one another and the world around us through stories. Our nation's founding values, too, center on individuals and their inalienable rights. Our government and laws were meant to serve them, not the other way around. So it is on individuals and their lived experiences that this books focuses.

No one group, party, or impulse is to blame for the recent changes in our nation's approach to law. These days, we are a people who trust one another less and less. When a problem arises, we are no longer so inclined to rely on individual judgment, our neighbors, or our local institutions to address it. When an idea becomes popular, it seems our first impulse is to embody it in law and debut the new rule on a national stage. In our eagerness for quick solutions, we sometimes look to agency officials rather than our elected representatives. Sometimes, too, we do so with a demand for strict conformity and little effort to accommodate different views. All of these impulses have become deeply entrenched in our society. And they are developments thoughtful people of any stripe can appreciate hold serious consequences for the integrity of our law and the lives and liberties of every American.

Really, the questions at the heart of this book are ancient ones. At the dawn of our republic, James Madison contemplated the dangers to individual freedom, equal treatment of persons, and respect for law itself when a nation's laws are allowed to grow "so voluminous that they cannot be read, or so incoherent that they cannot be understood . . . or undergo such incessant changes that no man, who knows what the law is today, can guess what it will be tomorrow."[13] But if the questions Madison posed are old ones, they also seem to me ones with special relevance to our times.

When sitting down to write this introductory note, I couldn't help but laugh when I had another encounter with the Leopard. The Hip Pocket Incident is legal lore. At the time, it made national headlines. I had heard and read about it, but I wanted to see the oral argument transcript for myself. That, however, turned out to be more difficult than I imagined. After striking out in a search of various online databases, I tried the Supreme Court Library. No luck there, either. Even the Library of Congress didn't have a copy.[14] In the end, I had to rely on old newspaper articles and accounts from scholars.[15]

Over the years, I have asked myself what I can do about the problem of too much law. Ultimately, I always circle back to the same answer: not much. As a judge, my job is to apply the law. I cannot change the underlying impulses that have led us as a society to regulate ever more, criminalize ever more, and punish ever more. The best I can do is share with you what I have seen from my unusual vantage in our legal system. Judges are not supposed to live "isolated from . . . society" but are encouraged to engage in a "wide range" of life's activities and "contribute to the law, the legal system, and the administration of justice."[16] Many of my colleagues and predecessors have done just that, offering thoughtful books on an array of topics.[17] It is in that same spirit I offer this book.

But if any real and lasting change is possible, it will not come from judges like me. It will come from people like those whose stories are recounted here. As Havel witnessed during the fall of communism, many of the deepest changes in his own society came from "unknown . . . people who wanted no more than to be able to live within the truth, to play the music they enjoyed, to sing songs that were relevant to their lives, and to live freely in dignity and partnership. . . . They had been given every opportunity to adapt to the status quo. . . . Yet they decided on a different course."[18]

—NMG

CHAPTER 1

AN INTRODUCTION
TO LAW'S EMPIRE

The worse the society, the more law there will be.
In Hell there will be nothing but law.

—GRANT GILMORE[1]

Fish and Felonies

EARLY ONE MORNING IN 2010, SANDRA YATES WAS DOING LAUNDRY when she noticed something alarming: seven agents in bullet-proof vests, hands primed on holstered guns, were approaching her bungalow on Anna Maria Island, Florida.

It turned out they were looking for her husband.

"He's out crabbing," she told them, mystified by what they could want with John, a 58-year-old commercial fisherman who had worked his way up from deckhand to captain of his own small crew.

Sandra and John met as teenagers thirty-six years earlier in Ohio. John's father owned a bait shop, and together father and son spent many weekends fishing on Lake Erie. As Sandra put it, John "more or less grew up on the water." The couple married, had a child, and moved to Florida to follow family and stake out a new life. John got a job doing what he loved most—fishing—while Sandra worked as a paralegal. By the time the agents showed up, the couple had lived in Florida for more than twenty-eight years.

John and Sandra Yates. © Thomas Bender, USA TODAY NETWORK

When Sandra called John to let him know that officers were looking for him, he was just as confused as she was. After all, he had a nearly blemish-free record as a fisherman, and he couldn't remember having done anything that might interest the authorities. John remained just as confused when he returned to shore and agents handcuffed and transported him two hours away to Fort Myers for booking.[2]

There, John finally learned the charges against him. Among other things, he stood accused of violating the federal Sarbanes-Oxley Act and faced a potential term of twenty years in prison.[3]

Now, you might be wondering: *Sarbanes-Oxley? Isn't that some sort of law about financial crimes?*

If you poke around the internet (as Sandra did late into the night in the days after her husband's arrest), you will find the Act described as designed "to help protect investors from fraudulent financial reporting by corporations." You will also learn that Congress adopted the law in the wake of a financial scandal that brought down the accounting firm Arthur Andersen.[4] Some say the firm engaged in a document-shredding frenzy after being tipped off about an impending federal investigation into work it had performed for its client Enron.[5]

All that might lead you to ask: *What does any of this have to do with a small-time fisherman?*

The story starts back in 2007. One day, while John was fishing in the Gulf of Mexico on his boat, the *Miss Katie*, a state wildlife agent (cross-deputized by federal authorities) came alongside.[6] As John tells it, the agent boarded the boat for a "safety inspection" and then asked John to open up the fish hold. The agent said he wanted to measure the fish—all two thousand pounds of them.[7]

After spending hours rummaging through the pile, the agent declared his verdict. According to his measurements (which John disputed), 72 red grouper were under the 20-inch harvesting minimum set by then-current federal regulations. True, even by the agent's count only three fish were under 19 inches and each was at least 18.75 inches. But all the same, 72 undersized fish it was. The agent ordered John to store the undersized fish in separate crates, issued a citation, and left.

After John returned to dock a few days later, the agent measured the fish again. This time, though, the agent found 69 undersized fish, not 72. What's more, the agent's measurements didn't *quite* match those he had taken days earlier while on board. From that and other evidence, the agent grew suspicious that the fish at the dock were not the same fish he had measured at sea. Still, nothing seemed to come of it. John didn't hear anything more from authorities for almost *three years*—that is, until the day armed agents showed up at his front door.[8]

At this point, you still might be wondering what any of this has to do with the Sarbanes-Oxley Act. As John learned after his arrest, however, that law is written in broad terms. The Act doesn't just make it unlawful to destroy financial records or documents "with the intent to impede, obstruct, or influence" a federal investigation. It also

The Miss Katie

prohibits the destruction of any other "tangible object" for the same purpose.[9] And, according to the government, John had done just that.

The government's theory ran this way: John or a member of his crew must have thrown overboard the undersized fish the agent had identified while out on the water. Before returning to port, the crew must have then replaced those fish with new (and still undersized?) substitutes from their remaining catch. On the basis of this theory, the government argued, John had destroyed "tangible objects"—yes, fish—with the intent of impeding a federal investigation.[10]

Needless to say, John saw things differently. On his account, it was hardly surprising that the agent's two sets of measurements didn't quite align. Fish expand and contract when they are moved into and out of cool storage and onto hot decks or docks. According to John, the agent wasn't exactly a fish-measuring expert, either; among other things, he didn't properly account for the lengthy lower jaws of red grouper.[11] To this day, John considers the government's theory that he threw undersized fish overboard only to replace them with new, still undersized substitutes "about the . . . stupidest thing I've ever heard."[12]

Stupid or not, it turned John and Sandra's lives upside down. On top of facing prison time, John lost his job—no one would hire a potential felon out of favor with the federal government. He was "contaminated," as Sandra put it. The couple lost their principal source of income and soon their house. They stopped taking family vacations with the grandchildren they were busy raising and tried to make ends meet by opening a used furniture store called Off the Hook Cortez. John refurbished furniture and Sandra painted it. To prepare for trial, Sandra stayed up late into the nights researching the law and corresponding with attorneys and agency officials.[13]

It was tough going. The family's ordeal was not made any easier knowing that federal officials had recently revised their regulations. When the agent boarded John's boat in 2007, the minimum harvesting size for red grouper was 20 inches. But by the time John was arrested three years later, that had changed. The new rule? Eighteen inches.[14] Even by the lights of the agent's measurements, not a single one of John's fish was that small.

Still, the government pressed ahead with its case. In time, prosecutors offered a plea deal that would allow John to plead guilty to an offense involving the forcible opposition of a federal officer.[15] But John saw no basis for that charge. He wanted to clear his name and insisted on standing trial.[16]

It did not go well. Over a year after his arrest and four years after the agent boarded his boat, a jury found John guilty of the Sarbanes-Oxley offense. At sentencing, the court imposed a term of thirty days behind bars (prosecutors had asked for closer to two years). The court also sentenced John to three years of supervised release, ordered him to submit a DNA sample, and subjected him to other restrictions.[17] The prosecution team issued a press release touting its victory.[18]

By now, it was nearing Christmas 2011. John sought permission to report to prison after the holiday so he could spend time with his grandchildren, eight and twelve years old at the time. The request was denied. So John sat in prison over Christmas. What's more, at age 59 he was required to wear an ankle bracelet marking him as an escape risk.

After serving his sentence, John was ready to move on. The case had consumed his family for too long. But Sandra was determined to appeal. She didn't want government officials to "do to someone else what they did to us." Even when their appeal failed, Sandra wouldn't give up.[19] She persuaded John and his attorney (today, a federal judge) to petition the Supreme Court to review John's Sarbanes-Oxley conviction.[20] It was the longest of long shots; the Supreme Court agrees to hear only about one percent of the thousands of petitions it receives every year.

But seven years after that agent boarded the *Miss Katie*, John and Sandra finally saw a sliver of hope: in 2014, the Court announced it would hear their case.

A Nation of Laws

More on the Yates family in a moment. First, let's take a step back. John's story might seem unusual. But is it? Maybe you've heard about the six-year-old who landed in court for picking a tulip by the bus stop. Or the ten-year-old whose lemonade stand was shuttered for lack of a business license.[21] Or any of the hundreds of similar cases.

The truth is, something's happening in our country. Law is multiplying, and its demands are growing increasingly complex. So much so that ordinary people are often caught by surprise, and even seasoned lawyers, lawmakers, and (yes) judges sometimes struggle to make sense of it all.

Of course, our country has always been a nation of laws. As children, we learn about the Boston Tea Party, how colonists objected to unjust laws announced by a capricious king, and how our founders chafed at taxation without representation. But we sometimes forget that they *demanded* laws, too. When the thirteen colonies decided to part ways with Great Britain, they detailed their reasons in the Declaration of Independence. High on the colonists' list of grievances was King George III's refusal to assent to laws proposed by colonial assemblies.

When it came time to draft the Constitution, the founders paid special attention to lawmaking as well. They didn't start by addressing how to elect our president or who would lead troops into battle in times of war. They didn't even begin by recording the freedoms we treasure, like the right to be free from unreasonable searches, to speak freely, and to live out our religious beliefs in peace. Instead, in Article I they established Congress and proceeded to outline detailed procedures for how our national government was to make new laws.

In some respects, nothing about this was a given. Plenty of other nations did (and continue to do) it differently. Like the colonies, France rebelled against a king in the eighteenth century. That country went through eight constitutions in the span of twenty-four years.[22] The first began with a list of certain guaranteed rights and then moved on to various matters of citizenship. Only in Title III did it discuss legislative powers. Today, Canada's constitution begins with a discussion of executive authority and doesn't get to the principal powers of lawmaking until about Article 91. Russia's constitution doesn't address lawmaking until around Article 94.[23]

In other respects, though, our Constitution's special focus on lawmaking makes perfect sense. As the political theorist Hannah Arendt put it, "law is much more important in this country than in any other," because Americans are "united neither by heritage, nor by memory, nor by soil, nor by language, nor by the same place of origin." What unites us is a common commitment to self-governance under a Constitution the people themselves have approved.[24] "In America," as Thomas Paine wrote, only "the law is king."[25]

We take rightful pride in this heritage. As middle school students, we learn about the founders' vision that a free and diverse people can rule themselves wisely through laws produced by their elected representatives. As adults, we cherish these ideals and count on them to order our daily lives.

So what happened? How did we get here? How can a fisherman face the possibility of decades in federal prison under the Sarbanes-Oxley Act for allegedly throwing fish overboard and not one of the dozens of officials who touches his case says, "Wait a minute . . ."? How can that same fisherman then go on to lose his livelihood—and lose his case before a jury and then again before an appellate court? And how can it be that his story isn't an uncommon one today?

A Paper Blizzard

At the most basic level, law in our country has simply exploded. Think Congress is wracked by an inability to pass legislation? Less than a hundred years ago, all of the federal government's statutes fit into a single volume. By 2018, the U.S. Code encompassed 54 volumes and approximately 60,000 pages.[26] Over the last decade, Congress has adopted an average of 344 new pieces of legislation each session. That amounts to about 2 to 3 million words of new federal law each year.[27] Even the length of bills has grown—from an average of around 2 pages in the 1950s to 18 today.[28]

That's just the average. Nowadays, it's not unusual for new laws to span hundreds of pages. The No Child Left Behind Act of 2001 ran more than 600 pages, the Patient Protection and Affordable Care Act almost a 1,000 pages, and the Consolidated Appropriations Act, 2021—which included a covid-19 relief package—more than 5,000 pages. About the last one, the chairman of the House Rules Committee quipped that "if we provide[d] everyone a paper copy we would have to destroy an entire forest." Buried in the bill were provisions for horse racing, approvals for two new Smithsonian museums, and a section on foreign policy regarding Tibet. By comparison, the landmark protections afforded by the Civil Rights Act of 1964 took just 28 pages to describe.[29]

Still, these figures from Congress only begin to tell the story. Federal agencies have been busy, too. They write new rules and regulations implementing or interpreting Congress's laws. Many bear the force of law. Thanks in part to Justice Brandeis, agencies now publish their proposals and final rules in the Federal Register; their final regulations can also be found in the Code of Federal Regulations. When the Federal Register started in 1936, it was 16 pages long.[30] In recent years, that publication has grown by an average of more than 70,000 pages *annually*.[31] Meanwhile, by 2021 the Code of Federal Regulations spanned about 200 volumes and over 188,000 pages. How long would it take a person to read all those federal regulations? Some estimate "over three years . . . And that is just the reading component. Not comprehension . . . not analysis."[32]

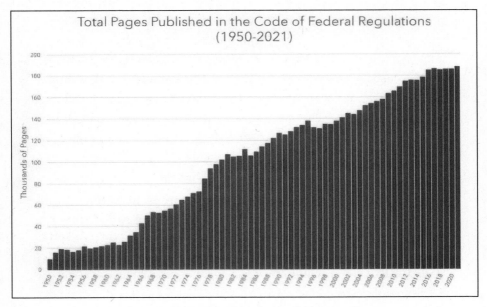

The growth of the Code of Federal Regulations, as published by the Regulatory Studies Center at the George Washington University.

Even these numbers do not come close to capturing all of the federal government's activity. Today, agencies don't just promulgate rules and regulations. They also issue informal "guidance documents" that ostensibly clarify existing regulations but in practice often "carry the implicit threat of enforcement action if the regulated public does not comply."[33] In a recent ten-year span, federal agencies issued about 13,000 guidance documents.[34] Sometimes these documents appear in the Federal Register; sometimes they don't. Sometimes they are hard to find anywhere. Echoing Justice Brandeis's efforts, a few years ago the Office of Management and Budget asked agencies to make their guidance available on searchable online databases.[35] But some agencies resisted. Why? By some accounts, they simply had no idea where to find all of their own guidance.[36] Ultimately, officials abandoned the idea.[37]

Judicial decisions, as well, contain vital information about how all our laws and rules operate. Today, most of these decisions can be found on searchable electronic databases, but some come with high subscription fees. If you can't afford those, you may have to consult a library. Good luck finding what you need there: reported federal decisions now fill more than 5,000 volumes. Each volume clocks in at about 1,000 pages, for a total of more than 5 million pages. Back in 1997, Thomas Baker, a law professor, found that "the cumulative output of all the lower federal courts . . . amounts to a small, but respectable library that, when stacked end-to-end, runs for one-and-one-half football fields."[38] One can only wonder how many football fields we're up to now.

As you might imagine, much in this growing mountain of law isn't exactly intuitive, either. Did you know that it's a federal crime to enter a post office while intoxicated? Or to sell a mattress without a warning label?[39] And if you're a budding pasta entrepreneur, take note: by federal decree, macaroni must have a diameter between .11 and .27 inches, while vermicelli must not be more than .06 inches in diameter. Both may contain egg whites—but those egg whites cannot constitute more than two percent of the weight of the finished product.[40]

If officials in the federal government have been busy, it's not as if their counterparts at the state and local levels have been idle. Virginia prohibits hunting a bear with the assistance of dogs on Sundays. In Massachusetts, be careful not to sing or render "The

Star-Spangled Banner" as "a part of a medley of any kind"—that can invite a fine.[41] Meanwhile, the New York City Administrative Code spans more than 30 titles and the Rules of the City of New York more than 50. In 2010, *The New York Times* reported on the regulatory hurdles associated with opening a new restaurant in the city. It found that an individual "may have to contend with as many as 11 city agencies, often with conflicting requirements; secure 30 permits, registrations, licenses and certificates; and pass 23 inspections." And that's not even counting what it takes to secure a liquor license.[42]

To appreciate the growth of our law at all levels, consider the lawyers. In recent years, the legal profession has proven a booming business. Between 1900 and 2021, the number of lawyers in the United States grew by 1,060 percent, while the population grew by about a third that rate.[43] Since 1950, the number of law schools approved by the American Bar Association has nearly doubled.[44] The number of lawyers in Washington, D.C.? That stands at about one for every 25 residents.[45] With the growth of law and its complexity, lawyers' salaries have had no trouble keeping pace, either. Equity partners in some of the nation's largest law firms now make on average over $1 million a year.[46] Demand for legal services is so great that most Americans today cannot afford even desperately needed legal advice.

Our legal institutions have become so complicated and so numerous that even federal agencies cannot agree on how many federal agencies exist. A few years ago, an opinion writer in *Forbes* pointed out that the Administrative Conference of the United States lists 115 agencies in the appendix of its *Sourcebook of United States Executive Agencies*. But the publication also cautions that there is "no authoritative list of government agencies." Meanwhile, the United States Government Manual and USA.gov maintain different and competing lists. And both of these lists differ in turn from the list kept by the Federal Register. That last publication appears to peg the number of federal agencies at 436.[47]

Reflecting on these developments sometimes reminds us of

Parkinson's Law. In 1955, a noted historian, C. Northcote Parkinson, posited that the number of employees in a bureaucracy rises by about five percent per year "irrespective of any variation in the amount of work (if any) to be done." He based his amusing theory on the example of the British Royal Navy, where the number of administrative officers on land grew by 78 percent between 1914 and 1928, during which time the number of navy ships *fell* by 67 percent and the number of navy officers and seamen dropped by 31 percent. It seemed to Parkinson that in the decades after World War I, Britain had created a "magnificent Navy on land." (He also quipped that the number of officials would have "multiplied at the same rate had there been no actual seamen at all.")[48]

Does Parkinson's Law reflect our own nation's experience? In the 1930s, the Empire State Building—the tallest in the world at the time—took 410 days to build. A decade later, the Pentagon took 16 months.[49] In the span of eight years during the Great Depression, President Franklin D. Roosevelt's Works Progress Administration built some 4,000 new schools, 130 new hospitals, 29,000 new bridges, and 150 new airfields; laid 9,000 miles of storm drains and sewer lines; paved or repaired 280,000 miles of roads; and planted 24 million trees.[50]

Compare those feats to more recent ones. In 2022, an opinion piece in *The Washington Post* observed that it had taken Georgia almost $1 billion and twenty-one years—fourteen of which were spent overcoming "regulatory hurdles"—to deepen a channel in the Savannah River for container ships. No great engineering challenge was involved; the five-foot deepening project "essentially . . . required moving muck." Meanwhile, raising the roadway on a New Jersey bridge took five years, 20,000 pages of paperwork, and 47 permits from 19 agencies—even though the project used existing foundations.[51] The same newspaper reported that in recent years Congress has required more than 4,000 annual reports from 466 federal agencies and nonprofits. According to lawyer and author Philip K. Howard, one report on the printing operations of the Social Security Administration took 95 employees more than four months to complete. Among other things, it dutifully informed Congress of the age and serial number of a forklift.[52]

"Show Me the Man and I'll Show You the Crime"

Not only have our laws grown rapidly in recent years. As we will see in coming chapters, so have the punishments they carry. You might think that federal criminal laws are reserved for the "worst of the worst"—individuals who have committed acts so egregious that they merit not just the attention of state authorities but federal authorities, and not just civil fines but potential prison time. But if that's your intuition, start by asking yourself this question: How many federal crimes do you think we have these days?

It turns out no one knows. Yes, every few years some enterprising academic or government official sets out to count them. They devote considerable resources and time (often years) to the task. But in the end, they come up short. Every time.

In 1982, the Department of Justice undertook what stands as maybe the most comprehensive count to date. A lawyer spent more than two years reading the U.S. Code—at that time, some 23,000 pages. At the end of it all, the best the lawyer could say was that there were *about* 3,000 federal crimes.[53]

A little more than forty years later, the U.S. Code is roughly *twice* the length it was in 1982, and contemporary guesses put the number of federal crimes north of 5,000.[54] As the American Bar Association has put it, "whatever the exact number of crimes that comprise today's 'federal criminal law,' it is clear that the amount of individual citizen behavior now potentially subject to federal criminal control has increased in astonishing proportions in the last few decades."[55]

Part of the reason no one can easily count the number of federal crimes is that our federal criminal code was "not planned; it just grew." We do not have any single place to which people can turn to discern what our criminal laws prohibit.[56] Sure, there's Title 18 of the U.S. Code, and it is labeled "Crimes and Criminal Procedure." But in truth, criminal laws are scattered here and there throughout various federal statutory titles and sections, the product of different pieces of legislation and different Congresses. Really, our federal criminal law is "a loose assemblage of . . . components that were built hastily to respond to perceptions of need and to perceptions of the popular will."[57]

That's not the only confounding factor, though. Many federal criminal statutes overlap entirely, are duplicative in part, or when juxtaposed raise perplexing questions about what they mean. Take fraud. We have a federal mail fraud law. We have a federal wire fraud law. We have federal bribery and illegal gratuities laws. We also have a federal law forbidding the deprivation of "honest services," though no one is exactly sure what it does (or does not) add to all those other laws about fraud. On top of all this, more new laws criminalizing fraud are proposed in just about every session of Congress.[58]

Once more, too, Congress's output represents just the tip of the iceberg. Our administrative agencies don't just turn out rules with civil penalties attached to them; every year, they generate more and more rules carrying criminal sanctions as well. How many? Here again, no one seems sure. But estimates suggest that *at least* 300,000 federal agency regulations carry criminal sanctions today.[59]

If you were to sit down to read through all of our criminal laws and regulations—or at least flip through them—you would find plenty of surprises, too. You would learn, for example, that it's a federal crime to "injure[]" a government-owned lamp in Washington, D.C., consult with a known pirate, or advertise wine by suggesting its intoxicating qualities.[60] The truth is, we now have so many federal criminal laws covering so many things that one scholar suggests that "there is no one in the United States over the age of 18 who cannot be indicted for some federal crime."

In case you think that's an exaggeration, he adds: "That is not an exaggeration."[61]

It's a state of affairs that sometimes makes it hard not to wonder how far we have left to travel to a world described by Lavrentiy Beria, the chief of Joseph Stalin's secret police, who was reputed to have bragged, "Show me the man and I'll show you the crime."[62] Don't think it can happen here? Ask John Yates, who was convicted for an offense he'd probably never heard of, one that few would have imagined would apply to him, and one that robbed him and his family of the life they cherished.

Beyond the Numbers

Numbers tell part of the story, but only a part. Today, the law touches our lives in very different ways than it once did.

In the past, the rules that governed what happened in our homes, families, houses of worship, and schools were found less in law than in custom or were left to private agreement and individual judgment. Even in the areas of life where law has long played a larger role, its character has changed. Once, most of our law came from local and state authorities; now, federal law often dominates.

Later chapters explore these developments in more depth, but consider just a few examples here. In the past, a seventh grader who traded burps for laughs in class might have been sent to the principal's office; these days, law enforcement officers may make an arrest. A 24-year-old who downloads academic articles that don't belong to him isn't just reprimanded; now we threaten him with decades in federal prison.[63] On a more systemic scale, consider that for most of our history, responsibility for educating the young and setting public school policy rested almost completely in the hands of parents and local and state officials. Until 1979, the federal government didn't even have a cabinet-level Department of Education. Now that federal agency employs more than 4,000 people and has an annual budget of almost $70 billion.[64] While it shares much of that money with states and local schools, often it does so on the condition that they comply with an ever-growing list of federal mandates.

What's responsible for the changing character of our law? No doubt it's a complicated story and we live in an increasingly complex world. But just consider what America looked like when Alexis de Tocqueville traveled the country in the 1830s. As the historian Niall Ferguson has observed, Tocqueville "marveled" at the way early Americans "preferred voluntary association to government regulation."[65] As Tocqueville himself recorded, "not only do they have commercial and industrial associations . . . they also have a thousand other kinds: religious, moral, grave, futile, very general and very particular, immense and very small; Americans use associations to give fetes, to found seminaries, to build inns, to raise churches, to distribute books . . . [and] create hospitals, prisons, schools." In short, Tocqueville concluded, "everywhere that, at the head of a new undertaking, you see the government in France and a great lord in England, count on it that you will perceive an association in the United States."[66]

These days, many of those old civic bonds are fraying. In his book *Bowling Alone*, Robert Putnam reports that "both civic engagement and organizational involvement experienced marked declines during the second half of the twentieth century." In recent years, those declines have "continued uninterrupted."[67] A few decades ago, over 70 percent of Americans were members of a church, synagogue, or mosque; today fewer than half are.[68] The Elks, a fraternal order that boasts six presidents among its past members, has "struggled" in recent years "with [a] massive decline in membership."[69] The Freemasons have shed three million from their ranks since the 1950s—a 75 percent decline.[70]

Accompanying this decline in civic association, we have experienced a profound decline in trust in one another.[71] We are less inclined to respect or even tolerate different ideas about how to live, raise children, and pray. Increasingly, studies show, we consider those who disagree with our own political views to be "immoral" or "unintelligent."[72] In one recent survey, roughly half of surveyed voters expressed the view that individuals who support "the other party" pose a "threat[] to the American way of life"; about 40 percent said the use of violence may be warranted to "prevent" those who hold competing views "from achieving their goals."[73] Rather than trust individuals to judge what is best for their own happiness, health, and safety, we have become increasingly comfortable doing what the "experts" tell us—and increasingly comfortable with forcing others to do the same.

It's hard not to wonder whether the explosion in our laws owes at least something to these developments. After all, when trust in individual judgment, civic institutions, and social norms fades, where else is there to look for answers but the law? Perhaps, too, the law does more, and does more at the national level, because it can. Communication across the continent has become a simple thing; so has the capacity to store and search vast amounts of information and monitor the movement of individuals—all of which allows authorities to direct and track compliance with their rules in ways that were unthinkable even a generation ago.

Whatever the combination of causes, one thing seems clear: If in this country law has always been king, its empire has never been so vast. More than ever, we turn to the law to address any problem we perceive. More than ever, we are inclined to use national authorities to dictate a single answer for the whole country. More than ever, we are willing to criminalize conduct with which we disagree. And more than ever, if elected officials seem slow to act, we look to other sources of authority to fill the void.

"Miracles Do Not Cluster"

The chapters that follow do not just trace these developments through the experiences of individuals like John and Sandra Yates. They also seek to explore what those developments mean for our lives and liberties and law itself. But as a starting point, consider what those who wrote our Declaration of Independence and Constitution hoped for us.

One of the "essential purposes" of our founding documents, Justice William O. Douglas famously wrote, "was to take government off the backs of people and keep it off."[74] Historically, after all, Americans have cherished the right to form their own opinions, speak their minds freely, and worship (or not) without interference. We like to think of our homes as our castles, generally subject to invasion only with a lawful warrant. We take for granted that authorities cannot deny our freedom without the assent of an impartial jury and due process.

At least initially, though, our Constitution didn't mention many of these rights. Most found expression only later in the Bill of Rights. James Madison was instrumental in drafting both documents, but he harbored some skepticism about the second.[75] As he saw it, any liberties the federal government might promise in a Bill of Rights would only ever be just that: promises.[76] The most effective way to protect our liberties, he thought, wasn't by recording them on a piece of parchment; it was by devising a system of government calculated to respect them. Madison's study of history persuaded him that people are naturally ambitious and tend to seek power over not just their own lives but others'. That fact of human nature, he believed, meant that the only sure way to protect our individual rights and keep government "off the backs of people" was to pit ambition against ambition.[77]

To that end, the Constitution Madison helped draft divided governmental powers both vertically and horizontally. It did so vertically by leaving most lawmaking power in the hands of state and local authorities—those closest to the people (a division of power called federalism). To the central government in a remote capital, the Constitution afforded only certain limited and enumerated powers: the power over foreign affairs, for example, along with other matters of a distinctly national character.

Within the central government, Madison proceeded to divide power horizontally among three branches (legislative, executive, and judicial). Even within those branches, he checked and balanced power still further, nowhere more notably than when it came to the business of making law. As our Constitution envisioned it, any new law would have to win approval from two separate houses of Congress, composed of elected representatives chosen by different constituencies for different terms. Even then, a new law would have to earn the president's approval or sufficient congressional support to override a veto.

Making new laws was *supposed to be* a difficult business. As Madison saw it, by requiring such a long and deliberative process, one so dependent on consensus, the Constitution would ensure that any new law—any new restriction on liberty—enjoys wide social acceptance, profits from an array of views during its consideration, and as a result proves more stable over time. The need for compromise inherent in the design also aimed to protect minorities by ensuring that their views and voices and votes couldn't be ignored. All in all, Madison hoped that the Constitution's arduous requirements would result in less law and more freedom—and at the same time yield laws that are wiser, more respected, and more apt to protect minority rights.[78]

For Madison, down any other path lay "calamitous" risks. In governments where lawmaking is easy, he wrote, laws can quickly become "so voluminous that they cannot be read, or so incoherent that they cannot be understood," and they may "undergo such incessant changes that no man, who knows what the law is today, can guess what it will be tomorrow." The "sagacious, the enterprising, and the moneyed few" may be able to anticipate, influence, and even profit from so much shifting law. But the "industrious . . . mass of the people" can do none of those things. In the end, law serves as an instrument only "for the *few*, not for the *many*," sapping and ultimately destroying confidence in public institutions and law itself.[79]

Madison hoped differently for our new nation. He sought to ensure that Americans would live under the rule of law but not be crushed by law. Today everyone likes to throw around the phrase "rule of law," but just what does it mean? Even political theorists debate the question. But there are a few important features that nearly everyone can agree on.

As Madison appreciated, the rule *of* law does not mean rule *by* law. Adolf Hitler blanketed Germany with laws—many secret and unknowable except to those in the Führer's favor.[80] The rule *of* law demands more than that. It requires laws that are publicly declared, knowable to ordinary people, and stable. So, for example, new legislation generally cannot be applied retroactively to past conduct you cannot alter but only to future behavior you can control. The rule of law is usually understood, as well, to guarantee that disputes about what a particular law means will be decided by independent and neutral judges, so that even the unpopular and most vulnerable among us receive a fair hearing.[81] These are just a few examples. In an effort to capture the spirit of the rule of law, the Oxford University philosopher Joseph Raz once called it a set of principles designed to "constrain the way government actions change and apply the law—to make sure, among other things, that they maintain stability and predictability, and thus enable individuals to find their way and to live well."[82]

Note that last condition. The rule of law is not an end unto itself. In large measure, it is about protecting individual liberty. "Observance of the rule of law," as Raz said, "is necessary if the law is to respect human dignity," a respect that "entails treating humans as persons capable of planning and plotting their future."[83] Or, to borrow from Hannah Arendt (who devoted much of her life to studying totalitarian regimes), the rule of law seeks to protect "man's power to begin something new out of his own resources."[84]

In drafting our Constitution, Madison and his colleagues prized these ideals. They sought to ensure that our laws would be publicly declared, knowable in advance, and the product of democratic processes. They sought to ensure that disputes about their meaning would be resolved by neutral judges. But perhaps most of all, they sought to keep "government off the backs of people" and allow them room to author their own lives. As Gouverneur Morris put it during the Constitutional Convention, "the excess rather than the deficiency of laws [is] to be dreaded" most.[85]

On any account, the framers' experiment was an uncertain one. At our nation's founding, the notion that a people could govern themselves wisely and with due respect for individual liberties was nothing short of revolutionary. Past republics had sometimes flickered brightly only to die away quickly. Few around the world thought that democratic majorities would long respect minority rights or avoid devolving into mob rule and tyranny. Daniel Webster once called our republic a miracle. But he also warned that "miracles do not cluster" and "that, which has happened but once in six thousand years" of human history "cannot be expected to happen often."[86] Even a quick look at our world today confirms his assessment. The conviction that people can both govern themselves and respect individual liberty along the way still faces skeptics and challenges.

Paradoxically, one of those challenges may lie in law itself. Some law is surely essential to our nation's flourishing and our well-being as individuals. But what happens to rule-of-law values when we demand ever more from the law, when we insist on national rules before considering local solutions, and when we permit unelected officials to make more of the rules that govern us? What happens to our individual freedoms and to our aspirations for equal treatment under law? And what happens to our respect for law itself? Put another way: What rule-of-law values do we place at risk when we forget *why* the Constitution left so much authority to state and local authorities, *why* it sought to make lawmaking so hard, and *why* it insisted on vesting the lawmaking function in elected representatives accountable to the people in regular elections? These, too, are questions explored in the pages that follow.

Meden Agan

John Yates was working in the couple's furniture shop in 2015 when he learned of the Supreme Court's decision.[87] By the margin of just a single vote, the Court had ruled in his favor. As the majority saw it, the Sarbanes-Oxley Act may prohibit the destruction of logbooks, spreadsheets, financial records, and other objects designed "to record or preserve information." But for all its expansiveness, the law does not reach red grouper thrown overboard.[88]

In a sense, it was a huge victory for the Yates family. The highest court in the land had overturned John's Sarbanes-Oxley conviction.

He and Sandra had won all the vindication our legal system can afford.

Still, you might forgive them for seeing things differently. The family's ordeal had lasted eight years. They had endured proceedings before three courts and thirteen different judges. "I feel good," John said after the Court's decision. "But you've got to look at it from my situation. I've already done the time. I've already paid the price. I lost a lot of wages because of this"—at least $600,000, he estimates. Really, as Sandra said, "we lost everything we had." John hasn't been back on a commercial fishing boat since his conviction. The couple now lives in a triple-wide trailer and depends on Social Security income and the extra jobs Sandra manages. Meanwhile, Sandra estimates that taxpayers spent as much as $11 million prosecuting the case.[89]

What happened to the federal officials who pursued John for all those years? After complaints emerged of "heavy-handed and unfair enforcement" against other fishermen like John, the inspector general of the Department of Commerce launched an internal investigation. His final report dryly concluded that the agency's enforcement officials had created a "highly-charged regulatory climate and dysfunctional relationship between [the agency] and the fishing industry."[90] But, he added, the investigation hadn't been easy. It seems that a key enforcement official had destroyed many of his files in the middle of the investigation. (An anonymous whistleblower described it as a "shredding party.") We can find no public record of criminal charges being brought against anyone for the destruction of *those* tangible objects. But when announcing the department's findings to Congress, the inspector general said the quiet part out loud: How do you think enforcement officials would have reacted "if a fishing company they were investigating had done the same thing"?[91]

In 2012, while John was appealing his case, Sandra pleaded her family's case to the government this way:

We are raising two grandchildren. We are simple people. The actions of these agents were damaging. These children have been affected also. Monies that would have been for them are gone. They have not even been afforded even family vacations any more. . . . Our lives are forever changed by this, and I don't believe these officers give a hoot who they hurt or why. [John] is a sixty-year-old man that has been beat up by these rogue agents. Jobs are tough enough to get when you are in your prime. He has been reduced to odd jobs. I am the primary provider for the family and I am old and tired, but I will not lie down or give up. We are meager people and don't want much, but fair and professional treatment should be mandatory for all.[92]

Sandra's words are powerful, maybe even more so when you consider the fact that there was nothing particularly unusual about John's case, at least from one point of view. Federal agency officials had adopted a regulation setting the minimum harvesting size at 20 inches, only later changing it to 18 inches. Another agency official concluded that John had 72 undersized fish on board and 69 at the dock. Meanwhile, Congress had adopted a broad law forbidding the intentional destruction of any "tangible object" in the face of a federal investigation. Without a doubt, a good argument could be made that John's alleged conduct violated this mix of statutory and regulatory rules.

From another perspective, though, Sandra and John's experiences, like those of many others you will meet in the coming pages, invite us to consider how well we are doing as a nation in our aspiration to live under the rule of law where ordinary people have room to grow, plan, and make their own way. Yes, our founders desperately wanted a nation of written laws. But from their study of history, they also appreciated the dangers that follow when lawmaking becomes too easy, when it is a task too far removed from the people, and when laws become too hard to find and too difficult to understand. The Roman emperor Caligula used to post his new laws on columns so high and in a hand so small that the people could not read them. The whole point was to ensure the people lived in fear—that most powerful of a tyrant's weapons. Our founders wanted no part of that for us. As much as they revered written laws, they also knew that when we turn to law to solve every problem and answer humanity's age-old debates about how we should live, raise our children, and pray, we invite a Leviathan into our lives.

The ancient Greeks famously lived by a philosophy of moderation; they inscribed the phrase *meden agan*—"nothing in excess"—on the temple of Apollo at Delphi.[93] It's a principle worth reflecting on when it comes to our laws today. If we don't, we may find ourselves asking a question Friedrich Hayek once posed: "Is there a greater tragedy imaginable than that, in our endeavor consciously to shape our future in accordance with high ideals, we should in fact unwittingly produce the very opposite of what we have been striving for?"[94]

CHAPTER 2

FAR FROM HOME

When a community loses its memory, its members no longer know one another. How can they know one another if they have forgotten or have never learned one another's stories? If they do not know one another's stories, how can they know whether or not to trust one another? People who do not trust one another do not help one another, and moreover they fear one another. And this is our predicament now.

—WENDELL BERRY[1]

The Copper Kings and the King of Poisons

SHAUN HOOLAHAN WORRIED ABOUT HIS DOG, BESSIE. FOR YEARS, grass struggled to grow on parts of his two-acre property: "I could fertilize, water, and just nothing would grow there." Bessie used to like lying in the bare spots. But then, Shaun said, she began developing tumors "all over her body," including a large lump on her chest. In time, a cancerous toe had to be amputated.[2] "That[] got me wondering," he said.[3]

Across town, Frank and Vickie Cooney wondered about Frank's cancer. "I noticed some strange things started happening because, well I got cancer in 2014 the first time, [and it] was prostate cancer, then a year later I [came] down with a brain tumor," Frank told a reporter. "And then . . . I [came] down with a very rare bone cancer." The couple worried about their children and grandchildren, too. "They were out in that dirt on four-wheelers, on bikes," Vickie said. "So what did it do to them?" Meanwhile, Rose Nyman explained that a "lot of my school chums have died of cancer, and I can't help but mak[e] the connection."[4]

What connected Shaun, the Cooneys, and Rose was that they all lived in or around perhaps the largest hazardous waste site in the country. The site, now administered under the federal Superfund cleanup program, covers a huge swath of southwestern Montana in and around the town of Butte.[5] In recent years, the region has suffered economically as well as environmentally. Over 20 percent of residents in the surrounding county live below the poverty line. Between 1970 and 2010, the population declined by about 40 percent.[6]

The reasons for the region's current challenges lie in the past. Many historians have recounted the tale, among them C. B. Glasscock, Michael P. Malone, and Michael Punke. When prospectors found gold near Butte in the 1860s, the town quickly sprung up as a

Butte, Montana, circa 1900

mining camp. Like other emerging communities in the West, it was rough country. One newspaperman from the East reported that "every businessman in Butte and every miner is a walking arsenal. He carries a brace or two of pistols in his belt and a Bowie knife in his right boot."[7] Meanwhile, some estimate that the harsh winters and hard living conditions meant about "ten percent would die between the months of September and May."[8]

By the 1870s, the easy gold was gone and interest turned to silver. To get at it, deep shafts had to be drilled and the ore milled and smelted.[9] Men of industry arrived with capital and technology, transforming Butte and the surrounding hills into a major industrial site. Two of those men, William A. Clark and Marcus Daly, became towering figures in the region. In time, Clark became one of the richest Americans of his day and built a 34-room home in Butte, today a bed-and-breakfast called the Copper King Mansion.[10] The old Corcoran Gallery in Washington, D.C., once housed his art collection.[11] But Clark's pursuits were not always so high-minded. To become a U.S. senator, he once bribed members of the Montana State Legislature; his son quipped that they'd "send the old man to the Senate or the poorhouse." Once uncovered, the scheme helped fuel the movement for the Seventeenth Amendment and the popular election of senators. Mark Twain found Clark "as rotten a human being as can be found anywhere under the flag; he is a shame to the American nation, and no one has helped to send him to the Senate who did not know that his proper place was the penitentiary, with a ball and chain on his legs."[12]

Marcus Daly, an Irish immigrant, was the one who first recognized the region's real industrial potential. One day in 1882, after bending down to pick up a rock blasted from a mining site, he turned to his lieutenant and exclaimed: "Mike, we've got it." What he'd got turned out to be "the largest deposit of copper sulphide that the world had ever seen." "No one knows it yet," Daly was rumored to have said, "but I have discovered the richest hill on earth."[13]

In the years following his discovery, new copper mines, mills, and smelters popped up with astonishing speed. The population of Butte soared. It doubled in the five years after Daly's arrival in 1876. Then it doubled again by 1886. In the nearby town of Anaconda, Daly built "the great . . . smelter," with a 585-foot smokestack that heralded Butte's emergence on the nation's stage.[14] It was the tallest brick smokestack in the world at the time, taller than the Washington Monument.[15] Immigrants flocked to the area, and at one point Daly's enterprises employed three-fourths of the wage earners in the state.[16]

Marcus Daly and William A. Clark

The copper industry brought theaters, a college, and wealth to the region. But the industry also brought something else. As one historian noted, "smoke from the smelters . . . was so thick that streetlamps were sometimes kept illuminated during the day. The smoke, loaded with arsenic, killed every tree—*every* tree—and every blade of grass. Except on St. Patrick's Day, Butte was devoid of green." In addition to arsenic, the smelter smoke contained sulfur. "Butte, literally, smelled like hell."[17] Another historian described cats that "licked the all-pervading grime from their whiskers and were poisoned by the arsenic it contained," as well as cattle that "graz[ed] on the withering grass [that] seemed literally to plate their teeth with copper."[18] As told at the time by the *Engineering and Mining Journal*, "the unfortunate traveler from South Butte traces his way not by land-marks, for these are utterly invisible, but by the hacking cough of his forerunner, who though a few feet away is completely veiled in smoke." In time, Butte earned a second nickname. It wasn't just the "richest hill on earth." It was also the "devil's throne."[19]

Still, "Butte could survive the second" nickname "because the first was proving true." By 1890, Montana produced 50 percent of the nation's copper, and soon the yearly output of metals was enough to load a freight train 20 miles long. Tunnels eventually stretched 900 miles, so long that it would take a motorist driving at 25 miles per hour more than 35 hours to pass through them all. "Anyone who knew about the West knew about Butte, fabled for its wealth, its toughness, its sinfulness, and its squalor."[20]

Miners in Butte, Montana

Butte copper didn't just make men rich and the region famous; it played a pivotal role in the nation's life. The site was considered so important to the country's efforts in World War I that troops commanded by then captain Omar Bradley were sent to guard it: copper meant bullets. Butte also supplied copper vital for the nation's growing web of telegraph and telephone wires. During World War II, the War Production Board put copper into an "urgency rating band"; only the Manhattan Project ranked higher. The site's copper was so important that men who otherwise would have been drafted were left to work the mines as "soldiers of production."[21]

But in the decades after the war, Butte's fortunes changed. As one historian related, "Butte, Montana—two oceans and half a continent removed from the rest of the world—would be buffeted by global forces long before those forces became 'globalization.'" Copper mines opened in other regions of the world while the demand for copper dropped. By the end of September 1980, the giant Anaconda smelter closed for good.[22] Many local residents—nearly a quarter of whom lost their jobs—remember it as the "most bitter of all days." "They cut off our primary reason for existence," an Anaconda optometrist said, adding that his patients approached him "with great embarrassment about stretching out payments for their medical bills."[23]

During its run, the region produced billions of dollars' worth of copper, silver, gold, and other minerals.[24] But by 1907, the Anaconda smelter also emitted more than 30 tons of arsenic, lead, and other contaminants *every day*—a figure that rose to 578 tons by 1978.[25] As *The Washington Post* recounted, "in the aftermath of the closure, as the region reeled economically and socially, residents began to piece together how much environmental damage the mega-mining had done." Residents talked of "mass sickness and death" among livestock, of yards and fields that wouldn't grow grass.[26] C.B. McNeil, a fourth-generation Anacondan, spoke of how his boat tipped over in the Clark Fork River while he was duck hunting. The river ran red from Butte's mine waste. "My watch stopped the next day," he recounted. "I took it into the jeweler and returned a few days later to pick it up. He simply shook his head and said, 'C.B., the insides of your watch have been dissolved.'"[27]

Today, the Anaconda smokestack stands alone in a state park as a reminder of the region's past. It can be viewed only from a distance—the soil around it remains too hazardous for public access.[28] The smelter itself was demolished; only the pleas of locals saved the stack.[29]

In the 1980s, the federal Environmental Protection Agency (EPA) designated an enormous area around Butte—about 300 square miles—as a Superfund site. The agency began working with the current corporate owner, Atlantic Richfield Company, on a cleanup plan.[30] It was a daunting task. About 20,000 acres of soil were "severely impacted by airborne emissions and millions of gallons of ground water were polluted," posing "well documented risks to human health and the environment."[31] Nearly forty years of cleanup work followed. Finally, in 2016, Atlantic Richfield announced that it had just about finished work on private landowners' properties. The company estimated that it had spent about $450 million.[32]

So why, after all that cleanup work, was Shaun Hoolahan still worried about his dog, Bessie, lying in his yard? Much of the answer has to do with how much arsenic remained in the soil. As early as 2000 BC, the Greek word *arsenikos* (meaning "potent") was "synonymous with poison," and for ages the substance has been known as the "king of poisons" as well as the "poison of kings."[33] Some suspect the toxin was responsible for the murder of Alexander the Great (others dispute the theory). Rumor even has it that the arsenic poisoning of husbands in early-nineteenth-century England was so much in vogue that the House of Lords tried to pass a law forbidding women from purchasing the substance.[34]

Today, some states set residential cleanup levels for arsenic at .04 parts per million (ppm). Certain localities consider 100 ppm too toxic even for their landfills. Yet in Montana, the EPA required Atlantic Richfield to remove only 18 inches of soil in residential yards—and the company had to do so only if soil samples reflected an arsenic level exceeding 250 ppm. For pasturelands—pretty much everything beyond residential yards—the EPA set the cleanup threshold at 1,000 ppm.[35] When asked how the agency chose its thresholds, an EPA representative said the numbers fell within what officials considered an "acceptable cancer risk range."[36]

Try talking about "acceptable cancer risk ranges" to the parents of

The Anaconda smokestack, 1939

the children at Tammy Peters's day care. Her playground wasn't eligible for cleanup under the EPA's plan because the "weighted average" of arsenic samples in her yard was below 250 ppm—even though some samples registered over 290 ppm, well above what many localities consider too dangerous even for their landfills. Many other Butte-area residents found themselves facing a similar dilemma.

Unhappy with the EPA's directives and the company's progress, a group of about one hundred landowners banded together in 2008 and sued Atlantic Richfield in state court. They didn't seek to interfere with the EPA's cleanup efforts under federal law; they simply sought to invoke state laws that they thought entitled them to a more thorough cleanup. They estimated that cleaning up their land properly, in accordance with state law, would cost Atlantic Richfield about $58 million.[37] As one resident, Serge Myers, put it, "We just want[ed] our yard to be clean and healthy for our kids."[38] You might have thought that the group's lawsuit had a shot, too. After all, it rested on well-recognized common-law theories. And historically, states have generally enjoyed primacy when it comes to regulating their own lands.

The company saw things differently. It argued that the federal government had superintended all of its work and that Montana law was powerless to alter or supplement the company's obligations. After almost a decade of legal wrangling, the Montana Supreme Court rejected the company's defense. The court explained that the landowners weren't seeking to "stop, delay, or change the work EPA is doing"; they were "simply asking to be allowed to present their own plan to restore their own private property to a jury of twelve Montanans who will then assess the merits of that plan." The Montana Supreme Court ordered the case, finally, to go to trial.[39]

Yet before the case could proceed to trial, Atlantic Richfield asked the U.S. Supreme Court to consider the matter. And in 2019, the Court agreed to do just that. In the proceedings that followed, the federal government joined sides with Atlantic Richfield. Together, they argued that federal law prohibits owners of land containing hazardous substances from pursuing additional "remedial action" without the EPA's permission—permission the landowners in Montana hadn't received. So landowners within almost 300 square miles in Montana could do *nothing* to clean their own properties—even at their own expense—without federal approval.

In the end, a majority of the Court agreed with Atlantic Richfield and the government's reading of the Superfund statute.[40] A federal law designed to promote the cleanup of contaminated lands thus became a tool to thwart a local effort to do just that. While I disagreed with the Court's reading of the law, from one point of view the result is entirely understandable. After all, a law empowering a single central authority to direct cleanups is certainly efficient. And if there had been strong national standards in the first place, perhaps the rampant pollution in and around Butte could have been avoided.

But what about Shaun Hoolahan, Rose Nyman, the Cooneys, and so many others like them? What are they supposed to do when faraway officials say that they and their children face an "acceptable cancer risk range" even as they watch family members, friends, and neighbors felled by disease? Surely the national government has an important role to play when it comes to protecting our environment. Surely, too, scholars can debate exactly where in this field local power must give way to federal. But does any of that mean states and individuals should be quite as powerless as Montana and its citizens are when it comes to cleaning up their own land? Historically, states have enjoyed considerable leeway to administer their own laws regulating their own lands through their own courts—and landowners have been free to clean up their properties at their own expense.[41] But not anymore within a vast region of Montana. Now the federal government alone may decide what "remedial actions" can be undertaken. "There is stuff that you cannot do because they stop you," Serge Myers, a 74-year-old great-grandfather explained. "If we had the money, my yard would be cleaned. I really would clean it. I'd hire the best they had to clean the darn thing."[42]

Where "Neither Landmarks nor People" Look Familiar

What happened to landowners in Butte now happens to many people. To resolve their rights, individuals often cannot appeal to state elected officials or to a local jury of their peers. Instead, they must seek answers from someone in a far-off capital. Someone who might not know much about local conditions and values, who might not have as much invested in local communities, who might not be meaningfully accountable to them. If law has grown dramatically in recent decades, one of its most notable features is *how* it has grown. So many questions once resolved by state and local institutions—if not by family, friends, and neighbors—must now find their way to Washington, D.C., for answers.

Just how far has this transfer of authority gone? Pietro Nivola of the Brookings Institution once put it this way: Federal law is now "effectively in the business of determining the minimum drinking age for motorists, setting the licensing standards for bus and truck drivers, [and] judging the fitness tests for recruits of local police or fire departments." It's in the business, too, of "enforcing child support payments, establishing quality standards for nursing homes, removing lead paint from housing units, replacing water coolers in school buildings, [and] ordering sidewalk ramps on streets." And it is in the business of "influencing how much a community has to pay its snowplow operators or transit workers, planning athletic facilities at state universities, . . . telling localities in some states how to deploy firefighters at burning buildings, [and] instructing passengers where to stand when riding municipal buses."[43]

The federal government's growing influence manifests itself in some pretty concrete ways. Next door to the White House sits the Eisenhower Executive Office Building. It once housed the State, Navy, and War Departments. Now the same building cannot even hold all of the White House staff. The State Department has moved to its own colossal building spanning 2.5 million square feet.[44] Meanwhile, the headquarters of the Department of Defense is so vast that even top officials keep getting lost in it. There's a George C. Marshall story and a Dick Cheney story. General Dwight D. Eisenhower, Supreme Commander of the Allied Expeditionary Force in Europe in World War II, got lost in it, too: "I walked and walked, encountering neither landmarks nor people who looked familiar."[45]

Entire books have been written about the demise of federalism. For some, its death knell sounded during the Civil War. For others, the story is about changes that took place in the first half of the twentieth century: the introduction of the federal income tax, the New Deal, two world wars, and expansive interpretations of the Constitution's Commerce Clause by the Supreme Court. But whatever happened long ago, more recent developments must be accounted for as well.

The fact is, much of the federal government's expansion has taken place in just the last few decades. Between 1960 and 1979 alone, federal per capita domestic spending rose by 73 percent (adjusting for inflation).[46] During the same period, civilian employment in the executive branch (excluding the Post Office and Department of Defense) rose by more than 50 percent. Today, some peg the civilian federal workforce at just under three million, almost all of whom work in the executive branch.[47] But even that number fails to account for the swell of federal contractors, which by 2015 numbered over three million. The use of contractors has grown so much that some scholars call them a "shadow" federal workforce. Perhaps unsurprisingly, the numbers are so vast that, in 2018, one federal agency reportedly didn't "have a clear understanding of how many contractors" it employed. Perhaps more surprisingly, according to one researcher, that same agency has used contractors to figure out whether it should use contractors.[48]

Here's another way to think about the shift to Washington. Studies suggest that between 1969 and 2022, expenditures on lobbying the federal government increased from $40 million (in today's dollars) to around $4 *billion*.[49] Meanwhile, in 1969, 5 of the richest 25 counties and independent cities in the United States were located in the Washington, D.C., area; more recently, that number doubled to 10.[50]

Since the 1960s, Congress has adopted an array of new laws and created a host of powerful new federal agencies to address matters previously left to the states.[51] Here is just a partial list of some of the seminal legislation enacted during just two decades, the 1960s and 1970s. Many of these laws are now household names, many do vital work, and in many ways it is difficult to imagine life without some of them. Yet all are relatively new additions to our social order.

Age Discrimination in Employment Act of 1967

Clean Air Act

Clean Water Act

Consumer Credit Protection Act

Consumer Product Safety Act

Controlled Substances Act

Department of Transportation Act

Economic Opportunity Act of 1964

Economic Stabilization Act of 1970

Elementary and Secondary Education Act of 1965

Employee Retirement Income Security Act of 1974

Endangered Species Act of 1973

Environmental Quality Improvement Act of 1970

Equal Credit Opportunity Act

Equal Employment Opportunity Act of 1972

Family Educational Rights and Privacy Act

Federal-Aid Highway Act of 1968

Federal Election Campaign Act of 1971

Federal Land Policy and Management Act of 1976

Food and Agriculture Act of 1965

Food Stamp Act of 1964

Gun Control Act of 1968

Higher Education Act of 1965

Housing and Urban Development Act of 1965

Land and Water Conservation Act of 1965

Marine Mammal Protection Act of 1972

National Environmental Policy Act of 1969

National Forest Management Act of 1976

Occupational Safety and Health Act of 1970

Older Americans Act of 1965

Organized Crime Control Act of 1970

Safe Drinking Water Act

Wild and Scenic Rivers Act

Wilderness Act

Not only has the federal government in relatively recent times assumed vast new responsibilities over matters once left to the states, it also has taken the reins in less direct ways. Unlike state and local governments, which operate with limited funds, the federal government enjoys the power to print money. And federal authorities have increasingly employed this power as a lever over state policy. Between 1960 and 2019, federal grants to states rose from $70 billion (adjusted for inflation) to over $700 billion—a 900 percent increase.[52] Regularly, these grants come with strings attached that require states to enforce all manner of federal rules and standards.

These days, for example, the federal government employs this tool to require states to do everything from setting a minimum drinking age to forcing medical workers to get a covid-19 vaccination on pain of losing their jobs.[53] In Wisconsin, close to half of the Department of Children and Families's employees are reportedly paid with federal funds; at the state's Department of Health Services, a fifth receive their paychecks thanks to federal dollars. Overall, state governments now receive on average about a third of their revenue from the federal government—subject to Washington's terms and conditions.[54] As former Nebraska Governor Ben Nelson remarked of his time in office: "I honestly wondered if I was actually elected Governor or just branch manager of the State of Nebraska for the federal government."[55]

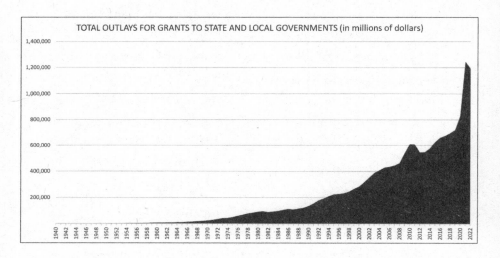

TOTAL OUTLAYS FOR GRANTS TO STATE AND LOCAL GOVERNMENTS (in millions of dollars)

Total outlays for grants to state and local governments have soared since the 1970s.[56]

"If Just One of Them Had Run for Sheriff"

When the founders set about drafting the Constitution, they faced the question of where to allocate power. Few wanted to concentrate all authority at the national level; they feared a single, centralized power would pose too much of a risk to individual liberty and invite the sort of tyranny they experienced at the hands of the English Crown. Yet the colonists' first attempt at a governing structure, the Articles of Confederation, left the federal government too weak to competently discharge even basic national duties like raising an army or conducting foreign affairs. How to strike the right balance between central and local control became one of the principal tasks of the Constitutional Convention.

Ultimately, the framers "split the atom of sovereignty" between national and state governments.[57] The federal government received more and clearer authority to raise armies, regulate interstate commerce, and conduct foreign affairs. But even under the new Constitution, the framers envisioned a national government with only "few and defined" authorities; it was state governments that would enjoy "numerous and indefinite" powers.[58]

That structure wasn't chosen to protect states for their own sake. It was a key part of Madison's project to diffuse power among competing institutions and in that way make intrusions on individual freedoms more difficult. Federalism serves other ends, too. As Tocqueville put it, "every central government worships uniformity: uniformity relieves it from inquiry into an infinity of details."[59] But in a large nation of immigrants of different ethnicities and religions and with different ways of life, details matter. Federalism provides a way for us to mediate our differences and live together in peace. Those in Massachusetts may choose to live under very different rules than those in Wyoming. From many, federalism allows us to become one: *e pluribus unum*.

Federalism offers still other benefits. It respects the fact that those closest to a problem often have the best sense of how to resolve it. Officials in Washington may have studied arsenic's toxic qualities, but maybe people in Montana appreciate the problem in ways those without arsenic in their backyards cannot. Even for seemingly national problems, federalism can serve a vital role: it allows different states to try different solutions, creating a marketplace of ideas from which the nation as a whole may learn. As Justice Louis Brandeis wrote, "it is one of the happy incidents of the federal system that a single courageous state may, if its citizens choose, serve as a laboratory; and try novel social and economic experiments without risk to the rest of the country."[60]

Of course, anything useful can be abused, and federalism is no exception. The cry of "states' rights" was used to justify slavery and Jim Crow laws and to defy federal civil rights legislation. Madison may not have had those problems in mind, but from the start he worried that, without a strong federal check, majorities in comparatively homogeneous states could more easily abuse the liberties of minorities.[61] The competition that federalism invites among states can also lead to a regulatory race to the bottom. And this diffusion of power can generate inefficiencies when businesses and individuals who work across state lines are forced to comply with an array of different rules.

Still, the link between federalism and freedom has animated human thinking for a long time. "Roman cities . . . enjoyed particular autonomy from central control," and "the great Italian, Dutch, and Hanseatic cities of the early modern period enjoyed wide-ranging self-government and, in some cases, functioned as independent states."[62] The Roman Catholic Church has long embraced the idea of "subsidiarity" as well, "the principle that a central authority should have a subsidiary function, performing only those tasks which cannot be performed effectively at a more intermediate or local level."[63] Indeed, in 1931, as totalitarianism was gaining ground in Europe, Pope Pius XI reaffirmed that it was "an injustice and at the same time a grave evil and disturbance of right order to assign to a greater and higher association what lesser and subordinate organizations can do."[64]

Circling back to more recent times, think about the covid-19 pandemic. The federal Occupational Safety and Health Administration—an agency previously concerned with workplace safety standards—asserted the authority to issue a mandate requiring some 84 million Americans to mask and test at their own expense or take newly developed vaccines rushed to market in something called Operation Warp Speed.[65] Meanwhile, the Centers for Disease Control and Prevention, a federal agency charged with disease prevention, got into the business of managing local landlord-tenant relations.[66] Both moves represented novel expansions of federal power into areas previously left to individual choice or local law.

Put to one side the wisdom, legality, and politics of the agencies' moves; consider them only from a federalism perspective. A vaccination mandate might be issued at different levels of governing bodies. It could be imposed by a parent, a private business, a school board, or a town. It could be imposed by state authorities or the federal government. As you move up the hierarchy of power and widen the affected community, different costs and benefits accrue. The lower you go, the more variances in opinions and values can be accounted for. Different individuals may have different convictions about what they will put into their bodies. They may form different judgments about the sufficiency of data to support the efficacy and safety of novel technologies. Different areas may be populated by people of different religious beliefs that may affect their thoughts about the vaccines on offer. Those who live in rural and sparsely populated places may reach different judgments about the necessity of vaccination than those who live in cities and dense neighborhoods.

By contrast, when decision-making is consolidated in agencies in Washington, D.C., it becomes harder to account for all these differences. To be sure, a centralized decision promises a quick and efficient response. That may be a vital benefit when it comes to a disease that knows no state lines. But centralization is not costless, either—to our ability to tolerate and accommodate different views, to experiment with and learn from different approaches, to the promise of self-government and individual liberty. Some researchers have suggested, for example, that the different approaches toward mask mandates taken in states such as Florida and California provided critical data about the mandates' efficacy on the spread of the virus, as well as their impact on the mental health and development of children and other vulnerable populations.[67]

Federalism often reminds us of a passage in *The Best and the Brightest*, David Halberstam's book about President John F. Kennedy's administration and the Vietnam War. "Among those dazzled by the Administration team," Halberstam wrote, was Vice President Lyndon

Johnson. After attending his first cabinet meeting, Johnson visited U.S. House Speaker Sam Rayburn and told him "with great enthusiasm how extraordinary" the new team was, "each brighter than the next." Reportedly, Rayburn responded, "Well, Lyndon, you may be right and they may be every bit as intelligent as you say, but I'd feel a whole lot better about them if just one of them had run for sheriff once." Halberstam later called it his favorite story in the book, "for it underlines . . . the difference between intelligence and wisdom, between the abstract quickness and verbal fluency which the team exuded, and the true wisdom, which is the product of hard-won, often bitter experience."[68]

Perhaps the story also underlines the different virtues our federal and local governments can offer. Maybe there's some data supporting agency officials when they talk of "acceptable cancer risk ranges" from the safety of their offices in Washington, D.C. But maybe, too, ordinary people in Montana have a wisdom born of experience that we should not be so quick to ignore.

"Rights Are Built, Not Born"

Ever heard the phrase "from Kalamazoo to Timbuktu"—or the old song bearing the same title—and wonder where Kalamazoo is located? A city of about 75,000, it sits in southwestern Michigan. Kalamazoo was once a prosperous place, a hub of agriculture, papermaking plants, and pharmaceutical development. But then an all-too-familiar story played out: plants closed and the region shed jobs. According to recent data, about a quarter of the population falls below the poverty line, and about 70 percent of the city's students qualify for free or reduced-price lunch.[69] Like others in towns across the country that have faced a similar plight, officials in Kalamazoo began scrambling for ideas to improve the city's future. "We flirted with every fad," reported one local economist. "The whole history of all the recent trends in economic development is right here," he told a reporter, pointing to a ten-page list of the 64 revitalization efforts undertaken between 1997 and 2004. "We've done everything."[70]

Then something happened: individuals stepped up. In 2005, the city partnered with anonymous donors to create the Kalamazoo Promise for children attending public schools. Under the Promise, students who finish high school receive money to attend any public college in the state; how much depends on how long they've been in the district's school system. Children who have attended since kindergarten have their entire tuition covered; those who have been in the district's system since the sixth grade get 80 percent coverage.[71] The Promise doesn't depend on income, disciplinary history, or really much of anything at all. The Promise may be, as *The New York Times* put it, "the most inclusive, most generous scholarship program in America." When the scholarship was announced over the loudspeakers in one high school, students broke out in tears. "It seemed unreal," one student reported. "Before the announcement, a lot of my classmates weren't going to go to college. Afterward, everyone applied." A father of three recalled that the day the Promise was announced, "the kids were up celebrating until 2 or 3 in the morning."[72]

Recent recipients of the Kalamazoo Promise scholarship

The program has proven to be life-changing. As of 2019, it's paid out about $117 million and has sent some 7,000 students to college. The program has had another effect, too: it has given a "significant economic boost" to the city. Only one year after the Promise was introduced, the school district's enrollment jumped by 10 percent, and the Promise's administrator reported receiving "calls daily from families interested in moving into the district." New teachers were hired, facilities were upgraded, and high school test grades improved. Home sales jumped by 6 percent in a year. Inspired by the program's success, donors established similar programs in communities across the country.[73]

Why tell this story? Here is a local response—a vision by ordinary individuals—tailored to a local problem, an experiment that came to serve as a model for other communities facing similar challenges. Truly, Kalamazoo served as a laboratory of democracy. Our history is replete with similar examples. Many towns, counties, and states granted women the right to vote long before the ratification of the Nineteenth Amendment.[74] The territory of Wyoming, the first to allow women the right to vote, went so far as to refuse to enter the Union without women's suffrage. "We will remain out of the Union one hundred years rather than come in without the women," its legislature fired off to Congress when asked to rescind women's voting rights as a condition of statehood.[75] Minimum-wage laws and child labor laws were also adopted at the local level before being embraced nationally.[76] New York State helped start the movement in this country to end debtors' prisons. Georgia led the nation in lowering the voting age to 18.[77]

Sure, the federal government can experiment, too, and we certainly have plenty of examples of it changing its mind (especially on high-profile issues when political parties swap control). But it's often hard, not to mention risky, to engage in trial-and-error experiments on a national scale. Dozens of permutations of a policy solution can be run across towns and states at any given time. States and municipalities also have a limited ability to borrow—"They are ultimately restrained by the willingness of their citizens to be taxed"—and may be quicker to abandon unsuccessful policy experiments. By contrast, when one side wins at the federal level, there is often no place left to explore other ideas or room to tolerate different views. Federal standards can ossify, too. As James L. Buckley, a former senator and federal appellate judge, put it, "once a federal law and its attendant regulations are in place, they are very difficult to change. This is so because of the laborious processes that bring them into being and because even the worst of them are apt to be protected by an 'iron triangle,' consisting of the legislators who brought them into being, the bureaucrats who oversee them, and those who benefit from the status quo, however flawed."[78] (We talk further about this phenomenon, and the concept of regulatory capture, in chapter 5.)

Some say federalism is for Republicans and centralization for Democrats. But if that idea may have had some salience at points in the past, it's hard to look around today and conclude that there's a right/left valence to federalism. Whatever the merits of the following ideas, notice that without federalism Colorado couldn't experiment with policies requiring a percentage of electricity sold in-state to come from renewable energy sources, and California couldn't experiment with more demanding animal welfare laws for livestock whose meat is sold in-state.[79] As Professor Heather Gerken of Yale Law School observed in pointing to similar examples (such as the $15 minimum wage and the movement to put body cameras on police officers), "it is useful to remember that rights are built, not born. . . . And social movements are almost always built from the ground up, moving through local and state sites before hitting the national stage."[80]

California State Supreme Court Justice Goodwin Liu reminds us of a particularly poignant example. For decades before and after the U.S. Supreme Court's 1896 decision in *Plessy v. Ferguson*, federal courts routinely upheld deeply unjust segregation laws as consistent with the federal Constitution. "What is lesser known," Justice Liu reminds us, is that "despite *Plessy* . . . , between the period from about the mid-1800s to 1900, there were several dozen state court decisions about school segregation. More than half of those cases granted relief to the black plaintiffs, largely on state constitutional or statutory grounds, within the confines of *Plessy*." In fact, as Justice Liu continues, the road to *Brown v. Board of Education* was paved with state court decisions. So much that, "in 1955, when the U.S. Supreme Court rendered its disposition in the *Brown* cases, it reversed . . . three federal district courts and affirmed . . . one state high court. I think that alone should give us pause in thinking about who are the heroes and who are the villains."[81]

The pattern more or less repeated itself when it came to racially biased juries. Again as Justice Liu notes, not long after *Brown*, the Supreme Court issued a decision that many lower federal courts interpreted as placing a "crippling burden of proof" on criminal defendants who sought to establish that they had been victims of unconstitutional racial bias in the jury selection process.[82] A number of state courts, however, took a different view and applied a more modest burden of proof on state court defendants under their state constitutions.[83] More than twenty years passed before, finally, the Supreme Court overruled its initial decision and moved federal law in the direction many state courts were already headed.[84]

In truth, the push and pull between national and local authorities that federalism allows has nothing to do with benefiting one party or another; it has more to do with the fact that no single government can always get it right. Protecting federalism means ensuring that when one government loses its way, another can help light the way back.

Carrie Buck

If Kalamazoo and the backdrop of *Brown v. Board of Education* illustrate how states and localities can sometimes lead, Carrie Buck's experience reflects the kind of costs that can come with federal intervention. Judge Jeffrey Sutton movingly recounts Carrie's story in his book *51 Imperfect Solutions*.[85]

It's a story that begins in the nineteenth century, when the idea of sterilizing people deemed "unfit" to procreate gained wide acceptance in intellectual circles.[86] Francis Galton, a cousin of Charles Darwin, first coined the term "eugenics," a word derived from the Greek *eugenes*, meaning "good in birth."[87] Eugenicists believed in a "scientific" approach to improving society—quite simply, bad genes, carried by so-called defective individuals, should be weeded out, allowing for "good genes" to flourish.[88] At its core, the eugenics movement was founded on the notion that a modern nation should "be planned and rationalized according to modern principles of biology, sociology, and economics."[89] To its proponents, eugenics was nothing less than "a way of using science to make a better world."[90]

Eugenics captivated the country's scientific and academic elite.[91] Between 1914 and 1928, the number of college courses on eugenics grew from 44 to 376,[92] and prominent professors at the nation's most prestigious universities helped lead the movement. As *Harvard Magazine* has since acknowledged, Harvard served in some ways as the movement's "brain trust." Its "administrators, faculty members, and alumni were at the forefront of American eugenics—founding eugenics organizations, writing academic and popular eugenics articles, and lobbying government to enact eugenics laws. And for many years, scarcely any significant Harvard voices, if any at all, were raised against it." Eugenics theories were popular at other leading universities, too; the president of Stanford and prominent professors at Yale threw their weight behind the movement and served as its leaders.[93]

Meanwhile, journals like *Science* and *Scientific American* ran prominent articles praising eugenic policies. Some of the articles included openly racist language and calls to close off democratic institutions to those "unfit" to govern.[94] Economic elites also had a strong incentive to join the movement. Many shared the conviction that, if governments continued "to place and keep under custodial care in state institutions all females who have become incorrigibly immoral, it will soon become a burden much greater than the state can carry."[95]

Notable public figures, including Theodore Roosevelt, John D. Rockefeller, and Margaret Sanger, subscribed to eugenics theories.[96] Meanwhile, prominent voices against the movement were few and far between. The author and philosopher G. K. Chesterton was one such lonely voice. He raged against eugenics in his 1922 pamphlet *Eugenics and Other Evils* and accused eugenicists of both misusing science and ignoring the humanity of the individual: "The Eugenist, for all I know, would regard the mere existence of Tiny Tim as a sufficient reason for massacring the whole family of Cratchit."[97] For his troubles, Chesterton was accused of being an "irrationalist."[98]

Despite its popularity in elite scientific, academic, and economic circles, the eugenics movement faced an uneven welcome in states across America. Some states adopted laws authorizing doctors to perform involuntary sterilizations. But many never did, and at least three governors vetoed eugenics legislation. Even in those states that allowed involuntary sterilizations, the practice differed wildly in early years. In some places, such as Nevada and South Dakota, no involuntary surgeries were performed between 1907 and 1921. Meanwhile, in the same time span, California sterilized 2,558 people (nearly 80 percent of the nation's total).[99]

When eugenics laws faced legal challenges in state courts, they often fared poorly. One prominent case involved a New Jersey statute signed into law by then Governor Woodrow Wilson. Under the law, a state agency—the "Board of Examiners of Feeble-Minded (including idiots, imbeciles, and morons), Epileptics, Criminals and other Defectives"—ordered the forced sterilization of an epileptic woman named Alice Smith. "Procreation by her" was, the Board ruled, "inadvisable."[100] When the case landed before the New Jersey Supreme Court in 1913, however, the court issued a unanimous opinion striking down the law and questioning the ethics of the whole affair.[101] That decision set an example several other state courts emulated, and by the early 1920s, the forced sterilization of so-called defectives appeared to be on "its last legs." Many people were coming to believe the practice "would soon come to an end" by the repeal or invalidation of eugenics laws or their simple neglect. As Judge Sutton writes, "had this happened, the heroes of the story would have been the state courts and the state and federal constitutions."[102]

But it didn't happen. Instead, eugenicists launched a renewed campaign to prove their case on a national scale. Relying on "hard data" and "science," they sought to demonstrate the dangers of letting nature take its course. They wrote articles, testified before legislatures, and adopted a new litigation strategy. No longer would they simply try "to avoid constitutional losses in fifty state supreme courts"; instead, they sought "to win one constitutional battle in the National Court."[103]

Eugenics advocates chose Carrie Buck of Virginia for their test case. From their perspective, her case seemed straight out of "Central Casting," as one historian put it.[104] Not only had Carrie been judged feeble-minded after being examined by experts and subjected to something called the Stanford Binet-Simon test, experts had also concluded that Carrie's mother and her child suffered from similar problems. Surely everyone could see the burden that families like hers inflicted on society and the wisdom of eugenics as a response. After the state designated Carrie for sterilization, a guardian appointed to represent her had to select a lawyer to defend her interests. Who did he choose? An attorney who had served on the board responsible for *approving* many prior sterilization requests.[105] What's more, the lawyer apparently joined his (nominally) opposing counsel in representing to the board that "this particular case was in admirable shape to go to the court of last resort, and that *we could not hope to have a more favorable situation than this one.*"[106]

Ultimately, they got their wish. Virginia's highest court approved the sterilization request, the U.S. Supreme Court exercised its discretion to hear the case, and in 1927 eight justices affirmed.[107] The nation's most celebrated judge of the day, Oliver Wendell Holmes, Jr.—once called by an admiring historian the "Yankee from Olympus"—wrote the decision.[108] His opinion comprised only five paragraphs, most of which recited facts and procedural history. Only two paragraphs contained any reasoning. Without mentioning the abundance of contrary state court decisions already on the books, Justice Holmes summarily dismissed Buck's legal claims and deferred to the experts' scientific and moral arguments. Nor did he did stop there; he proceeded to offer a haunting defense of forced sterilization. "It is better for all the world," he wrote for the Court, "if . . . society can prevent those who are manifestly unfit from continuing their kind. . . . Three generations of imbeciles are enough."[109]

Like many from his background, Justice Holmes had long admired the eugenics movement. As early as 1915, he had published a law review article in which he had written, "I believe that the wholesale social regeneration which so many now seem to expect, if it can be helped by conscious, coordinated human effort, cannot be affected appreciably by tinkering with the institution of property, but only by taking in hand life and trying to build a race. That would be my starting point for an ideal for the law."[110] Elsewhere, Holmes had written that "Malthus was right. . . . Every society is founded on the death of men. . . . I shall think socialism begins to be entitled to serious treatment when and not before it takes life in hand and prevents the continuance of the unfit."[111] In the aftermath of *Buck v. Bell*, he commented to a friend, "One decision that I wrote gave me pleasure, establishing the constitutionality of a law permitting the sterilization of imbeciles."[112]

Carrie Buck with her mother at the Virginia State Colony
for Epileptics and Feeble-minded

The Supreme Court's decision to intervene in *Buck v. Bell* landed like a bomb in public debates over forced sterilization. Buoyed by the Court's ringing endorsement of the practice and the imprimatur of no less a figure than Justice Holmes, the waning eugenics movement took off again: Within two years, a dozen states enacted new eugenics legislation. Within four years, 28 states had such laws. And after watching the Court defend involuntary sterilization with such vigor, some state courts hesitated to reach different judgments even under their own state constitutions.[113] The practice began to fall into disrepute once more only after, decades later, the world learned about the horrors of eugenics practices in Nazi Germany.[114]

Oliver Wendell Holmes, Jr.

What to make of it all? Carrie Buck's fate is a reminder of many old truths about the inherent value of individuals, their lives, and their liberties. But perhaps, too, it stands as a reminder that taking up an issue on the national stage carries with it risks, especially when

you seek to resolve it hastily and with certitude about the science of
the day. You may be sure there is One Right Answer. But any mistake
about the science or what represents progress can have a devastating
effect nationwide.

For all there is to lament in this story, however, it's worth noting
this: When Nazi Germany embraced eugenics, it had a strong national government and few citizens willing to stand in the way. The
forced sterilization of 400,000 people followed in just twelve years.
By contrast, in the much larger United States, where power was dif-
fused among states, perhaps 60,000 forced sterilizations took place
over seventy-five years.[115] Each was a tragedy. Many involved poor
women and minorities.[116] Yet it's hard not to wonder how many more
of these tragedies would have occurred without at least some initial
pushback from state courts, governors, and legislators.

What became of Carrie Buck? In the 1970s, K. Ray Nelson served
as the director of the Virginia facility where she had been confined.
An advocate for those with mental disabilities, Nelson decided to
seek her out. He first made contact with Carrie's sister, Doris. Doris
reported that she and her husband had tried unsuccessfully for years
to have children. It was only after meeting Nelson that Doris, then
in her sixties, learned that what she had thought had been an ap-
pendectomy performed on her at age 16 had actually been a forced
sterilization.[117]

Doris pointed Nelson to Carrie. Life "had not been kind to
her"—she lived "in a hovel on a dirt road" with an alcoholic husband,
having "tak[en] jobs so demanding that she weighed barely a hundred pounds." But it also turned out that Carrie "had advanced each
year with her grade" until she was removed from school and "in her
later years, she had become actively involved in reading groups and
in solving crossword puzzles, and she liked music and dramatics."
It wasn't "her genes but society and the state that had determined
her destiny." In fact, evidence gathered by historians suggests that
neither Carrie nor her relatives were "feeble-minded" (whatever that
means). Her trial had been a sham; her attorney had done much
in his career to promote sterilization and a good deal less in his

representation of Carrie to protect her from it.[118] It appears her only true fault was that she was poor and judged a burden on society. But in that, her fate is instructive, too, a reminder that calls for sacrificing the individual to the demands of collective interests, science, and progress can prove a fad, one whose effects may be borne by the most vulnerable among us.

Part of Something Worth the Trouble

Federalism's often overlooked virtues don't just include permitting policy responses tailored to local conditions (Butte's lesson), creating room for experimentation from which we all might learn (Kalamazoo), and serving as a check against hasty missteps at the federal level (the tragedy of *Buck* and the path to *Brown*). The framers designed our Constitution with ordinary individuals, their liberties, their right to self-governance, and their need to feel connected to their institutions in mind—and federalism was a key part of that plan as well. Federalism allows more people more ways to exercise their democratic muscles, feel ownership in our republican institutions, and grow attached to them. And it is through this active participation in our government that we learn and pass along from generation to generation the habits required to sustain our democratic experiment.

In our federal government, fewer than six hundred people in a land of more than 300 million can serve as an elected official at any given time. Running for federal office has never been cheap, either; just ask William A. Clark about his Senate race in Montana in 1899. These days, a winning campaign for the U.S. House of Representatives costs on average $2 million, one for U.S. Senate over $15 million.[119] Yes, there are plenty of opportunities to serve as a federal employee or contractor. But many of those jobs are in Washington, D.C. And, yes, you can comment on some of the rules our many federal agencies propose. But who except powerful interests with lawyers and lobbyists can afford to spend their time scouring the Federal Register for "notices of proposed rulemakings"? And how many among us really think that taking the trouble would make a difference anyway? Today, 33 percent of proposed federal agency rules don't garner a single public comment; close to 80 percent are the subject of ten or fewer public comments.[120]

By contrast, there are almost countless ways to participate in state and local government. It's not just that there are vastly more elected positions available (more than 500,000).[121] Citizens can attend meetings in person—school board, city council, you name it—and stand before local officials and make their voices heard. Don't like the local tax increase; the plan to rezone your neighborhood; your public school's curriculum? You can say so directly to the people responsible. You can also serve part-time and on a volunteer basis. For example, like many other cities, Baltimore has a Civilian Review Board that reviews complaints against police officers; Collingswood, New Jersey, has a Historic Preservation Committee tasked with preserving the town's architectural history; Winston-Salem, North Carolina, has a Youth Advisory Council to serve as a conduit between youth and the city's government.[122]

The very existence of state and local groups like these demonstrates respect for individuals, their wisdom, and their capacity to govern themselves. They also help instill essential democratic virtues: how to listen as well as speak, to compromise as well as win or lose, to lead as well as follow, to make rules as well as accept those others have made. By participating in democratic processes, we come to appreciate their value. As Alexis de Tocqueville put the point long ago, "local assemblies of citizens constitute the strength of free nations. Town-meetings are to liberty what primary schools are to science; they bring it within the people's reach, they teach men how to use and how to enjoy it."[123]

The power and benefits of this kind of civic participation are demonstrable. Some years ago, a study about jury service found that citizens who serve as jurors are more likely to vote after their service.[124] Another found that "the experience of consequential face-to-face talk" during jury service helps "make private individuals into public citizens by reinforcing their confidence in fellow citizens and public institutions."[125] Still another and even more local study at the University of Northern Colorado found that students involved in at least one campus organization are more likely to consider the university a community; "in short, it seems that to feel connected to the big," it helps "to be active in the small."[126] None of these findings or countless others like them would have come as a surprise to our forefathers. Through our Constitution's federal structure, they sought to bring people "constantly into contact, despite the instincts which separate them," by "giv[ing] each part of the land its own political life so that there should be an infinite number of occasions for the citizens to act together and so that every day they should feel that they depended on one another."[127]

When Tocqueville traveled across America in the 1830s, he was astonished by the bustling energy of our democracy. But his optimistic portrait came with worries, too. Over time, Tocqueville feared, Americans might find themselves increasingly absorbed in their individual pursuits and well-being, rather than committed to participating in public life with their fellow citizens.[128] If those conditions took hold, he feared, a new form of despotism—one which feeds on the isolation of individuals—could find a hospitable environment: After all, he noted, "despotism . . . is never more secure of continuance than when it can keep men asunder."[129] Into the vacuum formerly occupied by an active citizenry, Tocqueville foresaw the possibility of a paternalist central government emerging, one that "is alone responsible for securing their enjoyment and watching over their fate," one that would "entirely relieve them from the trouble of thinking and all the cares of living." In its final form, Tocqueville envisioned a government that:

> extends its embrace to include the whole of society. It covers the whole of social life with a network of petty, complicated rules that are both minute and uniform, through which even men of the greatest originality and the most vigorous temperament cannot force their heads above the crowd. It does not break men's will, but softens, bends, and guides it; it seldom enjoins, but often

inhibits, action; it does not destroy anything, but prevents much from being born; it is not at all tyrannical, but it hinders, restrains, enervates, stifles, and stultifies so much that in the end each nation is no more than a flock of timid and hardworking animals with the government as its shepherd.[130]

As Tocqueville understood, our republican experiment faces danger when people feel isolated from their fellow citizens and unable to effect change in their daily lives; when they become so fearful of the consequences of stepping into public life that they prefer to do as they are told and go unnoticed; when decisions are made by a distant few rather than in institutions closer to the people and accessible to them.

Cautionary signs stand before us. Open the newspaper on any given day and you may see headlines like "Why Does No One Vote in Local Elections?" or "In the U.S., Almost No One Votes in Local Elections."[131] Today, only about 27 percent of eligible voters participate in municipal elections,[132] and "recent results suggest it's slowly becoming even worse."[133] In 2021, New York City witnessed the lowest turnout in its mayoral election in nearly seven decades. A few years earlier, only about 27 percent of voters participated in Philadelphia's mayoral election.[134] Nor are these cities outliers.[135] And "the numbers get even worse as you go down the ladder to county, school board and special elections."[136]

A nonprofit foundation conducted a series of focus groups of millennials to explore the reasons for these developments. One common answer? "Many participants view[] local government as an afterthought at best."[137] It's not just millennials, either. "Voters may just need more reason to care," one article concluded, citing a poll of Los Angeles residents finding that "many would get more involved . . . if they thought it would make any difference."[138] Meanwhile, more than 60 percent of respondents in a 2012 Pew Research Center poll stated that the federal government controls too much of daily life.[139]

Contrast many of today's findings about participation and interest in local government with the enthusiasm Tocqueville witnessed. He saw New England towns that "partition[ed] municipal power among a great number of citizens," "scatter[ing] power in order to interest more people in public things."[140] He observed with admiration that "Americans of all ages, all stations in life, and all types of dispositions are forever forming associations."[141] The sum total of public life inspired loyalty and attachment to fellow citizens, town, state, and nation: individuals saw something that they were a "part of and that [was] worth [their] trouble to seek to direct."[142]

That final observation may hold the key. To sustain our republican experiment, to avoid the fate so many other democracies have suffered and Tocqueville feared for ours, participation in self-government must be both practically possible and worth the trouble. We must feel invested in our republican enterprise and learn the habits that enable it to endure. Federalism is not the be-all, end-all answer. But it's hard to argue with a recent report about what some observers, including the surgeon general, have called our nation's "loneliness epidemic" (more on that in chapter 5). It concluded that "we are long overdue for a rethinking of our responsibilities to others and our collective well-being, for reminders of an idea that was central to our founding and is at the heart of many great religious traditions: We have commitments to ourselves, but we also have vital commitments to each other."[143] It's hard not to wonder, too, whether an important part of that conversation should include asking whether, as a nation, we afford our families, friends, neighbors, and local communities enough opportunity to participate in deciding how we live.

CHAPTER 3

BUREAUCRACY UNBOUND

No public business of any kind could possibly be done at any time, without the acquiescence of the Circumlocution Office. . . . If another Gunpowder Plot had been discovered half an hour before the lighting of the match, nobody would have been justified in saving the parliament until there had been half a score of boards, half a bushel of minutes, several sacks of official memoranda, and a family-vault full of ungrammatical correspondence, on the part of the Circumlocution Office.

—CHARLES DICKENS[1]

Casey the Rabbit and Hemingway's Six-Toed Cats

MARTY HAHNE WAS EIGHT YEARS OLD WHEN HE FOUND A BOOK about Harry Houdini at a garage sale. Soon, he was hooked. He read the book "cover to cover" and began making "monthly trips to the magic shop." Within a few years, Marty began offering his own shows. After college and stints working on cruise lines, he realized that magic was his calling and settled down to "his first love" of "entertaining family audiences."[2] Somewhere along the way, Marty acquired a rabbit for his show; at one point there was Charlie, and then came Casey, a three-pound Netherland dwarf rabbit. The rabbits were the source of all the trouble.

In 2005, a woman with a badge approached Marty after he finished a children's show at a local library in Missouri. As Marty later recounted to *The Washington Post*, "She said, 'Show me your license.' And I said, 'License for ... ?' . . . She said, 'For your rabbit.'" Marty was perplexed: "I told her I could understand needing a license if I was using tigers, but I was using a bunny rabbit, a three-pound bunny rabbit."

Marty and one of his rabbits

It turned out that the woman was an agent from the U.S. Department of Agriculture.[3] Many years earlier, Congress had passed a law requiring, among other things, dealers of certain animals intended for research to secure a federal license.[4] Of course, Marty had no designs like that for Charlie or Casey. But by the time the agent approached him, Congress had amended the law. Now the law required "exhibitors," such as "carnivals, circuses, and zoos," to apply for and receive a license, too.[5]

You might wonder what any of that had to do with Marty. His local magic shows weren't exactly in the same league as carnivals, circuses, or zoos. Still, agency officials responsible for enforcing the law had issued their own detailed set of rules. And the rules defined "exhibitors" to include not just carnivals, circuses, and zoos, but also "animal acts" and "educational exhibits." So however one might read the statute itself, the agency's rules appeared to require even a small magic-show business like Marty's to meet federal licensing demands.[6]

Duly chastened, Marty applied for and received a federal license for his rabbit. As part of the process, he had to submit to surprise inspections of his home, and if he took the rabbit out of town for an extended period, he had to send his itinerary to the agency.[7] Apparently, Marty's first home inspection—at which the inspector wielded a hefty guidebook—didn't go well. Casey's travel cage was missing stickers reading "live animal"; it was also missing other stickers with arrows pointing up to show how to carry the cage.[8] Marty told the inspector that he already knew how to carry the cage—by the handle on top. The agent was not amused, so Marty asked how to procure the stickers. The inspector said the agency would send a few. Sometime later, a box of 200 showed up.[9]

After Hurricane Katrina in 2005, federal regulators decided to revise their rules.[10] Congress hadn't changed the law in any relevant way. But after more than four years of planning, the agency published new rules requiring animal exhibitors to develop disaster contingency plans. Those plans had to identify potential emergencies; outline tasks to be carried out in response to them; identify a chain of command to fulfill those tasks; and "address how response and recovery will be handled in terms of materials, resources, and training needed."[11]

Again, Marty dutifully complied. With the help of a disaster management expert, he drafted a 28-page contingency plan for Casey. The expert thought the plan "pretty short" given the agency's requirements. Even so, the plan covered everything from chemical leaks and floods to tornadoes and heat waves.[12] Meanwhile, Marty reached out to agency officials wondering why he—a one-man act— needed a written, agency-approved contingency plan for his rabbit when he already had one. "It is called common sense," as he told a reporter. "We live in Missouri. We have tornadoes here, so we have a safe room in our basement. I told the [agency] supervisor that I spoke with that, if there is a tornado, my 12-year-old Chihuahua— she's our baby—is first in, then the cats and, if there is time, the rabbit." That didn't sit well with the agency. "The supervisor told me that the rabbit, being the only licensed animal, is the most important in their eyes."

In the end, Marty seemed pretty resigned to it all, lamenting to one reporter that "I always thought I had a fun, easy job, and I would never have to worry about the government bothering me about it. But our government has gotten so intrusive, their tentacles are everywhere."[13] Well, maybe not quite everywhere. It turns out that if Casey had been an iguana, say, none of this paperwork would have been necessary under agency rules. Nor would Marty have needed a license or a contingency plan if he had raised Casey with the intent of boiling him for stew—animals raised for food are excluded from those requirements.[14] As Marty put it to the inspector, "You're telling me I can kill the rabbit right in front of you, but I can't take it across the street to the birthday party" without a license?[15]

It's not just pet rabbits that can prove troublesome. For years, Ernest Hemingway lived in Key West, Florida.[16] There, he produced some of his most famous works, including *For Whom the Bell Tolls*. Today, his old home is a museum, famed not only for its prior inhabitant but also for its six-toed cats. Dozens roam the property and can be found lounging in the garden or nestled in furniture.[17] Some say the cats are descendants of Hemingway's own six-toed cat named Snow White.[18] It seems that feline had been a gift from a ship's captain, sailors' legend having it that six-toed cats bring good luck.[19]

In a nod to Hemingway's own tradition, the museum names its cats after famous people. There's been a Marilyn Monroe, a Cary Grant, a Grace Kelly.[20] By all accounts, the cats are loved and well cared for. A local veterinarian tends to their medical needs, and a cemetery on the grounds has gravestones bearing the names of the departed.[21] When Hurricane Irma hit Key West, staff members remained at the museum to care for the cats.[22] Visitors love them. "Hemingway gets you here the first time," one repeat tourist reported. "But the cats keep us coming back."[23]

Hemingway was reputed to have once said that "a cat has absolute emotional honesty. . . . People hide their feelings for various reasons, but cats never do."[24]

For years, the cats kept federal officials coming back as well. During a visit in fall 2003, an official from the U.S. Department of Agriculture issued the same message to museum staff that Marty received: the museum needed a license to keep its cats. What's more, the agent said, the cats should be confined to cages or individual shelters for their safety.[25]

The museum staff recoiled. The cats had lived good lives roaming the property for more than forty years. A number were over nineteen years old at the time. Caging them, the staff worried, would amount to nothing short of animal cruelty.[26]

Months later, the federal agent returned with more suggestions for cat "containment." Apparently, the museum needed to hire a night watchman for the cats. Or reduce the number of cats. Or increase the height of the historic brick wall that surrounded the property (something the museum, a National Historic Site, could not do because of *another* agency's rules).[27]

More months went by. The federal agent returned again, this time with her supervisor. The pair informed museum staff that "containment" remained an issue. Because the existing wall couldn't be altered, they suggested adding a "hot wire" to the top to shock cats attempting to leave the property.[28] That proved a disaster. As CBS News reported, "cats apparently hunker down when they get in the shock zone. A Hemingway cat got burned. The Hemingway Home staff says the [agency] should've known better. After all, they claimed to be the experts."[29]

As the saga unfolded, the museum applied for a license. But agency officials told the staff that their application was being canceled—and that the museum would have to wait for six months to file a new one. In the meantime, officials reportedly warned the museum that it could face fines of $200 a day for each cat on the property, amounting to some $10,000 daily.[30]

The museum filed an appeal with the agency, but the agency declined to set a hearing. So the museum started over again and filed a new application. The agency rejected that application, too, this time because it wasn't "filled out correctly." Undaunted, the museum filed a third application.

In connection with that third application, a federal agent conducted another inspection. This time, the agent's report did not focus on "containment" as the primary issue but suggested measures like building elevated "resting surfaces" for the cats. The museum agreed to make the changes. But after a cat escaped from the property and died, the agency once again refused to grant the museum a license. The agency also informed the museum that fines were accruing and that it was considering confiscating the cats.[31] "I can't imagine," the museum's lawyer noted at one point, "why the federal government would have an interest in a handful of local cats."[32]

Somewhere in the middle of it all, the agency asked People for the Ethical Treatment of Animals (PETA) to assess the situation. But it seems that assessment didn't exactly help the agency's case. "What I found," the PETA inspector reported, "was a bunch of fat, happy and relaxed cats."[33] Federal agents conducted their own undercover surveillance, too, sometimes posing as tourists and surreptitiously photographing the cats. *The New York Times* reported that one photo depicted a cat sitting harmlessly on the pavement, accompanied by a caption reading "Picture of six-toed cat taken in restaurant/bar at end of Whalton Lane and Duval. May or may not be a Hemingway Home and Museum cat."[34] Agents allegedly even rented a guesthouse bordering the museum and asked the owner for a room with windows overlooking the museum so they could videotape the activities.[35] "It just got insane," the museum's lawyer commented to the *Times*. "The agents are coming down here on vacation, going to bars and taking pictures of cats."[36]

The whole ordeal dragged on for five years before the agency granted the museum a license after it made a few modifications to the property.[37] In an effort to forestall future disputes with the federal government, the museum proceeded to file its own lawsuit in which it challenged the agency's oversight authority. While the law Congress adopted clearly required zoos and carnivals to secure a federal license, the museum argued, nothing in the law permitted the agency to impose licensing rules on a historical site that happened to care for cats. A federal appellate court hearing the case acknowledged the museum's "somewhat unique situation" and "sympathize[d] with its frustration," but in the end deferred to the agency's expansive interpretation of its licensing authority under the law (more on that kind of deference later in the chapter).[38] In all, the museum reportedly spent at least $200,000 dealing with agency officials and their animal regulations. No word on how much the episode cost tax-payers, but CBS News documented fourteen trips by agents and a $17,000 cat evaluation.[39]

The Trouble with *Schoolhouse Rock!*

Remember the *Schoolhouse Rock!* videos? There's one with a cartoon figure of a bill sitting on the steps of Capitol Hill explaining how our federal legislative process works: the committee debates, the votes in the House of Representatives and the Senate, the need for the president's signature or a veto override.

It's a wonderful introduction to our system of government. But for all the video gets right, there's an anomaly at its core. The video follows the progress of a long-languishing bill designed to require school buses to stop at railroad crossings. At last and with much pride, the bill finally succeeds in becoming a law.[40] As it happens, though, we have no specific federal law like that. Instead, we have an agency rule, one issued by the Department of Transportation and buried deep within the Code of Federal Regulations (Title 49, Section 392.10, to be exact).[41]

Casey the rabbit, the Hemingway cats, and the truth about *Schoolhouse Rock!* illustrate another notable feature of our law today. Not only have the last few decades witnessed a shift in power from local to federal authorities, but even within Washington a dramatic transfer of power has taken place from elected representatives to unelected agency officials. These days, federal agencies don't just enforce the laws Congress writes; they also engage in activities that look a lot like legislating and judging. In important ways, all three of the powers Madison and the founders took care to separate have become commingled in agency hands.

Start with the agencies' quasi-legislative powers. Today, executive officials regularly issue sweeping rules like those Marty Hahne and the museum encountered.[42] Some, of course, are the result of directives straight from the top; President George W. Bush's administration implemented limits on federal funding for human embryonic stem cell research, while President Barack Obama's administration issued the Deferred Action for Childhood Arrivals policy that reshaped immigration enforcement priorities.[43] Both policies made front-page news. But the vast majority of executive branch decisions are not like that. They may be deeply consequential for thousands or millions of people, but they do not attract the kind of public attention that might sway elections. Just ask Marty.

Increasingly, too, these rules are produced without effective presidential oversight. As Judge Neomi Rao, who once headed the Office of Information and Regulatory Affairs, has explained, "a single bureaucrat can at times exercise an authority that exceeds that of a member of Congress. . . . Meaningful burdens can be imposed by regulations that do not reach the threshold for [this Office's] review or even consideration by an agency head or other political official."[44] A report by the Pacific Legal Foundation found that 71 percent of the nearly 3,000 rules issued by the Department of Health and Human Services between 2001 and 2017 were issued by lower-level officials rather than Senate-confirmed agency leaders; at the Food and Drug Administration the figure was 98 percent.[45] Hundreds of those regulations were deemed "significant" by the Office of Management and Budget, and, according to Senate testimony by one of the report's authors, "the FDA's own estimates found that the 23 most economically significant rules issued by non-Senate-confirmed employees have had a combined cost of $17.7 billion."[46]

The sheer scale of agency output is staggering. Remember all those laws we saw in chapter 2 that Congress passed in the 1960s and 1970s? Many of them authorized the creation of powerful new federal agencies with vast new powers; federal regulatory output has exploded ever since. Take one recent year by way of illustration. In 2015, Congress adopted about one hundred laws.[47] The same year, federal agencies issued 3,242 final rules[48] and published another 2,285 proposed rules.[49]

Today, forest rangers operate with thick books of rules.[50] Makers of ketchup, peanut butter, vodka—you name it—contend with rules that regulate down to the smallest detail. Ketchup must have a pH of 4.2 +/- 0.2 at certain stages of its formulation, and peanut butter may not have a fat content that exceeds 55 percent. Even the way the fat content is measured is closely regulated—it must be measured according to the rules "prescribed in *Official Methods of Analysis of the Association of Official Analytical Chemists*, 13th Ed. (1980)."[51] But good news for vodka aficionados: officials recently amended rules that once required vodka to be "without distinctive character, aroma, taste, or color."[52]

You might ask how we got so recently and so quickly to a point where unelected bureaucrats can make so many legally binding rules covering so many aspects of our lives. Well, the story's complicated. Small pieces of it fill long books, and we cannot begin to capture it all. But even a quick glimpse back tells quite a tale.

Not long after the Constitution's ratification, Congress took up a debate about the new nation's postal system.[53] Around 75 post offices and 2,400 miles of postal roads already existed—and in a nod to the new nation's view of the importance of the affair, Benjamin Franklin had been named the country's first postmaster general.[54] One of the questions Congress faced concerned where to site a number of new postal routes.[55] Should the route from Taunton to Newport go through Warren and Bristol or some other towns? How about the route from Baltimore to Hagerstown?[56] One congressman, Massachusetts's Theodore Sedgwick, found the whole affair silly. Why not, he proposed, simply appropriate funds for roads "by such route as the President of the United States shall, from time to time, Cause to be established"?[57]

You might think that an eminently sensible solution. But some congressmen (including James Madison, no less) protested that the proposal would improperly delegate legislative power to the executive branch.[58] One insisted that the Constitution required the government to be "administered by Representatives, of the people's choice; so that every man, who has the right of voting, shall be in some measure concerned in making every law for the United States."[59] Another observed sarcastically that, if the proposal succeeded, he would advance another that would "save a deal of time and money," for "if this House can . . . leave the business of the post office to the President, it may leave to him any other business of legislation; and I may move to adjourn and leave all the objects of legislation to his sole consideration and direction."[60] In the end, the Postal Act of 1792 gave the postmaster discretion on many fronts, but it also contained a long and dreary recitation of postal routes.[61]

Today, the postal route debate seems a world away. Few think the Constitution requires Congress to decide details like that. Surely, too, our agencies have much to offer when it comes to advising Congress about making new laws and administering old ones. But the episode does offer some sense of how far we have traveled from the debates of Madison's day to our own. In Article I of our Constitution, the People vested "All" federal "legislative Powers . . . in a Congress." A few decades after the postal route debate, Chief Justice John Marshall wrote for the Supreme Court that this assignment means "important subjects" must be "entirely regulated by the legislature itself," while Congress may leave "details" (like postal routes) for other officials "to fill up."[62] For years, the Supreme Court described the principle that Congress "cannot delegate legislative power" to executive branch officials as "vital to the integrity and maintenance of the system of government ordained by the Constitution."[63]

But it has been decades since our courts have done much to enforce that rule. And perhaps thanks in part to that omission, the pendulum has swung toward far-reaching delegations of legislative authority to agency officials. These days, Congress sometimes leaves agencies to write legally binding rules with little more guidance than "go forth and do good."[64] Laws tell agencies to regulate as "the public interest, convenience, or necessity" requires; others task them with setting "fair and equitable" prices; still others authorize agencies to determine "just and reasonable rate[s]."[65] One law that made its way to the Supreme Court recently even leaves the nation's chief prosecutor more or less free to decide for himself what kind of criminally enforceable registration requirements should apply to about half a million people.[66] Thanks to broad delegations like these, agencies can write, change, and change again rules affecting millions of Americans—all without any input from Congress.

While he was an early advocate for administrative power, Justice William O. Douglas explained that later in life he came to "realize[] that Congress defaulted when it left it up to an agency to do what the 'public interest' indicated should be done. 'Public interest' is too vague a standard to be left to free-wheeling administrators. They should be more closely confined to specific ends or goals."[67] But that wish, too, seems now a world away. If laws governing major facets of our society were once largely the work of elected representatives and the product of democratic compromises, nowadays they often represent only the current thinking of relatively insulated agency officials in a distant city. It's a result that, as Justice William J. Brennan, Jr., once observed, can pose a quandary: "Whereas the colonists challenged the king, today's citizens may find it impossible to know exactly who is responsible."[68]

Powers United

Here's the thing, though. These days, federal agencies don't just write and enforce legally binding rules. Often, they act as prosecutor and judge, too. So the same agency that sent agents to investigate the Hemingway cats isn't *just* the same agency that wrote a legally enforceable rule effectively equating a small museum to a zoo. It's *also* the same agency before which the museum had to appeal its case.

Admittedly, if you are unhappy with an agency's treatment of your case, *and* if you persist through all of its internal review processes, *and* if you have enough time and money, you can *usually* bring your complaint to federal court for review before an independent judge. But what are the chances of being able to endure and afford all that? Between 2010 and 2019, the Social Security Administration denied over 60 percent of disability applications,[69] yet only about one percent of claims are decided on the merits in federal court according to recent data.[70] And it's hard to think that there are so few appeals because agency procedures are so unerring when news reports indicate that, in recent years, "federal judges considering appeals for denied benefits found fault with almost six in every ten cases."[71]

Don't think this affects you? Professor Jonathan Turley has suggested that Americans today are "ten times more likely" to wind up in a case before an agency than a court.[72]

So suppose you receive a citation from an agency official and want to appeal. The agency judge might wear a robe and sit behind a bench. But often he is just another agency employee. Tomorrow, he could be transferred to another post—perhaps writing rules or enforcing them. Or he might end up moving into and out of the very industry whose cases he's responsible for passing upon.[73] Or maybe, too, agency bosses will signal displeasure if he doesn't rule according to their expectations: promotions might be lost, cases might be shifted to others.[74]

Not long ago, *The Wall Street Journal* reported on a Securities and Exchange Commission (SEC) judge who "came under fire from [the agency's chief judge] for finding too often in favor of defendants." In the end, she retired.[75] In other agencies, a director unsatisfied with a result reached by his administrative judges can have others— including himself—step in and retry the case.[76] As a former president of the American Bar Association once observed, "so long as [an agency] judge has offices in the same building as the agency staff, so long as the seal of the agency adorns the bench on which that judge sits, so long as that judge's assignment to the case is by the very agency whose actions or contentions that judge is being called on to review, it is extremely difficult, if not impossible, for that judge to convey the image of being an impartial fact finder."[77]

There's more. The usual rules of evidence—including the rule against the introduction of hearsay—don't always apply in agency adjudications.[78] And private parties don't always have a right to the discovery of relevant evidence.[79] As Professor Philip Hamburger of Columbia Law School put it, "Whereas constitutional law has long given defendants evidentiary protections, the administrative tribunals . . . flip[] these around to give the government special advantages."[80]

Given all that, it perhaps comes as no surprise that agencies have an unusually strong track record before their own tribunals. From October 2010 to March 2015, the SEC won about 90 percent of its contested in-house proceedings compared to 69 percent of its cases in federal court.[81] According to *The Wall Street Journal*, one SEC judge even warned individuals during settlement discussions that they "should be aware he had never ruled against the agency's enforcement division"; the *Journal*'s analysis revealed that the judge had, in fact, found defendants "liable in every contested case he has heard."[82]

It's not a story specific to any one agency. In 2015, a then commissioner of the Federal Trade Commission (FTC) gave a speech about the agency's mandate to prohibit "unfair methods of competition." He noted that, over approximately the last two decades, "in 100 percent of cases where the administrative law judge ruled in favor of the FTC staff, the Commission affirmed liability; and in 100 percent of the cases in which the administrative law judge found no liability, the Commission reversed"—a "strong sign," the commissioner went on, "of an unhealthy and biased institutional process."[83] Meanwhile, a special master looking into Coast Guard proceedings reported on fishermen's "common belief" that they stand "little or no chance of success" because administrative law judges (ALJs) and the agency "work hand-in-hand." "This same sentiment was expressed to me," the special master continued, "probably more graphically, by every lawyer, fisherman and fish dealer I interviewed who has had experience in appealing a case to a Coast Guard ALJ. With few exceptions, every Coast Guard ALJ decision I reviewed during this investigation upheld [the agency] on the issue of liability and the originally assessed penalty."[84]

Walk for a moment in Michael Biestek's shoes. Imagine that you have applied for Social Security disability benefits. Imagine that you have proven that you suffer from serious health problems and cannot return to your old carpentry job. Imagine that the agency denies your benefits application and you appeal. Like many cases before a Social Security administrative judge, yours turns on whether a significant number of other jobs remain that someone of your age, education, experience, and with similar physical limitations, could perform. When it comes to that question, the Social Security Administration bears the burden of proof. To meet its burden, the agency offers the testimony of an agency contractor it calls a "vocational expert." The expert asserts that there are 120,000 "sorter" and 240,000 "bench assembler" jobs nationwide that you could perform even with your disabilities.

But where did those numbers come from? The agency contractor says she relied on data from the Bureau of Labor Statistics and her own private surveys. But it turns out that the Bureau can't be the source; the data it keeps aren't so specific. The source—if there is one—must be the contractor's private surveys. So you ask to see them. The contractor refuses; she says they're confidential client files. You reply by pointing out that any confidential information can be easily redacted. But rather than order the data produced, the agency judge jumps in to say that won't be necessary. Even without the data, the judge says, the contractor's mere say-so warrants "great weight" and is more than enough evidence to deny your application. So your claim is dismissed based on the strength of what more or less amounts to secret evidence.[85] (When Mr. Biestek's case eventually reached the Supreme Court, Justices Ruth Bader Ginsburg, Sonia Sotomayor, and I dissented.)

William Humphrey

At this point you might ask: So what if all three major powers of government are often practically united in agency hands? Can't at least our elected president oversee their work? After all, Article II of our

Constitution vests the executive power in the president and makes him electorally answerable to "We the People." As James Madison put it, the Constitution anticipates a "chain of dependence," with "the lowest officers, the middle grade, and the highest . . . depend[ing] . . . on the president, and the president on the community"—all so that the "chain of dependence" "terminates in the supreme body, namely, in the people."[86]

It's a nice theory. But over time, we have done much to sever Madison's chain of dependence. It's not just the result of the problems already discussed: the exponential growth of the executive branch and all the layers of bureaucracy now standing between a politically accountable appointee and the official who in practice calls the shots. Madison's chain of dependence has also suffered because many "independent" agencies today (think alphabet soup: FTC, SEC, FCC, etc.) are, by statutory design, immune from normal presidential oversight. For that development, there may be many people to thank, but perhaps no one more than William Humphrey.

In 1933, President Franklin D. Roosevelt took office after one of the largest landslide victories in U.S. history.[87] By that time, Congress had already experimented with delegating vast powers to "independent" agencies. One of those agencies was the Federal Trade Commission, an agency President Woodrow Wilson helped create in 1914.[88] The agency's broad legislative mandate included, among other things, regulating "unfair" trade practices.[89] By 1933, however, President Roosevelt considered the agency ripe for reform. Instead of providing expert conclusions free from politics, he thought the agency's commissioners had become too friendly to business interests. In particular, one long-serving commissioner caught Roosevelt's eye: William Humphrey. The President wanted him out.[90]

That summer, the President wrote a letter asking Humphrey for his resignation. But Humphrey refused to go. Not exactly the model of an ascetic, apolitical expert, Humphrey had served in Congress (as a Republican) and worked in Washington, D.C., as a lobbyist for years. He was so well connected that he thought his old friends in Congress would protect him. But President Roosevelt wasn't one to back down, either, and in October he sent a "brisk note" informing Humphrey, "you are hereby removed."

Humphrey responded by retaining the services of William "Wild Bill" Donovan.[91] Most famous for his later leadership of the Office of Strategic Services in World War II, Donovan was already a highly decorated veteran of World War I, a former crime-fighting federal prosecutor, and one of the nation's leading lawyers.[92] The pair argued that the FTC was supposed to be a body of experts insulated from politics.[93] By law, a commissioner could be fired only for "inefficiency, neglect of duty, or malfeasance in office."[94] And the President's discharge letter had not accused Humphrey of any of that. As Humphrey put it, "I feel exasperated that I should be removed for purely political reasons." Humphrey fired off a furious letter to the President and set about filing a lawsuit. In the meantime, he continued to attend commission meetings and periodically filed demands for his unpaid salary.

Even Humphrey's death wasn't enough to end his crusade. In 1934, his executor took over the case and sought Humphrey's unpaid salary for his heirs. Eventually, the case made it all the way to the Supreme Court. Stanley Reed was the Solicitor General at the time, responsible for overseeing the government's cases before the high court. Upon taking office, Reed visited with his boss, Attorney General Homer Cummings. Reportedly, Cummings advised Reed that "you are going to win some cases in the Supreme Court and you are going to lose some. For your first case, pick out one that you can win." Reed chose Humphrey's case. As Reed later explained, he thought it was a case that "couldn't be lost," even against so estimable an opponent as "Wild Bill" Donovan.[95]

It's easy to see why Reed thought as he did. Only a decade earlier, the Supreme Court had decided a similar case called *Myers v. United States*. It, too, had involved a federal official who claimed the President had wrongfully fired him in defiance of laws designed to protect his independence. The case was so similar to Humphrey's that, by the time it reached the Supreme Court, the official at the heart of the suit was dead and the only question that remained concerned whether his heirs were entitled to his salary. In *Myers*, Chief Justice (and former President) William Howard Taft wrote a definitive decision vindicating Madison's chain of dependence. Under the Constitution, he explained, the chain of command in the executive branch must run inexorably upward to the president and from him to the American people. Perhaps experts can play a valuable role in advising policy makers. But without the power to remove those serving under him, the Chief Justice wrote, a president cannot "discharge his own constitutional duty of seeing that the laws be faithfully executed."[96]

Despite that landmark precedent, Reed's battle with Donovan didn't go as planned. In May 1935, the Court sided with Humphrey's executor in an opinion written by Justice George Sutherland (who, incidentally, Reed later succeeded on the Court).[97] Justice Sutherland dismissed much of *Myers* as nonauthoritative dicta and described the FTC as an "administrative body" that acts "in part *quasi*-legislatively and in part *quasi*-judicially" and therefore "cannot in any proper sense be characterized as an arm or an eye of the executive." As Justice Sutherland put it, the FTC's commissioners are "called upon to exercise the trained judgment of a body of experts"; they are to "act with entire impartiality" and enforce "no policy except the policy of the law." To operate effectively, Justice Sutherland continued, the commission must be free of the "coercive influence" of the president; any other result would threaten "the independence of a commission which is not only wholly disconnected from the executive department, but which . . . was created by Congress as a means of carrying into operation legislative and judicial powers, and as an agency of the legislative and judicial departments."[98]

For those who believed in the ideal of administrative agencies free from presidential oversight, Justice Sutherland's opinion was "a thrilling triumph." It "echoed down the corridors of the independent tribunals and administrative bodies of the government . . . throw[ing] a mantle of protection over a large group of public officers who are called upon to exercise independent judgment."[99] The victory was laced with irony, too. Justice Sutherland was not exactly known for his embrace of progressive philosophy. For his perceived hostility to the New Deal, some had derisively labeled him one of the "horsemen of the apocalypse."[100] But in the course of handing this particular defeat to President Roosevelt, Justice Sutherland endorsed a decidedly expansive view of agency authority.

While the decision had its fans in some quarters, others had a hard time wrapping their heads around it. If the FTC wasn't within the executive branch, in which of the Constitution's three branches did it reside? How can an agency exercise "quasi-legislative" and "quasi-judicial" powers without having to follow the Constitution's provisions governing the exercise of the legislative and judicial powers? And how can any agency do all that free of presidential oversight and thus electoral accountability to the American people? Robert H. Jackson, later appointed to the Supreme Court by President Roosevelt, reported that, though the case was "damn little" at one level, it "made Roosevelt madder at the Court than any other decision."[101]

Understandably so. President Roosevelt appreciated that the Court's new approach threatened to leave agencies not only with largely free rein from Congress, but with little presidential oversight.[102] As he put it in a 1937 report to Congress, "the practice of creating independent regulatory commissions" was "threaten[ing] to develop a 'fourth branch' of the Government for which there is no sanction in the Constitution."[103] Some even argue that President Roosevelt's effort to pack the Supreme Court had a lot to with the Humphrey episode. As two journalists put it, "the President saw in the decision the most direct of all possible trespasses on his powers as Chief Executive; he was completely infuriated."[104]

"The First Important Step"

The fusing of the three powers of our federal government into a "fourth branch" hasn't been the doing of one party or another. It is a phenomenon that has progressed by degree year in and year out through one administration after another. President Richard M. Nixon, for example, oversaw such a massive growth of federal administrative power that his chief economic advisor remarked that "probably more new regulation was imposed on the economy during the Nixon administration than in any other presidency since the New Deal."[105]

Occasionally, too, objections have come from "both the left and the right."[106] Thomas Sowell, a conservative thinker, argued that "it is hard to imagine a more stupid or more dangerous way of making decisions than by putting those decisions in the hands of people who pay no price for being wrong."[107] David Graeber, a liberal academic and former leader of the Occupy Wall Street movement, warned of what bureaucracies do to the human spirit and reminded us that the rebellions of the 1960s were "first and foremost against bureaucratic authority; all saw bureaucratic authority as fundamentally stifling of the human spirit, of creativity, conviviality, imagination."[108] More humorously, President Harry S. Truman once grumbled that "I thought I was the president, but when it comes to these bureaucrats, I can't do a damn thing." On getting ready to hand over the keys to the White House, he reportedly added about his successor, "He'll sit here and he'll say, 'Do this! Do that!' *And nothing will happen.* Poor Ike—it won't be a bit like the Army."[109] Still, bipartisan criticisms like these have done little to slow the momentum.

In the 1930s, influential academics, lawyers, and members of Congress on both sides of the aisle started expressing concern about this state of affairs, especially the "combination of judge, jury and prosecutor" functions in agency hands.[110] In 1938, a committee of the American Bar Association (ABA) chaired by Roscoe Pound, a former dean of Harvard Law School, issued an influential report.[111] The report cautioned that "the idea of checks and balances is inseparable from a well ordered society" and that "it is a mistake to think it an obsolete idea of the seventeenth and eighteenth centuries . . . something belonging only to a past era of small simple things."[112] Observing what was then transpiring in Europe, the report quoted an author who warned that:

In some countries democracy has been brazenly cast aside. Elsewhere the rise of executive government has not overtly been at
the expense of popular control, but nevertheless the same general
characteristics are discernible: administration is put beyond
democratic control. In the fascist countries executive government
is freed of popular review by reference crudely to principles of
leadership . . . in other countries more subtly by reference to the
importance of the expert in solving complex problems.[113]

The report did not shy away from what it thought of these developments. It called the idea of leaving so much responsibility to the
"professed ideal of an independent commission of experts above politics and reaching scientific results by scientific means" a dream that
bears "no correspondence with reality."[114] All forms of governmental
power, the report argued, are susceptible to error and abuse and demand checks and balances. Nor, as the ABA committee warned in
an earlier work, should we "have some 73 . . . courts in Washington,
most of them exercising legislative and executive as well as judicial
powers. A man should *not* be judge in his own case and the combination of prosecutor and judge in these tribunals *must* be relentlessly
exposed and combated."[115]

After years of debate and deliberation around these concerns,
Congress eventually passed the Administrative Procedure Act (APA)
of 1946.[116] The new law did not rein in broad legislative delegations
to executive agencies. It did not impose substantive limits on agency
rulemaking powers. It did not prohibit agencies from appointing
their own adjudicators to decide cases brought by their own enforcement agents. And it did not ensure that agencies would be more
meaningfully accountable to the president. Instead, the APA only
and more modestly sought to bring procedural regularity to agency
actions.

For our purposes, three features of the APA are important. First,
the law provides that agencies may exercise their "quasi-legislative"
powers and announce new rules with the force of law only through

the "formal" or "informal" rulemaking procedures outlined in the APA itself.[117] In formal rulemaking, an agency must follow demanding "trial-like procedures."[118] In informal rulemaking, an agency typically does not have to attend to those niceties; instead, it must simply provide public notice of any proposed rule it intends to adopt, allow an opportunity for comment, and then offer a "concise general statement of [the] basis and purpose" of the final rule.[119]

Second, the APA sets forth similar rules for the exercise of "quasi-judicial" powers by agency officials.[120] Formal adjudication requires an "adversarial, trial-type process": parties may present evidence and cross-examine witnesses, and cases are often presided over by administrative law judges, who enjoy a degree of independence.[121] In informal adjudication, few APA procedural protections apply.[122] These adjudications "vary substantially, ranging from 'semiformal' proceedings . . . to those . . . that are non-adversarial and procedurally bare."[123] What's more, these proceedings may sometimes take place before agency officials who do not enjoy even the limited independence that administrative law judges do.[124]

Third, the APA provides that those injured by an agency's action can generally escalate their complaints to an independent judge in federal court.[125] However, the role of judges in assessing agency actions is limited.[126] They are authorized to ask questions only like: Did the agency follow the APA's procedures? Are its decisions "arbitrary, capricious, [or] an abuse of discretion"? Are they "in accordance with law"? Can the agency show that its decision is supported by "substantial evidence"?[127]

Congress adopted the APA unanimously, and some have claimed that it was enacted "in an atmosphere of happy accord."[128] But that unanimity masked a more subtle truth. Everyone was well aware that the APA's ambitions were modest, and few imagined the law would supply a final and complete answer to the challenges posed by the growing administrative state.[129] As the senior Republican member on the House Judiciary Committee put it, "we feel it is the first important step in the direction of dividing investigatory, regulatory,

administrative, and judicial functions in Government agencies." A
Democrat expressed much the same sentiment, calling the new law
"merely the beginning" of reform.[130]

Little of that further reform has materialized in the almost eighty
years since the APA's passage. Nor have even the law's modest aspirations been fully realized. These days, the APA's formal rulemaking and adjudication processes seem ancient relics. Agencies almost
never use them.[131] Why bother with formal processes when less demanding ones are available? We have seen, too, what adjudications
can look like these days: some agencies almost always win before
their own tribunals; some supervisors can replace administrative
judges if they don't like their decisions; some agency decision makers may move into and out of the industries they regulate; some
agencies may even withhold critical evidence from litigants like
Mr. Biestek.

Increasingly, agencies do not even bother with the APA's informal
procedures. Instead, they rely more and more on "guidance documents." In the APA, Congress exempted guidance documents from
any procedural requirements on the theory that they wouldn't carry
the force of law, only provide helpful insight into the agency's thinking. But because guidance documents are so easy to issue—an agency
can more or less just type them up—their use has proliferated. Some
say that, for any given agency, guidance materials now span 20, 40,
or even 200 times the number of pages of promulgated rules.[132] This
may seem an insignificant development, except for the fact that
both regulators and the regulated often treat guidance as binding,
and many of these guidance documents are not easily available to
the public. Reminiscent of the Hip Pocket Incident, some have been
found only in the desk drawers of agency employees.[133]

Time has been no more kind to the APA's promise of judicial review. Yes, the APA generally permits individuals who exhaust internal agency proceedings to bring their complaints to court.[134] But
given the time and expense required to get to court, few cases make
it that far. As two professors have explained, "Whatever legitimacy

the Article III courts promise must seem like a distant mirage for the vast majority of immigrants, claimants, and others as they litigate in obscure hearing rooms, far away from the grandeur of the federal courts."[135]

Even for those who do manage to make it all the way to federal court, the APA's original promise of independent judicial proceedings has often proved to be something of a mirage. Take the APA's rule instructing judges to set aside any agency action that is "not in accordance with law." From the nation's earliest days, federal courts resolved any reasonable doubt about whether someone had violated a penal law in favor of the individual and against the government ("the rule of lenity": more on this in chapter 4). Courts traditionally resolved doubts about a legal document's meaning against the party who wrote it (*contra proferentem*).[136] And our law generally respected the age-old principle that no one should be the judge of his own case (*nemo judex in causa sua*).[137] As Chief Justice John Marshall put it, too, judges long took the view that "it is emphatically the province and duty of the judicial department to say what the law is" in the cases that come before them.[138]

Over time, however, courts retreated from those traditional rules in favor of new ones that benefitted the government. Almost forty years after the APA's adoption, for example, the Supreme Court decided a case called *Chevron v. Natural Resources Defense Council*.[139] In its aftermath, some read the Court's decision as requiring judges to begin deferring to an *agency's* "reasonable" resolution of any legal ambiguity.[140] So rather than resolving doubts about the law's meaning in favor of individuals, rather than construing any ambiguities against those who write the rules, and rather than providing their own independent judgment of the law's meaning, courts started allowing federal agencies to judge the meaning of the very laws that govern them. That's what happened in the Hemingway museum case: the court there rejected the museum's challenge to the agency's rules by explaining that it considered itself obliged to defer to the agency's interpretation of Congress's governing statute.[141]

In time, courts even began deferring to agencies when they *changed* their views about a statute's meaning.[142] One administration could read the law to mean one thing, the next could read it to mean something else altogether; the written law itself might not have changed a whit in between, and still courts would defer to the agency. Some scholars have argued that these deference doctrines are premised on a misreading of the APA and carry serious costs to rule-of-law values. As Judge Raymond Kethledge has put it, a final interpretation of the law by our judicial system is "both impartial and relatively predictable. But an agency's often is neither."[143] Others have suggested that these deference doctrines can be reconciled with the APA and offer counterbalancing benefits.[144] But whatever one's view, a notable study has found that the impact of these doctrines can be profound: In cases where federal appellate judges found a statute ambiguous and applied *Chevron* deference, agencies won 93.8 percent of the time. By contrast, when judges expressly declined to apply *Chevron* deference and decided for themselves what the law means, the agency win rate dropped to 38.5 percent.[145]

A similar story can be told about disputes over facts. The APA charges federal courts with reviewing agency decisions to ensure that they are supported by "substantial evidence."[146] That phrase was a familiar one around the time of the APA's adoption.[147] Courts had long examined jury verdicts under the same standard.[148] Under its terms, a reviewing judge generally asks whether a reasonable fact finder could have come to the same conclusion the jury did given the evidence presented at trial.[149] That deferential standard makes a good deal of sense when a judge is reviewing the work of a neutral jury with no stake in the outcome of a case. But isn't it fair to ask whether that same standard is appropriate when assessing the work of an interested party to a dispute, one with incentives to find the facts in its favor? Just ask Michael Biestek, who lost his claim for disability benefits on the strength of little more than an agency contractor's assertion that plenty of jobs were available to him—an assertion that itself rested on little more than claims about secret evidence.

A Marine Recruit and an Immigrant

Just how toothless has judicial review of agency decisions become? Consider what happened to Kevin George and Pankajkumar Patel.

Mr. George was a young recruit to the U.S. Marines Corps who left the military after doctors found that his service aggravated a pre-existing mental illness. In time, Mr. George applied for service-related benefits. Agency officials at the Department of Veterans Affairs held him ineligible under an agency-created rule. Later, the agency was forced to admit that its rule couldn't be reconciled with Congress's long-standing statutory directions. At that point, Mr. George asked the agency to revisit its decision denying him benefits.[150] After all, he observed, Congress has provided that a veteran may ask the agency "at any time" to correct administrative benefits decisions infected with "clear and unmistakable error."[151]

The agency refused to reconsider its decision. Yes, the rule the agency had relied on to reject Mr. George's application for benefits was inconsistent with Congress's statutory directives. And, yes, Congress had told the agency to correct any veteran benefits decision infected with a clear and unmistakable error. But, the agency said, its officials had correctly applied the agency's (legally mistaken) rule when they initially decided Mr. George's case.[152] And, by that chain of logic, agency adjudicators reasoned, the agency had not committed a clear and unmistakable error worthy of correction. Ultimately, the Supreme Court agreed with the agency's self-assessment, so Mr. George was out of luck. (Along with Justices Stephen Breyer and Sonia Sotomayor, I dissented).[153]

If Mr. George's case illustrates how deferential courts can be to agencies' legal mistakes, Pankajkumar Patel's case tells a similar story when it comes to their factual errors. Mr. Patel lived in the United

States for decades. Together with his wife and three sons, he made his home in Georgia. As a young man, Mr. Patel had entered the country illegally. But eventually he sought to make that right by applying for lawful permanent residency. Under the law, the Board of Immigration Appeals generally enjoys discretion to grant relief in cases like Mr. Patel's.[154] But an applicant is not eligible for relief if he has, among other things, "falsely represent[ed] . . . himself . . . to be a citizen of the United States" to obtain a "benefit under . . . State law."[155]

That last feature of the law, agency officials argued, posed a problem for Mr. Patel. At some point, it turned out, Mr. Patel had applied to renew his Georgia driver's license and checked a box stating that he was a U.S. citizen. He tried explaining to immigration officials that it had been an innocent mistake; he hadn't intended to falsely represent himself to anyone. In fact, he emphasized, there had been no need for him to lie about his immigration status to state authorities.[156] Under Georgia law, he was entitled to receive a driver's license without being a citizen, and state authorities had not found him guilty of misleading them.[157] Still, a federal immigration judge working at the Department of Justice found as a matter of fact that Mr. Patel had intentionally misrepresented his status to Georgia authorities and that he was therefore ineligible for discretionary relief and subject to deportation.

Mr. Patel appealed the decision internally and then to a federal court.[158] Much was at stake for him: the opportunity to remain with his family in this country, where he had lived for decades and made a life. Mr. Patel argued, in part, that the immigration judge's decision rested on a clearly mistaken factual finding about whether he intentionally misled Georgia authorities, stressing again that he had simply checked the wrong box and had no incentive to lie. But the federal court reviewing his case ruled that even if the agency's factual finding was gravely wrong, no judge had the power correct it—in fact, no federal judge had the power to even *hear* his case.[159] In the end, by a vote of 5 to 4, the Supreme Court agreed with that assessment.[160] (I was in dissent again.)

The upshot? As one commentator put it, Mr. Patel's request was a "simple one." He wanted "a federal judge—someone who is not beholden to the same attorney general tasked with deporting him . . . to review the life-and-death decisions that immigration officials make every day in immigration court." Instead, Mr. Patel found himself subject to removal from a country he had lived in for thirty years based on what might have been an agency's factual mistake—one that no court could even review, let alone correct. Nor did the decision affect just him. Under the Court's logic, that same commentator warned, "Thousands of immigrants like Patel will be locked out of court, forced to pay for the haphazard mistakes of harried immigration officials who will face no consequences."[161] And in case you wonder whether stories like Mr. George's and Mr. Patel's are unusual, the Supreme Court decided both cases within the span of a single month.

"The Father of Public Administration"

Where did this way of doing government come from? Many notable figures in our history have played important roles in the story. But if any one person deserves credit for getting the ball rolling, it might be Woodrow Wilson. As a young academic, Wilson wrote an article in 1887 that later helped earn him the nickname "the father of public administration."[162] In it, he argued for a new "science of administration" that would "straighten the paths of government."

Wilson had a model in mind for this "science." But, he said, it had not "grown up" on "this side [of] the sea." As he saw it, American political thinkers had spent too much time "dogmatiz[ing] . . . about the *constitution* of government" and too little time looking for ways to ensure government operates with the "utmost possible efficiency." For his model of inspiration, Wilson looked to Europe. (Though not to Great Britain; it was apparently lousy at his "science of administration.")[163] Perhaps most of all, he admired Prussian bureaucracy.[164] He believed that in Prussia "administration ha[d] been most studied and most nearly perfected." And while he offered some words of caution about adopting the Prussian model wholesale—"We should not like to have had Prussia's history for the sake of having Prussia's administrative skill"—Wilson believed its administrative model could and should be "Americanize[d]."[165]

There was just the small matter of the Constitution. The founders' carefully wrought system of checks and balances seemed to foreclose a regime that would place so much power in one set of (unelected) hands. Wilson acknowledged the problem but surmised that if the members of the Constitutional Convention could be reunited in his day, they would be "the first to admit that the only fruit of dividing power had been to make it irresponsible."[166] "For Wilson," as Professor Ronald J. Pestritto has explained, "the separation of powers, and all of the other institutional remedies that the founders employed against the danger of faction, stood in the way of government's exercising its power in accord with the dictates of progress."[167]

What's more, Wilson faulted the Constitution for trying to resolve too many questions by vote rather than by scientific judgment. To his eyes, the mass of the people were "selfish, ignorant, timid, stubborn, or foolish" and "rigidly unphilosophical." In a democratic republic, "a truth must become not only plain but also commonplace before it will be seen by the people who go to their work very early in the morning." Making matters worse, Wilson believed, was the fact that the right to vote was being extended to more and more Americans. Maybe the propertied men of the founding era could be trusted, but now? As he put it:

> To know the public mind of this country, one must know the mind, not of Americans of the older stocks only, but also of Irishmen, of Germans, of negroes. In order to get a footing for new doctrine, one must influence minds cast in every mould of race, minds inheriting every bias of environment, warped by the histories of a score of different nations, warmed or chilled, closed or expanded by almost every climate of the globe.[168]

Wilson's views on this topic weren't confined to a single article; they suffused his writings.[169] In his diary, for example, he complained that "universal suffrage is at the foundation of every evil in this country."[170] And over the course of his career, he opposed female suffrage, supported Jim Crow laws, and tolerated segregation by his cabinet secretaries in their departments.[171]

To Wilson, the answer to the United States' governance problems lay in new administrative structures largely insulated from democratic influence, ones that would "deliver us from the too great detail of legislative enactment" and "give us administrative elasticity and discretion."[172] As Professor Pestritto has explained, Wilson sought the creation of new authorities that would "see[ ] to the daily rulemaking and regulation of public life." "Administration, after all, is properly the province of scientific experts in the bureaucracy; the experts' competence in the specific technological means required to achieve those ends on which we are all agreed gives them the authority to administer or regulate progress, unhindered by the realm of politics."[173]

Wilson's influence is hard to overstate. He attracted many powerful followers in the academy and among statesmen. Like many others, James Landis, who served as both dean of Harvard Law School and chairman of the Securities and Exchange Commission (more on him in chapter 7), became convinced that our "simple tripartite form of government" was "inadequa[te]" "to deal with modern problems."[174] Ultimately, Wilson himself led the movement to the White House, where he put his theories into practice by creating new independent agencies like the Federal Trade Commission that later caused President Roosevelt such trouble.[175]

If Wilson's ideas were highly influential, they were also pretty revolutionary. The founders knew that men are not angels and we are all individually prone to error.[176] But their answer to that dilemma was very different from Wilson's. In 1907, Francis Galton observed that at a county fair the average of all the entries in a "guess the weight of the ox" contest proved remarkably accurate. It beat not just nearly all individual entrants' guesses but also those of "cattle experts."[177] Today, that observation is captured by the phrase "the wisdom of crowds."[178] *That* was the sort of wisdom the framers sought to capture in the representative democracy they built.

What about efficiency? It's not as if the framers failed to consider the need for efficient administration. They vested responsibility for *enforcing* the law in a single president rather than a committee in part for just this reason. Without having to consult others, they thought, a single president would enjoy the power—and be unable to hide from the responsibility—of vigorously enforcing our laws. But to the framers, the *creation* of laws called for a very different sort of leadership.[179] Before asking a vigorous executive to enforce any new law, the framers thought a slow and careful process in order, one designed to protect minority voices and capture the wisdom of the people. Nor was the framers' design just about optimizing decisional outcomes. As they saw it, the people have a *right* to make the rules governing their lives through their elected representatives. And any system of lawmaking that neglected this right would tend to invite contempt for the law itself to "steal[] into the hearts of the people."[180] In this nation, as the Declaration of Independence put it, government was to derive its just powers from the consent of the governed.

What about Wilson's idea that administrators can help us avoid the need for cumbersome lawmaking processes thanks to their unbiased, apolitical scientific expertise? As Justice Elena Kagan observed before assuming the bench, that notion "today seems almost quaint."[181] Really, it came to seem quaint pretty quickly. By the time President Roosevelt entered office in 1933, who really thought that Wilson's Federal Trade Commission was stocked with apolitical trade policy savants rather than old political hands like William Humphrey?

It's easy to imagine the framers would have found Wilson's thoughts on the subject pretty quaint, too. The framers acknowledged a few self-evident truths in our Declaration and the Bill of Rights. But beyond that, they knew, there lies a vast number of policy questions on which even reasonable and well-informed minds will disagree. Rather than build a government premised on the assumption that elites can and will apolitically discern for us all a single right answer to a particular policy question, the framers thought it safer and more consonant with human nature to proceed on an assumption that those who participate in government will be ambitious for power—and that their ambitions should not be efficiently unleashed but always checked and balanced.[182] Giving us all a chance to participate, to reason and debate, to listen and learn, and to deliberate together, they also believed, promised to produce wise laws, ones more accommodating of different views, and ones more likely to enjoy wide respect and prove durable over time. And once more, the framers thought all that was nothing less than our inalienable right.

None of this is to say that Wilson didn't have a point. Ours *is* an increasingly complex world. But if Wilson diagnosed a problem, it's fair to ask questions about the wisdom of his proposed cure. In 1945, Friedrich Hayek posed the same question Wilson had more than a half century earlier: "*Who* is to do the planning" for society? He offered a more nuanced answer: while acknowledging that experts have an important role to play in advising lawmakers and implementing the policies they select, Hayek insisted that the "scientific knowledge[] [that] occupies now so prominent a place in public imagination . . . is not the only kind that is relevant." We should remember that another kind of knowledge is critical, too: "The knowledge of the particular circumstances of time and place. . . . We need to remember only how much we have to learn in any occupation after we have completed our theoretical training, how big a part of our working life we spend learning particular jobs, and how valuable an asset in all walks of life is knowledge of people, of local conditions, and special circumstances."[183]

"Rule by Nobody"

In his 2011 State of the Union address, President Obama spoke of the growth of federal administrative agencies in recent years—and by implication the difficulty any president faces in trying to oversee it all. The President observed that we now have 12 different agencies that deal with exports and at least 5 responsible for housing policy. He added, "The Interior Department is in charge of salmon while they're in fresh water, but the Commerce Department handles them when they're in saltwater. I hear it gets even more complicated once they're smoked."[184] Thinking the President had exaggerated, fact-checkers busily got to work. In the end, they rated his statement "mostly true"—but only because it "unders[old] the complexity."[185]

President Obama's speech got big laughs.[186] And at one level it *is* funny. But for ordinary people trying to navigate a federal bureaucracy—one that holds immense and often largely unreviewable power over important parts of their lives—the joke conveys a bitter truth. The director of the Immigrants' Rights Clinic at the University of Chicago Law School, for example, told this story to *The Hill* about the steps she had to go through just to get an appointment for her client to be fingerprinted in connection with an asylum order. She started by filing a fingerprinting request with U.S. Citizenship and Immigration Services. After a month passed without a reply, she sent another request. Still nothing. So she called the agency hotline. They told her to call the agency's local office in Chicago. When she did, that office said it had no power to schedule the appointment and directed her to the national processing center. When she reached out to that center, a representative referred her back to the agency hotline.

Here's what happened next:

When I called the hotline again, I was told that no one was responsible for booking the appointments at the present time and that I should call back in six weeks to see if new guidance had been issued. I asked to speak with a supervisor. I was told that a supervisor would call me back in the next 42 days and that I should keep my phone with me at all times. If I missed the call, I would have to start the process again.

When the supervisor called weeks later, he said that I needed to contact my client's deportation officer. I called the deportation officer, and he said he wasn't responsible for making the appointments, either. When I begged for his help, he finally said that he would do me a favor—and he set up the appointment in less than five minutes. He ended the call with: "You know, any of those people you talked to could have set up the appointment."

The lawyer concluded, "A system in which it takes four months to schedule an appointment isn't just broken. It is barely a system at all."[187] David Graeber, describing his own bureaucratic odyssey, put it this way: "They set demands they insist are reasonable, and then, on discovering that they are not reasonable . . . conclude that the problem is not with the demands themselves but with the individual inadequacy of each particular human being who fails to live up to them."[188]

The academic and author Edwin J. Feulner, Jr., once argued that Hayek's "greatest contribution lay in the discovery of a simple yet profound truth: man does not and cannot know everything, and when he acts as if he does, disaster follows."[189] We wouldn't call our current state of affairs a disaster—though Mr. George and Mr. Patel might disagree. But maybe our society's increasing deference to claims of bureaucratic expertise threatens something even more vital than our promise of democratic self-government or rule-of-law values: our nation's respect for the *individual*—for the dignity that exists within each of us, whatever our quirks, warts, and failings—and our conviction that the individual's inalienable rights may not be bargained away, even in the name of efficient public administration.

Many years ago, a wise judge, Learned Hand, said that he would find it "most irksome to be ruled by a bevy of Platonic Guardians, even if I knew how to choose them, which I assuredly do not. If they were in charge, I should miss the stimulus of living in a society where I have, at least theoretically, some part in the direction of public affairs."[190] It's a reflection that poses this question: What happens when we forget what that stimulus feels like; when we lose our appetite for participation in public life; when we become so accustomed to taking directions from a "bevy" of experts that we cannot imagine doing things any other way? For her part, Hannah Arendt answered that question with a warning, one about a world in which "there is nobody left with whom one can argue, to whom one can present grievances, on whom the pressures of power can be exerted. . . . [T]he rule by Nobody is not no-rule, and where all are equally powerless we have a tyranny without a tyrant."[191]

CHAPTER 4

THE SWORD OF DAMOCLES

The value of a sword of Damocles is that it hangs—not that it drops.

—JUSTICE THURGOOD MARSHALL[1]

Bobby Unser in the Wilderness

THE SAN JUAN MOUNTAINS TOWER OVER SOUTHWESTERN Colorado. They sit in a region of the Rockies renowned for its stark and varied beauty, with wildflower meadows, meandering creeks, and high mesas set against the backdrop of snow-covered summits.[2]

Bobby Unser was one of the many outdoor enthusiasts who flocked to the area. For those too young to remember, Bobby was a legendary race car driver from a legendary racing family. His father, two uncles, three brothers, and children all competed. Altogether, the Unser family won the Indianapolis 500 nine times. Bobby was responsible for three of those wins, but those were only a fraction of his triumphs.[3] Among other things, he regularly won the "most danger-filled race of all," the annual Pikes Peak International Hill Climb, which winds up twelve miles of twisting roads to the top of one of Colorado's most iconic mountains.[4]

Bobby grew up in Albuquerque, New Mexico. His family moved there when Bobby was a toddler, and his father opened a gas station and repair shop along the famed Route 66.[5] When his father retired, Bobby took over the business. Even after he became famous, Bobby continued to live in the area.[6]

Bobby Unser was known as the "King"
of the "Race to the Clouds" on Pikes Peak.
Here, he celebrates his 13th win in 1986.[7]

One day in December 1996, Bobby set out from his ranch with a friend and fellow racer, Robert Gayton. They loaded two snow-mobiles onto a trailer and headed across the state line to a spot in the San Juan range, intending to take advantage of the sunny day. Robert was a novice at the sport, so Bobby planned an easy trip to a nearby mesa. After a few practice spins by the parking lot, the friends headed out on a trail.[8]

After they reached the mesa, the weather turned. As Bobby later recalled, "all of a sudden the wind came up, as it often does in that part of the world." A ground blizzard ensued. Visibility dropped to near zero and the wind started howling, maybe sixty or seventy miles per hour.[9] Quietly, Bobby worried for his friend: "Robert had never ridden before, so if he gets more than ten feet behind me, he's probably going to die."[10] As the two struggled to find their way back to the parking lot, Robert drove off into a ravine and his snowmobile got stuck. The pair had little choice but to leave the machine behind and double up on Bobby's.[11]

Soon their luck turned from bad to worse. Bobby's brand-new snowmobile began sputtering. "I [would] get it running for a little bit; it would run half a city block, maybe a block, and it would quit again, and each time it got to where it was harder to get started." The two men, both skilled mechanics, struggled to keep the machine going. Finally, it died and darkness began descending. "We are in trouble, no question about it," Bobby later recalled. The pair abandoned the second snowmobile and started walking down the mountain. "The direction has to be down," Bobby thought, because "for sure we would die if we stayed in the high country."

Eventually, the men realized they were lost and unlikely to make it to safety that night, so they stopped to build a snow cave. They spent a long, cold night huddled there.[12] When morning broke, they resumed walking. By then the snow was waist deep in places. Robert didn't think he'd make it. Meanwhile, Bobby became sick; he vomited so much that he started bringing up blood. After a treacherous 18 hours, suffering from frostbite and dehydration, the men stumbled on a barn. Miraculously, it had a landline phone and they were able to call for help.[13]

Rescuers found Robert's snowmobile abandoned in the ravine. After making it back home and recuperating, Bobby started thinking about his own machine. It was, after all, brand new, and he had spent some $7,000 on it. Ultimately, he contacted officials of the U.S. Forest Service in Albuquerque for help locating it. Though they spent some time poring over maps together, they made little headway. In the end, an official told Bobby that he'd contact colleagues in the Colorado office who might be able to help.

Bobby met with the Colorado officials the next day.[14] Together, they again hunched over maps. Bobby described it as a "pleasant afternoon." But as things wound down, the mood changed. After they agreed on a likely spot where the snowmobile might be found, Bobby recalled that one of the officials "reache[d] under the table and pull[ed] out a pre-written ticket."[15] "And *then* they introduced themselves as being police officers for the National Forest Service."[16]

What the officials hadn't told Bobby earlier was that they had been investigating him for violating a federal ban on the use of motor vehicles in a wilderness area.[17] Back in 1964, Congress enacted the Wilderness Act to protect designated wilderness areas from certain uses. One such protected area is the South San Juan Wilderness, near where Bobby and Robert had left on their trip to the mesa.[18]

Bobby had known all this and taken care to plan his trip across land where it was legal to snowmobile. If he and Robert had veered off course, he insisted, it wasn't with an intent to trespass across protected wilderness; they had simply gotten lost in the storm. When officials told him that he had committed a crime, Bobby recalled, he couldn't "believe this is even happening." What particularly upset him was that the meeting had turned out to be something of a trap.[19] And not just one with a civil fine attached; instead, officials charged Bobby with a *federal crime*—one that threatened him with up to six months behind bars.

Quitting wasn't Bobby's style, though, and he decided to take his case to trial. The prosecution against him hinged on where the snowmobiles had traveled and were eventually found. But as the trial progressed, it became apparent that witnesses couldn't agree. Ultimately, the trial judge found the "most credible" testimony came from one of the rescue team members. The judge then used a piece of wire to measure the distance on a map from the parking lot to the area the witness identified before concluding that, yes, Bobby had traversed protected land.[20] On that basis, the judge found Bobby guilty and imposed a $75 fine.

Most people might have left matters there. Not Bobby. He appealed to the Tenth Circuit (my old court), which had some serious concerns about the trial proceedings. Among other things, the court noted that the trial judge had pretty clearly "misread the scale of the map." Still, the Tenth Circuit affirmed Bobby's conviction, and that was that.[21] Bobby estimated that by the end of it all, the government had spent $1 million to brand him a criminal and secure a $75 fine.

Years later, he still spoke of the affair. "I've never been in trouble. I mean, I'm as clean a person as you could ever have. And yet to take a person like that and threaten to throw him in jail [and] ruin his career. . . ."[22] In 2021, Bobby died at the age of 87 at his home in Albuquerque.[23] He'll forever be known as a legend in the world of racing. But because of one ill-fated trip, he'll also be known as a federal convict.

Three Felonies a Day

Reasonable people can debate whether Bobby Unser deserved to be fined. But did he deserve to be charged criminally and face potential incarceration as a 62-year-old man, all for (possibly) blundering off course in a storm? Criminal law is "the heavy artillery of society."[24] A too-lenient penal code risks jeopardizing the safety of the community. A too-harsh one risks effecting a deep injustice on those it ensnares. As Professor Herbert Wechsler once wrote in making those observations, the criminal law's "promise as an instrument of safety is matched only by its power to destroy."[25]

Once, our criminal laws were reserved for enforcing a relatively small number of pretty intuitive and widely accepted norms: do not kill, do not steal, do not rob, and so on; conduct, as the legal scholar Henry M. Hart, Jr., once put it, that deserves "a formal and solemn pronouncement of the moral condemnation of the community."[26] Today, we have strayed far from that ideal. It's not uncommon these days to pick up a newspaper and read about a man who was imprisoned for not finishing the siding on his own home. Or a subway passenger who was handcuffed and booked for eating French fries in a subway station. Or individuals arrested for sharing food with the homeless in a public park. ("One of the police officers said, 'Drop that plate right now,' as if I were carrying a weapon," one of the arrestees later said.)[27] In Louisiana, a group of monks found out the hard way that making burial caskets without a license can lead to prison time (more on that in chapter 5).

Increasingly, too, the police are called even when children misbehave. In chapter 1, we saw one such case that made its way to me while I served as a judge on the Tenth Circuit. A 13-year-old thought it'd be fun to disrupt class with a cascade of burps. His classmates howled with laughter, but the teacher was justifiably dismayed. In the past, the boy's parents might have been called, the principal involved. Today? The teacher called authorities, who handcuffed and arrested the boy for the crime of "interfer[ing] with the educational process" in violation of state law.[28] In other cases, teenagers have been handcuffed for violating a school's dress code. Special education children have been pepper-sprayed for climbing on school furniture.[29]

Are these examples outliers? Maybe. But maybe they point to a truth, too. If the "heavy artillery" of the criminal law was once largely reserved for addressing obviously morally culpable behavior, today it's often applied to censure behavior that, if deserving of censure at all, used to be addressed through less forceful means—parental or community mediation or civil penalties. Looking at the growth of our criminal laws, Professor Douglas Husak estimates that 70 percent of adult Americans today have committed an imprisonable offense— many, maybe most, without even knowing it.[30] That estimate might be conservative. The attorney and journalist Harvey Silverglate has argued that the average American now commits three felonies a day.[31]

Just as criminal law was once reserved for relatively few and serious offenses, it was also once largely the province of state authorities. States were thought to possess general police powers, while the federal government enjoyed only a handful of expressly enumerated powers.

At the nation's founding, the first federal criminal statute contained fewer than fifty crimes (the exact number depends on how you count them).[32] Now, as we have seen, some scholars peg the number of federal statutory crimes at more than 5,000. Many are rarely enforced, but without sunset rules like some states have (see chapter 7), they remain ominously on the books.

All of this is relatively new as well. As a 1998 American Bar Association task force put it, "more than forty percent of the federal criminal provisions enacted since the Civil War have been enacted since 1970." The task force found that development "startling."[33] But if it was startling in 1998, in the ensuing years the exponential growth of criminal law has come to seem almost commonplace. For all the claims about congressional languor we hear about on the news, Congress has been busy adding an average of 56 new federal crimes to the books every year.[34]

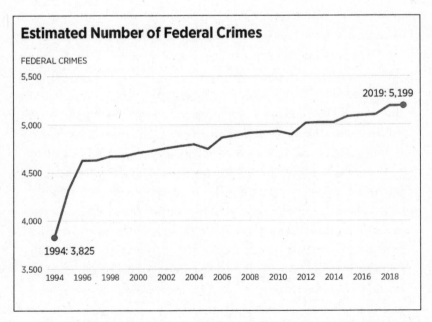

Not your parents' criminal code: The number of federal crimes has sky-rocketed since even the early 1990s. Source: The Heritage Foundation, Count the Code: Quantifying Federalization of Criminal Statutes.

As in so many other areas, too, Congress has increasingly delegated its criminal lawmaking powers to executive agencies. Now, many criminal laws are not the direct product of elected representatives accountable to us; they're the handiwork of agency officials. Remember the law Bobby Unser was alleged to have violated? Congress didn't write it. Instead, Congress delegated to the Secretary of Agriculture the task of making "provisions for the protection" of certain federal lands. To find the provision that ensnared Bobby, you have to turn to a section deep within the Code of Federal Regulations: Section 261.16(a) of Title 36 in Bobby's day.[35] Nor does anyone have a clue how many federal regulatory crimes are out there. As we have seen, the best anyone can do is guess that they number over 300,000.[36]

To be sure, no one institution or group is responsible for the proliferation of our criminal laws. They have exploded at the federal level, but they have grown dramatically at the state and local levels as well. As we come to trust one another less, our fears lead us to demand more protections from one another. And with ever more criminal laws comes an ever-growing criminal justice bureaucracy to enforce them. As one scholar has described it:

> Enforcement of criminal laws requires resources at every step of the way—police officers to investigate and apprehend suspects, prosecutors to bring them to justice, public defenders to represent the indigent, court reporters to record hearings, trial judges to preside over the proceedings and sentence convicted defendants, probation officers to prepare presentencing reports and supervise unincarcerated offenders, appellate judges to hear criminal appeals, an entire prison system to house convicted offenders and defendants awaiting trial, a parole board to determine when an offender is ready for early release, a commission to establish sentencing guidelines, and specialized bureaucracies for specialized crimes and crime-fighting programs.[37]

Along the way, the number of federal prosecutors and police divisions has ballooned. According to the National Association of

Criminal Defense Lawyers and the U.S. Chamber Institute for Legal Reform, "the ranks of federal prosecutors [have grown] from 1,500 in 1980 to roughly 7,500 today."[38] That's a *fivefold* increase during a time span when the nation's population didn't even double.[39] And while "most people have probably heard of the FBI, the Secret Service, and the DEA, . . . the truth is many [federal] regulatory agencies [now] have some law enforcement power."[40] The Department of Education, whose mission is to "promote student achievement," once noted on its website that it has agents who "exercise full law enforcement authority—carrying firearms, taking sworn statements, applying for and executing search and arrest warrants."[41] And remember the agent who boarded John Yates's boat? He was cross-deputized with the National Oceanic and Atmospheric Administration. Around the time of John's arrest, that agency reportedly had more than one hundred full-time personnel with firearm and arrest authority.[42] Before 1970, neither of these two agencies even existed in anything like their present form.

One Out of Forty-Seven

Not only have we adopted more criminal laws at an astonishing clip in recent years, but the punishments our criminal laws carry have also grown markedly. Beginning in earnest in the second half of the twentieth century, legislatures began to adopt laws that had, as Judge Jed Rakoff has noted, "two common characteristics: they imposed higher penalties, and they removed much of judicial discretion in sentencing." Notable among these laws were statutes imposing mandatory minimum terms of imprisonment for certain crimes.[43]

Today, sentencing changes like these can propel some sentences into the stratosphere. A defense attorney in Florida told *The Economist* that, looking at his clients' prison terms, it appeared to him that the United States was conducting "an experiment in imprisoning first-time non-violent offenders for periods of time previously reserved only for those who had killed someone." One of his clients who had been convicted of fraud was sentenced to 845 years. "I got it reduced to 835," the lawyer said with a sigh.[44] A group that looked across state prison systems found "a consistent upward trend in the amount of time people spend in state prisons" and that the "longest prison terms are getting longer."[45] Another group found that one out of every seven of those now incarcerated is serving a life sentence—more people in total than were serving *any* sentence in 1970. And while crime tends to be a "young man's game," 30 percent of those serving life sentences were found to be over the age of 55.[46]

Thanks to developments like these, the United States is now a world leader when it comes to incarceration. Our incarceration rate is not only eight times as high as the median rate in western European democracies, it is higher than the rates found even in some of our closest competitors such as Turkmenistan and Rwanda.[47] Like those of many states, federal prisons have been operating for years around or above 100 percent capacity.[48] And those who emerge from our prisons often confront collateral consequences that haunt them for years—including the loss of voting rights, licenses, public benefits, jobs, and access to housing.[49]

Just how new is all this? For a good portion of the twentieth century, incarceration rates in this country were pretty flat—so much so that, as Professor David Cole has explained, some criminologists imagined that they'd always be the same. From the 1940s to the 1960s, the prison population actually decreased. But since the 1970s, it has "mushroomed."[50] In all, more than a million Americans today are behind bars.[51] When those on parole or probation are included, the Department of Justice estimates, one out of every forty-seven adults is under "some form of correctional supervision."[52]

Nor, again, do the numbers tell the whole story. Much has been written about how, when the number of crimes increases and the punishments they carry grow more severe, respect for criminal law as a whole decreases. As far back as 1967, a presidential commission convened to study the nation's criminal justice system warned that a "substantial cost of overextended use of the criminal process is the risk of creating cynicism and indifference to the whole criminal law."[53] Or as Professor William Stuntz once put it, "too much law amounts to no law at all," for "when legal doctrine makes everyone an offender, the relevant offenses have no meaning independent of law enforcers' will. The formal rule of law yields to the functional rule of official discretion."[54]

Take what happened during the covid-19 pandemic as a microcosm. Before the pandemic, many legislatures across the country adopted laws granting executive officials discretion to declare states of emergencies. Many governors, mayors, and others deployed those emergency powers during the pandemic and used them to announce their own new rules. Some observers defended the rules as essential; others questioned them. Either way, the rules often shifted from week to week and from town to town in ways difficult for people to track. In some jurisdictions, people were arrested or criminally charged for doing what in any other time could only be described as "living life." One researcher looked into the practices of a single city and found that one man had been cited for "[s]itting in front of his home listening to music"; another for "being on a city street unnecessarily with two other individuals"; and yet another group for "milling around aimlessly."[55] Many of the targeted individuals were members of less powerful constituencies or minority groups. Government officials targeted churches but not favored businesses.[56] And early in the pandemic, *Time* magazine pointed to studies finding that "people of color were 2.5 times more likely to be punished for violations of covid-19 orders than white people."[57]

Much more could be (and has been) said about the hidden costs of expanding the reach of criminal law and the wreckage it can leave behind for individuals, their families, and their communities. But here, consider just one man's story. As recounted by Trent England, Andrew M. Grossman, Erica A. Little, and others, as a young man George Norris fell in love with orchids. Eventually, he quit his job as a construction worker with the hope of turning his passion into a living. He worked hard, traveling to Peru, Ecuador, and Mexico in search of exotic plants, building his business slowly over time. Eventually he made a name for himself, collectors increasingly turned to him, and his small business began to flourish. Then one day in October 2003, his life turned upside down.

That day, six federal agents dressed in black body armor and bearing firearms pulled up to his home in three pickup trucks. Two went around the back of the house, while another approached the front door. When George opened the door, the agents announced that they were executing a search warrant and swept in, ordering George to sit in the kitchen while an agent watched over him.[58] His wife was out at the time, but a neighbor soon alerted her about the brewing trouble (apparently agents had been asking passersby what they knew about "the criminal activity" going on at the house). When she called her husband, she found him "frightened" and "confused"; "there was no telling what this was about."

Mrs. Norris later testified that the agents had "ransacked" their home, dumping drawers full of belongings onto the floor, all before carting away some 37 boxes of the couple's possessions, including Mr. Norris's computer. It took about five months for the Norrises to learn that George was under investigation for importing orchids without proper documentation.[59] After federal authorities indicted him on seven counts, George surrendered to officials, who placed him in handcuffs and leg shackles—by that point he was 67 years old—and confined him in a cell with three other arrestees. One was suspected for murder; two for dealing drugs. When he told his cellmates he was in for orchids, they erupted with laughter. One quipped: "What do you do with these things, smoke 'em?"

George tried to fight, but the legal bills racked up. Eventually, he changed his not-guilty plea to guilty. "I absolutely hated that," he later said. "The hardest thing I ever did was stand there and say I was guilty to all these things. I didn't think I was guilty of any of them." He was sentenced to seventeen months in prison (the government had asked for about double that time). He was then and forever labeled a federal felon. He reported to prison in January 2005; was temporarily released while an appellate court heard his case; then returned to prison to serve the remainder of his term. For seventy-one days, officials reportedly segregated him in solitary confinement (though, as it turned out, he was actually with two other inmates thanks to overcrowding). The reason? Some say it was because he had brought sleeping pills into prison—this despite the fact that he suffered from Parkinson's disease. Finally, George was released in April 2007.[60] His wife later testified that:

> The hardest part is I lost the man I married. He came home from prison and he ate and he slept and he sat on the couch and looked at the TV, but he wasn't really watching it. . . . It was like having him in a coma, almost. He wouldn't water a plant, he wouldn't call the grandkids, he wouldn't invite a friend over, he didn't want to go out to dinner. Nothing.[61]

The family struggled with their finances, having used their savings to pay for George's defense. George's business was done, his greenhouse abandoned; he simply didn't have it in him anymore. "I don't sleep like I used to; I still have prison dreams," he later told an interviewer. And then in a quiet voice he added, "It's utterly wrecked our lives." By the way, those agents, the ones who arrived at the Norrises' door, armed and in body armor? Some were from the U.S. Fish and Wildlife Service.[62]

Of course, not every federal felon is like George Norris. Many sitting behind bars are serving time for violent crimes or conduct that most would recognize as reprehensible. Doubtless, too, new criminal laws are sometimes needed to address new social developments (the internet, for example). And surely the federal government has a role to play in the criminal field, including to thwart criminal schemes that cross state lines or to secure fundamental rights protected by the federal Constitution. But are more criminal laws and longer sentences the answers to every problem?

An "Evil-Meaning Mind"

Even beyond all the new laws and longer sentences, our criminal justice system is changing in more subtle but telling ways. In the next few sections, consider three examples, each of which involves a shift away from a presumption in favor of the individual and liberty and toward collective interests and greater punishment.

Begin with Joseph Morissette. In the years after World War II, Joseph lived with his wife and son in a small town in Michigan. A veteran of the war, the 27-year-old supported his young family by working at a fruit stand during the summer and as a trucker and scrap iron collector in the winter.[63] One day in December 1948, he went hunting with his brother-in-law on a tract of uninhabited land known to locals as good deer habitat. The area had been used by the U.S. Air Force as a practice bombing range where simulated bombs made up of metal cylinders filled with sand and black powder were dropped onto ground targets. Once used, the spent casings were thrown haphazardly into piles so they would be "out of the way." By the time Joseph ventured onto the land, some of the casings had been lying there for years.

Joseph didn't come home with any deer that day, but he did stumble on a heap of spent casings. Thinking he would at least cover the expenses of his hunting trip by salvaging some, he loaded them onto his truck. In the end, he realized $84 from his venture, about $1,000 today.[64] All of that was done in broad daylight, without any effort at concealment.

When FBI agents eventually came calling, Joseph spoke candidly, explaining that he thought the casings had been abandoned. Unimpressed, officials indicted him for stealing government property in violation of federal law. The trial judge wasn't impressed, either, with Joseph's insistence that he had acted innocently. Whether Joseph believed the casings had been abandoned or intended to steal them, the judge ruled, was neither here nor there. Ultimately, the court convicted Joseph and sentenced him to two months in prison or a fine of $200.

In time, the case made its way to the Supreme Court—and, once there, the justices united in throwing out Joseph's conviction. Writing for the Court, Justice Robert H. Jackson explained that a criminal offense generally requires proof of an "evil-meaning mind" as well as "an evil-doing hand." Put simply, with only limited exceptions, the government must show that the defendant committed a particular act (*actus reus*) with a particular mental state (*mens rea*). Because that hadn't happened in Joseph's case, the Court explained, his conviction couldn't stand. The prosecution might have proved that he had committed a proscribed act, but it hadn't proved that he had acted with anything worse than an innocent state of mind.

The "evil-meaning mind" requirement was hardly something new or particular to Joseph's case. It was, as Justice Jackson stressed, an ancient feature of Anglo-American law that rested on a "belief in freedom of the human will."[65] To *choose* to do something, our law has long recognized, is to embrace and endorse it, to make it part of your life's story in a very different way than undertaking the same act innocently or accidentally. As a society steeped in respect for the individual, we have traditionally taken account of this in our criminal laws.

Just consider an example involving two defendants, one who intentionally kills another person and a second who takes a life through some negligent action. Both actions yield the same result. But in a society concerned with the individual as well as societal interests, liberty as well as safety, and intentions as well as consequences, we recognize that a person who *purposefully* harms another is very different from one who does so *negligently*. Or, as Oliver Wendell Holmes, Jr., put it, "even a dog distinguishes between being stumbled over and being kicked."[66]

Professor Herbert Wechsler once spoke of *mens rea* requirements this way: "To condemn when fault is absent is barbaric. It is the badge of tyranny, the plainest illustration of injustice."[67] The influential model penal code Wechsler helped assemble in the 1960s endorsed just that view, indicating that a *mens rea* requirement should presumptively attach to material elements of a crime.[68] More than that, the code carefully laid out different grades of *mens rea* ranging from intent to knowledge to recklessness to negligence—all because we recognize that calibrating a just punishment often turns on the nature of the defendant's state of mind.[69]

While scholars have dug up some criminal offenses before the mid–nineteenth century in England and the United States that required no proof of *mens rea*, those crimes were "to be found only occasionally, [and] chiefly among the nuisance cases." In his 1933 article "Public Welfare Offenses," Professor Francis Bowes Sayre observed that, by his time, the number of offenses without *mens rea* requirements had grown. He attributed the shift to "the demands of an increasingly complex social order," along with "the trend of the day away from nineteenth century individualism toward a new sense of the importance of collective interests." Still, Sayre found, these new "public welfare" offenses generally threatened only "light monetary fines rather than imprisonment." To go further than that and "subject defendants entirely free from moral blameworthiness to the possibility of prison sentences," Sayre added, would be "revolting to the community sense of justice."[70]

Yet if that was once our society's compromise between individual and collective interests, it is a compromise that has been "unraveling" ever since. In recent decades, scholars have documented a remarkable growth in "public welfare" offenses with meager or no *mens rea* requirements.[71] One study, for example, looked at "446 non-violent, non-drug criminal offenses proposed in the 109th Congress and found that 57 percent of those had either no, or only a very weak, *mens rea* requirement"; in the end, 23 were enacted.[72] Many of these new "public welfare" offenses also carry with them the possibility of heavy fines and serious terms of incarceration. As one scholar has put it, in our day "traditional public welfare offenses . . . have been upgraded to felony status."[73] Just compare Joseph Morissette with Bobby Unser. Back in 1952, the Supreme Court was unwilling to entertain the possibility that the federal government might send Joseph to prison for two months without any hint he had meant to do wrong. Meanwhile, in the 1990s the federal courts upheld Bobby's conviction for an offense without any *mens rea* requirement that carried a six-month potential term of incarceration.

Fair Notice?

If that's one subtle shift in our criminal laws, here is another. Historically, English courts were loath to punish a man if he didn't have fair notice of the law's demands.[74] In the United States, this fair notice promise was understood to inhere in the Constitution's guarantee of due process of law.[75] As Justice John Marshall Harlan II wrote, "in a civilized state the least that can be expected of government is that it express its rules in language all can reasonably be expected to understand."[76] Like the *mens rea* requirement, the fair notice demand was long considered essential to the protection of individual liberty and intrinsic to the idea that just punishment follows blameworthy choices.

One part of our law's fair notice demand is expressed in vagueness doctrine. For centuries, judges have declined to enforce statutes or rules that are so vague that ordinary people cannot tell what conduct is out of bounds. The doctrine is still alive today, but the changed character of our criminal laws strains its ideals.[77] Today, it's not just that an ordinary person may have trouble understanding *a* particular law or *a* particular regulation. Fair notice problems now run deeper than that.

Recall from chapter 1 that we have no "federal criminal code" to which people can turn to discern the law's demands.[78] Instead, criminal prohibitions are peppered throughout the U.S. Code and federal regulations.[79] And what was lawful today can become unlawful tomorrow in ways that are not always easy to keep up with. Just consider what happened to Carlton Wilson. He bought firearms legally, yet his circumstances changed years later so that his once lawful possession became a federal crime. When officials prosecuted him under what the federal appellate court called "a relatively new and obscure" law, they didn't blink when Mr. Wilson told them he hadn't known about the law. "Ignorance of the law is no excuse," the maxim goes—and for his ignorance Mr. Wilson landed in prison for more than three years.[80]

Nor is it always a defense when the government itself has approved your course of conduct. According to congressional testimony, the Environmental Protection Agency once created a hotline to field questions about a particularly complex law governing the disposal of hazardous waste. But there was a catch. The agency said it couldn't guarantee the accuracy of its advice, and prosecutors said that reliance on the agency's incorrect information wouldn't qualify as a defense.[81] Another agency, the Internal Revenue Service, for a period gave wrong answers about a third of the time to callers on its hotline. When asked about its error rate, agency officials reportedly, and without a hint of irony, "pointed to the growing complexity of the nation's tax laws and the numerous and rapid tax-code changes that have been made in recent years."[82] That agency's hit rate later improved to over 90 percent, but by then another issue arose: only a fraction of callers (11 percent in 2021) could get through to an agency representative.[83]

Beyond the criminal law's sheer size is the fact that some of our most potent statutes are nearly impossible for even judges and lawyers to understand. Take just two examples. The first we encountered briefly in chapter 1. It criminalizes "scheme[s] or artifice[s]" to "deprive another of the intangible right of honest services."[84] What does that mean? For years after the law's enactment, lower court judges debated the question and reached wildly different judgments.[85] When the Supreme Court finally took up the issue, a Department of Justice lawyer explained the agency's view that the law criminalized "divided loyalties" in the workplace. Justice Stephen Breyer responded by pointing out that "perhaps there are 150 million workers in the United States. I think possibly 140 [million] of them would flunk your test."[86] Ultimately, the Court rejected the government's expansive interpretation of the statute and adopted a narrower construction that largely restricted the law's application to schemes involving bribes and kickbacks accepted by individuals who owe a fiduciary duty to their employer.[87] But even that didn't solve all the problems. Does the law cover only public officials who owe a fiduciary duty to the government? Does it apply to private individuals who contract with the government? Or does it apply to *everyone* who owes some sort of fiduciary duty to his employer? Even today, no one can be sure.[88]

How about "aggravated identity theft"? Perhaps most people would agree that someone who deliberately steals another person's identity and racks up massive charges in her name engages in wrongful conduct that may merit a stint behind bars. But the federal statute criminalizing identity theft is written so broadly that, as the government has sought to read it, the label "aggravated identity thief" could be affixed to almost every adult American: every bill splitter who has overcharged a friend using a mobile payment service such as Venmo; every contractor who has rounded up his billed time by even a few minutes; every college hopeful who has overstated his involvement in the high school glee club.[89]

Maybe this state of affairs would be tolerable were it not for that maxim that ensnared Carlton Wilson: "Ignorance of the law is no excuse." It's an ancient proposition premised on an assumption that most people know right from wrong in a criminal justice system that reflects fundamental community norms. As Professor Hart once explained, if our penal code "does a sound job of reflecting community attitudes and needs, actual knowledge of the wrongfulness of the prohibited conduct will usually exist."[90] The idea is a simple one: You cannot get away with murder by claiming you didn't know there was a statute forbidding you to kill. In a civilized society, we presume you have understood that much from an early age.

What happens, though, when the criminal law grows so much that it no longer reflects just everyday intuitions but holds even seemingly ordinary conduct unlawful? In those circumstances, Hart argued that any defense of that old maxim must "necessarily shift[] its ground from a demand that every responsible member of the community understand and respect the community's moral values to a demand that everyone know and understand what is written in the statute books. Such a demand is *toto coelo* different." It is a different demand that poses us with new questions, too: If a criminal law does not reflect common intuitions, how can an ordinary person be expected to know about it—or even know to look for it? Has criminality now sometimes become just "a matter of ill chance, rather than blameworthy choice"?[91]

The Rule of Lenity

Still another ancient principle of Anglo-American criminal law has long sought to balance the scale between individual and collective interests: the rule of lenity. If vagueness doctrine aims to protect individuals against laws that *do not* fairly define prohibited conduct, the rule of lenity applies to laws that *do* define prohibited conduct but are susceptible to different interpretations. In cases like that, the rule encourages judges to pick an interpretation that is respectful of the individual.

The rule of lenity played a prominent role in this country for most of our history. Spin through criminal cases from the founding era, and you will see it applied again and again by some of our most highly revered judges.[92] But as with so much else, something has changed in recent years. "One of the oldest canons of interpretation" is now described by some scholars as an "afterthought or curiosity" in federal jurisprudence, "no more than a tie-breaker at best; a throwaway doctrine at worst."[93]

Consider how things used to work. In 1820, the Supreme Court took up the case of a seaman charged under a federal statute that prohibited manslaughter on the "high seas." But, as it turned out, the seaman had killed someone on a river in China, 35 miles above the mouth of the river. Chief Justice John Marshall freely admitted that Congress might have intended to cover the seaman's conduct. Still, he said, "penal laws are to be construed strictly" because of "the tenderness of the law for the rights of individuals," and because every person has a right to suffer only those punishments dictated by "the plain meaning of words" found in the law. Because a reasonable doubt existed about whether "high seas" encompassed foreign rivers, Chief Justice Marshall concluded, that doubt had to be resolved in favor of the individual, not the government; all individuals, even unsavory ones, are entitled to fair notice of the law's demands.[94]

Today, some seek to replace this traditional version of the rule of lenity with a weaker one. While in the past any reasonable doubt about the law had to be resolved in favor of liberty, some now argue that lenity should apply only when the law contains a "grievous" ambiguity. All of which means that a person can be imprisoned for transgressing an ambiguous legal rule, one not obvious to many or maybe even most people, so long as the law isn't later deemed "grievously" ambiguous by a judge. Sometimes, too, judges will thumb through reams of legislative history or speculate about a statute's purpose to resolve perceived ambiguities *before* consulting the rule of lenity. Exactly the sort of enterprise Chief Justice Marshall refused to countenance back in 1820 when he admitted that Congress very well might have intended to include the sailor's conduct but held that insufficient to overcome the rule of lenity.[95]

Just compare the way the Supreme Court resolved that case with the way it resolved another one in the late 1990s. In *Muscarello v. United States*, the Court faced a statute imposing a five-year mandatory prison term on any person who "uses or *carries* a firearm" "during and in relation to" a "drug trafficking crime."[96] The defendant had transported marijuana in his truck to sell to others. At the time, he also had a gun in a locked glove compartment. Did the defendant "*carry* a gun" during and in relation to his drug-trafficking crime and thus trigger a mandatory five-year prison term? The Court said yes, dismissing the rule of lenity along the way. To be sure, the Court admitted, the term "carry" can have different meanings in different contexts. To be sure, too, in some senses the term "carry" might seem to require more than having a gun locked away nearby. But, the Court concluded, there was no "grievous" ambiguity.[97]

Aaron Swartz

From a young age, Aaron Swartz proved to be unusually gifted. He could read by age three, built and programmed an ATM in elementary school, and a few years later created an online user-generated encyclopedia—an early sort of Wikipedia. By fourteen, he was helping write code for a nonprofit founded by Professor Lawrence Lessig (formerly of Stanford, now at Harvard). In the span of the next few years, Aaron was accepted to Stanford, dropped out, codeveloped Reddit, and, once that was sold, became a teenage millionaire.[98]

Aaron had little interest in money, though, and soon turned to activism, dedicating himself "to limiting the amount of power institutions could wield over individuals." Among other things, he collaborated with the founder of a nonprofit that sought to provide free access to public government documents not covered by copyright law.

Along the way, Aaron became particularly interested in the federal government's Public Access to Court Electronic Records (PACER) system. Typically, PACER required members of the public to pay for electronic access to documents filed in open court proceedings. Aaron thought those materials should be available for free, and in the fall of 2008 he downloaded large volumes of them. As *The New York Times* reported, the government "was not pleased." Federal officials investigated Aaron's conduct and even surveilled his parents' home. Eventually, however, the government dropped its investigation and Aaron's lawyers reportedly told his family that it didn't seem any laws had been broken.

A little later, Aaron connected his computer to MIT's networks—by then, he was a fellow at nearby Harvard.[99] Much as he had done with PACER, he began downloading articles from JSTOR, an online library containing academic articles, books, and research materials. For the next several months, JSTOR worked with the university to identify the person responsible for the downloads.[100] After enlisting the help of law enforcement (the Secret Service got involved), MIT installed a hidden camera that recorded Aaron's activities. Soon after that, he was arrested.[101]

The motive for Aaron's conduct remains unclear, but many suspected that he intended it as an act of civil disobedience in line with his belief in open access to ideas and information.[102] Regardless, once caught, he returned the articles to JSTOR and the company considered the matter closed, telling the U.S. Attorney's Office that it "preferred that no charges be brought."[103]

Federal officials had other ideas. They charged Aaron with wire fraud and three counts under the Computer Fraud and Abuse Act of 1986.[104] Federal officials also subpoenaed Aaron's then girlfriend, believing she knew about his activities. Eventually, prosecutors floated a deal that offered Aaron four to six months in prison if he agreed to plead guilty to multiple felonies. The prosecutors argued it was a good deal. On their theory, Aaron had taken articles worth some two million dollars, conduct that exposed him to years in prison under applicable sentencing guidelines. Aaron's lawyer saw things differently: "I said, 'What he took from JSTOR wasn't worth anything! It was a bunch of, like, the 1942 edition of the *Journal of Botany*!' The idea that Aaron should be sentenced the same way as someone who tries to beat someone out of two million dollars in a security-fraud scam? Someone who steals money from people?"[105]

In the end, Aaron refused the prosecutors' deal. What he couldn't stomach, friends and family said, was the idea that he'd be labeled a felon.[106] He also worried how he would fare in prison. "Aaron was a small man," his lawyer explained. "He was sensitive. He was shy. He was intellectual. He didn't seem to be like a very strong candidate for federal prison." "But beyond all that," his girlfriend added, "he just really thought he was innocent."[107]

After Aaron declined their offer, prosecutors added another nine counts to their charges against him, exposing him now to decades in prison and millions in fines.[108] As these events unfolded, Aaron's mother fell ill and his money began to dwindle.[109] He hated the prospect of asking others for financial help, yet going to trial wouldn't be cheap. "I had a clear sense of how devastating this was to him," his father said. "Because of the financial cost, because of the uncertainty of the penalties, because of how it changed his life and the effect it had on his relationships. All of those things were very hard for him."

On January 11, 2013, a few months before trial, Aaron committed suicide.[110] His family released a statement, declaring his death "not simply a personal tragedy" but "the product of a criminal justice system rife with intimidation and prosecutorial overreach."[111] The U.S. Attorney released her own statement: "I must . . . make clear that this office's conduct was appropriate in bringing and handling this case."[112]

Aaron Swartz

In the days after Aaron's suicide, his former mentor, Professor Lessig, penned a tribute to Aaron, describing him as "brilliant, and funny. A kid genius. A soul, a conscience." But Lessig did more than eulogize Aaron; he also asked all of us to consider what had driven Aaron to do what he'd done:

[Aaron] is gone today, driven to the edge by what a decent society would only call bullying. I get wrong. But I also get proportionality. . . .

[T]he question this government needs to answer is why it was so necessary that Aaron Swartz be labeled a "felon." For in the 18 months of negotiations, that was what he was not willing to accept, and so that was the reason he was facing a million dollar trial in April—his wealth bled dry. . . .

Fifty years in jail, charges our government.[113]

Aaron's case is a tragedy, his death an incalculable loss for his family and friends. It also illustrates a number of notable trends in our criminal justice system.

In the first place, notice that surveillance video contributed to Aaron's arrest. Private institutions that conduct surveillance (such as MIT) may not be bound by the same rules as law enforcement. And surely no one wants a world in which criminals can easily hide their crimes. But should we blind ourselves to the fact that at the same time criminal laws have expanded to touch more and more aspects of our daily lives, the tools the government can use to track suspects have also increased exponentially? Even in the 1990s, witnesses pretty much had to guess where Bobby Unser had driven his snowmobile and a judge had to use wire to measure distances on a map. Today, we live in a world where cell phones, cell tower records, and automated license plate readers can track and record our every move. Some researchers even estimate that one in two Americans may be found in a law enforcement facial recognition database.[114]

Consider, too, how judicial interpretations of the Fourth Amendment over the last half of the twentieth century intersect with these new technologies. Without securing a warrant premised on probable cause of a crime, police can pick through your curbside trash. They can access your bank records and maybe even your medical records and DNA. They can hover a helicopter (or now a drone?) 400 feet over your backyard, too.[115] Why isn't a warrant required? Because courts have held that no person has a "reasonable expectation of privacy" that would be invaded by this conduct—a standard the Court created in the 1960s to delineate what counts as a search or seizure deserving of constitutional protection.[116]

Even old-fashioned searches are now easier. To search your home, the government still usually needs a warrant supported by probable cause of a crime. But when the menu of available crimes to pick from expands, the protection of the home diminishes. Just think back to George Norris, whose house was ransacked for the crime of having inaccurate paperwork for his orchids.

If it's become easier for the government to *find* a crime, that's nothing compared to how easy it's become to *prosecute* one. Bobby Unser and Aaron Swartz are rarities these days for declining plea deals. In recent years, about 97 percent of felony convictions at the federal level and 94 percent of felony convictions at the state level have come by way of plea agreements.[117] It's yet one more relatively new development in our criminal justice system. In his article "Plea Bargaining and Its History," Professor Albert Alschuler traced the history of plea bargaining and concluded that it "was essentially unknown during most of the history of the common law." In fact, "for many centuries Anglo-American courts did not encourage guilty pleas but actively discouraged them." That started to change around the end of the nineteenth century, but, once again, transformational change came only in the latter half of the twentieth.[118] As one scholar recounted in 2005, while the federal guilty plea rate "stayed flat during some periods and even declined significantly during the 1950s and 1960s," it experienced "a relentless climb from the early 1970s."[119]

This newly aggressive reliance on plea bargaining to adjudicate guilt represents a radical shift for a nation that professes to value trial by jury as the gold standard for testing culpability. "The Trial of all Crimes," Article III of the Constitution says, "except in Cases of Impeachment, shall be by Jury." Our founders valued the jury trial so highly that they repeated its guarantee in the Bill of Rights. In the Sixth Amendment, defendants are assured not just the right to a "speedy and public trial" by an "impartial" jury but also certain rights during trial itself, among them the right to confront witnesses against them and to have the assistance of counsel for their defense.

On the surface, our devotion to the trial may seem unshaken. We still venerate the great trial lawyers of the past and consume vast quantities of television courtroom dramas. So how is it that the criminal trial has in short order become a feature more of fiction than fact? Surely this development has something to do with the changes to our criminal laws we have already discussed—including the growing number of criminal offenses, lowered *mens rea* standards, and the rise of ever more draconian penalties. Often, prosecutors can now pick from a smorgasbord of criminal offenses and heap on many overlapping charges, some with low or no *mens rea* requirements, all carrying their own potential penalties, sometimes including formidable mandatory minimum prison terms.

Pause for a moment over Aaron's predicament. He faced the possibility of years in prison under the initial counts the prosecutors assembled. Meanwhile, the government offered him a four-to-six-month sentence if he agreed to plead guilty. The pressure to accept a deal like that is obvious, especially when a prosecutor can add more charges carrying more prison time if a defendant refuses to plead guilty (as the prosecutor did in Aaron's case). Nor is the predicament Aaron faced unusual. A 2018 study estimated that the average sentence a defendant receives for embezzlement after a federal trial is about eight times as long as the sentence a defendant receives when he pleads guilty (4.7 years versus 0.6). For antitrust violations the difference is 12.1 years compared to 1.4 years. Much the same goes for many other offenses.[120] Surveying the field, one federal judge has remarked that the sentences prosecutors are able to threaten if a defendant goes to trial can be "so excessively severe they take your breath away."[121]

Should we care? Plea deals save taxpayers the expense of trials. They allow prosecutors to process more cases and keep more criminals off the street.[122] But nothing in life is free, and with these benefits come costs. In an early plea-bargaining case from the 1970s, the

Supreme Court heard a case involving Paul Hayes. He was indicted on a forged check charge (amount at stake: $88.30) and was offered a five-year recommended sentence if he agreed to plead guilty. He refused, professing his innocence. At that point, the prosecutor made good on a threat he had made during bargaining if Hayes didn't "save the court the inconvenience and necessity of a trial": he returned to the grand jury and secured an indictment for an additional charge under the state's three-strikes law, which carried a mandatory sentence of life in prison. At trial, Hayes was convicted and duly sentenced to life—even though one of the convictions triggering the three-strikes law had resulted in probation and the other a stint in a state reformatory beginning as a teenager. The Court found the prosecutor's threat permissible, reasoning that "whatever might be the situation in an ideal world, the fact is that the guilty plea and the often concomitant plea bargain are important components of this country's criminal justice system."[123]

In the wake of that case, similar tactics have proliferated. In his posthumously published book *The Collapse of American Criminal Justice*, Professor Stuntz highlighted instances in which the government induced one defendant to plead guilty by "threatening to incarcerate his sick wife for the balance of her life" and threatened to imprison another defendant's "parents for trying to help him evade capture—an offense that is almost never enforced against anyone, much less against suspects' families." After detailing more cases like these, Stuntz went on to argue that "outside the plea bargaining process, such threats would be deemed extortionate. Within that process, such threats [have become] par for the course."[124]

John Zenger

Our founders favored jury trials for a reason. With a jury, questions of guilt or innocence are not resolved by negotiations with officials who hold the cards and enjoy largely unreviewable discretion in playing them. Instead, the decision whether to bring the full force of the government's penal powers to bear on an individual depends on the judgment of private citizens—peers of the accused who can look at the sum total of the evidence, including the government's conduct, and decree whether a man deserves punishment. A jury's verdict of acquittal is final; no official can appeal it. In a public trial, police and prosecutorial misconduct can be brought to light, dubious evidence tested, and official overreach turned aside. Really, it is another feature of our separation of powers designed to pit power against power to ensure that no one enjoys too much authority and the awesome might of the government is not abused. For just these sorts of reasons, Thomas Jefferson once said that he considered trial by jury "the only anchor, ever yet imagined by man, by which a government can be held to the principles of its constitution."[125]

As we close this chapter, consider how things once looked. John Zenger was a German immigrant and printer in prerevolutionary America. When William Cosby, the British colonial governor of New York, summarily removed from office a state judge whose decisions displeased him, the former judge banded together with allies and established a newspaper, the *New-York Weekly Journal*, with Zenger as its printer.[126] Unlike its rival paper, which supported the governor, the *Weekly Journal* published critical articles and lampoons of Cosby. Irked, Cosby maneuvered to have Zenger arrested for seditious libel and thrown in jail. The presiding judges, who served at the pleasure of the governor, set bail far above Zenger's means and then disbarred his two attorneys.[127] Zenger's prospects looked bleak.

But then Zenger's allies managed to secure for him the representation of a leading colonial lawyer, Andrew Hamilton. At the trial that followed, one of the judges instructed the jury to consider only whether Zenger published the offending issues of the *Weekly Journal*. Given that instruction, there seemed no question of Zenger's guilt—and, indeed, when Hamilton rose to speak on behalf of his client he

The trial of John Zenger

admitted that Zenger had published the articles in question.[128] But he also famously implored the jury:

> The question before the Court and you, Gentlemen of the jury, is not of small or private concern. It is not the cause of one poor printer, nor of New York alone, which you are now trying. No! It may in its consequence affect every free man that lives under a British government on the main of America. It is the best cause. It is the cause of liberty.[129]

After a short deliberation, the jury found Zenger not guilty. Cheers erupted in the courtroom; Hamilton was hailed as a hero; and Zenger, released from jail, promptly went back to printing the *Weekly Journal.* One of his first orders of business was publishing an account of his trial.[130]

What does Zenger's experience have to offer us today? Prosecutors perform a vital function in our society. But perhaps Zenger's trial is a reminder of some of what can be lost when guilt is negotiated behind closed doors by officials who enjoy tremendous leverage and largely unreviewable discretion. These arrangements may be the result of good intentions in pursuit of useful social purposes. But the law of unintended consequences is an unforgiving one, and, as Justice Louis Brandeis once put it, "experience should teach us to be most on our guard to protect liberty when the Government's purposes are beneficent."[131] When criminal offenses multiply, penalties mount, *mens rea* requirements disappear, and the force of vagueness doctrine and the rule of lenity recede, the intentions may be good ones, too. But tinker too much with the balance of power our Constitution envisioned and you risk ushering us into a precarious world.

CHAPTER 5

THE FORGOTTEN AMERICANS

How much more precious is a little humanity
than all the rules in the world.

—JEAN PIAGET[1]

Your Farm or Your Faith

IN 1737, THE *CHARMING NANCY* DOCKED IN PHILADELPHIA HARBOR after an 84-day transatlantic voyage from Rotterdam. The ship carried 21 Amish families fleeing religious persecution in the Old World and seeking the freedom to live out their faith in a new one.[2] The journey had been perilous; according to some sources, of the 312 passengers who had set out from Europe, at least 24 had died—most of them children.[3] When recording notable events along the voyage, one diarist focused principally on the deaths: "We landed in England the 8th of July, remaining 9 days in port during which 5 children died. Went under sail the 17th of July. The 21st of July my own Lisbetli died. Several days before Michael's Georgli had died. On the 29th of July three children died. On the first of August my Hansli died and Tuesday previous 5 children died. On the 3rd of August contrary winds beset the vessel from the first to the 7th of the month three more children died."[4]

Many of the Amish in our country today can trace their ancestors to passengers on that voyage or a handful of others like it. Those who risked the trip were often attracted to William Penn's "holy experiment" of religious toleration in the Pennsylvania Colony, whose charter posited that "no People can be truly happy, though under the greatest Enjoyment of Civil Liberties, if abridged of the Freedom of their Consciences, as to their Religious Profession and Worship."[5] To the Amish, that promise meant everything. In the seventeenth century, the Amish splintered off from Anabaptists, who had challenged traditional Christian orthodoxy and faced fierce hostility from authorities. Many Anabaptists were imprisoned and tortured; others were executed or enslaved. Some cities even hired "Anabaptist hunters" to capture suspected believers.[6] The Amish themselves were persecuted in similar ways.[7]

Even in America, the Amish have faced pressures to conform. Wars, the rise of the welfare state, novel technologies, and modern educational expectations—each has forced the faithful to confront whether and how to adapt their religious convictions to changing conditions. Many Amish have refused military conscription on pain of punishment. Others have declined to participate in the Social Security program even after pressure from the IRS. When, during the Great Depression, the government proposed paying farmers to let their land lie fallow, some Amish resisted, finding it a "cruel" policy when so many were starving. Those who did comply often refused the government's reimbursements: "I don't think it's right to take money that isn't earned," one farmer told a reporter.[8] When states sought to impose compulsory schooling laws, a group of Amish families objected and ultimately won a victory in a Supreme Court opinion that extolled the virtues of freedom and toleration: "There can be no assumption that today's majority is 'right' and the Amish and others like them are 'wrong.' A way of life that is odd or even erratic but interferes with no rights or interests of others is not to be condemned because it is different."[9]

Perhaps most famously, the Amish have resisted adopting technological innovations, if to different degrees in different communities. Each community adheres to its own body of religious rules for daily life called the *Ordnung*. When a community disagrees over whether to adopt a new technology, fractures can follow. Over time, approximately forty different Amish communities have emerged within the United States.[10] Among the most traditional of these groups is the Swartzentruber Amish, who account for about 7 percent of the U.S. Amish population today.[11]

The Swartzentruber Amish refuse to embrace even technologies that other Amish groups have adopted.[12] As one minister has said, "We don't like to change. When you change, that's when you get into trouble." Many Swartzentruber Amish forgo indoor plumbing and electricity, do not own phones or cars, and use farming techniques harking back to the early 1900s. In part because of these restrictions, the Swartzentruber Amish communities are among the poorest in the Amish world.[13] One researcher described a successful furniture maker who responded to a backlog of orders not by expanding his business (which would have required hiring outside help) but by removing the wooden sign advertising his wares. In its place he put a new sign—"worms 3 cents"—"A boost to his young son's new business."[14]

In recent years, members of the Swartzentruber Amish have faced trouble from agency officials in Fillmore County, Minnesota. In 2014, Amos and Mattie Mast bought a parcel of land on which they hoped to raise their young family. Like many Swartzentruber Amish, the Masts weren't particularly well off and the land they purchased didn't have a house on it. It did, however, have an old building that had once been used as a schoolhouse, and, lacking other good options, the family moved into it while converting the structure to a home.[15]

The county objected. It had recently adopted new rules, pursuant to a statewide mandate, requiring homes to have modern septic systems for the disposal of "gray water"—household water used for washing dishes, laundry, and the like. Of course, the old schoolhouse didn't have a system like that, and Amos and Mattie believed that installing one would violate their faith. (Toilets were another matter; the family used an outhouse, and that was never the subject of dispute.)[16]

In an effort to accommodate the county, the Masts offered to dispose of their household gray water using a mulch basin system. Employing that kind of technology, they said, would not offend their faith. And, they stressed, some twenty states authorize mulch basins for the disposal of gray water.[17] The family also pointed out that, in Minnesota itself, thousands of campers, hunters, fishermen, and owners of rustic cabins are entirely exempt from gray water septic system mandates.[18]

The county wasn't having it. Officials told the Masts that they could not remain in their home permanently without a compliant modern septic system. Cease-and-desist letters followed. After a bit, officials even asked a court to remove the family from the land. (For good measure, officials told Amos that he was illegally selling handwoven crafts and baskets without a $250 "rural home-based business permit.")[19]

The Masts pleaded with the government not to make them leave. They explained that they had three small children aged three years, two years, and three months, and implored officials to consider "the public interest in preventing parents and their three children [from] becoming homeless in November." The Masts also noted their confusion: Wouldn't the gray water discharge of a family of five be less than that of the thirty-some students who had previously occupied the schoolhouse? Was there really an "imminent public health threat"—as the county put it—in their remaining on the land while negotiations continued, especially when so many others were exempt from the county's mandate?[20]

Their pleas went nowhere. Unable to reach common ground with the county, the Masts eventually joined forces with a number of other Swartzentruber Amish in the area who had fallen into the crosshairs of officials. The group filed a lawsuit alleging that state and local officials had accorded insufficient weight to their religious beliefs.[21]

In response, the county filed a counterclaim seeking a judicial order to remove *all* the families without modern septic systems from their homes.[22] The county also set about trying to prove that the Bible doesn't *really* say what the Amish think it says. (Among other things, the county argued that the Bible compels respect for secular authority.) And the government sought to prove that the Swartzentruber Amish don't *really* follow their own rules restricting the use of modern technology.[23] To that end, the government even asked the court to let their officials rummage around local Amish homes to see what technologies might be hidden there. The prosecution's biggest scoop? Perhaps the fact that, after some interrogation at trial, Mattie Mast acknowledged that she uses disposable diapers when traveling with her children.[24]

In the end, the Masts prevailed. But the road wasn't short or smooth. They lost on trial and appeal, and after the Supreme Court remanded their case to the state court, they lost yet again. Only after a second appeal did they finally succeed.[25] The whole episode took almost a decade before they carried the day.

The Twin "Evils"

In the last few chapters, we saw some of the costs associated with the rapid growth in our law—to rule-of-law values, to our aspirations for self-government, to the Constitution's separation of powers and rights promised to us as inalienable, to respect for law itself. But there's another, sometimes hidden cost that warrants attention. It has to do with equality.

When law expands rapidly in size and complexity, when important rules can change (and change back again) with ease and little warning, when important guidance is sometimes found only in an official's desk drawer, who are the winners and losers? In one sense, everyone may suffer. But who suffers the most? New septic system regulations may represent little more than a modest expense and a paperwork hassle for many people. Owners of rustic second homes may even have sufficient influence to win an exemption from the rules. But small and less powerful groups like the Amish often have a harder time making their case, and new rules can represent to them not just an expense or a hassle but an existential crisis. They may be forced to choose between losing their homes and violating their faith.

James Madison may not have anticipated the Masts' plumbing problems, but he had firm convictions about what too much law means for ordinary people. As he saw it, a nation awash in rapidly changing laws is a nation destined to favor the few, the wealthy, and the well-connected at the expense of the many, the vulnerable, and the unpopular. Madison's convictions on this score were the product of hard study. The first of twelve children, he was a voracious reader and eager student of history. One biographer noted that his education was grounded in the classics and the Bible and that he tried to "follow the lead of the Gospels in placing the individual at the heart of existence."[26]

It might have been easy to underestimate Madison. By some reports, he was our most diminutive president (standing about five feet, four inches) and contemporaries such as George Washington and Thomas Jefferson (both about six feet, two inches) towered over him. Madison was often sickly in his youth and at times thought himself destined for a short life. But in the end, he outlived most of the Constitution's other framers. He also prepared for the Constitutional Convention like no one else. Not only did he arrive early, he devoted long hours to studying ancient republics and the constitutions of the various states. He even prepared in advance the Virginia Plan, which played a large role in framing the Convention's deliberations.[27] During the proceedings, he kept notes that remain our best evidence of what transpired.[28] Later, he not only wrote the Bill of Rights, he also drafted an address for George Washington, Congress's response to it, and (yes) Washington's reply.[29] It's no exaggeration to say that when the founders needed a serious piece of thinking and writing done, James Madison was their man.

In preparing for the Convention, Madison compiled a list of "vices" in state and colonial political systems that he hoped the nation might avoid when drafting a new constitution. High on his list were the twin "evil[s]" of "multiplicity and mutability" in law. As he saw it, even in their "short period of independency," some states already "ha[d] filled as many pages [of law] as the century which preceded it"; laws had changed so quickly that they were sometimes "repealed or superseded . . . even before a knowledge of them [could] reach[] the remoter districts within which they were to operate."[30] As he later argued in Federalist No. 62, a government that permits its laws to grow so exuberantly and change so often is nothing less than "poison[]" to "the blessings of liberty." "The sagacious, the enterprising, and the moneyed few" may be able to track all the changes and even turn them to their benefit. But either way, they gain an "unreasonable advantage" over the "mass of the people." And that is a path, he worried, sure to corrode and eventually shatter the "attachment and reverence" citizens hold for their institutions and law itself.[31]

The Knowledge Gap

How exactly do the "multiplicity and mutability" of our laws impact the few and the many differently? In chapter 4, we explored how the growth and changes in our criminal law have created more and more traps for the unwary. Even those with money and sophistication can sometimes find themselves stepping into one of those traps unwittingly. But with more resources to access legal advice, they can often mitigate the risk in ways ordinary people like John Yates and Joseph Morissette cannot. Here, let's put the criminal side of the equation aside and consider just the price to equality that our growing law can carry for Americans who are fortunate enough never to find themselves facing a prosecutor.

One place to start might be this: By the government's count (probably an underestimate), Americans today spend 9.78 *billion* hours a year completing federal paperwork.[32] Harvard Law School Professor Cass Sunstein offers this way to think about that daunting figure:

Suppose that we assembled every resident of Chicago and insisted that for the entirety of 2019, each one must work forty hours a week engaged in just one task: filling out federal forms. By the end of 2019, the 2.7 million citizens of Chicago will not have come within four billion hours of the annual paperwork burden placed on Americans.

This paperwork burden has "massive negative effects," Sunstein explains, making it difficult for people to "enjoy fundamental rights . . . , to obtain licenses and permits, to obtain life-changing benefits, or to avoid crushing hardship." But who suffers the most? "As a practical matter," Sunstein observes, "the answer is often the poorest among us." The poor are less likely to have the resources and time to contend with the law's complexities and its demands. As Sunstein notes, other groups, such as elderly persons experiencing cognitive decline, may suffer disproportionately as well.[33] We might add to the list marginal groups with unpopular views like the Amish.

The trouble, of course, runs much deeper than paperwork. By the time you get to filling out paperwork, you usually have a sense of the rules you must satisfy and the forms you must complete. But today just *finding* the relevant law, regulation, guidance, or form can pose a serious challenge. As we saw in chapter 1, anyone wanting to find the federal laws and rules that govern them must consult (at a minimum) the U.S. Code and the Code of Federal Regulations. Both sets of books are behemoths, unmanageable for any single person to read, though the latter is worse—more than 120,000 pages worse. Still, at least they are written down in a series of published volumes. The same isn't true of guidance documents, which are scattered everywhere from blog posts to internal reference manuals.[34] And it's not hard to see who is most disadvantaged when law becomes so voluminous that just finding the relevant provisions becomes an ordeal.

Consider the straits Alfonzo De Niz Robles found himself in when his case came before me as a judge on the Tenth Circuit. A Mexican citizen married to a U.S. spouse, Mr. De Niz Robles sought to apply for lawful permanent residency in the United States. His situation was hardly unique. But trying to identify the relevant legal rules for his case proved almost impossible.

Start with this problem. Two different federal statutes appeared to speak to Mr. De Niz Robles's situation. The first indicated that individuals like him may remain in this country while they apply to the attorney general for permanent residency. But the second suggested that Mr. De Niz Robles and others like him must serve a ten-year waiting period *outside* the country before applying for admission.[35]

What was Mr. De Niz Robles supposed to do?

Helpfully, some years earlier the Tenth Circuit had considered a case about the interaction between these warring statutory commands. In the end, the court had held that the first provision trumped the second.[36] Given that, Mr. De Niz Robles did what most anyone would do: he remained in this country as he applied for permanent residency. At this point, you might think the story a little complicated but likely to yield a happy ending.

Not quite. For more than six years, the government sat on Mr. De Niz Robles's application. Finally, the Board of Immigration Appeals (BIA), acting on behalf of the attorney general, denied it. The agency didn't do so because of anything particular to Mr. De Niz Robles or any defect in his (considerable) paperwork. Instead, it sought to revisit the way the Tenth Circuit had resolved the conflict between the two conflicting statutes.

In the agency's view, the court had made a mistake. Properly read, the agency insisted, the second statute trumped the first, so individuals like Mr. De Niz Robles had to satisfy a ten-year waiting period outside the country before applying for admission. The agency further insisted that its views on how the law works deserved *Chevron* deference (see chapter 3). In fact, the agency not only told the Tenth Circuit that it had to defer to its view of the law, the agency also insisted that the court had to apply its view retroactively to Mr. De Niz Robles's case.

The upshot? Mr. De Niz Robles had already spent more than six years in this country waiting for action on his application; he had done so relying in good faith on federal court precedent.[37] But according to the agency, all that time had been wasted. Now he would have to start over with a ten-year waiting period outside the country, effectively turning his application process into a 16-year odyssey. "It was, like,

'Today you can wear a purple hat but tomorrow you can't,'" Mr. De Niz Robles's wife said about the agency's conduct. "It was mind-boggling."[38]

Unsurprisingly, Mr. De Niz Robles challenged the agency's view. And eventually, my old court provided him with some relief. Maybe, we said, Supreme Court precedent required giving agencies so much deference that they can effectively overrule federal appellate court decisions. But, we held, agencies may overrule federal courts only prospectively; they cannot apply their new rules retroactively to existing cases like Mr. De Niz Robles's. Individuals in his shoes were entitled to rely on existing judicial precedent.

Of course, none of that promised to help future immigrants. And in reality it didn't do much to help Mr. De Niz Robles. After our court's decision and close to a nine-year wait, he was still waiting for an answer from the BIA about his application for permanent residency.[39] By then his family had spent more than $40,000 on legal fees as the case bounced from agency to court and back to the agency again. Shortly before his case was set for yet another hearing, a reporter asked Mrs. De Niz Robles if she had a message to convey. She began to cry. "Look at the families," she said. "I just hope that they can come up with something that is justice."[40]

Just trying to describe all the ins and outs of Mr. De Niz Robles's case is hard. Imagine living it. In our legal system today, we ask ordinary individuals to find the relevant statutes, spot the contradictions, identify the relevant judicial precedent resolving those contradictions, and then anticipate potential changes an administrative agency might insist on years down the line. Maybe sophisticated corporations with elite lawyers can manage to navigate a world like that for the skilled foreign workers they seek to employ. But how can ordinary people be expected to keep up?

Apples and Compliance Costs

Suppose you manage to navigate the relevant law and complete all the paperwork perfectly. There still remains the cost of complying with so many laws from so many sources that are changing so often and so quickly. And those compliance costs, too, often have disparate impacts.

Some years ago, *The New York Times* wrote about a fifth-generation apple orchard owned by the Ten Eyck family in Altamont, New York. The patriarch of the family explained how, over the years, his business had become subject to more and more rules and regulations from more and more agencies: federal, state, and local. The *Times* ran the numbers and identified some 5,000 rules and restrictions relevant to orchards at just the federal level.

"The number of rules on ladders alone!" Mr. Ten Eyck said, pointing to "an assortment of rules, guidances, standards and training requirements associated with ladders, including how to achieve proper angling." He pointed as well to the farm's required safety plan; it calls for an employee to scour the orchard for mouse and deer droppings, the equivalent, he said, to looking for an earring on the ground. Why that particular requirement? Apparently to ensure that farm employees do not accidentally step on the droppings, then step on a ladder rung, then put their hand on the rung, then put that hand on an apple. Other rules specify the type of wedding rings that can be

Peter Ten Eyck II of Indian Ladder Farms

worn and prohibit chewing gum. Describing one visit from investigators that consumed about forty hours of family and staff time during the busy harvest season, *The New York Times* noted that "this is life on the farm. . . . With thick rule books laying out food safety procedures, compliance costs in the tens of thousands of dollars and ever-changing standards from the government and industry groups, local produce growers are a textbook example of what many business owners describe as regulatory fatigue."

Where does all this lead? One attorney who advises farmers explains that "so many of the farmers I've spoken with tell me that stricter and stricter regulations have put many of their neighbors and friends out of business, and in doing so cost them their homes, land and livelihoods." He worries especially about the impact on small farmers, predicting that "more of our fruits and vegetables will be grown by large domestic producers who can afford to comply with the regulations—at the expense of smaller competitors—and by produce farmers abroad."[41] After all, who is best suited to follow and implement 5,000 federal rules and countless state and local ones: a family farmer or a farming conglomerate?

Small apple farmers aren't alone in their struggles. Remember John Yates? A special master appointed by the Secretary of Commerce to review potential cases of prosecutorial misconduct against fishermen concluded that the regulations fishermen face are so "complex, complicated, constantly changing, and in some cases, contradictory" that many are "paranoid every time they come ashore to offload their catch that they will be met at the dock by a Special Agent who will look for and find a violation." Nor, the special master concluded, is their paranoia entirely unfounded; the cases he reviewed "support this conclusion."[42] Meanwhile, an earlier study by the Office of Inspector General of the Department of Commerce noted that many fishermen believe officials are "intentionally putting small fishermen out of business in favor of corporate fishing entities," while other studies of specific fisheries point to waves of consolidation.[43] "We've been frozen out," one smaller fisherman said of all the rules. "This system has given it all to the big guys."[44]

Stepping back from apples and fish to look at the larger picture, the lawyer and author Philip K. Howard pointed out some years ago that, according to the Small Business Administration, small businesses face annual regulatory costs 36 percent higher per employee than those faced by larger firms.[45] Other studies echo that finding.[46] Close to half of small-business owners say they have halted or delayed an investment or opportunity because of uncertainty over the regulatory landscape.[47] As an opinion piece in *The Washington Post* put it, "for decades, large businesses have been taking market share from small businesses, and the corporations at the top of the pyramid have been consolidating into ever-bigger megacorporations."[48]

Even the federal government has acknowledged research finding "that more heavily regulated industries experience fewer new firm births and slower employment growth than less heavily regulated industries, and . . . small firms are more likely to exit an industry in response to regulation than large firms."[49] All this has had a predictably disproportionate impact on vulnerable communities and the less wealthy: In 2019, the Small Business Administration estimated that 99.9 percent of minority-owned businesses were small businesses, and a 2015 study indicated that middle-class families account for over half of all new business ventures.[50]

Caskets and Capture

To be fair, those who make the laws, write the rules, and insist on the proper paperwork often act with the best of intentions. Charged with specific tasks—ensuring safe orchards or sound fishing practices— officials may simply seek to fulfill their mandates. But a narrow focus on pursuing one set of goals can sometimes fail to account for other considerations important to a healthy society—considerations like equality of opportunity and fairness.

Sometimes, though, the problem runs deeper than that. Sometimes, powerful interests can capture regulatory processes and use them to entrench their positions at the expense of others who are less fortunate.[51] Hundreds of academic articles and books have been written about the phenomenon of regulatory capture, but the basic concept isn't hard to understand. George Stigler, a Nobel Prize–winning economist, put the point simply: Once concentrated groups recognize that regulation is inevitable, they often employ their influence to ensure that regulatory outcomes maximize their welfare at the expense of other, more diffuse and less well-organized interests.[52] And when regulatory work is performed largely behind closed doors, when it is concentrated in democratically unaccountable hands, when the processes for rulemaking grow increasingly complex, the opportunities for powerful interests to influence the outcome grow.[53] Judge Douglas Ginsburg has explained the effect of regulatory capture on consumers this way:

> Regulation is an item of trade, supplied by politicians who traffic in the state's monopoly on the use of force, and demanded by producers who can use regulation to extract rents from consumers. Regulation occurs because consumers, being numerous and each having a small stake in preventing it, are typically not organized as effectively as producers and hence systematically lose in the legislative struggle.[54]

To see how regulatory capture can play out in practice, meet the monks of Saint Joseph Abbey in rural Louisiana. In 2005, Hurricane Katrina wreaked havoc on a pine forest that provided timber and a source of income for the 36 Benedictine monks who called the abbey home. In the hurricane's aftermath, the monks began looking for other ways to support themselves. For years, they had made simple wooden caskets in which to bury their departed colleagues. Now, they decided, they would expand their operation and offer two options to the public: a "traditional" casket priced at $2,000 and a "monastic" option available for $1,500. The abbey's tailor contributed by sewing the pillowcases, and a deacon blessed each casket before delivery. All in all, it was a pretty good deal: the monks produced a quality casket, and their prices beat those of many local rivals.

Abbot Justin Brown and Deacon Mark Coudrain
with the Abbey's caskets

That, however, proved a problem. Not long after the monks started offering caskets to the public, the Louisiana State Board of Embalmers and Funeral Directors intervened.[55] The Louisiana State Legislature had created the Board in 1914 to regulate "the care and disposition of the deceased."[56] But by the time of its dispute with the abbey, eight of the nine Board members were funeral industry participants.[57] And they were none too happy with the new clerical competition. The Board wrote a letter to the abbey stressing that, under state law, only licensed funeral homes were entitled to sell caskets to the public. And becoming a licensed funeral home in Louisiana was no easy thing. Among other things, a funeral home had to have a "parlor" that could hold thirty people; a "display room" for six caskets; embalming facilities; and a full-time funeral director who had completed thirty credit hours at an accredited college, finished an apprenticeship, and passed a test administered by the International Conference of Funeral Service Examining Boards.

The monks weren't interested in opening a funeral home; they only wanted to sell caskets. But because they hadn't complied with the regulations, the Board issued a cease-and-desist order commanding them to stop selling caskets.[58] The Board subpoenaed two abbey officials to testify and threatened them with fines and potential time behind bars.[59] The monks tried lobbying lawmakers to change state law and permit nonprofit charities like theirs to sell caskets. But the monks met opposition on that front as well—not from the public but once more from funeral directors. During all these developments, the monks quietly kept on selling their caskets.[60] That led an angry Board to dispatch an investigator to take sworn statements from those who had purchased the caskets and to take pictures of the caskets "before any evidence could be buried."

All for what? Between 2007 and 2010, the monks sold sixty caskets in a state that sees 40,000 annual deaths. Yet it seems even that small number represented a threat to entrenched industry interests. After all, if the monks were not stopped, other potential rivals might enter the casket market. Local funeral directors were so concerned that some took to disparaging the monks' products. They questioned whether the monks even made the caskets or whether it was all a marketing gimmick. And, they emphasized, casket sales are "complicated"; after all, said one, "a quarter of America is oversized [and] I don't even know if the monks know how to make an oversized casket."[61] Not everyone has the time, the tenacity, or the resources to fight entrenched industry interests that have taken hold of the regulatory reins and turned them to their benefit. But at least this particular story had a happy ending—eventually. After a federal lawsuit and six years of wrangling with the Board, in 2013 the monks finally won the legal right to enter the Louisiana casket market.[62]

Lawyers Everywhere and Nowhere

Making your way in a world filled with shifting laws is difficult without lawyers. Often you need a lawyer just to locate the relevant law and understand it. If an agency's interpretation of the law is buried in a guidance document, you'll hardly have a chance of finding it without the assistance of someone in the know. If the law is ambiguous, you cannot begin to guess how an agency might resolve it without the help of someone familiar with the regulators' habits. And if you get caught up in an enforcement action over your septic system, farm, or casket business, who will you call? As laws proliferate in number and complexity, access to legal services becomes increasingly vital.

All of which suggests that a moment of self-reflection might be in order. How well are we lawyers doing at helping the public navigate a system we are responsible for administering (if not creating)? Are we doing more to right inequalities or to perpetuate them?

We all enjoy lawyer jokes, but maybe part of their appeal is that the truth is so much harder to confront. Partners in high demand at big-city law firms can command more than $2,000 an hour. Even in places you might not expect, prices can be eye-watering: a 2017 report from Kansas put the median rate across the state at $225 per hour.[63] Doubtless it's higher now. These rates mean that any hope of vindicating legal rights in court is beyond the means of most people. A 2013 study pegged the median cost of real estate disputes taken through trial at around $66,000 and the median cost of employment disputes at around $87,000. To put these figures into perspective, the median household income in 2022 hovered around $70,000.[64] Contributing to the costs are judicial delays and court backlogs. In civil cases, the time from filing a case to a scheduled trial date has nearly doubled since just the early 1990s.[65]

Put simply, low- and middle-income Americans face an access-to-justice crisis. The United States ranks near the bottom of the developed world when it comes to access to counsel in civil cases.[66] Studies suggest that over 80 percent of the civil legal needs of lower-to-middle-income individuals are unmet in some jurisdictions, and over 76 percent of cases in state court have at least one self-represented party.[67] Unsurprisingly, those forced to represent themselves usually fare far worse than those with legal representation.[68] All of this invites other predictable consequences: as two institutes working on access-to-justice issues put it, there is a "strong, almost linear relationship between household income and negative consequences associated with legal problems" and "certain socio-demographic and racial/ethnic groups are particularly disadvantaged in terms of access to justice."[69] Translation: Maybe those with considerable means can get the legal help they need, but most individuals are left to navigate by themselves—and good luck with that.

We can already hear some of our friends at the bar warming up their reply. Yes, they will say, our hourly rates are high. But those rates are the product of market demand, and it's unfair to blame us for charging what the market allows. On the surface, that reply might seem fair enough. But scratch the surface, and it falls apart. In the United States, we lawyers (along with Louisiana funeral home directors) enjoy the privilege of regulating our own marketplace. And many of the regulations we insist upon artificially restrict the output of legal services, ensuring high market prices for our services while providing little in the way of compensating benefits to our clients. To get a sense of the problem, ask just three questions.

First, how do we lawyers treat innovative competitors? Take LegalZoom by way of example. The company helps individuals and small businesses create relatively simple legal documents such as wills, leases, and premarital agreements at a fraction of what a lawyer would charge.[70] But in spite of largely positive consumer reviews, the firm has been forced to contend with a raft of lawsuits seeking to have it banned in many states.[71] Why? Lawyers have long and successfully lobbied for broadly written laws prohibiting nonlawyers from engaging in the "unauthorized practice of law."[72] And lawyers have used these laws as cudgels to thwart new entrants that threaten to undercut their prices.[73] Of course, it might make sense to limit *some* legal work to fully accredited lawyers. A client facing a complex trial in state or federal court probably should retain a qualified trial lawyer. But is that same rule appropriate when it comes to addressing basic legal needs?

Second, how do we treat other outsiders who might help make legal resources more affordable? In many jurisdictions, rules prohibit lawyers and law firms from accepting outside investment from non-lawyers. In theory, these rules serve the laudable goal of ensuring that lawyers are not influenced by the demands of investors when representing clients.[74] But in practice, our self-imposed rules often greatly restrict the available supply of legal services and "contribute[]" to the low innovation and high cost of services that characterize the U.S. legal market today."[75] Other sensitive industries manage the risk of undue investor influence through tools short of a total ban on outside investment. So, for example, you can get basic medical and accounting services at "shops" found in and coordinated with your local superstore, but you will not find everyday legal services available there. Within a short time after the United Kingdom dropped its ban on outside investment in 2007, studies showed new "alternative business structures" had emerged and quickly captured 20 percent of consumer and mental health legal work and nearly 33 percent of the personal injury market. All of which suggests that the new firms were doing exactly what you would expect: expanding access to legal services, decreasing prices, and helping meet the needs of underserved poor and middle-class clients.[76]

Third, what about our law schools? Today, most states require future lawyers to obtain both a bachelor's degree and a law degree.[77] Typically, that amounts to seven years of higher education. Between 1980 and 2019, the cost of an undergraduate degree skyrocketed by 169 percent. Between 1985 and 2019, the cost of a private law school education nearly tripled. And that's accounting for inflation.[78] Today, the average student walks out of law school burdened with about $140,000 in debt.[79] According to one organization tracking these figures, "it is impossible for the average lawyer working in the public sector to pay off federal student loans if they follow" government-recommended repayment plans.[80] Given all that, is it any wonder that so many members of the bar charge such high prices?

Nor is it obvious that all of these expensive educational requirements are necessary to protect our clients' interests. Apparently, the idea of mandating three years of postgraduate law school education originally had a lot to do with the fact that medical school ran four years; some argued that law school should be treated comparably—an argument that seems to have rested more on professional pride than empirical proof or practical necessity.[81] Once out of school, different lawyers provide very different kinds of services; some may spend their careers helping clients navigate family or small-claims court, others may specialize in complex intellectual property disputes. Yet rather than developing different educational paths tailored to different career paths, our professional rules generally force future lawyers to secure an undergraduate degree that may be entirely unrelated to law and then to spend a uniform three years in legal training—much of which they spend studying areas of law in which they "will never see a single client." As one commentator has said, it may not be a "bad thing for every law school graduate to be equally prepared to represent a criminal on death row, draft a will or negotiate a public offering of securities," but is it sensible?[82] Again, our colleagues in the United Kingdom don't think so. If they wish, law students there can pursue a variety of postgraduate degrees focusing on specialty areas. But they can also earn a basic law degree after just three years of *undergraduate* study.[83]

Charles Dickens's book *Bleak House* traced the interminable legal case of *Jarndyce and Jarndyce* as it slowly bled everyone involved dry. Dickens himself spent time working as a clerk in a law office and drew on that experience in his writings. His views may be a bit stronger than our own, but his hyperbole has a point—and a warning—for our profession. As Dickens saw it, "the one great principle of the . . . law is, to make business for itself. There is no other principle distinctly, certainly, and consistently maintained through all its narrow turnings. Viewed by this light it becomes a coherent scheme, and not the monstrous maze the laity are apt to think it."[84]

Covid-19 Winners and Losers

When news hit in late 2019 that a novel coronavirus was circulating globally, existing trends in our law accelerated and sharpened.

Whatever else one might say about what happened, some things stand out: as a nation, we sought answers less from ourselves, our friends, and our neighbors, and more from central authorities; we looked less to elected representatives and more to agency officials; we demanded not carefully deliberated solutions but quick action; and along the way, we sometimes enacted rules that privileged the few over the many.

In the early months of 2020, executive officials at every level—national, state, and local—issued emergency edicts.[85] Some but not all of those decrees could trace their legal authority to legislation delegating emergency powers to executive officials under specified circumstances.[86] Initially, many of the decrees ran for short durations (say, thirty days) in conformity with existing legislation.[87] Later, however, various executive officials asserted the authority to renew their temporary edicts repeatedly.[88] Two and a half years after a pandemic was declared, a number of states were still enforcing emergency orders.[89] The federal government didn't end its national public health emergency declarations until the spring of 2023—more than three years after their initial adoption.[90] Through it all, legislatures were rarely involved. Agencies did not always bother with providing advance notice of their new rules; nor did they always seek public comment on them.[91] Instead, we lived in a world of intense Wilsonian administrative efficiency. Executive officials simply issued edicts. Huge numbers of them. Extraordinary ones, too.

At the federal level, our representatives in Congress initially enacted a temporary moratorium on certain tenant evictions but later chose not to extend the program. Unsatisfied, officials at the Centers for Disease Control and Prevention (CDC) declared their own moratorium—and then extended it again and again.[92] Meanwhile, the Occupational Safety and Health Administration adopted emergency regulations of its own mandating covid-19 vaccines for 84 million Americans, even though (once more) Congress had already considered that course and declined to pursue it.[93]

At the state and local levels, governors and other executive officials issued decrees shuttering schools and businesses, restricting travel, and mandating the use of face masks.[94] Outdoor playgrounds were closed. Some were fenced off. Still others were encircled with thick yellow tape reminiscent of crime scenes.[95] If the edicts were ignored, more measures were quickly taken. The town of San Clemente, California, dumped 37 tons of sand into the local skate park to prevent children from taking a spin. In Malibu, police arrested and handcuffed a lone paddleboarder offshore.[96]

Keeping up with all the shifting executive edicts was no easy feat. Officials modified and revised their rules over and over again, sometimes on a weekly basis.[97] A year into it all, *The New Yorker* described what it was like to run a restaurant in Manhattan. "For months," the magazine reported, restaurants "endured a baffling crossfire of changing rules and regulations, from a gantlet of city and state agencies." State officials banned indoor dining, then allowed it under various restrictions, then banned it again. In response to one such ban, the mayor issued a memo interpreting its terms and advising that guests were, as the magazine put it, "prohibited from going inside to use the rest room, and restaurant workers were effectively not allowed to take their staff meals anywhere but the kitchen." After "an outcry ensued," state officials responded that the mayor was wrong and that they hadn't mandated anything of the sort. At another point, "there was a run on propane patio heaters" after the mayor announced an extension of the city's outdoor dining program. Later, though, the city issued rules clarifying that the heaters had to be kept far away from buildings, streets, and even persons—rendering them more or less useless. "The rules change by the hour," one restaurant owner complained. "You don't know what tomorrow is going to be."[98]

In some quarters, even the free exchange of ideas over these shifting measures proved unwelcome. Facebook suspended users for questioning the effectiveness of masks.[99] Various media outlets flagged as misinformation suggestions that covid-19 had originated in a lab, only to reverse course later when evidence for the "lab hypothesis" could no longer be easily dismissed.[100] LinkedIn, whose self-described mission is to "connect the world's professionals," censored views critical of the official covid-19 response, including a post from a then professor

Sand dumped into the skate park of South Windsor, Connecticut

of medicine at Harvard Medical School linking to an interview of his with a comment: "It's a very strange time we have entered into. . . . Basic principles of public health are thrown out the window while the working class is thrown under the bus."[101] Doctors, epidemiologists, Nobel Prize winners, even our representatives in Congress: it seemed that no one was exempt. Over a year into the pandemic, YouTube removed a video by a sitting senator that questioned the effectiveness of masks (and suspended his account for a week).[102] That same site removed two videos from a Senate committee hearing on the treatment of covid-19—but not before one of them racked up 8 million views.[103] In Florida, the state's surgeon general saw Twitter block his post about potential side effects of the covid-19 vaccine.[104]

Can it come as any great surprise that in this environment— where so many laws were made and changed so quickly, where new mandates came more often by way of executive decree than legislative compromise, where open public debate was stifled—those with political clout, popular points of view, or wealth often fared better than others? Take Nevada's reopening plan in 2020. It permitted breweries, bowling alleys, and other favored secular institutions to reopen at 50 percent capacity, yet limited indoor religious worship services to "no more than fifty persons" regardless of the size of the building. So casinos in Las Vegas could host thousands of patrons, but Calvary Chapel Dayton Valley was left unable to conduct even a brief service with ninety congregants, a number that amounted to about 50 percent of its capacity.[105]

Nevada wasn't an isolated example. For a period, California forbade *all* indoor worship in much of the state while allowing most indoor businesses to continue to operate with capacity restrictions. Officials justified the ban by pointing to factors that supposedly distinguished religious worship from secular activities. In particular, California stressed that religious services sometimes involve singing. Yet instead of addressing singing in church, the state flatly banned all indoor religious services. And it did so at the same time it appeared to allow indoor singing at some of the state's most powerful companies: music, film, and television studios.[106]

In New York, a color-coded executive decree had similar winners and losers. In "red" zones, no more than ten people could attend religious services but businesses deemed "essential" could host unlimited numbers of patrons. Just what businesses were "essential"? Liquor stores, hardware stores, bike stores, acupuncturists, and more. In "orange" zones, the disparity was even starker: houses of worship were capped at 25 people, while even "nonessential" businesses could go about their affairs without any limits. This despite the fact that some houses of worship were designed to accommodate more than a thousand people.[107]

Early on, one professor recalled walking down a main street in his small town of Amherst, Massachusetts—one that, like the streets of small towns dotted across the United States, was filled with small businesses. "What will be left of that vibrant downtown," he wondered, "when we emerge from the coronavirus crisis?" The professor predicted the "reinforc[ement]" and "exacerbat[ion]" of "what were already the two key economic trends of our lifetime: consolidation and inequality," with the winners being mostly "executives of large corporations, partners at private-equity firms and investors in both—in short, the very rich." In contrast, he continued, "working-class and lower-skilled workers will experience lasting economic harm," all of which will "further hollow out what was once known as the American Dream."[108]

How did those predictions pan out? By April 2021, with many restrictive policies still to unfurl, the Federal Reserve reported that roughly 200,000 more businesses had closed permanently compared to historical levels. About two-thirds were individual businesses, with barbershops, nail salons, and other personal service providers suffering the most.[109] The Federal Reserve reported that minority-owned businesses had been hit especially hard.[110]

Our response to the pandemic carried with it other disparate impacts as well. Often, risks were transferred rather than eliminated. That dinner you had delivered to your home? Someone had to make it; someone had to deliver it. Social distancing? It's a lot more manageable from the comfort of a second home in the country than a small city apartment. Online Zoom classes for your six-year-old? No doubt less of a problem for families with funds for home help, tutors, and fast internet connections. (Or better yet, skip the Zoom and go for a $25,000 in-person pod.)[111] Mask mandates? Easier to support when you can work maskless from home in your sweatpants and don't have to spend ten hours on a factory floor to make ends meet.

Where there were losers, there were winners. In the first year of the pandemic, Amazon, for example, "hired thousands of employees—including lawyers," perhaps in part to navigate all the rapid rule changes.[112] The company's stock price soared, and Jeff Bezos's net worth rose about $80 billion between March 2020 and October 2021. Collectively, the country's billionaires added about $2.1 trillion to their net worth during the same period, a 70 percent increase from their collective prepandemic fortunes. Millionaires didn't fare poorly, either: Credit Suisse reported that the number of "ultra-high net worth individuals"—those with assets over $50 million—had grown by 24 percent, the highest rate of increase in decades.[113]

Covid-era restrictions distilled to their essence recent trends in our lawmaking practices, providing a glimpse of what happens when laws are made and remade with ever-increasing speed outside the legislative process. They offer a glimpse, too, into the different effects ever-changing laws can have on "the sagacious, the enterprising, and the moneyed few" as compared with "the industrious . . . mass of the people."[114] Public administration may have been vigorous and efficient. But it did not come without a price.

CHAPTER 6

THREE FREEDOMS

"Don't you wish you were free, Lenina?"

"I don't know what you mean. I am free. Free to have the most wonderful time. Everybody's happy nowadays."

—ALDOUS HUXLEY, *BRAVE NEW WORLD*[1]

Ordered Liberty

JOHN LOCKE WROTE THAT "THE END OF LAW IS NOT TO ABOLISH OR restrain, but to preserve and enlarge Freedom"; "where there is no Law, there is no Freedom."[2] Many people since, George Washington reputedly included, have described what we seek from law in similar terms, calling it "ordered liberty."[3]

To illustrate the point, in 2014 Georgetown University Professor Randy Barnett invited his readers to consider the Sears (now the Willis) Tower in Chicago: Think of the thousands of people moving at any given moment in a building that rises more than a hundred stories and brims with offices, retail shops, and restaurants. The building's hallways, stairs, and elevators (there are nearly a hundred of the last, and they make more than 42,000 trips a day) all work together to help people find their chosen destinations. Without this structure, Professor Barnett reminded us, people "could not accomplish their purposes or, for that matter, any useful ends."[4]

In much the same way, when done well, our laws may constrain us in some ways, but without them we could not begin to pursue our own aspirations in life. To put the point more bluntly, most of us are happy to trade (say) the freedom to kill others in return for a law securing our own physical safety. The same goes for most age-old laws, like those against assault and theft. We know intuitively that the absence of laws such as these—or the failure to enforce them—would do more to impair than facilitate our ability to chart our way in the world.

Admittedly, there's a paradox in play. The freedoms we cherish cannot exist without some law, but they can also be imperiled by too much law. At that end of the spectrum, the risk does not come from bad men who would do us harm; it comes from those who would script the details of our lives in the name of better securing our safety, our happiness, or their own particular vision of progress. The last chapter explored the impact of the growth of law on our nation's promise of equality under law. This one asks an even more fundamental question: If the "end of law" is the protection of ordered liberty, how well is our legal structure doing at realizing that goal?

In one way or another, perhaps every chapter in this book speaks to that question. But let's take it on even more directly by considering three stories. Each is about the struggle of ordinary Americans to chart their own path in a world with so much law. And each centers around one of three rights long thought essential in any society dedicated to ordered liberty: first, the right, as Justice Louis Brandeis put it, "to think what we like and say what we please";[5] second, the right to gather and associate with one another, recognizing that we are intensely social beings who rarely flourish in isolation; and finally, the right to plan and pursue our own lives without harm to others, or what our Declaration of Independence calls the "pursuit of Happiness."[6] John Stuart Mill, for one, argued that "no society in which these liberties are not . . . respected[] is free, whatever may be its form of government."[7]

Foster Care and the Freedom to Differ

Writing at the height of the Second World War in *West Virginia State Board of Education v. Barnette*, Justice Robert H. Jackson observed that "struggles to coerce uniformity of sentiment in support of some end thought essential to their time and country have been waged by many good as well as by evil men." As Justice Jackson noted, such struggles rarely end well: history shows that "as first and moderate methods to attain unity" prove unsuccessful, "those bent on its accomplishment must resort to an ever-increasing severity." Ultimately, "those who begin coercive elimination of dissent soon find themselves exterminating dissenters. Compulsory unification of opinion achieves only the unanimity of the graveyard."[8]

It's difficult to read Justice Jackson's words without seeing in them an effort to contrast our nation's experiment in liberty with the experiments in fascism and communism then playing out in Europe. Here, our founders valued the "freedom to think as you will and to speak as you think"—and they valued that freedom "both as an end and as a means": an end because the right to think and speak freely belongs inalienably to each of us; a means because thinking and speaking freely are essential to self-government.[9] By allowing a wide array of views room to flourish, the founders understood, "we may test and improve our own thinking both as individuals and as a Nation."[10] As Justice Jackson recognized, our First Amendment was designed to avoid the "strife" that so often accompanies efforts to compel unity of thought and speech "by avoiding [its] beginnings."[11]

Of course, the right to think and speak means little if it protects only popular views or ones held by elites. For the right to mean anything, it must mean the right to disagree. (As George Orwell once quipped, "If liberty means anything at all it means the right to tell people what they do not want to hear.")[12] Perhaps, too, through history people have disagreed on few things more than matters of faith. Many immigrants to this country, past and present, have made grueling journeys to our shores for the very purpose of securing the right to practice religious beliefs so unpopular at home that they faced persecution, punishment, even death. Think back to the Amish we met in chapter 5.

Our First Amendment recognizes this reality by protecting religious speech twice in a single sentence—first by singling out the "free exercise" of religion for protection by name and then by prohibiting laws "abridging the freedom of speech" more generally.[13] Hard experience had taught the framers that "government suppression of speech ha[d] so commonly been directed *precisely* at religious speech that a free-speech clause without religion would be Hamlet without the prince."[14] In some ways then, the right to think and express religious beliefs is a kind of canary in the First Amendment coal mine. When the spirit of the times breeds censure, it is often the first to go.

What has the spirit of *our* times meant for the freedom to hold and express unpopular ideas?

Consider the experience of three women from Philadelphia, Toni Simms-Busch, Sharonell Fulton, and Cecilia Paul. Each found a place in her heart and home for foster children. After graduating from college, Ms. Simms-Busch took a job as a social worker. In that role, she later testified, she saw the desperate need for foster parents and resolved to help. Ms. Fulton's journey was different but led to the same destination: "I went to church and I prayed about it and I believe that it was my faith that led me to it." Over a span of twenty-six years she fostered forty children.[15] As she explained, "Mostly what I've done is emergency placement, so that means [the children] have been taken from their family, and they don't understand why. They're hurting. . . . My goal with the children is to reach out, find a way . . . show them some love, be there when they need you."[16]

Like the other women, Ms. Paul had deep connections to Philadelphia. After college, she worked as a nurse at a children's hospital before leaving to raise her own family. But she missed helping other children, so she, too, turned to fostering. Ultimately, Ms. Paul fostered more than a hundred children, six of whom she adopted. Many of the infants she fostered came to her addicted to drugs and in need of special care.[17] In 2015, the city named her "Outstanding Foster Parent of the Year."[18] "I would be a completely different person if it wasn't for my mom," Thomas Paul, one of her now-grown adopted sons, said. "She was like an angel, really."[19]

Sharonell Fulton

After deciding to foster, each of these women partnered with Catholic Social Services (CSS). The group is "an arm of the Catholic Church," and the women were drawn to the organization in part because of their own faith. "I knew," Ms. Simms-Busch said, "that we would share the same foundational beliefs."[20]

CSS dates its mission of assisting families in need back to the 1790s, when the Roman Catholic Church in Philadelphia, among other faith-based orders, began caring for children left orphaned or neglected after the yellow fever epidemic.[21] Today, the nonprofit continues to see "caring for vulnerable children as a core value of the Christian faith and therefore views its foster care work as part of its religious mission and ministry."[22]

For much of our nation's history, foster care was provided largely by private charities like CSS. In fact, when CSS (then named the Catholic Children's Bureau) formally started its work in 1917, it "made placements with little to no government involvement."[23] CSS officials later testified that the Missionary Sisters of the Blessed Trinity who staffed the bureau would learn of at-risk children needing homes, coordinate their placement with families, and track their progress.[24] Even decades later, when the government first became involved in the foster care arena, the bureau retained "tremendous" authority, deciding for itself questions of both removal and placement. It wasn't until the second half of the twentieth century that the city took a "more active role" in the process.[25]

Today, the city assumes protective custody of children removed from their homes. It then contracts with private agencies to place the children into foster homes.[26] On average, more than 3,000 children find themselves in the city's foster care system every year; often they have been abused or neglected, sometimes severely.[27]

By 2018, the city had contracts with more than twenty different foster care agencies.[28] Because each "has slightly different requirements, specialties, and training programs," the city encourages prospective foster parents to "browse the list of foster agencies to find the best fit."[29] Foster care agencies are responsible for certifying prospective parents as fit to foster, a process that takes months to complete.[30] By law, an agency must evaluate an applicant's background, "existing family relationships," "attitudes and expectations," and "mental or emotional stability."[31] In the end, the agency decides whether to "approve, disapprove or provisionally approve the foster family."[32]

To the best of anyone's knowledge, not a single complaint has been lodged against CSS in the history of its operations.[33] To the contrary, as the city itself has put it, CSS is a "point of light" in its foster care system.[34] Ms. Simms-Busch has worked with nearly all the foster agencies in the city but considers CSS's level of care "unique."[35]

By way of example, she has described how "when my [CSS social care] worker comes, he spends time with my boys, he plays with them, he interacts with them. . . . When my two-year-old sees my worker coming, he runs to him. He does not run to many people, so that's a good thing."[36] Ms. Paul's adopted son Thomas recalls visits from his CSS social care workers that helped him and other children "out of their darkness." Once when Ms. Fulton took in new foster children on Christmas Eve, the nonprofit delivered wrapped presents to her door so they wouldn't be without gifts the next morning. Sometimes, too, children come to foster homes with nothing but the clothing on their backs. CSS helps supply clothing or an allowance to purchase items beyond what the city provides.[37]

Today, the foster care system in the United States faces a crisis. There are far more children in need of homes than foster families willing to take them in.[38] The shortage is so acute that by some counts, nearly 57,000 children in the foster care system (about one in seven) live in group homes rather than with foster families.[39] In California, children have been made to sleep on city office conference tables or mats on the floors.[40] In Washington, reports indicate that foster children as young as two years old have had to spend nights in hotels: 211 hotel stays were reported in just one month in 2016. The lack of available long-term foster homes also leads to more moves for children: One study documented the not-uncommon plight of a four-year-old moved among ten different families and various hotel rooms in the span of three months.[41]

Perhaps unsurprisingly, children in group homes often fare worse than those in foster family settings. They're less likely to graduate from high school, more likely to be arrested for crimes, and more likely to develop mental health problems.[42] *The Washington Post* described the situation this way: because of the "shortage of foster parents," "case workers and courts have been funneling children into crowded emergency shelters, hotels, out-of-state institutions and youth prisons—cold, isolating and often dangerous facilities not built to house innocent children for years." The executive director of a non-profit child advocacy organization was reported to have said simply, "We are just destroying these kids."[43]

Philadelphia isn't immune to these challenges. In March 2018, the crisis there became so severe that city officials put out an "urgent" call for foster parents (it needed about 300 more). One agency staffer explained the situation this way: "We'll get 200 requests a month from [the city] and we'll be able to place maybe 10 of them. . . . We're sending infants sometimes to infant shelters."[44]

Just days before issuing its urgent call, however, the city declared a freeze on new foster placements through CSS. Why? Apparently, city officials had gotten wind from a *Philadelphia Inquirer* reporter that CSS does not vet same-sex couples for certification as foster parents.[45] As a Catholic organization, CSS adheres to the view that "marriage is a sacred bond between a man and a woman."[46] And because it understands certification "to be an endorsement of [foster families'] relationships," CSS declines to "certify unmarried couples— regardless of their sexual orientation—or same-sex married couples. CSS does not object to certifying gay or lesbian individuals as single foster parents or to placing gay and lesbian children." What's more, no same-sex couple had even asked the agency for certification. Were they to do so, CSS representatives have stated, they would happily refer such a couple to another agency in the city—just as they sometimes do for various other reasons, such as geographic proximity.[47]

Still, the paper's reporting touched off a flurry of activity in the city government. Almost immediately, the city council adopted a resolution asserting (not entirely accurately) that CSS has "policies that prohibit the placement of children with LGBTQ people based on religious principles."[48] The city's Commission on Human Relations launched an investigation, and the Commissioner of the city's Department of Human Services met personally with CSS representatives. At the meeting, the CSS representatives highlighted the fact that the nonprofit had been serving children in need in Philadelphia without complaint for more than a hundred years. Still, shortly after the meeting came the call: the city would no longer refer children to CSS for new placements.[49] Just before the announcement, the agency reported serving about 120 children across one hundred foster homes at any given time.[50]

CSS and the families it worked with were devastated. Helping children was a core part of CSS's "religious mission and ministry," with many faithful believing that they have an obligation to assist children in need.[51] But because of the freeze, CSS stopped recruiting and certifying new families and, according to the agency, beds in the homes of its current families lay empty. By mid-June, the nonprofit reported 26 available spots for children in need of a home, a number it projected to increase to about 35 by the end of the month.[52] There were even cases, CSS later stated, in which city officials had sought to "block[] children entering foster care from reuniting with siblings who were placed with CSS families" and to "block[] children re-entering foster care from returning to CSS foster parents they knew and loved."[53]

Toni Simms-Busch, Sharonell Fulton, and Cecilia Paul spoke about the impact on their own lives and those of the children they sought to help. In June, Ms. Paul said that her home had been empty for three months because of the freeze, that she had never gone that long without a referral, and that she felt "very lost, very lost."[54] For Ms. Simms-Busch, the developments were "heartbreaking," given that "there are homes that could be open" to children in need.[55] Ms. Fulton worried that the children she was then fostering (four and five years old) might be moved to another home. All three women reported that, if CSS's foster care services were forced to close, they were unsure that they'd continue to foster with another agency; CSS had been, after all, like "family."[56]

By the end of June, CSS's contract with the city expired and the city refused to sign a new one (beyond a "maintenance" agreement for children still in CSS homes). That is, the city said, unless CSS agreed to change.[57] The city pointed out that Bethany Christian Services, the largest Protestant adoption and foster agency in the nation, had acceded to the city's demands and revised its certification standards.[58] The not-so-subtle message: CSS should, too. (Bethany explained its decision on its website: "The reality is that the government runs the foster care system, and we cannot serve children in foster care without contracting with the state. So we faced a choice: continue caring for hurting children who need a safe family, or close our foster care program completely.")[59]

In reply, CSS representatives said that the group couldn't change how it thought or expressed itself about marriage, something its religious tradition treats as a sacrament. When it became clear that the city wouldn't back down, CSS felt it had no choice but to take the matter to court. The group argued that the city's referral freeze violated its First Amendment rights.[60] "To be clear," the group's lawyer explained, CSS wasn't seeking to impose its beliefs on anyone else. Instead, it was saying, "Please let me stand aside."[61] The group's ideas about marriage might not be popular, but CSS stressed they were nothing new and the agency had served the Philadelphia community well for many years—long before the government had even entered the foster care field. By 2018, however, none of that was enough.

How did it work out in the end? In the spring of 2021, the Supreme Court unanimously held that the city's refusal to renew its contract with CSS on the basis of the group's religious ideas violated the First Amendment. But consider what it took. The group had to endure years of litigation. It had to persist, too, through losses both in the trial court and on appeal.[62] In the meantime, children in need were left unserved and available beds in loving homes sat empty.

A "Nation of Joiners"

For most of our history, America has been, as the historian Arthur Schlesinger put it, a "nation of joiners."[63] We remember Benjamin Franklin as a signer of the Declaration of Independence and the Constitution, the publisher of *Poor Richard's Almanack*, and the inventor of the lightning rod and bifocal glasses. But we sometimes forget the many other activities that mark him as witness to the spirit Schlesinger spoke of: Franklin formed a club for artisans; a subscription library (where he was head librarian for a time); and a volunteer fire department. He was the first president of the Academy and College of Philadelphia (later the University of Pennsylvania) and founded the American Philosophical Society.[64] None of those activities or comparable ones by other founders detracted from their reverence for the individual; our country's famed individualism has never meant, as Schlesinger reminded us, "the individual's independence of other individuals, but [instead] his and their freedom from governmental restraint."[65]

When it set about drafting the First Amendment shortly after the Constitution's adoption, Congress included the freedom to assemble alongside the free exercise of religion and freedom of speech, understanding that they all march together. These rights are so closely aligned that, at the time, some argued there was no need to single out the right to assemble for separate treatment. As Representative Theodore Sedgwick from Massachusetts put it, "If people freely converse together, they must assemble for that purpose; it is a self-evident, unalienable right which the people possess; it is certainly a thing that never would be called in question." Others, however, insisted on mentioning the right to assemble—not because they disputed Sedgwick's premise but because people *had* been prevented from gathering freely in the past and, as Representative John Page of Virginia contended, "If the people could be deprived of the power of assembling under any pretext whatsoever, they might be deprived of every other privilege contained in the clause."[66]

As we have seen in earlier chapters, our habit of associating with one another has withered in recent decades. Many of the places where we once gathered and found support and meaning are shadows of their former selves. Church attendance has fallen precipitously; long-standing social clubs such as the Elks and the Rotary Club struggle for members; even poker, bridge, and bingo nights have been replaced by online Wordle and internet gambling. In the wake of all this, a marked decline in trust in one another has followed. In 1972, half of Americans believed that their fellow citizens could be trusted. In 2020, that number stood at one-third.[67] As Robert Putnam observed in *Bowling Alone*, it's hard not to make a connection between these trends. When we do not regularly engage with one another, when we feel the tug of social connections less and less, how much easier is it, as Putnam put it, for us to fall prey to the thought that we are "surrounded by miscreants"?[68]

These are worrying trends for many reasons, but one of them concerns our capacity for self-government. While democracy depends on the freedom to think and speak freely, it also depends on trusting that those with whom we disagree are not "miscreants"; it depends on listening to and engaging with those who hold different views. And our civic associations are the places where that trust and those habits were once learned. "When Alexis de Tocqueville visited the United States in the 1830s," Putnam noted, "it was the Americans' propensity for civic association that most impressed him as the key to their unprecedented ability to make democracy work."[69]

As troubling as our retreat from civic life may be, most of us take for granted that *if we want to*, we can gather with others more or less as we wish. But the nation's experiences during the covid-19 pandemic rendered even that conviction less certain. In the last chapter, we looked at the covid-19 era with an eye to what the proliferation of rules and edicts means for our aspirations for equal treatment of persons under law. Here let's examine the episode from a different perspective and consider what it meant for people like Chris Reed.

Before March 2020, Mr. Reed met weekly with other recovering addicts at the "sober bar" he ran in northern Illinois. Together, the group would socialize over live music and "lean on each other in their daily struggles to keep from relapsing." Then, seemingly overnight, everything changed. Like so many across the nation, Mr. Reed was ordered to close his business immediately and indefinitely.[71]

Put to one side the effect the closure had on Mr. Reed's finances or the sense of worth that so often comes with a job. What about his gatherings for recovering addicts? The group tried to continue operating online, but it wasn't the same. "I just celebrated ten years" free from substance abuse, Mr. Reed told a reporter at the time. "I thought I was the only person who had these issues and then I started going to meetings and I started to see all these other people who had gone through similar things and connecting with them, whether it was just going out to dinner or coffee after a meeting. There was a certain level of camaraderie. That's just something you can't produce with the Zoom meetings."[72] He wasn't the only one worried about what the loss of physical interaction would mean to addiction recovery efforts. "It's one thing to be socially isolated, but it's another thing to be socially isolated and trying to get sober. That's an unfathomable thing," another recovering addict said.[73] Still another reported being "scared": "Online just won't be the same. We won't have the fellowship that we so desperately need."[74]

Early on, some doctors predicted that the shuttering of in-person meetings would badly damage recovery efforts. "We consider addiction a disease of isolation," explained one physician. "Now we're isolating all these people and expecting them to pick up the phone, get online, that sort of thing—and it may not work out as well."[75] Often, it didn't. By 2021, reports emerged that connections important to recovery that had been fostered in person weren't being duplicated online. "People are relapsing left and right," said one recovering addict. "The loneliness plays into it." Another echoed her words: "What is more supportive than walking into a room and seeing a human you can touch? What's been missing is body language, our ability to hug each other."[76]

Really, few aspects of life were unaffected. In many states, nearly every outlet that offered a chance for human interaction was shuttered: not just schools and nursing homes but libraries and bookstores, coffee shops and museums, malls, zoos, parks, and playgrounds.[77] Any place you might have once met someone for coffee; had an impromptu interaction with another person while standing in line or scanning a bookshelf; met a fellow mom or dad while out with the kids—all stood vacant, some of them never to return. Poignantly, *The New York Times* reported on the mother of a nine-year-old boy in a pediatric nursing home facility who had endured months without visits from her; she spoke of the decline he had suffered.[78] Nor were situations like that uncommon.

What were people to do? The official answer was "Go virtual." The CDC recommended remote learning for schools, and most states mandated it.[79] (At least for public schools; if you were rich enough or fortunate enough, you might have found another way.) State officials forced places of worship to rely on online services.[80] Doctors diagnosed patients via telemedicine, and the elderly in nursing homes were left to substitute visits from family with FaceTime.[81] But not only did those modes of interaction pale in comparison to human contact, many Americans simply couldn't access them. According to 2018 statistics from the U.S. Census Bureau, 8 percent of households have no computer—defined broadly to include smartphones—and 15 percent no broadband internet connection. The Bureau reported, too, that households with higher rates of connectivity tended to be those with higher incomes; lower internet subscription rates were associated with renters, "households with limited English speaking ability[,] and households with at least one person who was disabled."[82]

Even when in-person activities resumed, life remained far from normal. "Social distancing" entered everyday speech, soon to be followed by "mask up." California required masks and social distancing for private gatherings in a person's own home—when those gatherings were allowed at all.[83] Massachusetts, like some other states, required children as young as five to mask in public indoors, and even outdoors when social distancing wasn't possible.[84] Federal agencies required toddlers over the age of two—a critical stage in child development—to wear masks in its Head Start program, a mandate that remained in place until 2023.[85] Across the nation, children ate lunch behind plexiglass or without talking; sat and "played" isolated six feet apart; and went without seeing a smile for hours each day.

Some of this shuttering happened voluntarily, especially early on, when relatively little was known about covid-19. But as time passed, restrictions on our ability to gather—to learn together, eat together, pray together, struggle together, keep sober together—became increasingly a matter not of choice but of official fiat. Priests who had voluntarily closed the doors to their houses of worship but later wanted to reopen for congregations in need weren't permitted to do so. Public school administrators and teachers who had once been happy to try Zoom but then found it inadequate were forbidden from reopening their classrooms. Even on a more granular level official rules reigned. You may have wanted to host friends for a round of cards at your home; organize a playdate for your kids at the local playground; or take a mask-free walk through the park with grandma. But in many states, those activities were prohibited as well.[86]

Take the experience of Pastor Jeremy Wong of Orchard Community Church in Campbell, California. Before the lockdowns, he and his family hosted eight to ten members of his congregation for dinner each week, followed by Bible study and communal prayer. It was a deeply meaningful ritual for the participants.[87] By law, however, even those small gatherings were banned.[88] Government orders divided the state into tiers based on things such as covid-19 case rates and a "health equity metric" and decreed what gatherings were and weren't allowed in each tier.[89] In Tier I, *no* private indoor gatherings were permitted and outdoor gatherings were limited to three households. In the remaining tiers, indoor gatherings were "strongly discouraged," and their size was limited by law; in Tier II, for example, a maximum of three households could gather.[90]

Nor, as we saw in chapter 5, did officials always apply those restrictions evenhandedly. In Pastor Wong's case, his home state allowed hair salons, barbershops, and "personal care services" such as nail salons, tattoo parlors, body waxing and massage services to remain open, often without occupancy restrictions.[91] Some businesses could even allow clients to go maskless, prompting a judge who faced Pastor Wong's case to point out that in California "a beauty shop may host an *unrestricted* number of households, half of them bare-faced and in immediate proximity to the other half. But Wong, in a space of the same size—even an outdoor space— would be limited to three households, despite donning masks and maintaining a six-foot distance."[92]

For Pastor Wong, folding his Bible study group was a deep wound. "Communal worship, congregational study, and collective prayer are central tenets of my faith and ministry," he explained, and "these types of in-person gatherings are impossible to replicate in an on-line format." More than that, for the members of his congregation, "prayer and faith-based teachings [were] critical means to cope with and respond to the covid-19 crisis."[93] Like others across the nation, they were suffering, and as one journalist wrote, "trying to comfort churchgoers who had lost family members or jobs via Zoom—while liquor stores, dispensaries and hair salons stayed open—left [Pastor] Wong increasingly nonplused." For him, the gatherings were "important because they address needs of people . . . that things like medicine can't."[94]

What was the human toll of all this enforced isolation? As Jonathan Sumption, a former justice of the U.K. Supreme Court, observed, "Interaction between human beings is not an optional extra. It is the basic foundation of human society. It is the basis of our emotional lives, of our cultural existence."[95] School isn't just about learning your ABCs or studying William Faulkner; it's about learning to take turns and share, to stand up to a bully, to laugh with classmates, to offer friends a shoulder to lean on and find one to lean on yourself. Physical bookstores don't just allow you to buy a book, something online services can do just as well if not better; they provide for chance encounters, a recommendation, some banter, or even a simple greeting. Alcoholics Anonymous meetings don't exist just to hand over a coin or to talk addiction; they're about a touch on the shoulder or a reassuring hug. Few human interactions like these were left unscathed. Even age-old rituals like the celebration of birth or marriage or the mourning of death were interrupted. Forget bowling alone; people died alone.

Given what social beings we are, it is no surprise that studies have consistently found that a "lack of social connection poses a significant risk for individual health and longevity." One study reports that loneliness increases the risk of premature death as much as smoking 15 cigarettes a day.[96] Other studies suggest that people who are lonely are more likely to suffer from heart disease, stroke, and immune system problems; more likely to suffer from dementia and depression; and more likely to die early.[97] Not just a little more likely, either: the CDC estimates that social isolation is associated with a 50 percent increased risk of developing dementia and a 29 percent increased risk of developing heart disease, and loneliness among heart failure patients is associated with a nearly four times increased risk of death.[98] All this has long been known.

The effects of our nation's experiment with years of enforced social isolation may take decades to assess fully. But consider this: while other factors were surely in play, just a year after the imposition of our isolating regulations, reports emerged that suicides and depression among children had soared,[99] violence against women had risen dramatically,[100] and decades of progress in math and reading scores among school children had been erased.[101] Researchers even reported lower IQs among those born during the era of covid-19 restrictions, blaming the drop on less stimulation and "interaction with the world."[102]

Jimmy Gonzales visiting his wife, Isabel, in a nursing home; both in their nineties, they were forbidden to spend time together in the same room due to covid-19 policies.[70]

It wasn't just children. Others suffered, too. Nursing homes and long-term care facilities that shut their doors to visitors and scaled back on internal social activities saw some of their residents deteriorate rapidly. "We are seeing actual deaths as a result of the isolation," a state senator reported in late 2020, an observation echoed by many.[103] "We're hearing from a number of family members and [long-term care] ombudsmen that many residents are just losing the will to live," noted the director of public policy and advocacy for the National Consumer Voice for Quality Long-Term Care.[104]

What about recovering addicts like Mr. Reed? One study found that covid-19-era restrictions were "detrimental to mental health and substance use outcomes," highlighting especially their impact on the homeless.[105] By November 2021, the CDC reported that drug overdoses had reached new highs.[106] "These are numbers we have never seen before," the director of the National Institute on Drug Abuse said, noting, as *The New York Times* put it, that "the fatalities have lasting repercussions, since most of them occurred among people aged 25 to 55, in the prime of life."[107] Later, the CDC reported that overdose deaths increased by *30 percent* in the first year of the pandemic. An accompanying report dryly observed that "the pandemic and vital public health mitigation measures designed to reduce disease spread potentially led to unintended social and economic consequences (e.g., depression, health care disruption), which can increase overdose risk."[108]

Some argue that our isolating regulations were essential to stop the spread of covid-19. Others say they went too far. But put that debate to the side. Whatever one thinks of all that, one thing seems clear: our rules made an already lonely society lonelier.

Nor did We the People adopt these decrees dictating how and with whom we could gather.[109] Most were issued by executive officials—many of whom, by virtue of their socioeconomic class and power, were better equipped than most to cope with the often devastating effects of their own rules. Violators were threatened not just with civil penalties but with criminal sanctions. In some places, agents surveilled church parking lots, recorded license plate numbers, and issued no-tices warning that attendance at even outdoor services satisfying all state social distancing and hygiene requirements could amount to criminal conduct. Officials issued vaccination mandates and threat-ened to fire those who failed to comply—even nurses and doctors who cared for covid-19 patients at risk to themselves before any vaccine was available. Military service members who refused to be vaccinated were threatened with dishonorable discharge and confinement.

Through it all, at least one more thing became clear: fear and the desire for safety are powerful forces. They can lead to a clamor for action—almost any action—as long as someone does something to address a perceived threat. A leader or expert who claims he can fix everything if only we do exactly as he says can prove an irresistible force. We do not need to confront a bayonet; we need only a nudge before we willingly abandon the right to govern ourselves through our elected representatives and accept rule by decree. Along the way, we will ac-cede to the loss of many cherished civil liberties—including the right to leave our homes and live, play, laugh, and grieve with one another. We may even cheer on those who ask us to forfeit our personal freedoms. It's not a new story, of course. In the twentieth century, Europeans abdicated their liberties to strongmen. Even the ancients warned that democracies can degenerate into autocracies in the face of fear.

A few weeks into the lockdowns, *The New York Times* published an op-ed titled "I Miss Singing at Church." But it wasn't just about singing. "I miss things I did not know I would," the author began. She continued:

> I miss walks with friends, how I could look in a friend's eyes and see light in them, not flattened into two dimensions. I miss the sadness or laughter those eyes reveal up close, the hard days, the mirth. . . .
>
> I miss the congregation singing at the church where I've served as a priest for three years. . . . And though I'm an introvert, I miss gathering together, watching the sanctuary slowly fill, hearing the soft murmur of the crowd, the trills of children, the coughs, the handshaking, strangers sitting side by side.[110]

The author went on to detail the simple human interactions—trivial things, really, most of them—that make up an hour, a day, a week, and eventually a life. "If an American should be reduced to occupying himself with his own affairs, at that moment half his existence would be snatched from him; he would feel a vast void in his life," Tocqueville once remarked.[111] Seldom in our history had that truth been more obvious.

Braiding and Threading

If too much law risks impairing the freedom to speak our minds, exercise our religious faiths, or just associate with one another, it can also interfere with the ability of ordinary Americans simply to make their way in the world.

We've seen examples of this already. Remember John Yates, who was left unable to continue in a job he loved—one that offered not just financial security but also a sense of pride and community—in part because the government sought to extend financial fraud legislation to red grouper. But in case you think his case an outlier, consider that our laws today increasingly require individuals to obtain state-issued permits or licenses before they can even *begin* working. Some of these laws, of course, help ensure competence and quality. But not infrequently other factors are at play.

Take Isis Brantley. She began braiding hair at the age of six. Her community in Texas was, she later put it, "very low income . . . but with very high morals and values." As a single parent, her mother raised her and her four siblings and encouraged them to keep "learning more about our culture, and just loving ourselves and embracing who we were." Growing up, Ms. Brantley and her sister honed their braiding skills by practicing on local community members.[112] By the time Ms. Brantley arrived at college, her talents had begun attracting attention. "I found a new life for myself," she later said.[113] In 1981, she opened her first shop and later moved her business to a small community center in Dallas, calling it the Institute of Ancestral Braiding.[114]

The practice of hair braiding dates back thousands of years in Africa, where "traditionally, a person's hairstyle might reflect anything from their tribal membership to their social rank to their marital status." In some societies, "only family members could braid one another's hair"; in others, "a community or family hairdresser would braid everyone's." "Thus, just as one's hairstyle reflected one's community, braiding itself helped build and sustain communities." Like Ms. Brantley, many braiders learn their craft at an early age, often from family members, and perfect their skill through years of practice.[115]

Isis Brantley fought to work and teach her craft.
Of his own battle, Ashish Patel remarked, "All I ever wanted
was a fair chance to pursue my American Dream."

Steeped in this history, hair braiding for Ms. Brantley has never been just about business. "My motto," she likes to say, "is healing through hair."[116] Ms. Brantley's talents are widely acknowledged (Grammy Award winner Erykah Badu is a fan), but she never jealously guarded her craft. Instead, she hired "women who didn't have jobs off the streets" to work in her salon, letting them watch her work and teaching them along the way.[117] Over the years, Ms. Brantley helped women struggling with "drug abuse, financial duress, and mental health challenges."[118] To many she touched, she is something of a "spiritual god-mother."[119]

One day in 1997, however, after she had been in business for more than a decade, the life she had built was shattered.[120] Seven police officers—five uniformed and two undercover—"raided" her salon, Ms. Brantley later recounted, "like some really strong force." In front of clients, the officers handcuffed her and told her she was "going to jail." Which was, in fact, exactly where they took her.[121]

Ms. Brantley's offense? Hair braiding without a license.

It turned out that, earlier in the year, authorities had changed their administrative rules. Now anyone wishing to provide hair-braiding services in Texas first had to attend a licensed cosmetology school and pay at least $3,000 for 300 hours of training. Never mind that it wasn't clear what those schools had to offer hair braiders.[122] Never mind, too, that the average annual salary of a hair braider is $37,000[123] and securing a cosmetology license could require a practitioner to forgo an income for more than seven weeks, assuming eight hours of schooling five days a week.

Ms. Brantley decided to fight back. After all, she didn't dye, relax, or even cut hair; her methods were based on natural techniques and required no chemicals or sharp instruments. Her only tools were her hands. "This is an ancestral art form," she explained.[124] And she didn't see why she or anyone else seeking to make a living from her craft needed a "permission slip," much less one prohibitively costly for many.[125] As she saw it, hair braiding was a lifeline for many women in her community, an honorable way to put food on the table.

While Ms. Brantley faced her own troubles, another fight was brewing in other corners of the state. Authorities were also busy cracking down on eyebrow threaders. Threading is another centuries-old practice, this one rooted in the Middle East and South Asia. It was little known in much of the United States until relatively recently, when immigrants to the country began opening kiosks and salons dedicated to the craft. In threading, a single strand of cotton thread is twisted into a loop, then brushed along the skin, entwining and removing unwanted hair. Again, no chemicals, heat, or sharp objects are involved.[126]

Like braiding, threading isn't usually a path to riches; threaders make an average of around $33,000 a year.[127] Still, it has offered many of its practitioners, often recent immigrants, a way to help make ends meet. As with hair braiding, threaders often learn the craft at an early age from family or friends; by the time they practice it commercially, many have been threading for years.[128] Among those caught up in the Texas crackdown, Tahereh Rokhti and Nasim Rajabali had already been threading for around thirty years, while Nazira Momin and Vijay Lakshmi Yogi had been practicing their art for twenty and eight years, respectively. Each is an immigrant or first-generation American with roots in India or Iran. Also swept up was Ashish Patel, who had come to this country from India and started a threading business with his partners.[129]

Why the crackdown? Once more, authorities had decided to categorize threading as the practice of "cosmetology," which meant that commercial threaders needed a license. The state had regulated cosmetology since the 1930s with the stated intent of "prevent[ing] the spread[] of contagious and infectious diseases," and it now claimed that "the practice of threading raises significant public health concerns."[130] By pulling a hair from the root, officials asserted, threading "caus[es] trauma to the hair follicle," making it a "potential portal[] of entry for a multitude of infectious agents." Unlicensed threaders, officials said, faced up to $5,000 per violation per day.[131]

To secure a license, threaders were told that they had to take at least 750 hours of instruction in an approved program, followed by two sets of exams. The training programs cost at least $3,500—a price tag that, once more, doesn't include the income a student must forgo to attend hundreds of hours of classes.

What did all that training cover? A licensed program had to "devote at least 225 hours of instruction to facial treatments, cleansing, masking, and therapy; 90 hours to anatomy and physiology; 75 hours to electricity, machines, and related equipment; 75 hours to makeup; 50 hours to orientation, rules, and laws; 50 hours to chemistry; 50 hours to care of clients; 40 hours to sanitation, safety, and first aid; 35 hours to management; 25 hours to superfluous hair removal; 15 hours to aroma therapy; 10 hours to nutrition; and 10 hours to color psychology."[132] Apparently, that last bit involved instruction in how to "connect[] colors with emotions and behavior."[133]

What *didn't* the training programs have to cover? Threading.[134] What's more, threading wasn't even a mandatory topic on the state's practical and written cosmetology exams.

In response to the state's crackdown, Ms. Rokhti abandoned threading and found a lower-paying job; Ms. Yogi was left unemployed.[135] For his part, Mr. Patel couldn't afford the fines that he would face if he continued to employ competent but unlicensed threaders—but he also couldn't find licensed cosmetologists who knew how to thread. In the end, he closed shop and abandoned plans to expand to additional locations.[136] "I grew up in India," Mr. Patel explained, "and I found it difficult to land a good opportunity to start my own business. That's why I came to Texas. I am only asking for a fair chance."[137]

Once upon a time, Texas required licenses only for medical doctors. Then it added dentists to the list. Over the years, more licensing requirements followed. Still, by 1945, the state insisted on licenses for just 43 non-alcohol-related trades, many with a clear public safety connection. It was only in the following decades that things really took off. By the 2000s, Texas licensed some 500 occupations.[138]

According to one assessment, Texas's licensing regimes on average require individuals to pass two exams and complete more than 300 days of training.[139] Many of the state's licensing regimes involve recurring fees.[140] And some are far more demanding, even requiring applicants to pass exams administered by those they seek to compete against. To qualify as a registered interior designer, for example, Texas insists on a college-level education and years of work experience. Aspiring interior designers who satisfy those conditions must then apply to the Texas Board of Architectural Examiners for permission to take an exam (cost: $225) and then sit for the exam (cost: upward of $295).[141] By comparison, peace officers in Texas—who may carry firearms and make arrests—are required to complete about 700 hours of training and emergency medical technicians around 150.[142]

Think Texas makes it hard? It's not even the state with the most licensing barriers.[143] In Annapolis, Maryland, you can't work as a fortune-teller without a license. No luck getting around the ban by wordsmithing your offerings, either: the city makes it clear that you need a license to work in "spiritualism, mind reading, fortune-telling, clairvoyance, astrology, horoscope preparation and reading, palmistry, phrenology, crystal gazing, hypnotism . . . psychometry or any similar business or art."[144] Louisiana requires aspiring florists to pass a licensing exam. That exam is no joke. Administered by the Louisiana Horticulture Commission (which includes licensed florists—once more, the very people with whom would-be florists hope to compete), the exam apparently has a pass rate of around 75 percent. At least some years ago, it apparently tested whether arrangements have the "proper focal point" and whether flowers are "spaced effectively."[145]

Sometimes the growth of licensing laws is attributable to industry capture of administrative rulemaking and policies. But sometimes, too, special interests secure preferential treatment directly from state and local legislatures. Either way, a 2015 report by the White House Council of Economic Advisers and the U.S. Department of the Treasury found that onerous licensing regimes can not only reduce the total employment in a field, they can also lead to increased prices for goods and services and do so without "increas[ing] the quality of [those] goods and services." The report further found that the burden of such schemes is often felt disproportionately. The report highlighted several groups that are especially disadvantaged: military spouses (who relocate frequently); immigrants (who may possess valuable talents but not the requisite funds or language skills to satisfy licensing constraints); and workers with a criminal record (whose record may foreclose licensing "regardless of whether the conviction is relevant to the license sought, how recent it was, or whether there were any extenuating circumstances").[146] Milton Friedman once declared "the overthrow of the medieval guild system . . . an indispensable early step in the rise of freedom in the Western world."[147] But looking at our contemporary licensing landscape, some might wonder exactly how far we've really come.

How did the story end for Ms. Brantley and the eyebrow threaders? Texas closed Ms. Brantley's salon, and for a time she found herself homeless with five children in tow.[148] But she wasn't one to give up. After a decade of legal wrangling, including a trial, she prevailed.[149]

Sort of. In 2007, the state legislature excused braiders from other licensing requirements and gave them the option of obtaining instead a "Hair Braiding Specialty Certificate of Registration," which required just 35 hours of instruction and no exam. Ms. Brantley was grandfathered in and deemed free to practice her trade.[150] But Ms. Brantley didn't just *do* hair braiding; recall, she also loved *teaching* hair braiding. Teaching was her way of passing "this great art down to the next generation, while helping mothers put food on their tables."[151] And even under the new Texas scheme, those seeking to become hair braiders still had to complete their 35 hours of training at a licensed barber school.

Winning *that* license was no easy feat for Ms. Brantley. Under state law, a barber school was required to have at least 2,000 square feet of floor space; ten workstations "that include a chair that reclines, a back bar, and a wall mirror"; and "a sink behind every two workstations." Ms. Brantley's salon didn't have any of that; it was cozier—800 square feet—with just three stations. The cost of complying? Ms. Brantley estimated that she would have to spend $25,000, on top of the cost of relocating and paying a higher rent at a new location.[152] "Texas has no problem with Isis teaching," her lawyer explained, pointing out that she had been invited to guest teach at licensed schools.[153] "It just has a problem with her working for herself."[154]

More battles followed. In the end, nearly *two decades* after her saga began, Ms. Brantley won the right to teach as well as practice her craft when Texas deregulated hair braiding altogether.[155] That final victory, she said, felt "wonderful. I can use my own hands and start my own business and help others who don't have much."[156] She added, "I just want the world to know what this . . . means. I don't think people know what it means to have economic liberty right now . . . and to be able to earn an honest living with this gift. My daughter literally worked her way through college, just as a braider. Extra money she needed, she didn't have to ask me for it. This is a gift, and an art, that you can carry and never become homeless or hungry."[157] It was a cause for celebration for Ms. Brantley and other braiders in Texas, though practicing their craft still requires a license in many states today.[158]

The threaders? In 2009, they banded together and brought suit against the state, contending that its licensing scheme violated their right under the Texas constitution "to earn an honest living in the occupation of one's choice free from unreasonable governmental interference." After early losses and years of litigation, the Texas Supreme Court took up their case and, in the end, agreed with them. Requiring 750 hours of training, it ruled, "is not just unreasonable or harsh, but it is so oppressive" as to be impermissible.[159] The threaders were "overjoyed." As Mr. Patel put it, "All I ever wanted was a fair chance to pursue my American Dream."[160]

CHAPTER 7

THE SPIRIT OF LIBERTY

*It is through good order that all peoples have ar-
rived at tyranny. It surely does not follow that
peoples ought to scorn public peace; but they
must not let it suffice for them.*

—ALEXIS DE TOCQUEVILLE[1]

James M. Landis

ON JULY 31, 1964, NEWS BROKE OF THE DEATH OF JAMES M.
Landis. His body was found floating in his backyard pool by
neighborhood children who had climbed over the fence.[2] If Landis is
unknown to many today, at the time he was a towering figure—not
only the former dean of Harvard Law School and an advisor to presidents, but one of the leading architects of the administrative state.
As one biographer put it, "In the history of regulation in America,
few names loom larger than that of James M. Landis."[3] His passing
at age 64 was, as an obituary noted, a "sad end to the career of a man
who had played major roles in the administrations of Presidents
Franklin D. Roosevelt, Harry S. Truman and John F. Kennedy."[4]

As documented by Thomas K. McCraw, Donald A. Ritchie, and
Justin O'Brien, Landis lived a remarkable life. Born to missionar-
ies in Japan, Landis didn't even set foot in this country until his

early teens. His father was a bit of a polymath—a teacher, philol-
ogist, and cartographer; his mother, German by heritage, taught
the language to her five children. Together, they instilled in Landis
a ferocious work ethic that contributed to both his later triumphs
and tragedies.

On arrival in America, Landis proved to be a dazzling student.[5]
Classmates at Princeton recounted that, when called on in class, he
answered "as if he had written the textbook." "Wealthier but duller"
students forked over a dollar and a half an hour to "hear him second-
guess the professors in pre-exam tutorial seminars." His own study
habits were more haphazard: he often waited until a few days before
exams to retreat into his room with coffee and books in hand—or
he eschewed studying altogether in favor of a nightlong poker game
before an early-morning exam. Little changed when he arrived at
Harvard Law School. His roommate observed that, after an evening
at the card table, Landis would return to his apartment, "lie down
on the floor, face down with pillows under elbows, reading his cases
for the next day's classes. When he fell asleep he would simply turn

James Landis

his head right or left on one of the pillows until he wakened and then continued reading." Still, it seemed to work: Landis graduated first in his class at both Princeton and Harvard. Roscoe Pound, the law school's dean at the time, called him the "strongest man I ever had under me. . . . [A] man of keen mind, very brilliant, steady, quiet, an exceptional student in every way."[6]

With an assessment like that, it was no surprise that Landis soon landed in the chambers of Justice Louis Brandeis as a young law clerk.[7] One of the most consequential cases the Court heard during the year that Landis clerked was *Myers v. United States*.[8] Recall from chapter 3 that in *Myers* the Court held that the president enjoys considerable power to remove those serving under him. Justice Brandeis dissented; he saw nothing impermissible about laws insulating agency officials from presidential control.[9] To help him prepare his dissent, Justice Brandeis dispatched Landis to gather historical evidence for his view. The Justice's resulting dissent burst with footnotes sourced by his brilliant clerk—so much so that Chief Justice William Howard Taft complained of the "enormous number of fine-print notes and . . . citations without number."

After a year clerking, it was back to teach at Harvard Law School, Landis proclaiming that he didn't want the "raccoon coats and chauffeurs" that came with law firm life. But it wasn't long before he grew restless with academic life, and in 1933 he got his chance at public service.[10] President Roosevelt asked his friend and Harvard Law School Professor Felix Frankfurter for help drafting new federal securities legislation. In turn, Frankfurter called on his former student. Landis happily agreed to assist with the project.[11] He arrived with his mentor at Washington, D.C.'s, Union Station on a Friday, intending to stay the weekend. He wound up staying four years. During that period, he not only helped draft seminal legislation granting agencies vast new powers. He also served as a commissioner of the Federal Trade Commission and later as chairman of the Securities and Exchange Commission—nicknamed "Landis's New Commission" for the role he played in creating it. By that point, he was married with a wife and children, yet his appetite for work left little time for family.[12]

When asked why her husband hadn't accompanied her to a party, his wife reportedly answered, "What husband?"[13]

Eventually, Landis returned to Harvard, this time as the youngest dean in its history. There he embarked on a series of public lectures defending the regulatory state and the power of experts.[14] As Justice Elena Kagan explained when serving as a Harvard professor:

> The need for expertise emerged as the dominant justification for . . . enhanced bureaucratic power. James Landis became the principal spokesman for the idea on his return . . . to the legal academy. "With the rise of regulation, the need for expertness became dominant[,]" Landis wrote, "for the art of regulating an industry requires knowledge of the details of its operation . . ." Political control—legal control, for that matter—posed the risk of unduly stifling this needed "expertness." Landis spoke admiringly of "[o]ne of the ablest administrators" he knew, who never read the statutes he administered, but simply "assumed that they gave him power to deal with the broad problems of an industry and, upon that understanding . . . sought his own solutions." Fear not this official, Landis implied, for "expertness" imposed its own guideposts, effectively solving the problem of administrative discretion. Expert professionals could ascertain and implement an objective public interest; administration could become a science.[15]

To Landis, the administrative state was the answer to what he perceived as the "inadequacy of a simple tripartite form of government to deal with modern problems."[16] It was a Wilsonian ideal.

His lectures were published as *The Administrative Process*, a book that earned Landis substantial acclaim (and not a little criticism) but that in many ways also represented the high-water mark in his life.[17] Soon an affair with an assistant led to his divorce. Friends and colleagues distanced themselves, and he resigned his Harvard posts, his departure from the school this time "final and in sorrow." For a time, he served as a commissioner at the Civil Aeronautics Board (CAB), an agency vested with broad powers to regulate the airline industry. But serving on that board was a step down for the one-time administrative superstar. He began drinking heavily and using sleeping pills. After less than two years on the job, his term expired and President Harry Truman declined to renew the appointment. Temporarily, his old friend Joseph Kennedy, Sr., gave him work.[18] In the hope of securing a more permanent professional footing, Landis decided to try his hand in private practice for the first time. So at the age of 48, he finally took the bar exam; it included a question about a statute he had helped draft.[19]

Much of Landis's private practice involved appearing before his former agency, the CAB. The experience proved to be eye-opening. "Some years ago," he noted, "I wrote a fairly popular book defending the administrative process on the ground that it would be expeditious and less costly than going to court. After this experience and several others with the CAB I almost feel it a moral duty to revise my estimate of that process made before my acquaintance with the organization."

In time, Landis got the chance to formalize his critique. When John F. Kennedy, the son of his old friend, won the presidency, he asked Landis to undertake a comprehensive survey of federal regulatory practices. Accepting the assignment, Landis launched himself feverishly into the project. Six weeks later, he was done. "In a sense, I've been working on this report all my life," he told reporters.[20]

As one biographer later put it, "the Landis report was breathtaking in its critique" and "stunned" the academic and legal community "by both its verve and far-reaching implications."[21] Another called it "a merciless dissection of the [agencies'] failures, informed not only by the author's years of study and experience but also by a bitter sense of the historical betrayal of the regulatory ideal."[22]

The report highlighted the growing scope and impact of federal regulatory agencies and the broad delegations Congress had afforded them. As Landis summarized, "The scope of responsibility entrusted to these agencies is enormous, exceeding in its sweep, from the standpoint of its economic impact perhaps, the powers remaining in the Executive and the Legislative." Furthermore, he wrote, "these delegations, once made, are rarely recalled or retracted." Instead, "the tendency is to expand them as more and more complex problems arise. The legislative standards under which the delegations are made are similarly increasingly loosened so that not infrequently the guide in the determination of problems that face the agencies is not much more than their conception of the public interest."

Beyond that, Landis identified at least ten more particular problems with agency practices. These included excessive costs and delays in securing answers from agencies; incompetent personnel, rather than the experts he had once anticipated; insufficient interagency coordination; and flawed decisional processes. He noted, for example, that "it is a general belief, founded on considerable evidence, that briefs of counsel, findings of hearing examiners, relevant portions of the basic records, are rarely read by the individuals theoretically responsible for the ultimate decision." He observed, too, that "the combination of the functions of prosecutor and judge" in administrative adjudication had "developed a belief that elements of fairness were too frequently absent."[23]

The report Landis handed in—thirteen years to the day after losing his seat on the CAB—made seismic waves in Washington. One of the chief authors of the Administrative Procedure Act hailed it as "the voice of one crying out in the wilderness," and agency officials, hearing of President Kennedy's enthusiasm for the report, rushed to "scrounge up copies." Newspapers covered Landis's work extensively. Reporters even trailed former President Truman on one of his early-morning walks, eager for his take. He conceded the report's critiques about the competency of some of his agency appointees but quipped, "Jim ought to know something about it. He was one of the appointees."

For a time, Landis joined the Kennedy administration to carry out the report's recommendations, and there was even talk of nominating him to the Supreme Court. But then disaster struck when it was revealed that he had sent love sonnets to (another, different) assistant. Whether things had progressed beyond the land of Byron remains unknown, but the letters landed in the hands of his love interest's husband, who named Landis as a "correspondent" in an ensuing divorce suit.[24] President Kennedy accepted Landis's resignation on September 1, 1961.[25]

More bad news followed. A routine background check into presidential appointees revealed that Landis had failed to file income tax returns for the years 1955 to 1960. He had set aside money and filled out most of the forms but had never gotten around to finishing the job. It seems he had harbored no intent to defraud; instead, the legal luminary simply procrastinated, distracted by other work. As all that became public and prosecutors mulled over charges, Landis's drinking, already heavy, began to take a toll. When the charges came, his lawyers suggested that he plead not guilty by reason of incompetency; certainly, a biographer has argued, the case could have been made. But Landis refused, fearing that doing so would imperil the ongoing regulatory reform efforts he had championed. Besides, he expected no worse than a fine and suspended sentence.

In that, he miscalculated. The judge handling his case imposed a sentence of thirty days in jail.[26] He even turned down Landis's request for a little time before beginning his term. Ultimately, Landis spent most of his sentence at the Columbia Presbyterian Medical Center receiving treatment for a neurological problem, and New York authorities later suspended his law license.[27] The whole episode was a devastating blow for a man once the subject of a *Fortune* article titled "The Legend of Landis."[28]

Three weeks after his suspension, Landis was found floating in his swimming pool. While some speculated it had been a suicide, the coroner ruled it accidental drowning likely caused by a heart attack.[29] Attorney General Robert F. Kennedy wept at his funeral.[30]

When it came to dealing with Landis, the administrative state he helped create did not exhibit the sort of inefficiency he criticized late in life, only perhaps a lack of humanity. In accordance with his wishes, his body was cremated and his ashes scattered in the home garden he had lovingly tended. But a dispute still lingered about his back taxes. He had paid the IRS some $94,000 in penalties (about $900,000 today).[31] The IRS, however, insisted that more than $70,000 remained outstanding. Landis had believed the agency's calculations to be mistaken and had spoken of contesting them. But after his death, no one was left with the will or perhaps the resources to carry on the fight. So in a final act of ruin, the agency closed its case by taking Landis's home—pool, garden, ashes, and all.[32]

Our Laboratories of Democracy

If Landis considered himself "quite a protagonist of the administrative process," he also became "perhaps its severest critic too."[33] Nor, as he discovered, do reforms come easily. Max Weber, a German political economist and proponent of administrative power, once acknowledged that "bureaucracy is among those social structures which are hardest to destroy"—or, one might add, simply reform.[34] Still, it would be a mistake to give up on the hope of reform for its difficulty.

An English doctor once described his practice this way:

> Among my patients are some refugees. . . . They have no doubts about the benefits of the rule of law, having experienced the opposite in their own flesh and blood. They know what a relief it is not to fear the nocturnal knock at the door and to pass a man in uniform without trembling with anxiety. They know also that the rule of law is an historical achievement, not the natural state of man. . . . Because of their own experience, they do not take it for granted. They know that it arose from a long philosophical and political development, one unique in world history. They know that it is a fragile achievement and easily destroyed.[35]

Our nation reflects that doctor's practice. We are a nation of immigrants, one built by men and women who fled oppression in pursuit of freedom and the rule of law. Our Constitution has done a better job mediating those twin ambitions than any other system of government yet devised. Its adoption was a miracle. And if the job of manifesting a miracle fell to our founders, the job of ensuring that it endures falls to each new generation. Yes, we may face challenges. But canvass the nation, and you will find a new generation of reform efforts by men and women of our own time that are no more partisan or divisive in spirit than those Landis and President Kennedy championed sixty years ago.

Start with what is happening at the state level. States remain our laboratories of democracy, no less than when Justice Brandeis spoke of them in those terms almost a century ago.[36] And when it comes to tackling the challenges posed by our mountain of laws, they are once more leading the way.

Is there anyone who thinks it's a good thing to maintain on the books a law that forbids cursing in front of women? Or one that penalizes playing the National Anthem out of tune?[37] Recognizing that our statutes and regulations have grown massively and sometimes haphazardly over time, a number of states, including New York and New Jersey, have created commissions to study the retirement of obsolete laws.[38] The commissions may not be perfect, but they have won notable victories, and their initial successes have induced other states to follow suit or even take the idea a step further.[39]

In 2019, for example, the Idaho Legislature opted against reauthorizing the state's administrative code and thus put the onus on the governor to decide which rules to keep and which to toss. After a process that involved some forty public meetings, 20 percent of the state's regulatory rules were abandoned and another 20 percent simplified.[40] Around the same time, Rhode Island eliminated a variety of outdated or costly rules—perhaps 30 percent of its administrative code.[41] Texas, meanwhile, sets a "sunset" date for most agencies, at which time an agency will be eliminated unless reauthorized by the legislature. The state's Sunset Advisory Commission reviews agencies annually to assess whether they remain effective and how their services might be improved. Since the commission's inception, approximately 42 agencies and programs have been eliminated and other agencies consolidated and streamlined.[42] A number of other states have experimented with their own versions of sunset laws, too.[43]

Many have also pursued licensing reform. Recall from earlier chapters the often debilitating effect some licensing regimes can have on people's ability to make a living: braiders and threaders asked to take on thousands of dollars of debt to complete courses having little to do with their art; florists unable to make a living after failing an exam administered in part by those with whom they hope to compete; monks who could not make caskets without satisfying extensive funeral home mandates unrelated to their intended offerings. After decades that saw states expand licensing requirements to more and more lines of work and impose ever more stringent conditions, the tide seems to be turning. As one journalist has noted, "occupational licensing reform is gaining traction," as something "on which Democrats and Republicans can often agree."[44] In 2019, Arizona began recognizing occupational licenses issued by other states, so already-licensed plumbers, cosmetologists, contractors, and others may work without having to take additional tests or undergo repetitive training.[45] In quick succession, a number of other states followed suit.[46] Idaho consolidated eleven separate licensing agencies into one. Florida and Ohio, among many others, eased or removed licensing requirements for a broad swath of professions: as of 2021, you no longer need a license to work as a timekeeper for a boxing match in the Sunshine State or as a cosmetic therapist in the Buckeye State.[47]

There is also some room for optimism when it comes to access to justice. As we saw in chapter 5, in a world with so much law, access to legal advice is vital—yet many Americans cannot afford it. Recognizing this reality, a number of states are beginning to take steps to address the problem. In 2020, for example, Utah established a regulatory "sandbox" for nontraditional legal service providers. During the pilot period, the state allowed these entities, such as law firms with nonlawyer ownership, to provide legal advice in certain practice areas. A year in, the Institute for the Advancement of the American Legal System observed that one of the first entities Utah permitted under its new law had begun providing "free and low-cost legal services to assist clients in completing court documents, and . . . related legal advice using chat-bots, instant messaging, and nonlawyer staff." "In just nine months," the Institute found, "more than 2,500 people have received help with housing, immigration, healthcare, discrimination, employment, and a gamut of other issues."[48] California now allows certain licensed "legal document assistants" to assist clients before certain tribunals. Colorado permits licensed nonlawyers to represent clients in unemployment proceedings. And to help streamline litigation and reduce costs, Arizona has devised a new rule requiring parties in civil suits to disclose documents "relevant to the subject matter of the action" within thirty days of a responsive pleading, and adds an ongoing duty of disclosure thereafter. It's a small but significant step toward reforming the expensive and lengthy pretrial discovery process that is often marked by multiple rounds of document requests, interrogatories, and motions practice.[49]

The Rest of the CAB Story

If reform efforts are under way at the state level, there is also reason for hope at the federal level. Just consider what Justice Stephen Breyer and Senator Edward Kennedy once did. It involved one of the most sweeping deregulatory efforts in our nation's history, shuttering an entire agency and unleashing vast new opportunities for millions in how they work and live.

When he arrived in 1974 to lead the staff of the relatively obscure Subcommittee on Administrative Practice and Procedure of the Senate Judiciary Committee, which Senator Kennedy chaired, Breyer suggested to his new boss two initiatives he might consider pursuing:

airline deregulation or Watergate-inspired procedural reforms. The Senator chose the first option, and Breyer went about setting up seven days of hearings. He invited airline executives, consumer advocates, and officials from the Civil Aeronautics Board, the very agency that James Landis had led and practiced before decades earlier.[50]

At the time, "no interstate air carrier could operate without" a hard-to-come-by "certificate of public convenience or necessity" from the agency. The agency also strictly regulated airline fares and routes. Virtually "any change an airline wanted to make in its fare or route structure required a formal application . . . and lengthy and complex administrative hearings and appeals, often followed by court proceedings."[51] What's more, as Landis observed, the agency's decisions weren't always exactly the products of reasoned judgment. One regulator recalled being assigned to draft the agency's decision awarding a route to a particular airline. Reportedly, he was told nothing except the airline's name and was left to invent reasons for the decision—reasons the board then adopted wholesale.[52]

*Future Supreme Court Justice Stephen Breyer and
Senator Kennedy at Breyer's confirmation hearing*

At the hearings, a surprising thing happened. As Breyer put it, "everyone was for" deregulation except for two groups: "One was the industry, or some of it. And the other was the board. And that itself spelled out a certain message."[53] Among those pressing for change were the famed consumer advocate Ralph Nader and the economist Alfred Kahn. After the hearing, Senator Kennedy and other key figures in both parties were convinced by the case for deregulation, and by the time Jimmy Carter won the presidency, "the stage was set."[54] In 1978, the Airline Deregulation Act became law. It eliminated the Civil Aeronautics Board and encouraged competition among airlines rather than regulation by agency officials.[55]

As always with change, there were winners and losers. But a few things stood out: In the forty years before the Act's passage, not a single new company had entered the market to provide passenger air service on a large scale. Within six years after the Act's passage, 134 new airlines were formed.[56] Not all survived, of course, and no little disruption followed. But those who have studied the industry report that, thanks to enhanced competition, many new routes and drastically lower fares emerged.[57] In fact, between 1978 and 2011, base ticket prices dropped by almost 40 percent in inflation-adjusted terms.[58] As a result, millions of people flocked to the skies for the first time. An activity that had once belonged largely to elites became one that many Americans more or less take for granted, one that has opened new vistas of opportunity, reconnected families, and allowed so many to experience for themselves new ideas and ways of life.

If it all sounds so simple and obvious today, no one should discount the challenge involved. Breyer tells the story of attending a seminar with George Stigler, the Nobel Prize–winning economist famed for his theories on regulatory capture. At the seminar, Stigler "proved" that it would be impossible to deregulate the airline industry; too many players had vested interests in keeping regulatory arrangements just as they were. But for Breyer, that assessment wasn't reason to lose hope; instead, it was "a certain challenge, because . . .

if something is wrong from the point of view of the public, well why shouldn't we change it?"[59]

Why not, indeed? The sweeping regulatory reform Edward Kennedy and Stephen Breyer helped achieve on a bipartisan basis in 1978 can serve as an inspiration and model for similar initiatives. And though the prospects for change of the sort they achieved may sometimes seem daunting, there is also reason for hope. Just consider: *Both* Presidents Obama and Trump championed regulatory reform. *Both* emphasized the importance of predictable, stable regulations that are accessible to ordinary Americans. *Both* also took notable actions in that direction. President Trump instituted a "two for one" regime under which agencies had to repeal two rules for every new one issued.[60] President Obama ordered agencies to "eliminate rules that don't make sense," and reported in his 2012 State of the Union address that those efforts had resulted in more than 500 reforms at a cost saving of more than $10 billion to the nation's economy over the following few years.[61] One of those changes involved revisions to a half-century-old rule that classified spilt milk as hazardous waste, resulting in expensive cleanup efforts for farmers.[62] ("With a rule like that, I guess it was worth crying over spilled milk," the President quipped.)[63] Some may quibble that reforms like these are trivial. But they matter for affected individuals—apparently, some farmers spent $10,000 annually to comply with the old spilt-milk rule.[64] Even more important, efforts like these provide reason for optimism that common ground can be found in regulatory reform efforts in the future, just as it was in 1978.

"The Fuel Necessary"

As World War II raged overseas, a federal judge we met back in chapter 3 gave a speech called "The Spirit of Liberty." Before nearly one and a half million people in Central Park, Judge Learned Hand observed that "liberty lies in the hearts of men and women; when it dies there, no constitution, no law, no court can even do much to help it."[65] At the time, democracies around the world were sliding into autocracies, and individual liberties most Americans took for granted were giving way to collective impulses. The only true guard against the same happening here, Hand knew, wasn't to be found in the halls of government; it was to be found in people who understand what a tremendous inheritance we have received and who have the will and courage to preserve it. As Thomas Jefferson put it, the only "safe depositor[ies]" of our form of government and the freedoms it promises are We the People.[66]

Why were so many people assembled in Central Park that day to hear a judge speak about freedom? Much of it had to do with Bronislava du Brissac. She was an immigrant to this country who had fled Poland after the Russian Revolution of 1917 and eventually settled on a farm on Long Island, New York. In gratitude for the opportunities the nation had provided her family, she set about in 1938 to organize a day featuring, as *Time* magazine described it, "patriotic speeches, songs, prayers, and a parade from Walt Whitman's birthplace to [her] farm." A year later, William Randolph Hearst began popularizing similar patriotic celebrations in his newspapers and calling on cities to emulate them. Many did just that.[67] In 1940, Congress issued a resolution setting aside the third Sunday in May as "I Am An American Day," explaining that "it is desirable that the sovereign citizens of our Nation be prepared for the responsibilities and impressed with the significance of their status in our self-governing Republic."[68] Judge Hand gave his famous speech to one such gathering.

Today, the event has been moved from May to September.[69] It's been renamed Constitution Day and Citizenship Day.[70] And it is not celebrated with anything like the enthusiasm of the past. In its heyday, though, the event drew huge crowds. In Baltimore, for example, General Douglas MacArthur led the city's first parade. According to some sources, by 1944 the gathering drew 23,000 people; the next year, 75,000. At its peak, approximately 500,000 people attended, as *The Baltimore Sun* put it, to celebrate "pride in being Americans."[71]

Similar events across the country featured appearances by Hollywood stars and other notable public figures.[72] In 1940, in an interview for an "I'm An American" series, Albert Einstein spoke of how "America will prove that democracy is not merely a form of government bound to a good Constitution, but also a way of life supported by a people who have a good tradition—a tradition of moral strength. And the fate of the human race is more than ever dependent on its moral strength today."[73] A few years later, in 1947, then Congressman John F. Kennedy offered a memorable speech at an event in Mineola, New York: "The fires of liberty were not self-starting," he told the gathered crowd, "nor are they self-perpetuating. . . . To safeguard the fires we must be aware of the fuel necessary for their continued burning. Such fuel is the recognition by each American of the extreme importance of our government and how it works." He finished by urging those "gathered here today [to] reaffirm our faith in American liberty by pledging ourselves to a more studied and conscientious awareness of government and the men who govern us."[74]

Doubtless, we face serious challenges on these fronts today. According to a recent study, only 38 states require a stand-alone civics class in their high schools; only 6 require a full-year class.[75] Less than half of Americans can name the three branches of our federal government, let alone explain why the separation of powers exists and how it is designed to protect their rights.[76] According to a 2016 study, close to 30 percent of millennials think it is "unimportant" for voters to "choose their leaders in free elections." Only 32 percent consider it "absolutely essential" in a democracy that "civil rights protect people's liberty."[77] Surveys suggest that over 60 percent of Americans today would flunk the test immigrants to this country must pass to become citizens.[78] In some quarters, even Fourth of July celebrations have come under attack.[79] Prominent voices regularly assert in leading media outlets that our Constitution is outdated and that there are "newer, sexier, and more powerful . . . systems" that promise more entitlements to the people or more powers to the government to deal with problems unique to our modern times.[80]

But if our civic education deficits are real, in recent years a number of groups have responded in the same spirit Stephen Breyer did with the CAB: by viewing them as a challenge to be overcome. These groups know what Jefferson knew—that "if a nation expects to be ignorant and free . . . it expects what never was and never will be."[81] They know, too, what studies consistently show—that "civic education, when done well, produces young people who are more likely to vote; work on community issues; become socially responsible; and feel confident speaking publicly and interacting with elected officials."[82] Consider the work of just three such groups (hardly a complete list, but groups I have come to admire after volunteering in their work in various capacities).

The National Constitution Center. Located in Philadelphia, the center lies just steps from Independence Hall. It's a relatively new institution, one that broke ground 213 years to the day after the Constitution was signed. By congressional mandate, the center is directed to "disseminate information about the U.S. Constitution on a nonpartisan basis in order to increase awareness and understanding of the Constitution among the American people."[83] As a centerpiece of these efforts, the center maintains an online Interactive Constitution that features scholars from across the legal and political spectrum discussing the Constitution's provisions.[84] Click on the Fourth Amendment, for example, and you will find not just its text but three other documents.[85] One, a "common interpretation," sets forth a largely undisputed interpretation of the amendment. Two others showcase scholarly disagreements. The Interactive Constitution doesn't just educate, then; it also models respectful civic dialogue. The site was launched in 2015 and has accumulated more than 71 million unique hits. During the 2020 election season, it received up to 100,000 unique hits *a day*. And each month about 100,000 people download the center's podcasts featuring interviews with constitutional scholars—again of all stripes.[86]

The center offers an array of other compelling online resources, including a "drafting table" that allows visitors to click through each sequential draft of the most notable provisions of the Constitution and an array of associated primary documents.[87] Together, the sources provide insight into the materials that inspired the founders and the paths of negotiation they traveled to arrive at a final compromise. Beyond that, there's a Supreme Court case law library, a historic documents library, and an entire course on constitutional law for high schools to draw on. The class begins with a unit on civil dialogue and proceeds through some of the nation's key foundational moments and most consequential judicial decisions.[88] Interested students and teachers can draw on a wealth of other online resources as well, including all of the readings that made up Jefferson's famed reading list.[89] (James Madison was the initial beneficiary of the list, having spent the months leading up to the Constitutional Convention reading "two trunks of books from abroad" that Jefferson had sent him about the history of "Ancient & Modern Confederacies.")[90]

iCivics. Justice Sandra Day O'Connor was a pioneer in more ways than one: raised on a cattle ranch in Arizona, she went on to become the first female justice in the Supreme Court's history, and late in life she worked to raise awareness of both breast cancer and Alzheimer's disease.[91] But as her children have observed, "Of all her accomplishments, Justice O'Connor consider[ed] iCivics to be her most important work and greatest legacy."[92] After retiring from the Court, she founded the organization because, as she wrote, "I've seen first-hand how vital it is for all citizens to understand our Constitution and unique system of government, and participate actively in their communities."[93]

Today, iCivics reaches nearly 140,000 teachers in all fifty states. Its lesson plans are downloaded a million times a year. It also offers online games centered around civic education themes. And all the material is free, no small thing in a nation that doesn't always prioritize funding for civic education.[94] (The federal government spends about five cents per student annually on civic education, compared to $54 per student for STEM classes.)[95]

The Colonial Williamsburg Foundation. In 1699, the Virginia General Assembly passed "an act directing the building [of] the Capitoll and the City of Williamsburg."[96] The city remained the colony's capital for the next 81 years and was the site of important early conflicts between colonists and royal forces.[97]

Today, the foundation maintains the city's historic district as "the world's largest American history museum."[98] Visitors can walk the streets that Washington, Jefferson, and Madison once trod; watch mock legislative proceedings in the restored capitol building, where colonists once protested parliamentary taxes and voted for independence; and sit in a tavern where many of our founders met as they contemplated revolution. Visitors can speak with "nation builders," men and women who, dressed in colonial garb, study and portray historical figures such as Washington, Madison, and James Armistead Lafayette, a onetime slave who won his freedom for his contributions to the war effort. They can also watch cabinetmakers, blacksmiths, weavers, and others using tools and methods from the eighteenth century.[99] And as of February 2023, visitors can see the Bray School, a recently discovered building that is likely the oldest remaining structure in the United States once dedicated to the education of Black children.[100] Beyond teaching through immersion for those able to visit in person, the foundation offers an array of educational resources for use nationwide. There is an institute that offers training for teachers across the country; online curricular offerings; a library with extensive primary sources; and a wealth of other digital programming. The foundation's podcast, *Ben Franklin's World*, is among the most popular podcasts worldwide. New episodes amass an average of 120,000 downloads, with over 11 million total downloads so far.[101]

Of course, none of these institutions or others like them can fully remedy our civic education deficit. For that, there must be an individual will to learn, as well as sustained efforts in our schools to teach.[102] But these groups do offer models for others to follow and resources for all to employ. Their work shows, too, that civic education doesn't have to be a partisan or boring affair. Instead, it can be about telling the full American story in all its complexity—and in that way it can help form citizens equipped to serve as sound stewards of the liberties entrusted to their safekeeping.

This sort of hard work can produce surprises, too. Sometimes we learn that our disagreements are not nearly as vast as we might have thought. Just consider what happened at the National Constitution Center in the fall of 2022. The center brought together three teams of leading constitutional scholars: "team libertarian, team progressive, and team conservative." It then asked each group to draft its ideal constitution for the twenty-first century. Notably, not a single group decided to start from scratch; not one chucked out the framers' basic tripartite and federalist form of government. Instead, each team returned to the basic Enlightenment ideal that inspired our founders: a government of limited and divided powers whose ability to encroach on individual liberty is checked and balanced at one turn after another. In presenting their constitution, "team progressive" explained its approach: "In our view, the original Constitution establishes a structure of divided government that is a necessary precondition for a constitutional democracy with robust protections for individual rights. . . . [S]imilar to the framers in 1787, we also are focusing on the structures of government over developing an exhaustive set of rights." The other teams said much the same.[103]

Out of Many, One

If the preservation of our liberties depends on civic education, civic education depends on civil dialogue. How can we teach and learn if we cannot speak our minds freely and listen to one another earnestly?

When the delegates to the Constitutional Convention arrived in Philadelphia in the summer of 1787, the prospect of failure loomed large; some feared that the "dissolution of the Convention was hourly to be apprehended."[104] Little wonder: the delegates hailed from different states, represented starkly different interests—small states versus large, agrarian interests versus urban—and held diverse views on how best to allocate power and preserve rights. There was also the looming question of slavery. Add to that potent mix the fact that the delegates were separated from their families, stuffed into a small assembly room for hours each day, all in a sweltering city "not known for its public sanitation." Bursts of anger and intemperance were not uncommon.[105] Despite all that, after four months of deliberation the delegates produced a national constitution unlike anything the world had seen. In an age when democracies were often derided as unstable and given to failure, those who spent that long, hot summer in Philadelphia produced the greatest and longest-lived democratic charter in history. While human and imperfect, it was, as Daniel Webster said, a miracle all the same.[106]

Independence Hall's Assembly Room, where the
Constitutional Convention met in the summer of 1787.

How did the delegates do it? Of course, there was discord and drama along the way. Often the chances of success looked bleak. Our framers were hardly saints (more on that in a minute). But as former Supreme Court fellow Derek Webb has recounted, beginning early on they worked hard to establish "civic friendship[s]" that carried over into the assembly room. They dined together. Some stayed in the same boardinghouse. They formed clubs "open to delegates from all the states, and their informal membership typically cut across sectional and ideological lines." After sharing meals together, delegates in these clubs would gather for discussion. No less important, once the Convention started, delegates agreed to a set of "ground rules of parliamentary procedure that facilitated respect, listening, and open-mindedness, initial gestures of respect and deference."[107] They promised not to leak their proceedings or play out their debates in the press.[108] And in one early sign of goodwill to other delegations, Virginia, by far the most populous state, agreed that each state should have an equal vote in the coming deliberations rather than have its vote weighted in proportion to its population.[109]

In the end, the Convention modeled our nation's greatest strength: *e pluribus unum*. Out of many, one. Here, we seek to capture the wisdom of the whole people through free debate and electoral competition. We require our laws to survive a daunting gauntlet to ensure they are vetted by the people's representatives and negotiated to accommodate a wide swath of competing interests, not just those currently in the majority. In this way, as Yale Professor Stephen Carter has put it, our democracy "can be seen not only as a type of government but as a system of manners, a form of social life." Indeed, "civil dialogue over differences is democracy's true engine: we must disagree in order to debate, and we must debate in order to decide, and we must decide in order to move. And it all works, as James Madison noted . . . only if we begin by understanding the necessity of disagreeing: 'As long as the reason of man continues fallible, and he is at liberty to exercise it, different opinions will be formed.'"[110]

On this front as well, one so essential to our nation's success, we face serious challenges. Often it seems that we have trouble simply tolerating viewpoints different from our own or trusting that those with whom we disagree love this country as much as we do. In a recent survey, nearly 20 percent of Americans reported that politics "has hurt friendships or family relationships."[111] Another 48 percent said that knowing the political views of another person tells them something (either "a lot" or "a little") about whether that individual "is a good person."[112] When in 2022 Democrats and Republicans were asked to describe each other, the Pew Research Center found that they tended to think of members of the other party as more "dishonest," "immoral," "closed-minded," and "unintelligent" than other Americans.[113] The center also found that "the number of negative traits Americans ascribe to members of the opposing party has increased substantially over the past six years."[114]

Troublingly, too, an increasing number of people no longer believe in the free speech values at the core of our democratic engine. A survey by John Villasenor of the Brookings Institution found that approximately 20 percent of college students think it's acceptable to use *violence* to silence speakers "known for making offensive and hurtful statements." When asked what kind of environment a college should foster, about half chose one that "prohibit[s] certain speech or expression of viewpoints that are offensive or biased against certain groups of people" over one that exposes students "to all types of speech and viewpoints." Looking at his survey results, Villasenor concluded that they "establish with data what has been clear anecdotally to anyone who has been observing campus dynamics in recent years: freedom of expression is deeply imperiled on U.S. campuses."[115]

It would be a mistake, though, to think the problem is confined to campuses. Increasingly, Americans of all ages express comfort with censorship of what others may write, say, read, or hear. According to a recent Pew Research Center poll, 55 percent of Americans think the government should "take steps to restrict false information online,

even if it limits freedom of information."[116] All told, we've traveled
no small distance since John F. Kennedy proudly declared that "we
are not afraid to entrust the American people with unpleasant facts,
foreign ideas, alien philosophies, and competitive values. For a nation that is afraid to let its people judge the truth and falsehood in an
open market is a nation that is afraid of its people."[117]

Many have hypothesized about the causes of this growing intolerance. Some have pointed to the rise of social media and attendant
echo chambers; an increase in wealth that can isolate and estrange
us; the stripping away of old forms of identity—God, nation, family,
and local community connections—that may leave people primed
to assume new ones.[118] But whatever the reasons for our growing
intolerance, we should all be concerned about where it leads. As the
journalist George Packer warned, "When politics becomes a perpetual tribal war, ends justify almost any means and individuals are
absolved from the constraints of normal decency."[119] If that's right,
it's a script we have seen before. As Learned Hand and John F.
Kennedy alluded to in their "I Am An American Day" speeches,
Europe in the 1930s and 1940s had men who treated politics as
war and thought the stakes of the day too high to tolerate dissent.
They, too, believed that the ends justified the means—and it did not
end well.

Still, if there is reason for concern, we should hardly catastrophize.
Our present challenges are not unprecedented. Democracies are
rich, complex places, and any government run by the people promises some rough and tumble—with slips and falls—along the way. As
Professor Carter reminds us, from its start our nation was "famous
for our bad manners." (After visiting the new nation in the 1830s,
the British author Frances Trollope wrote an entire book arguing
that we had no manners at all.)[120] Often, too, our founders *were*
pretty rough on one another when expressing political disagreements. Think of Thomas Jefferson and Alexander Hamilton's infa-
mous squabbles. ("So seditious, so prostitute a character," Hamilton
wrote of Jefferson. "A man whose history . . . is a tissue of mach-
inations against the liberty of the country," Jefferson shot back.)[121]

Don't forget Hamilton's fatal duel with a sitting Vice President. Or the fistfights (and canings) that sometimes broke out in the halls of Congress.[122]

Nor did our predecessors always stand above the temptation to use the levers of government to censor debate and dissent. After supplying us with a model of civil dialogue in Philadelphia in 1787, about a decade later the founding generation offered us a cautionary tale. During John Adams's administration and under the guise of national security, a Federalist-controlled Congress adopted the Sedition Act, a law that criminalized "false, scandalous and malicious" speech about the federal government.[123] During the law's brief and ignominious reign, it was used to suppress views of the administration's critics and their allies in the press. As described in *The Washington Post*, when Charles Holt, the editor of a Connecticut newspaper, took some verbal jabs at Secretary of the Treasury Alexander Hamilton ("Are our young officers and soldiers to learn virtue from General Hamilton? Or like their generals are they to be found in the bed of adultery?"), the government "promptly charged Holt with being a 'wicked, malicious seditious and ill-disposed person—greatly disaffected' to the U.S. government" and imprisoned him.[124]

If history offers some comfort that our present problems are not unique, our own times also suggest some reasons for hope. A 2018 study by the nonprofit group More in Common found that a majority of Americans are fed up with polarization and want less absolutism and more compromise.[125] And just as there's a renewed movement afoot to teach civic education, there is a corresponding effort to rekindle our commitment to free speech and civil dialogue. The National Constitution Center's model high school constitutional law class, for example, doesn't begin with founding-era documents; it begins with a unit on civil dialogue.[126] And remember those teams of libertarian, progressive, and conservative legal scholars the center assembled to draft their ideal constitutions for the twenty-first century? Not only did all three groups wind up producing documents that hew closely to our existing charter's central insights.

Remarkably, after a week of dialogue, they even managed to reach consensus on five proposed amendments to our Constitution. No less remarkably, each of their proposed amendments sought to build on Madison's central insight that liberty's best protection lies in pitting power against power. As Jeffrey Rosen and Sal Khan explained, "All three teams shared concerns about an imperial presidency and a runaway administrative state." They continued: "What unites all five amendments is a focus on the structures of government rather than individual rights. By preventing all power from being concentrated in one place, all are designed to ensure that each of the three branches can check the others or that all three branches are ultimately responsible to the people."[127]

"That Little Spark"

As we write, our nation is rapidly approaching the 250th anniversary of the Declaration of Independence. When 56 men gathered to sign that document in 1776, they didn't just signal their collective discontent with British rule or their view that "Governments . . . deriv[e] their just powers from the consent of the governed." On that day, they engaged in an act of immense personal courage in defense of the idea that each of us is "created equal" and enjoys the inalienable right to "Life, Liberty, and the pursuit of Happiness."

That conviction and those words have inspired freedom movements around the world and influenced declarations of independence in countries as diverse as Czechoslovakia and Vietnam.[128] Throughout our own history, they have served as a yardstick for measuring how well we are living up to our own stated ideals. President Abraham Lincoln appealed to the Declaration's promises before and during the Civil War. ("Near eighty years ago we began by declaring that all men are created equal; but now from that beginning we have run down to the other declaration, that for some men to enslave others is a 'sacred right of self-government.' . . . Our republican robe is soiled, and trailed in the dust. Let us repurify it. . . . Let us re-adopt the Declaration of Independence, and with it, the practices, and policy, which harmonize with it.")[129] Those who gathered at Seneca Falls in 1848 to propel the women's rights movement forward appealed to the Declaration, too. (Their motto: "All men *and women* are created equal.")[130] Dr. Martin Luther King, Jr., did the same when he stood before the Lincoln Memorial in 1963. ("I have a dream that one day this nation will rise up and live out the true meaning of its creed: We hold these truths to be self-evident, that all men are created equal.")[131]

The men who signed the Declaration could hardly have foreseen any of that. What they did know was that, by the simple act of signing their names, they had committed an act of treason.[132] "Do you recollect the pensive and awful silence which pervaded the house when we were called up, one after another, to the table of the President of Congress," Benjamin Rush later wrote to John Adams, "to subscribe what was believed by many at that time to be our own death warrants?" The "Silence & the gloom" were interrupted, Rush added, "only for a moment by Col. Harrison of Virginia who said to Mr. Gerry at the table, 'I shall have a great advantage over you Mr. Gerry when we are all hung for what we are now doing. From the size and weight of my body I shall die in a few minutes, but from the lightness of your body you will dance in the air an hour or two before you are dead.'"[133]

The gallows humor could not mask the hard truth that awaited. "For their dedication to the cause of independence, the signers risked loss of fortune, imprisonment, and death for treason." Five were taken captive.[134] One lost a son to the war; another had two sons captured by the British.[135] Nearly a third had their homes "destroyed or damaged," and "nearly all of the group emerged poorer."[136] Francis Lewis's property was destroyed and his wife imprisoned under brutal conditions; she died two years later.[137] John Hart's family fled as the British approached their New Jersey home. While troops occupied his farm, Hart lived on the run, "never deeming it safe to remain under the same roof two nights in succession."[138] During the battle of Yorktown, Thomas Nelson, Jr., saw that the British were using his home as their headquarters. Legend has it that he didn't hesitate to encourage colonial troops to open fire on it.[139] Damage from the cannon fire remains visible on the southeast side of the house more than two centuries later.[140] Nelson was "left a poor man" after the Revolution and ultimately "buried in an unmarked grave . . . so that his creditors could not hold his body as collateral." Reputedly, before he died, he was asked if he felt bitter about his experiences. He replied, "I would do it all over again."[141]

Who were these men? Not professional soldiers. About half were lawyers. Some were merchants; others landowners and farmers. Many stood to gain from remaining on the sidelines: They were "in the vigor of existence," some with considerable land and fortune, who had "all the offices and emoluments at the disposal of royalty within their reach."[142] Their signatures represented not only an act of immense courage but one of personal sacrifice.

Which leads to a final point: our democracy doesn't depend just on a people equipped with the knowledge necessary to engage in the hard work of self-government, or citizens able to speak freely and inclined to listen respectfully. It depends on the courage and sacrifice of men and women willing to stand up, even at a high personal cost, to defend the rights to democratic self-rule, equal treatment, life, liberty, and the pursuit of happiness that belong to us all. Washington's famous *Rules of Civility and Decent Behavior in Company and Conversation* may have begun with society niceties: don't roll your eyes, don't lift an eyebrow, don't spit in another's face. But they did not end there. Tellingly, they finished with a call to "labour to keep alive in your breast that little spark of celestial fire called conscience."[143]

The pages of our history are filled with stories of men and women who labored courageously against great odds to sustain "the fires of liberty." One of our heroes from our own profession is Justice John Marshall Harlan. His portrait at the Supreme Court depicts a dispirited man—and understandably so. In 1896, in *Plessy v. Ferguson*, the Supreme Court upheld state-imposed racial segregation. Only Justice Harlan dissented, firm in his conviction that "our Constitution is color-blind, and neither knows nor tolerates classes among its citizens."[144] Doubtless, his views about the innate equality of all persons won him few friends and many enemies in his home state of Kentucky. Many years later, of course, his views were vindicated in *Brown v. Board of Education*.[145] But he knew none of that in his own time. His journey was lonely and uncertain—and courageous.

Nor is it necessary to reach back to great figures in history. The courage of the men and women whose stories fill chapter after chapter of this book inspires us, too. Often against high odds and with little notoriety, in ways both large and small, they have struggled to realize a little more of the Declaration's promise in their own times and places.

Recall just one of them, Sandra Yates, whom we met in chapter 1. It's easy in retrospect and with the sterility of the written word to gloss over what she did, but think for a moment of the enormity of it. In an era when nearly all defendants plead guilty, she and her husband learned how to operate within our legal system and employ its tools to vindicate what they believed to be right and just. They did so without the backing of wealth or power; indeed, the government's charges effectively precluded John from making a living at his job. They proceeded against great odds, too: the officials they were up against enjoyed nearly endless resources, devoting perhaps $11 million and five years to the task of proving John's guilt.

At how many points would it have been easier simply to throw in the towel and say "Enough"? John faced one of those moments after he was released from jail. By then he didn't see what he could gain by pursuing an appeal; he had served his time. But when John faltered, Sandra was there to remind him of the importance of his case for others. They needed to press on, she insisted, to prevent officials from "do[ing] to someone else what they did to us."

In truth, *even after* John won at the Supreme Court, Sandra wasn't satisfied. The case had been a close one; John had prevailed by only a single vote. She wanted more: "I was upset it wasn't a higher number," she confessed.[146] For her, the long and lonely fight was about something greater than herself or her family. It was about making this nation a little truer to its founding ideals. The same spark of courage that ignited our democratic experiment in Independence Hall in the summer of 1776 lives on in people like Sandra Yates. We stand in awe of them. They are our real hope.

EPILOGUE

W HEN SPEAKING WITH GROUPS OF YOUNG PEOPLE OR EVEN
lawyers and fellow judges, I am often asked if I am an optimist or a pessimist when it comes to our nation's future. As you can
probably surmise by now, I struggle with the question. The problems
I have attempted to sketch in this book, however imperfectly, are real
and serious. While some law is essential to our democracy and liberties and the equal treatment of all people, too much law can undermine all of those things and even respect for law itself. The year
after he was expelled from the Soviet Union, Aleksandr Solzhenitsyn
gave an address in the United States in which he warned that while
the rise of an authoritarian state may seem unthinkable here, "It can
happen. It is possible. As a Russian proverb says: 'When it happens
to you, you'll know it's true.'"[1]

I am unsure only about that last part. If it does happen, it may
not be so obvious. It may not come by way of some dramatic event,
external threat, or internal revolt. It may come about slowly and
be exactly what we *want*. As Tocqueville warned, when we do not
trust one another and live isolated from our neighbors and communities, fear takes hold and nothing but the government remains
to watch over us. We *want* laws to assume responsibility for decisions once left to individuals, families, and private associations. We
want action, almost any action, whether from our elected leaders or
someone else. We *want* the comfort of uniform rules rather than un-
tidy local responses. In the end, we may still have institutions we
call states, Congress, the presidency, and courts. We may still have
a Bill of Rights and something we call law. All the familiar terms
may remain, but the meaning of those words will be hollowed out.
Instead of most of the rules regulating how we live being made at the

local level, almost everything of significance will be decided far from home. Instead of governing ourselves through our elected representatives, our laws will be made by officials who do not answer to us. Instead of having independent judges to decide our disputes, we will have ones who are forced to account to others. Instead of jealously guarding our rights to think, speak, pray, and pursue happiness, we will allow our liberties to become more and more circumscribed, all in the name of better protecting our own well-being. Instead of a rule *of* law designed to ensure fair notice, equal treatment, and room for individual flourishing, we will have rule *by* laws that can be applied and altered in ways that few can anticipate, that often favor the connected and moneyed, and that come to cover nearly every facet of our lives. Bit by bit we will move from a world in which law is revered into one in which it generates disaffection and feeds distrust. And that will be exactly what we want.

Despite my real concerns, though, I confess I remain an incorrigible optimist. America has overcome daunting odds time and again. At our nation's birth, almost no serious thinker in Europe thought a democracy could survive long without devolving into chaos or tyranny. Yet almost 250 years later, here we stand. For much of our history, the promise of equal treatment under the law looked more like an unserious fiction than an earnest ambition. Yet while much remains to be done, we have made many strides to realize that promise, from the Civil War to the Civil Rights Act of 1964. World wars, terrorist attacks, political assassinations, economic depressions, the fall of other countries to communism and fascism, and so much more have tested our nation, too. Still, America remains the greatest beacon of liberty the world has ever known. The ideals embodied in our Declaration of Independence—that each of us enjoys certain inalienable rights, that all of us are created equal, that governments derive their just power from the consent of the governed—have inspired billions of people around the world and captured truths that resonate in every human heart. I would never bet against the American people.

—NMG

ACKNOWLEDGMENTS

WHILE THERE ARE MANY PEOPLE TO THANK, THE STARTING place must be with my coauthor, Janie Nitze. Her family fled communist Czechoslovakia, seeking freedom in this country. I know of few who prize our Constitution and the liberties it promises more than she does; she is also one of the most remarkable lawyers of her generation. After earning an undergraduate degree in physics, a master's in statistics, and a law degree, all at Harvard, Janie clerked for both me and my colleague Justice Sonia Sotomayor. Janie has taught law, worked in private practice, and served as a Senate-confirmed member of the Privacy and Civil Liberties Oversight Board. She has also helped start an early childhood education program; is the mother of three young children; and is married to an equally remarkable young man, Paul Nitze, whom I first met when he was clerking for Judge Carlos Lucero, one of my colleagues on the Tenth Circuit. Somehow, Janie found time to work with me on this book; she is in every sense its coauthor. From outlining its scope to interviewing some of those whose stories are recounted here, overseeing the work of our research assistants, and working with me on every page, she was there through many long hours but always with a new idea and an infectious laugh. She is a true colleague and the best of friends.

Janie and I owe a profound debt to those whose stories are recounted in these pages. Their actions stand as models for the sort of courage it takes to preserve what Judge Learned Hand called the spirit of liberty. When challenges arose, they stood squarely to meet them, often against great odds and at no small personal cost, all without any expectation of public acknowledgment or praise. Some had lawyers, too, who worked tirelessly and often without charge on their behalf, modeling the kind of good our profession is capable of. We thank all of those who spent countless hours speaking to us about their experiences. This book would have been greatly impoverished without their generosity.

This book also owes a debt to my colleagues and law clerks at the Tenth Circuit and the Supreme Court. Many of the ideas examined here are the product of hearing and discussing years of cases together. We may not always agree, but their thinking always improves my own and I have enjoyed the journey with them immensely.

Janie and I profited as well from research assistants who helped us track down sources and confirm citations. My hope for the future of this country has a lot to do with the passion and skill I see in young people like them: Burke Craighead, Zachary Gluckow, Hayley Isenberg, Jack Kieffaber, Tom Koenig, Eli Nachmany, Tiffany Pages-Sanchez, Matt Phillips, Owen Smitherman, Nathaniel Sutton, Marisa Sylvester, and Stephen Vukovits. We profited, too, from Insun Hong's invaluable insights as we thought through our book cover design.

Janie and I are grateful to Rachel Barkow, David Feder, Louise Gorsuch, Hon. Raymond Kethledge, Dr. Jan Kucera, Matthew Latimer, Michael McConnell, James Neidhardt, Eric Nelson, Paul Nitze, Hon. Neomi Rao, Jeffrey Rosen, Hon. Jeffrey Sutton, Peggy Sutton, Hon. Amul Thapar, Hon. Timothy Tymkovich, and Keith Urbahn for kindly agreeing to read and comment on the manuscript. We are indebted as well to Ethan Torrey of the Supreme Court Legal Office for his careful review of the manuscript and advice throughout the drafting process.

My chambers team, which in recent years has included Jessica Bartlow, Kristin Thompson, Arielle Goldberg, Reagan Dupler, and Claire Nevill, makes coming to the office a joy in ways large and small, day in and day out. For that and their friendship along the way, I am truly grateful. They are family to Louise and me.

Finally, words cannot begin to capture my gratitude for Louise and our daughters. They are simply everything to me.

—NMG

Working on this book has been the highlight of my life in the law, and for the opportunity I am immensely grateful to the Justice. It says something special about him that in a city dominated by ghost-writers working in anonymity, he not only penned every word of this book but then insisted on giving me credit as coauthor anyhow. No clerk leaves his chambers without an acute awareness of the Justice's belief in the primacy of the individual in our constitutional frame-work. For teaching me that; for his mentorship and life advice; and for the friendship he and Louise have so graciously extended over these many years, I am thankful beyond words.

I echo the Justice's thanks to the many research assistants who helped invaluably along the way, as well as to the men and women who lived the cases described in this book and were willing to relive them again in interviews.

Paul and kids: you are my all.

Finally, I thank my mom and dad. To crib from an English doctor we earlier quoted, they know what it is to fear the nocturnal knock at the door and to tremble at a man in uniform. They know what liberty is because they've known its absence. I thank them for their unwavering support and for passing their love of, and hope for, this country down to me.

—JN

NOTES AND SOURCES

Whatever our aspirations for originality of thought, at its core this is a book about old ideas—ones our framers cherished and enshrined in the Declaration of Independence and Constitution. In the endnotes that follow, we have attempted to provide source materials for readers interested in pursuing particular strands of thought in greater depth. At the same time, some of the ideas we discuss are borrowed from sources too ingrained or dimly recalled to be faithfully recorded—but borrowed gratefully they remain. In addition, we have sought to minimize distraction by consolidating note numbers: If sequential sentences on the same topic derive from one or more sources, we often have consolidated sources in a single endnote. We trust the interested reader will be able to make the right connections.

Some passages in the book make use of material found in the Justice's judicial opinions or academic articles. These underlying sources, too, are referenced in the endnotes.

When quoting from source materials, we have at times omitted brackets and standardized grammar, capitalization, and style choices in the interest of readability. No change was made with the intent of modifying substance.

Finally, many of the stories related here are drawn from interviews, court materials, and media reports. We are grateful not only to those who so generously gave their time to speak with us but also to members of the press who devoted their time, energy, and resources to recording some of the challenges ordinary Americans can face in a world with so much law.

EPIGRAPH

1. Whitney v. California, 274 U.S. 357, 377 (1927) (Brandeis, J., concurring), *overruled by* Brandenburg v. Ohio, 395 U.S. 444 (1969).

PROLOGUE

1. DOUGLAS ADAMS, THE HITCHHIKER'S GUIDE TO THE GALAXY 9–10 (1979).
2. Lotte E. Feinberg, *Mr. Justice Brandeis and the Creation of the* Federal Register, 61 PUB. ADMIN. REV. 359, 359–60 (2001); *Building History,* SUPREME COURT OF THE UNITED STATES, https://www.supremecourt.gov/about/buildinghistory.aspx (last visited Feb. 17, 2024).
3. Lotte E. Feinberg, *Mr. Justice Brandeis and the Creation of the* Federal Register, 61 PUB. ADMIN. REV. 359, 360 (2001).
4. Panama Refining Co. v. Ryan, 293 U.S. 388 (1935); Mary Whisner, *Some Guidance About Federal Agencies and Guidance,* 105 LAW LIBR. J. 385, 390 n.27 (2013); Note: *Delegation of Power by Congress,* 48 HARV. L. REV. 798 (1935).
5. Lotte E. Feinberg, *Mr. Justice Brandeis and the Creation of the* Federal Register, 61 PUB. ADMIN. REV. 359, 365 (2001); *Dignity of Supreme Court Shattered by Laughs in Code Case,* EVENING STAR, Dec. 11, 1934, at 3; *Judiciary: Hip Pocket Law,* TIME, Dec. 24, 1934, at 12.
6. *Hearings Before Subcomm. No. II on the Judiciary, House of Representatives on H.R. 11337 and H.R. 10932,* at 15 (Feb. 21, 1936); Lotte E. Feinberg, *Mr. Justice Brandeis and the Creation of the* Federal Register, 61 PUB. ADMIN. REV. 359, 360 (2001).
7. Panama Refining Co. v. Ryan, 293 U.S. 388, 412 (1935).
8. *Judiciary: Hip Pocket Law,* TIME, Dec. 24, 1934, at 12.
9. *See generally* Lotte E. Feinberg, *Mr. Justice Brandeis and the Creation of the* Federal Register, 61 PUB. ADMIN. REV. 359 (2001); Urban A. Lavery, *The Federal Register, and the Need of Its Reform,* 2 LAW. & L. NOTES 1 (1948); *Judiciary: Hip Pocket Law,* TIME, Dec. 24, 1934, at 12.
10. Caring Hearts Personal Home Services, Inc. v. Burwell, 824 F.3d 968, 971 (10th Cir. 2016); Brief for Appellants at 10–11, Caring Hearts Personal Home Services, Inc. v. Burwell, 824 F.3d 968 (10th Cir. 2016) (No. 14-3243).
11. Buffington v. McDonough, 143 S. Ct. 14 (2022); Biestek v. Berryhill, 139 S. Ct. 1148 (2019); Gutierrez-Brizuela v. Lynch, 834 F.3d 1142 (10th Cir. 2016).
12. VÁCLAV HAVEL, *On Evasive Thinking* (June 9, 1965), in OPEN LETTERS: SELECTED PROSE 1965–1990 10–11 (Paul Wilson ed., 1991).
13. *The Federalist* No. 62 (probably James Madison), in THE FEDERALIST PAPERS 381 (Clinton Rossiter ed., 1961). Some have suggested that Alexander Hamilton wrote *The Federalist* No. 62. But the essay is more often attributed to Madison, and the edition of THE FEDERALIST PAPERS cited here identifies him as its probable author. I have followed its lead.
14. Back then, parties could often pay for transcriptions of the proceedings, but they weren't required to deposit a copy with the Court until 1968. NMG conversation with Supreme Court librarian, Aug. 17, 2023.
15. Even so, piecing together the narrative wasn't easy. As the government's lawyer later recounted in describing his "public humiliation" to Erwin N. Griswold, the justices at argument were fixated on "this question of publication of codes, orders, and regulations." Lotte E. Feinberg, *Mr. Justice Brandeis and the Creation of the* Federal Register, 61 PUB. ADMIN. REV. 359, 365 (2001). But which of those (codes, orders, or regulations) was being discussed at any given moment isn't always clear—to the reader decades later, but perhaps as well, given the haphazard state of the publication of government rules, to the parties then, too.
16. Commentary to Canon 4, *Code of Conduct for United States Judges* (effective March 19, 2019).
17. By some counts, Supreme Court justices have written or edited more than 350 books covering an array of topics ranging from psychiatry, medicine, and religion to law reform. *See* Ronald Collins, *353 Books by Supreme Court Justices,* SCOTUSBLOG (Mar. 12, 2012), https://www.scotusblog.com/2012/03/351-books-by-supreme-court -justices/. For a small sampling of some notable contributions on law and its administration by justices and other federal judges in relatively recent years, *see*

STEPHEN BREYER, ACTIVE LIBERTY: INTERPRETING OUR DEMOCRATIC CONSTITU-
TION (2005); STEPHEN BREYER, MAKING OUR DEMOCRACY WORK: A JUDGE'S VIEW
(2010); STEPHEN BREYER, THE AUTHORITY OF THE COURT AND THE PERILS OF POL-
ITICS (2021); STEPHEN BREYER, THE COURT AND THE WORLD: AMERICAN LAW AND
THE NEW GLOBAL REALITIES (2015); WILLIAM O. DOUGLAS, A LIVING BILL OF RIGHTS
(1961); WILLIAM O. DOUGLAS, AN ALMANAC OF LIBERTY (1954); WILLIAM O. DOUG-
LAS, TOWARDS A GLOBAL FEDERALISM (1968); WILLIAM O. DOUGLAS, WE THE JUDGES
(1956); ANTHONY KENNEDY, THE CONSTITUTION AND THE SPIRIT OF FREEDOM (1990);
JON O. NEWMAN, BENCHED: ABORTION, TERRORISTS, DRONES, CROOKS, SUPREME
COURT, KENNEDY, NIXON, DEMI MOORE, AND OTHER TALES FROM THE LIFE OF A
FEDERAL JUDGE (2017); RICHARD A. POSNER, AGING AND OLD AGE (1995); RICHARD A.
POSNER, BREAKING THE DEADLOCK: THE 2000 ELECTION, THE CONSTITUTION, AND
THE COURTS (2001); RICHARD A. POSNER, HOW JUDGES THINK (2008); RICHARD A.
POSNER, OVERCOMING LAW (1996); RICHARD A. POSNER, REFLECTIONS ON JUDGING
(2013); JED S. RAKOFF, WHY THE INNOCENT PLEAD GUILTY AND THE GUILTY GO FREE:
AND OTHER PARADOXES OF OUR BROKEN LEGAL SYSTEM (2021); WILLIAM H. REHN-
QUIST, ALL THE LAWS BUT ONE: CIVIL LIBERTIES IN WARTIME (1998); WILLIAM H.
REHNQUIST, GRAND INQUESTS: THE HISTORICAL IMPEACHMENTS OF JUSTICE SAMUEL
CHASE AND PRESIDENT ANDREW JOHNSON (1992); WILLIAM H. REHNQUIST, THE
SUPREME COURT (1987); ANTONIN SCALIA, A MATTER OF INTERPRETATION: FED-
ERAL COURTS AND THE LAW (1998); ANTONIN SCALIA & BRYAN A. GARNER, MAKING
YOUR CASE: THE ART OF PERSUADING JUDGES (2008); ANTONIN SCALIA & BRYAN A.
GARNER, READING LAW: THE INTERPRETATION OF LEGAL TEXTS (2012); JEFFREY
SUTTON, 51 IMPERFECT SOLUTIONS: STATES AND THE MAKING OF AMERICAN CONSTI-
TUTIONAL LAW (2018); JEFFREY SUTTON, WHO DECIDES? STATES AS LABORATORIES OF
CONSTITUTIONAL EXPERIMENTATION (2021); J. HARVIE WILKINSON III, COSMIC CON-
STITUTIONAL THEORY: WHY AMERICANS ARE LOSING THEIR INALIENABLE RIGHT TO
SELF-GOVERNMENT (2012).

18. VÁCLAV HAVEL, *The Power of the Powerless* (Oct. 1978), in OPEN LETTERS: SELECTED
PROSE 1965–1990 154–55 (Paul Wilson ed., 1991).

CHAPTER 1: AN INTRODUCTION TO LAW'S EMPIRE

1. GRANT GILMORE, THE AGES OF AMERICAN LAW 99 (2d ed. 2014).
2. JN interview with Sandra Yates.
3. Sarbanes-Oxley Act of 2002, Pub. L. No. 107-204, 116 Stat. 745 (2002); JN interview
   with Sandra Yates.
4. Will Kenton et al., *Sarbanes-Oxley Act: What It Does to Protect Investors*, INVESTO-
   PEDIA (May 8, 2022), https://www.investopedia.com/terms/s/sarbanesoxleyact.asp;
   Will Kenton et al., *Andersen Effect: Meaning, History in the Enron Scandal*, INVESTO-
   PEDIA (Oct. 26, 2021), https://www.investopedia.com/terms/a/anderseneffect.asp.
5. Will Kenton et al., *Andersen Effect: Meaning, History in the Enron Scandal*, INVESTO-
   PEDIA (Oct. 26, 2021), https://www.investopedia.com/terms/a/anderseneffect.asp.
6. Yates v. United States, 574 U.S. 528, 532–33 (2015).
7. Amaris Castillo, *Former Cortez Fisherman Shares His Side of Case That Has Reached
   U.S. Supreme Court*, BRADENTON HERALD (Nov. 6, 2014), https://www.bradenton
   .com/news/local/article34745838.html; JN interview with Sandra Yates.
8. Yates v. United States, 574 U.S. 528, 533 (2015); United States v. Yates, 733 F.3d 1059,
   1061–62 (11th Cir. 2013); John Yates, *A Fish Story*, POLITICO (Apr. 24, 2014), https://
   www.politico.com/magazine/story/2014/04/a-fish-story-106010; *see also* JN interviews with Sandra Yates and Judge John Badalamenti.
9. Sarbanes-Oxley Act of 2002, Pub. L. No. 107-204, § 802, 116 Stat. 745, 800 (2002).
10. Yates v. United States, 574 U.S. 528, 534 (2015); Brief of the United States at 7–8, 10,
    United States v. Yates, 733 F.3d 1059 (11th Cir. 2013) (No. 11-16093).
11. JN interview with Sandra Yates; *see also* Initial Brief of Appellant Yates at 17–18,
    United States v. Yates, 733 F.3d 1059 (11th Cir. 2013) (No. 11-16093).
12. Amaris Castillo, *Former Cortez Fisherman Shares His Side of Case That Has Reached
    U.S. Supreme Court*, BRADENTON HERALD (Nov. 6, 2014), https://www.bradenton
    .com/news/local/article34745838.html.
13. JN interview with Sandra Yates.

14. Yates v. United States, 574 U.S. 528, 534 (2015); 50 C.F.R. § 622.37(d)(2)(iv) (2022) (effective May 18, 2009).
15. *HB Fisher Serves Jail Time, Appeals Conviction*, THE ISLANDER (Jan. 25, 2012), https://www.islander.org/2012/01/hb-fisher-serves-jail-time-appeals-conviction/; JN interviews with Sandra Yates and Judge John Badalamenti.
16. JN interviews with Sandra Yates and Judge John Badalamenti.
17. Yates v. United States, 574 U.S. 528, 531, 534 n.1, 535 (2015); John Yates, *A Fish Story*, POLITICO (Apr. 24, 2014), https://www.politico.com/magazine/story/2014/04/a-fish-story-106010; JN interview with Sandra Yates. The jury variously acquitted and convicted John Yates of other charges.
18. *Cortez Commercial Fisherman Found Guilty by Jury*, U.S. DEPARTMENT OF JUSTICE (Aug. 9, 2011), https://www.justice.gov/sites/default/files/usao-mdfl/legacy/2011/08/31/20110809_Yates_FTM_GrouperConv.pdf.
19. JN interview with Sandra Yates.
20. JN interviews with Sandra Yates and Judge John Badalamenti.
21. Kenya Hunter, *Health Dept. Shuts Down Kids' Lemonade Stand in Richmond*, NBC 4 WASHINGTON (May 16, 2021), https://www.nbcwashington.com/news/local/health-dept-shuts-down-kids-lemonade-stand-in-richmond/2673569/; Trace William Cowen, *6-Year-Old Boy Sent to Court in North Carolina for Picking a Tulip*, YAHOO! NEWS (Mar. 24, 2021), https://news.yahoo.com/6-old-boy-sent-court-204227370.html.
22. Martin A. Rogoff, *A Comparison of Constitutionalism in France and the United States*, 49 MAINE L. REV. 21, 23, 60 (1997).
23. *France*: CONST. OF 1791 (Fr.), https://www.conseil-constitutionnel.fr/les-constitutions-dans-l-histoire/constitution-de-1791. *Canada*: CONST. ACT, 1867, art. 91 (Can.), https://laws-lois.justice.gc.ca/PDF/CONST_TRD.pdf; *see also* Honourable Justice John M. Evans, *Current Constitutional Issues in Canada*, 51 DUQ. L. REV. 323, 325 (2013) (explaining that "the provisions of [Canada's] formal constitution" are "contained in the Constitution Acts, 1867-1982"). *Russia*: CONST. OF THE RUSSIAN FED'N, ch. V, art. 94, http://archive.government.ru/eng/gov/base/54.html.
24. HANNAH ARENDT, THINKING WITHOUT A BANISTER: ESSAYS IN UNDERSTANDING, 1953–1975 490 (Jerome Kohn ed., 2018).
25. THOMAS PAINE, COMMON SENSE: ADDRESSED TO THE INHABITANTS OF AMERICA 36 (P. Eckler ed., 1914) (1776) (italics removed).
26. *GPO Produces U.S. Code with New Digital Publishing Technology*, GOVINFO (Sep. 23, 2019), https://www.govinfo.gov/features/uscode-2018#:~:text=The%20U.S.%20Code%20is%20a,of%20the%20Law%20Revision%20Counsel.
27. *Statistics and Historical Comparison*, GOVTRACK, https://www.govtrack.us/congress/bills/statistics (last visited Sep. 23, 2022).
28. *Legislative Productivity in Congress and Congressional Workload* ch. 6, 7, in *Vital Statistics on Congress*, BROOKINGS INSTITUTION (Feb. 8, 2021), https://www.brookings.edu/wp-content/uploads/2019/03/Chpt-6.pdf.
29. Consolidated Appropriations Act, 2021, Pub. L. No. 116-260, 134 Stat. 1182 (2020); Patient Protection and Affordable Care Act, Pub. L. No. 111-148, 124 Stat. 119 (2010); No Child Left Behind Act of 2001, Pub. L. No. 107-110, 115 Stat. 1425 (2002); Civil Rights Act of 1964, Pub. L. No. 88-352, 78 Stat. 241 (1964); Mary Clare Jalonick, *Too Big to Read: Giant Bill a Leap of Faith for Congress*, AP NEWS (Dec. 22, 2020), https://apnews.com/article/politics-james-mcgovern-legislation-coronavirus-pandemic-bills-0da216bf0352e92f8a62d8438fc9b519.
30. *The Federal Register: March 14, 1936–March 14, 2006* 3, 16, NATIONAL ARCHIVES, https://www.archives.gov/files/federal-register/the-federal-register/history.pdf (last visited Sep. 25, 2022).
31. *Reg Stats: Total Pages in the Code of Federal Regulations and the Federal Register*, REGULATORY STUDIES CENTER, COLUMBIAN COLLEGE OF ARTS & SCIENCES, GEORGE WASHINGTON UNIVERSITY, https://regulatorystudies.columbian.gwu.edu/reg-stats (last visited Sep. 25, 2022).
32. *What Is QuantGov*, QUANTGOV, https://www.quantgov.org/about (last visited Nov. 6, 2022); *see also* Patrick McLaughlin, *The Code of Federal Regulations: The Ultimate Longread*, MERCATUS CENTER, GEORGE WASHINGTON UNIVERSITY (Apr. 1, 2015),

https://www.mercatus.org/research/data-visualizations/code-federal-regulations
-ultimate-longread ("The average adult reads prose text at a rate of 250 to 300 words
per minute. If you read the *Code of Federal Regulations* at 300 words per minute on
a full-time basis, it would take you nearly three years to get through just the version
of the CFR published in 2012. That's about 58 times longer than it would take to read
through the five volumes currently published in George R. R. Martin's fantasy saga,
A Song of Ice and Fire. Or 220 times longer than it would take to read through *The
Lord of the Rings*.").

33. Exec. Order No. 13891, 84 Fed. Reg. 55235 (Oct. 9, 2019).

34. *Shining Light on Regulatory Dark Matter, U.S. House of Representatives Comm. on
Oversight and Gov't Reform Majority Staff Rep.* (Mar. 2018), https://www2.ed.gov
/policy/gen/reg/retrospective-analysis/guidance-report.pdf; Clyde Wayne Crews Jr.,
An Inventory of Federal Agency Guidance Documents, FORBES (Mar. 20, 2018),
https://www.forbes.com/sites/waynecrews/2018/03/20/an-inventory-of-federal
-agency-guidance-documents/?sh=55cad2695447.

35. Exec. Order No. 13891, 84 Fed. Reg. 55235 (Oct. 9, 2019).

36. *Capital Conversations: Hon. Paul J. Ray, OIRA Administrator*, FEDERALIST SOCIETY
(Oct. 13, 2020), https://fedsoc.org/events/capital-conversations-hon-paul-j-ray-oira
-administrator.

37. Exec. Order No. 13992, 86 Fed. Reg. 7049 (Jan. 20, 2021).

38. Thomas E. Baker, *Tyrannous Lex*, 82 IOWA L. REV. 689, 700 (1997).

39. 15 U.S.C. §§ 70c(a), 70i; 18 U.S.C. § 3061(c)(4); 39 C.F.R. § 232.1(g); *see also* MIKE
CHASE, HOW TO BECOME A FEDERAL CRIMINAL: AN ILLUSTRATED HANDBOOK FOR
THE ASPIRING OFFENDER 14 (2019); Eli Lehrer, *America Has Too Many Criminal
Laws*, THE HILL (Dec. 9, 2019), https://thehill.com/opinion/criminal-justice/473659
-america-has-too-many-criminal-laws.

40. 21 C.F.R. 139.110(a)(1) (egg white); 21 C.F.R. 139.110(b) (macaroni); 21 C.F.R. 139.110(d)
(vermicelli); 21 C.F.R. 139.112.192(a) (enforcement provisions); 21 U.S.C. § 333(a)(1)
(penalty).

41. VA. CODE Ann. § 29.1-521(a)(1)(ii) (2023), https://law.lis.virginia.gov/vacode/title
29.1/chapter5/section29.1-521/; MASS. GEN. LAWS ch. 264, § 9 (2023), https://
malegislature.gov/Laws/GeneralLaws/PartIV/TitleI/Chapter264/Section9.

42. Diane Cardwell, *A New Team Helps Steer Restaurateurs Through a Thicket of Red
Tape*, N.Y. TIMES (Dec. 27, 2010), https://www.nytimes.com/2010/12/28/nyregion
/28permits.html; *see also* PHILIP K. HOWARD, TRY COMMON SENSE: REPLACING THE
FAILED IDEOLOGIES OF RIGHT AND LEFT 116 (2019).

43. *Profile of the Legal Profession* 10 (2021), AMERICAN BAR ASSOCIATION (2021), https://
www.americanbar.org/content/dam/aba/administrative/news/2021/0721/polp.pdf;
Statistics of Population (Census of 1900), U.S. CENSUS BUREAU, https://www2.census
.gov/library/publications/decennial/1900/volume-1/volume-1-p2.pdf (last visited
Oct. 2, 2022); *QuickFacts: United States*, U.S. CENSUS BUREAU, https://www.census
.gov/quickfacts/fact/table/US/PST045221 (last visited Oct. 2, 2022).

44. *ABA-Approved Law Schools*, AMERICAN BAR ASSOCIATION, https://www.americanbar
.org/groups/legal_education/resources/aba_approved_law_schools/ (last visited
June 5, 2022); J. Gordon Hylton, *Looking at the Increase in the Number of Law
Schools and Law Students, 1950–2010*, MARQUETTE UNIVERSITY LAW SCHOOL (July 25,
2012), https://law.marquette.edu/facultyblog/2012/07/looking-at-the-increase-in-the
-number-of-law-schools-and-law-students-1950-2010/.

45. *Profile of the Legal Profession* 11, AMERICAN BAR ASSOCIATION (2021), https://www
.americanbar.org/content/dam/aba/administrative/news/2021/0721/polp.pdf.

46. JEFFREY A. LOWE, MAJOR, LINDSEY & AFRICA, *2020 Partner Compensation Survey*
18 (2020); *see also 2022 Partner Compensation Survey*, MAJOR, LINDSEY & AFRICA
(Oct. 18, 2022), https://www.mlaglobal.com/en/insights/research/2022-partner
-compensation-survey.

47. Clyde Wayne Crews Jr., *How Many Federal Agencies Exist? We Can't Drain the
Swamp Until We Know*, FORBES (July 5, 2017), https://www.forbes.com/sites
/waynecrews/2017/07/05/how-many-federal-agencies-exist-we-cant-drain-the
-swamp-until-we-know/?sh=6b49b651aa28; Federal Register, https://www.federal
register.gov/agencies (stating that the number of "agencies found" is 436) (last visited

Feb. 21, 2024); *see also* PHILIP K. HOWARD, TRY COMMON SENSE: REPLACING THE FAILED IDEOLOGIES OF RIGHT AND LEFT 204-05 (2019), Jennifer L. Selin & David E. Lewis, ADMINISTRATIVE CONFERENCE OF THE UNITED STATES, SOURCEBOOK OF UNITED STATES EXECUTIVE AGENCIES 12 (2d ed. 2018); THE UNITED STATES GOVERNMENT MANUAL (2022), https://www.govinfo.gov/content/pkg/GOVMAN-2022-12-31/pdf /GOVMAN-2022-12-31.pdf; *A–Z Index of U.S. Government Departments and Agencies*, USA.GOV, https://www.usa.gov/agency-index (last visited Feb. 21, 2024).

48. C. Northcote Parkinson, *Parkinson's Law*, THE ECONOMIST (Nov. 19, 1955), https:// www.economist.com/news/1955/11/19/parkinsons-law.

49. Claudette Roulo, *10 Things You Probably Didn't Know About the Pentagon*, U.S. DEPARTMENT OF DEFENSE (Jan. 3, 2019), https://www.defense.gov/News/Feature -Stories/story/Article/1650913/10-things-you-probably-didnt-know-about-the -pentagon/; George F. Will, *Can America "Do Big Things" Again? Ask the Regulators and Lawyers*, WASH. POST (June 15, 2022), https://www.washingtonpost.com/opinions /2022/06/15/mitch-landrieu-infrastructure-spending-challenge/.

50. *Works Progress Administration (WPA)*, HISTORY CHANNEL (June 10, 2019), https:// www.history.com/topics/great-depression/works-progress-administration.

51. George F. Will, *Can America "Do Big Things" Again? Ask the Regulators and Lawyers*, WASH. POST (June 15, 2022), https://www.washingtonpost.com/opinions/2022 /06/15/mitch-landrieu-infrastructure-spending-challenge/.

52. PHILIP K. HOWARD, TRY COMMON SENSE: REPLACING THE FAILED IDEOLOGIES OF RIGHT AND LEFT 121–22 (2019); David Fahrenthold, *Unrequired Reading: Many of the Thousands of Reports Mandated by Congress Will Only Gather Dust*, WASH. POST (May 3, 2014), https://www.washingtonpost.com/sf/national/2014/05/03 /unrequired-reading/.

53. GianCarlo Canaparo et al., *Count the Code: Quantifying Federalization of Criminal Statutes*, HERITAGE FOUNDATION (Jan. 7, 2022), https://www.heritage.org/crime-and -justice/report/count-the-code-quantifying-federalization-criminal-statutes#_ft nref61; Gary Fields & John R. Emshwiller, *Many Failed Efforts to Count Nation's Federal Criminal Laws*, WALL ST. J. (July 23, 2011), https://www.wsj.com/articles /SB10001424052702304319804576389601079728920; Ronald L. Gainer, *Report to the Attorney General on Federal Criminal Code Reform*, 1 CRIM. L. F. 99, 110 (1989).

54. *GPO Produces U.S. Code with New Digital Publishing Technology*, GOVINFO (Sep. 23, 2019), https://www.govinfo.gov/features/uscode-2018#:~:text=The%20U.S.%20Code %20is%20a,of%20the%20Law%20Revision%20Counsel; GianCarlo Canaparo et al., *Count the Code: Quantifying Federalization of Criminal Statutes*, HERITAGE FOUN- DATION (Jan. 7, 2022), https://www.heritage.org/crime-and-justice/report/count -the-code-quantifying-federalization-criminal-statutes#_ftnref18.

55. AMERICAN BAR ASSOCIATION, THE FEDERALIZATION OF CRIMINAL LAW 10 (1998).

56. Ronald L. Gainer, *Federal Criminal Code Reform: Past and Future*, 2 BUFF. CRIM. L. REV. 45, 57–58 (1998); *see also* GianCarlo Canaparo et al., *Count the Code: Quantifying Federalization of Criminal Statutes*, HERITAGE FOUNDATION (Jan. 7, 2022), https://www.heritage.org/crime-and-justice/report/count-the-code-quantifying -federalization-criminal-statutes#_ftnref18.

57. Ronald L. Gainer, *Federal Criminal Code Reform: Past and Future*, 2 BUFF. CRIM. L. REV. 45, 58 (1998); *see also* GianCarlo Canaparo et al., *Count the Code: Quantifying Federalization of Criminal Statutes*, HERITAGE FOUNDATION (Jan. 7, 2022), https://www.heritage.org/crime-and-justice/report/count-the-code-quantifying -federalization-criminal-statutes#_ftnref18.

58. 18 U.S.C. §§ 201, 1341, 1343, 1346; *Public Corruption & Honest Services Fraud Leg- islation*, NATIONAL ASSOCIATION OF CRIMINAL DEFENSE LAWYERS (Mar. 16, 2020), https://www.nacdl.org/Content/PublicCorruptionHonestServicesFraudLegislation.

59. John S. Baker, Jr., *Measuring the Explosive Growth of Federal Crime Legislation*, 5 FEDERALIST SOC'Y REV. 23, 25 (2004).

60. 18 U.S.C. § 1657; 40 U.S.C. § 8103(b)(4); 27 U.S.C. § 205(e); 27 C.F.R. § 4.64(a)(8)(iii); *see also* Ilya Somin, *Why the Rule of Law Suffers When We Have Too Many Laws*, WASH. POST (Oct. 2, 2017), https://www.washingtonpost.com/news/volokh-conspiracy /wp/2017/10/01/why-the-rule-of-law-suffers-when-we-have-too-many-laws/.

61. Gary Fields & John R. Emshwiller, *Many Failed Efforts to Count Nation's Federal Criminal Laws*, WALL ST. J. (July 23, 2011), https://www.wsj.com/articles/SB100014 24052702304319804576389601079728920.

62. *See* Ilya Somin, *Why the Rule of Law Suffers When We Have Too Many Laws*, WASH. POST (Oct. 2, 2017), https://www.washingtonpost.com/news/volokh-conspiracy /wp/2017/10/01/why-the-rule-of-law-suffers-when-we-have-too-many-laws/.

63. *See* A.M. *ex rel.* F.M. v. Holmes, 830 F.3d 1123, 1130 (10th Cir. 2016); Steven Hsieh, *Why Did the Justice System Target Aaron Swartz?*, ROLLING STONE (Jan. 23, 2013), https://www.rollingstone.com/politics/politics-news/why-did-the-justice-system -target-aaron-swartz-106848/.

64. Department of Education Organization Act, Pub. L. No. 96-88, 93 Stat. 668 (1979); *About ED*, U.S. DEPARTMENT OF EDUCATION, https://www2.ed.gov/about/landing .jhtml (last visited Feb. 4, 2023).

65. Niall Ferguson, *The Regulated States of America*, WALL ST. J. (June 18, 2013), https:// www.wsj.com/articles/SB10001424127887324021104578551291160259734.

66. 2 ALEXIS DE TOCQUEVILLE, DEMOCRACY IN AMERICA 489 (Harvey C. Mansfield & Delba Winthrop eds. & trans., University of Chicago Press 2000) (1835).

67. ROBERT D. PUTNAM, BOWLING ALONE: THE COLLAPSE AND REVIVAL OF AMERICAN COMMUNITY 2 (2020).

68. Jeffrey M. Jones, *U.S. Church Membership Falls Below Majority for First Time*, GALLUP (Mar. 29, 2021), https://news.gallup.com/poll/341963/church-membership -falls-below-majority-first-time.aspx.

69. *Canyon Elks Lodge #2887, Elk Lodge Historic Members*, CANYON ELKS LODGE #2887, https://www.canyonelkslodge.org/elk-history/historical-elks (last visited Feb. 4, 2024); *New Trends for Elks*, GREATER WILDWOOD, NJ 1896, https://www.elks.org /lodges/NewsStory.cfm?StoryID=27300&LodgeNumber=1896 (last visited Feb. 4, 2024); *see also* Taya Flores, *Fraternal, Service Groups Battle Declining Membership*, J. & COURIER (Oct. 11, 2014), https://www.jconline.com/story/news/2014/10/11 /fraternal-service-groups-battle-declining-membership/16874977/; DIVYA WODON, NAINA WODON, & QUENTIN WODON, MEMBERSHIP IN SERVICE CLUBS: ROTARY'S EX-PERIENCE 11 (2014).

70. Taya Flores, *Fraternal, Service Groups Battle Declining Membership*, J. & COURIER (Oct. 11, 2014), https://www.jconline.com/story/news/2014/10/11/fraternal-service -groups-battle-declining-membership/16874977/; Christianna Silva, *Freemasons Say They're Needed Now More than Ever. So Why Are Their Ranks Dwindling?*, NPR (Nov. 28, 2020), https://www.npr.org/2020/11/28/937228086/freemasons-say-theyre -needed-now-more-than-ever-so-why-are-their-ranks-dwindling ("In recent years, membership has dropped roughly 75% from a high of more than 4.1 million in 1959— when about 4.5% of all American men were members."); *see also* DIVYA WODON, NAINA WODON, & QUENTIN WODON, MEMBERSHIP IN SERVICE CLUBS: ROTARY'S EXPERIENCE 11 (2014); Alexander Towey, *The Rise, Decline, and Renaissance of Freemasonry in the United States During the 20th and 21st Century*, CALIFORNIA STATE UNIVERSITY (Nov. 16, 2022), https://scholarworks.calstate.edu/concern/theses/vt150r919 (master's thesis, California State University San Marcos).

71. ROBERT D. PUTNAM, BOWLING ALONE: THE COLLAPSE AND REVIVAL OF AMERICAN COMMUNITY 3 (rev. ed. 2020).

72. *Partisan Hostility Grows, Signs of Frustration with the Two-Party System*, PEW RESEARCH CENTER (Aug. 9, 2022), https://www.pewresearch.org/politics/2022/08 /09/as-partisan-hostility-grows-signs-of-frustration-with-the-two-party-system/.

73. *Center for Politics Study: Partisan Desires Override Support for Constitutional Freedoms and American Values*, UNIVERSITY OF VIRGINIA CENTER FOR POLITICS (Oct. 2023), https://centerforpolitics.org/news/center-for-politics-study-partisan -desires-override-support-for-constitutional-freedoms-and-american-values/; *see also Voice of the Voter Survey*, UNIVERSITY OF VIRGINIA CENTER FOR POLITICS (Oct. 2023), https://centerforpolitics.org/crystalball/wp-content/uploads/2023/10 /VoV-Presentation-FINAL.pdf.

74. W.E.B. DuBois Clubs of America v. Clark, 389 U.S. 309, 318 (1967) (Douglas, J., dissenting).

75. *See, e.g.,* Michael P. Zuckert, *Madison's Consistency on the Bill of Rights,* 47 NAT'L AFFS. 154 (2021).

76. *See, e.g.,* Letter from James Madison to Thomas Jefferson (Oct. 17, 1788), in 5 THE WRITINGS OF JAMES MADISON 1787–1790 272 (Gaillard Hunt ed., 1904) ("The restrictions however strongly marked on paper will never be regarded when opposed to the decided sense of the public, and after repeated violations in extraordinary cases they will lose even their ordinary efficacy.").

77. *See* Letter from James Madison to Thomas Jefferson (Oct. 17, 1788), in 5 THE WRITINGS OF JAMES MADISON 1787–1790 272 (Gaillard Hunt ed., 1904); *see also, e.g., The Federalist* Nos. 47, 48, 51 (James Madison), in THE FEDERALIST PAPERS 300–08, 320–25 (Clinton Rossiter ed., 1961).

78. *See, e.g., The Federalist* Nos. 47, 51 (James Madison) and 62 (probably James Madison), in THE FEDERALIST PAPERS 300–08, 320–25, 381–82 (Clinton Rossiter ed., 1961).

79. *The Federalist* No. 62 (probably James Madison), in THE FEDERALIST PAPERS 381–82 (Clinton Rossiter ed., 1961).

80. HANNAH ARENDT, THE ORIGINS OF TOTALITARIANISM 394, 399 (1973).

81. *See, e.g.,* JOSEPH RAZ, *The Rule of Law and Its Virtue,* in THE AUTHORITY OF LAW: ESSAYS ON LAW AND MORALITY 210, 213–14, 217 (1979).

82. Joseph Raz, *The Law's Own Virtue,* 39 OXFORD J. LEGAL STUD. 1, 2 (2019).

83. JOSEPH RAZ, *The Rule of Law and Its Virtue,* in THE AUTHORITY OF LAW: ESSAYS ON LAW AND MORALITY 221 (1979).

84. HANNAH ARENDT, THE ORIGINS OF TOTALITARIANISM 455 (1973).

85. 2 THE RECORDS OF THE FEDERAL CONVENTION OF 1787 585 (Max Farrand ed., 1911).

86. DANIEL WEBSTER, AN ANNIVERSARY ADDRESS, DELIVERED BEFORE THE FEDERAL GENTLEMEN OF CONCORD AND ITS VICINITY 6 (1806).

87. Chris Anderson, *Supreme Court Reverses Cortez Fisherman's Conviction,* SARASOTA HERALD TRIB. (Feb. 25, 2015), https://www.heraldtribune.com/story/news/2015/02/25/supreme-court-reverses-cortez-fishermans-conviction/29301170007/.

88. Yates v. United States, 574 U.S. 528, 532 (2015).

89. Chris Anderson, *Cortez Fisherman Struggles After Supreme Court Win,* SARASOTA HERALD TRIB. (Oct. 22, 2019), https://www.heraldtribune.com/story/news/2019/10/22/anderson-cortez-fisherman-struggles-after-supreme-court-win/2470913007/; JN interview with Sandra Yates.

90. National Oceanographic and Atmospheric Administration, *Review of NOAA Fisheries Enforcement Programs and Operations* 1, 3, OFFICE OF INSPECTOR GENERAL, U.S. DEPARTMENT OF COMMERCE (Jan. 2010), https://www.oig.doc.gov/OIGPublications/OIG-19887.pdf.

91. Memorandum from Todd J. Zinser to Dr. Jane Lubchenco, *Re: OIG Investigation #PPC-SP-10-0260-P, re: Destruction of OLE Documents During an Ongoing OIG Review* (Apr. 2, 2010); Allison Winter, *Lawmakers Want NOAA's Law Enforcement Chief to Quit in Wake of Scandal,* N.Y. TIMES (Mar. 4, 2010), https://archive.nytimes.com/www.nytimes.com/gwire/2010/03/04/04greenwire-lawmakers-want-noaas-law-enforcement-chief-to-61023.html.

92. Letter from Sandra Yates to Office of Inspector General, U.S. Department of Commerce, *Re: OIG Compl. No. PPC-CI-10-1339-H* (Aug. 21, 2012).

93. BURTON F. PORTER, THE GOOD LIFE: ALTERNATIVES IN ETHICS 138 (2001) (for translation); ROBIN SOWERBY, THE GREEKS: AN INTRODUCTION TO THEIR CULTURE 20 (1995) (for temple of Apollo).

94. FRIEDRICH A. HAYEK, THE ROAD TO SERFDOM, TEXT AND DOCUMENTS: THE DEFINITIVE EDITION 60 (Bruce Caldwell ed., 2014).

CHAPTER 2: FAR FROM HOME

1. WENDELL BERRY, *The Work of Local Culture,* in WHAT ARE PEOPLE FOR? ESSAYS BY WENDELL BERRY 157 (1990).

2. Sylvia Carignan, *Century of Toxic Gloom Drives Montanans Back to Supreme Court,* BLOOMBERG LAW (Oct. 1, 2019), https://news.bloomberglaw.com/environment-and-energy/century-of-toxic-gloom-drives-montanans-back-to-supreme-court.

3. Kathleen McLaughlin, *A Tiny Town's Long Struggle to Rid Itself of Toxic Waste Reaches the Supreme Court,* WASH. POST (Dec. 1, 2019), https://www.washingtonpost.com

/national-security/a-tiny-towns-long-struggle-to-rid-itself-of-toxic-waste-reaches
-the-supreme-court/2019/11/30/24d0e41e-1084-11ea-9cd7-a1becbc82f5e_story.html.

4. Nick Mott, *Anaconda Hears Details on Proposed Superfund Cleanup Plan*, MONTANA PUBLIC RADIO (Mar. 3, 2020), https://www.mtpr.org/montana-news/2020-03-03/anaconda-hears-details-on-proposed-superfund-cleanup-plan.

5. Atlantic Richfield Co. v. Christian, 140 S. Ct. 1335, 1345 (2020).

6. *QuickFacts: Anaconda-Deer Lodge County, Montana*, U.S. CENSUS BUREAU, https://www.census.gov/quickfacts/fact/table/anacondadeerlodgecountymontana/PST045221 (last visited July 17, 2022); Nick Mott, *Anaconda Hears Details on Proposed Superfund Cleanup Plan*, MONTANA PUBLIC RADIO (Mar. 3, 2020), https://www.mtpr.org/montana-news/2020-03-03/anaconda-hears-details-on-proposed-superfund-cleanup-plan.

7. MICHAEL P. MALONE, THE BATTLE FOR BUTTE 7–8 (1981); MICHAEL PUNKE, FIRE AND BRIMSTONE: THE NORTH BUTTE MINING DISASTER OF 1917 18–19 (2006).

8. MICHAEL PUNKE, FIRE AND BRIMSTONE: THE NORTH BUTTE MINING DISASTER OF 1917 19 (2006) (quoting DAN CUSHMAN, MONTANA—GOLD FRONTIER 69–70 (1973)).

9. MICHAEL PUNKE, FIRE AND BRIMSTONE: THE NORTH BUTTE MINING DISASTER OF 1917 20 (2006).

10. COPPER KING MANSION, http://thecopperkingmansion.com (last visited Sep. 17, 2022); *The Mansion*, COPPER KING MANSION, http://thecopperkingmansion.com/the-mansion (last visited Sep. 17, 2022).

11. *Antiquities to Impressionism: The William A. Clark Collection, Corcoran Gallery of Art*, NATIONAL GALLERY OF ART, https://www.nga.gov/research/publications/pdf-library/antiquities-to-impressionism.html (last visited July 17, 2022).

12. MICHAEL P. MALONE, THE BATTLE FOR BUTTE 129, 199 (1981); MICHAEL PUNKE, FIRE AND BRIMSTONE: THE NORTH BUTTE MINING DISASTER OF 1917 43 (2006).

13. MICHAEL P. MALONE, THE BATTLE FOR BUTTE 28 (1981); MICHAEL PUNKE, FIRE AND BRIMSTONE: THE NORTH BUTTE MINING DISASTER OF 1917 16, 21, 23–25 (2006).

14. C.B. GLASSCOCK, THE WAR OF THE COPPER KINGS 55, 75 (1935).

15. Brief for Treasure State Resources Ass'n of Montana et al. as Amici Curiae Supporting Petitioner at 12, Atlantic Richfield Co. v. Christian, 140 S. Ct. 1335 (2020) (No. 17-1498).

16. MICHAEL PUNKE, FIRE AND BRIMSTONE: THE NORTH BUTTE MINING DISASTER OF 1917 60–61 (2006); *see also* Francis Curran, *The Most Irish Town in America?*, IRISH TIMES (Mar. 16, 2011), https://www.irishtimes.com/news/the-most-irish-town-in-america-1.573655.

17. MICHAEL PUNKE, FIRE AND BRIMSTONE: THE NORTH BUTTE MINING DISASTER OF 1917 87–88 (2006).

18. C.B. GLASSCOCK, THE WAR OF THE COPPER KINGS 69–70 (1935).

19. C.B. GLASSCOCK, THE WAR OF THE COPPER KINGS 69, 71 (1935); MICHAEL P. MALONE, THE BATTLE FOR BUTTE 63 (1981).

20. C.B. GLASSCOCK, THE WAR OF THE COPPER KINGS 71, 182, 285 (1935); MICHAEL P. MALONE, THE BATTLE FOR BUTTE 53, 201 (1981).

21. Brief for Treasure State Resources Ass'n of Montana et al. as Amici Curiae Supporting Petitioner at 7–8, Atlantic Richfield Co. v. Christian, 140 S. Ct. 1335 (2020) (No. 17-1498); MICHAEL P. MALONE, THE BATTLE FOR BUTTE 34–35 (1981).

22. MICHAEL PUNKE, FIRE AND BRIMSTONE: THE NORTH BUTTE MINING DISASTER OF 1917 266–68 (2006).

23. Lydia Chavez, *When Arco Left Town*, N.Y. TIMES (July 25, 1982), https://www.nytimes.com/1982/07/25/business/when-arco-left-town.html.

24. C.B. GLASSCOCK, THE WAR OF THE COPPER KINGS 285 (1935).

25. *Anaconda Smelter, Anaconda, Montana, Superfund Case Study* 2 (Mar. 2016), U.S. ENVIRONMENTAL PROTECTION AGENCY (MAR. 2016), https://www.epa.gov/sites/default/files/2018-02/documents/anacondasmeltercasestudy-2016.pdf.

26. Kathleen McLaughlin, *A Tiny Town's Long Struggle to Rid Itself of Toxic Waste Reaches the Supreme Court*, WASH. POST (Dec. 1, 2019), https://www.washingtonpost.com/national-security/a-tiny-towns-long-struggle-to-rid-itself-of-toxic-waste-reaches-the-supreme-court/2019/11/30/24d0e41e-1084-11ea-9cd7-a1becbc82f5e_story.html.

27. Sylvia Carignan, *Century of Toxic Gloom Drives Montanans Back to Supreme Court*, BLOOMBERG LAW (Oct. 1, 2019), https://news.bloomberglaw.com/environment-and -energy/century-of-toxic-gloom-drives-montanans-back-to-supreme-court.

28. Atlantic Richfield Co. v. Christian, 140 S. Ct. 1335, 1362 (2020) (Gorsuch, J., concurring in part and dissenting in part).

29. Nora Saks, *"A Great Place to Work . . . A Dirty, No Good Hellhole,"* MONTANA PUBLIC RADIO (Aug. 10, 2018), https://www.mtpr.org/montana-news/2018-08-10/a-great -place-to-work-a-dirty-no-good-hellhole.

30. Atlantic Richfield Co. v. Christian, 140 S. Ct. 1335, 1347 (2020); *id.* at 1362 (Gorsuch, J., concurring in part and dissenting in part).

31. U.S. ENVIRONMENTAL PROTECTION AGENCY, REGION 8, HELENA, MONTANA, FIFTH FIVE-YEAR REVIEW REPORT: ANACONDA SMELTER SUPERFUND SITE, ANACONDA-DEER LODGE COUNTY, MONTANA ES-1 (2015).

32. Atlantic Richfield Co. v. Christian, 140 S. Ct. 1335, 1347 (2020); *id.* at 1362 (Gorsuch, J., concurring in part and dissenting in part).

33. *The Arsenic Rule: Background and Rule Provisions* 2, U.S. ENVIRONMENTAL PROTECTION AGENCY (2015), https://www.epa.gov/sites/default/files/2015-09/documents/train1 -background.pdf; Andrew Yosim et al., *Arsenic, the "King of Poisons" in Food and Water*, 103 AM. SCIENTIST 34, 34 (2015).

34. Joan Acocella, *Murder by Poison*, NEW YORKER (Oct. 7, 2013), https://www.newyorker .com/magazine/2013/10/14/murder-by-poison; Aline Nassif & Matthew Armitage, *Disease, Not Conflict, Ended the Reign of Alexander the Great*, INDEPENDENT (Aug. 7, 2005), https://www.independent.co.uk/news/science/disease-not-conflict-ended-the -reign-of-alexander-the-great-304278.html.

35. Atlantic Richfield Co. v. Christian, 140 S. Ct. 1335, 1362 (2020) (Gorsuch, J., concurring in part and dissenting in part); Response Brief for Gregory A. Christian at 8–9, Atlantic Richfield Co. v. Christian, 140 S. Ct. 1335 (2020) (No. 17-1498).

36. Matt Volz, *Montana Landowners Say Government Botched Arsenic Cleanup*, GREAT FALLS TRIB. (Feb. 24, 2017), https://www.greatfallstribune.com/story/news/2017/02 /24/landowners-say-epa-botched-cleanup-now-want-shot/98350772/.

37. Atlantic Richfield Co. v. Christian, 140 S. Ct. 1335, 1347–48 (2020); *id.* at 1362 (Gorsuch, J., concurring in part and dissenting in part).

38. Kathleen McLaughlin, *A Tiny Town's Long Struggle to Rid Itself of Toxic Waste Reaches the Supreme Court*, WASH. POST (Dec. 1, 2019), https://www.washingtonpost.com /national-security/a-tiny-towns-long-struggle-to-rid-itself-of-toxic-waste-reaches -the-supreme-court/2019/11/30/24d0e41e-1084-11ea-9cd7-a1becbc82f5e_story.html.

39. Atlantic Richfield Co. v. Christian, 140 S. Ct. 1335, 1348, 1350 (2020); *id.* at 1362 (Gorsuch, J., concurring in part and dissenting in part).

40. Atlantic Richfield Co. v. Christian, 140 S. Ct. 1335, 1357 (2020); Brief for the United States as Amicus Curiae Supporting Petitioner at 32–34, Atlantic Richfield Co. v. Christian, 140 S. Ct. 1335 (2020) (No. 17-1498); Brief for Petitioner at 32, Atlantic Richfield Co. v. Christian, 140 S. Ct. 1335 (2020) (No. 17-1498).

41. Atlantic Richfield Co. v. Christian, 140 S. Ct. 1335, 1362 (2020) (Gorsuch, J., concurring in part and dissenting in part).

42. Matt Volz, *Montana Landowners Say Government Botched Arsenic Cleanup*, GREAT FALLS TRIB. (Feb. 24, 2017), https://www.greatfallstribune.com/story/news/2017/02 /24/landowners-say-epa-botched-cleanup-now-want-shot/98350772/.

43. Pietro S. Nivola, *Why Federalism Matters*, BROOKINGS INSTITUTION (Oct. 1, 2005), https://www.brookings.edu/research/why-federalism-matters/.

44. *Eisenhower Executive Office Building*, THE WHITE HOUSE, https://www.whitehouse. gov/about-the-white-house/the-grounds/eisenhower-executive-office-building/ (last visited June 22, 2022); *Executive Director's Recommendation, Harry S. Truman Federal Building*, NATIONAL CAPITAL PLANNING COMMISSION (Sep. 8, 2016), https:// www.ncpc.gov/docs/actions/2016September/Truman_Bldg_Security_Improvments _Recommendation_6541_%20Sept2016.pdf.

45. *Pentagon Known for Being Hard to Navigate*, TWIN CITIES.COM PIONEER PRESS (Nov. 13, 2015), https://www.twincities.com/2009/02/21/pentagon-known-for-being -hard-to-navigate/; CENTER OF MILITARY HISTORY, UNITED STATES ARMY, REPORT BY

THE SUPREME COMMANDER TO THE COMBINED CHIEFS OF STAFF ON THE OPERATIONS IN EUROPE OF THE ALLIED EXPEDITIONARY FORCE, 6 JUNE 1944 TO 8 MAY 1945 (1994).

46. Veronique de Rugy, *The Rise in Per Capita Federal Spending*, MERCATUS CENTER (Nov. 12, 2014), https://www.mercatus.org/research/data-visualizations/rise-capita -federal-spending (showing that in 2014 real dollars, per capita spending in 1960 was $3,924. In 1979, it was $6,795).

47. *Executive Branch Civilian Employment Since 1940*, OFFICE OF PERSONNEL MANAGE- MENT, https://www.opm.gov/policy-data-oversight/data-analysis-documentation/ federal-employment-reports/historical-tables/executive-branch-civilian- employment-since-1940/ (last visited Mar. 3, 2023) (761,000 personnel in 1960 to 1,201,000 in 1979); Carol Wilson, *Federal Workforce Statistics Sources: OPM and OMB* 6, CONGRESSIONAL RESEARCH SERVICE (June 28, 2022), https://sgp.fas.org /crs/misc/R43590.pdf.

48. BRUCE CANNON GIBNEY, THE NONSENSE FACTORY: THE MAKING AND BREAKING OF THE AMERICAN LEGAL SYSTEM 124 (2019); DANIEL GUTTMAN & BARRY WILLNER, THE SHADOW GOVERNMENT (1976); Paul C. Light, *The True Size of Government: Track- ing Washington's Blended Workforce, 1984–2015* 3, THE VOLCKER ALLIANCE (2017), https://www.volckeralliance.org/resources/true-size-government-1; Letter from Greg Walden, Gregg Harper & John Shimkus, House of Representatives Committee on Energy and Commerce, to Scott Pruitt, U.S. Environmental Protection Agency (July 3, 2018) (on file with the authors).

49. Taylor Giorno, *Federal Lobbying Spending Reaches $4.1 Billion in 2022—the Highest Since 2010*, OPEN SECRETS (Jan. 26, 2023), https://www.opensecrets .org/news/2023/01/federal-lobbying-spending-reaches-4-1-billion-in-2022-the -highest-since-2010/ (2022 figures); *21% Rise Reported in Lobby Spending*, N.Y. TIMES (Aug. 9, 1970), https://www.nytimes.com/1970/08/09/archives/21-rise -reported-in-lobby-spending-1969-increase-is-attributed-to.html; *CPI Inflation Calculator*, BUREAU OF LABOR STATISTICS, https://data.bls.gov/cgi-bin/cpicalc.pl; *see also* Jonathan O'Connell & Anu Narayanswamy, *Lobbying Broke All-Time Mark in 2021 amid Flurry of Government Spending*, WASH. POST (Mar. 12, 2022), https:// www.washingtonpost.com/business/2022/03/12/lobbying-record-government -spending/ (2021 figures).

50. *Historical Income Tables: Counties*, U.S. CENSUS BUREAU (Oct. 8, 2021), https://www .census.gov/data/tables/time-series/dec/historical-income-counties.html; *2020 Amer- ican Community Survey: S1903 ACS 5-Year Estimates Subject Tables*, U.S. CENSUS BUREAU, https://data.census.gov/table?q=median+income+in+2020&g=010XX00US $0500000&tid=ACSST5Y2020.S1903 (last visited Sep. 12, 2023); *see also* Steven Ross Johnson, *The 15 Richest Counties in the U.S.*, U.S. NEWS & WORLD REPORT (Dec. 23, 2022), https://www.usnews.com/news/healthiest-communities/slideshows/richest -counties-in-america; Ann Schmidt, *The 20 Wealthiest Counties in the U.S., Including These Washington, D.C., Suburbs: Report*, FOX BUSINESS (Dec. 18, 2019), https://www .foxbusiness.com/money/washington-dc-suburbs-richest-counties.amp.

51. Exec. Order No. 10973, 26 Fed. Reg. 10469 (Nov. 3, 1961); Department of Housing and Urban Development Act, Pub. L. No. 89-174, 79 Stat. 667 (1965); Civil Rights Act of 1964, Pub. L. No. 88-352, 78 Stat. 241 (1964); Department of Transportation Act, Pub. L. No. 89-670, 80 Stat. 931 (1966); *Reorganization Plan No. 3 of 1970*, U.S. ENVIRONMENTAL PROTECTION AGENCY (1970), https://archive.epa.gov/epa/aboutepa /reorganization-plan-no-3-1970.html; Consumer Product Safety Act, Pub. L. No. 92-573, 86 Stat. 1207 (1972); Federal Election Campaign Act Amendments of 1974, Pub. L. No. 93-443, 88 Stat. 1263 (1974); Commodity Futures Trading Commission Act of 1974, Pub. L. No. 93-463, 88 Stat. 1389 (1974); Energy Reorganization Act of 1974, Pub. L. No. 93-438, 88 Stat. 1233 (1974); Department of Energy Organization Act, Pub. L. No. 95-91, 91 Stat. 565 (1977); Civil Service Reform Act of 1978, Pub. L. No. 95-454, 92 Stat. 1111 (1978); Department of Education Organization Act, Pub. L. No. 96-88, 93 Stat. 668 (1979); Exec. Order No. 12127, 44 Fed. Reg. 19367 (Mar. 31, 1979).

52. Robert Jay Dilger, *Federal Grants to State and Local Governments: A Historical Perspective on Contemporary Issues* 5, CONGRESSIONAL RESEARCH SERVICE (May 22, 2019), fas.org/sgp/crs/misc/R40638.pdf; *see also CPI Inflation Calculator*, BUREAU

OF LABOR STATISTICS, https://www.bls.gov/data/inflation_calculator.htm (last visited Feb. 10, 2024).

53. South Dakota v. Dole, 483 U.S. 203, 211–12 (1987); Biden v. Missouri, 142 S. Ct. 647, 650 (2022).

54. BADGER INSTITUTE, FEDERAL GRANT$TANDING 4, 16 (2018); *see also Where States Get Their Money: FY2021*, PEW CHARITABLE TRUSTS (Mar. 21, 2023), https://www .pewtrusts.org/en/research-and-analysis/data-visualizations/2023/where-states-get -their-money-fy-2021.

55. *The Tenth Amendment and the Conference of the States: Hearing Before the Subcomm. on the Const., Federalism, and Property Rights of the S. Comm. on the Judiciary*, 104th Cong. 7 (1995) (statement of E. Benjamin Nelson, Governor of Nebraska).

56. *Historical Tables* Table 12.2, THE WHITE HOUSE, https://www.whitehouse.gov/omb /budget/historical-tables/ (last visited Feb. 4, 2024).

57. U.S. Term Limits, Inc. v. Thornton, 514 U.S. 779, 838 (1995) (Kennedy, J., concurring).

58. *The Federalist* No. 45 (James Madison), in THE FEDERALIST PAPERS 292 (Clinton Rossiter ed., 1961).

59. 2 ALEXIS DE TOCQUEVILLE, DEMOCRACY IN AMERICA 363 (Francis Bowen ed., Henry Reeve trans., Cambridge: Sever and Francis 3d ed. 1863) (1835).

60. New State Ice Co. v. Liebmann, 285 U.S. 262, 311 (1932) (Brandeis, J., dissenting).

61. *The Federalist* No. 51 (James Madison), in THE FEDERALIST PAPERS 320–25 (Clinton Rossiter ed., 1961).

62. Joel Kotkin and Ryan Streeter, *Introduction: Reviving Localism in America*, in LOCALISM IN AMERICA: WHY WE SHOULD TACKLE OUR BIG CHALLENGES AT THE LOCAL LEVEL 2, American Enterprise Institute (Feb. 2018), https://www.aei.org/special -features/localism-in-america/.

63. *Subsidiarity*, OXFORD ENGLISH DICTIONARY (2d ed. 1989); *see also* Andrew Murray, *The Principle of Subsidiarity and the Church*, 72 AUSTRALASIAN CATHOLIC RECORD 163, 164 (1995); Joel Kotkin and Ryan Streeter, *Introduction: Reviving Localism in America*, in LOCALISM IN AMERICA: WHY WE SHOULD TACKLE OUR BIG CHALLENGES AT THE LOCAL LEVEL 2, American Enterprise Institute (Feb. 2018), https://www.aei .org/special-features/localism-in-america/.

64. Pope Pius XI, *Quadragesimo Anno: Encyclical of Pope Pius XI on Reconstruction of the Social Order*, LIBRERIA EDITRICE VATICANA (1931), https://www.vatican.va /content/pius-xi/en/encyclicals/documents/hf_p-xi_enc_19310515_quadragesimo -anno.html.

65. National Federation of Independent Business v. Department of Labor, Occupational Safety and Health Administration et al., 142 S. Ct. 661, 663 (2022); *Operation Warp Speed: Accelerated COVID-19 Vaccine Development Status and Efforts to Address Manufacturing Challenges*, U.S. GOVERNMENT ACCOUNTABILITY OFFICE (Feb. 11, 2021), https://www.gao.gov/products/gao-21-319.

66. Alabama Association of Realtors v. Department of Health and Human Services, 141 S. Ct. 2485, 2486 (2021).

67. *See, e.g.*, Joel M. Zinberg et al., *Freedom Wins: States with Less Restrictive COVID Policies Outperformed States with More Restrictive COVID Policies* 2–5, PARA- GON HEALTH SERVICES (2023), https://paragoninstitute.org/wp-content/uploads /2023/02/20230201_Zinberg_FreedomWinsStateswithLessRestrictiveCOVIDPolicies OutperformedStateswithMoreRestrictiveCOVIDPolicies_FINAL_202302091645.pdf.

68. DAVID HALBERSTAM, THE BEST AND THE BRIGHTEST xiv (1992); *see also* Howard Husock and Wendell Cox, *The Enduring Virtues of American Government Localism*, *in* LOCALISM IN AMERICA: WHY WE SHOULD TACKLE OUR BIG CHALLENGES AT THE LOCAL LEVEL 20, American Enterprise Institute (Feb. 2018), https://www.aei.org /special-features/localism-in-america/.

69. *QuickFacts: Kalamazoo City, Michigan*, U.S. CENSUS BUREAU, https://www.census.gov /quickfacts/fact/table/kalamazoocitymichigan/BZA115220 (last visited July 19, 2022); Steve Carmody, *Kalamazoo Promise Reaches a Milestone, and Faces a Challenge*, MICH- IGAN RADIO (Apr. 30, 2019), https://www.michiganradio.org/education/2019-04-30 /kalamazoo-promise-reaches-a-milestone-and-faces-a-challenge; Ted C. Fishman, *Why These Kids Get a Free Ride to College*, N.Y. TIMES (Sep. 13, 2012), https://www.nytimes .com/2012/09/16/magazine/kalamazoo-mich-the-city-that-pays-for-college.html. See

generally Michael D. Hais, Doug Ross, and Morley Winograd, *Go Local: Communities as Laboratories for Rescuing American Democracy*, in LOCALISM IN AMERICA: WHY WE SHOULD TACKLE OUR BIG CHALLENGES AT THE LOCAL LEVEL 64, American Enterprise Institute (Feb. 2018), https://www.aei.org/special-features/localism-in-america/.

70. Ted C. Fishman, *Why These Kids Get a Free Ride to College*, N.Y. TIMES (Sep. 13, 2012), https://www.nytimes.com/2012/09/16/magazine/kalamazoo-mich-the-city-that-pays-for-college.html.

71. Steve Carmody, *Kalamazoo Promise Reaches a Milestone, and Faces a Challenge*, MICHIGAN RADIO (Apr. 30, 2019), https://www.michiganradio.org/education/2019-04-30/kalamazoo-promise-reaches-a-milestone-and-faces-a-challenge; *Eligibility*, KALAMAZOO PROMISE, https://www.kalamazoopromise.com/eligibility#extentbenefits (last visited Oct. 18, 2023).

72. Ted C. Fishman, *Why These Kids Get a Free Ride to College*, N.Y. TIMES (Sep. 13, 2012), https://www.nytimes.com/2012/09/16/magazine/kalamazoo-mich-the-city-that-pays-for-college.html.

73. Steve Carmody, *Kalamazoo Promise Reaches a Milestone, and Faces a Challenge*, MICHIGAN RADIO (Apr. 30, 2019), https://www.michiganradio.org/education/2019-04-30/kalamazoo-promise-reaches-a-milestone-and-faces-a-challenge; Ted C. Fishman, *Why These Kids Get a Free Ride to College*, N.Y. TIMES (Sep. 13, 2012), https://www.nytimes.com/2012/09/16/magazine/kalamazoo-mich-the-city-that-pays-for-college.html; Kaomi Goetz, *In Kalamazoo, a Promise Boosts School Enrollment*, NPR (Nov. 29, 2006), https://www.npr.org/templates/story/story.php?storyId=6552216.

74. *See, e.g.*, Jessie Kratz, *Rightfully Hers: Woman Suffrage Before the 19th Amendment*, NATIONAL ARCHIVES (Aug. 15, 2019), https://prologue.blogs.archives.gov/2019/08/15/rightfully-hers-woman-suffrage-before-the-19th-amendment/; *After Suffrage*, MUSEUM OF FLORIDA HISTORY, https://museumoffloridahistory.com/learn/the-19th-amendment-at-100/after-suffrage/ (last visited June 23, 2022).

75. Wyoming Women's Suffrage Day, S.J.R. 3, 65th Leg., Gen. Sess. (Wyo. 2019).

76. *History of Child Labor in the United States—Part 2: The Reform Movement*, U.S. BUREAU OF LABOR STATISTICS (Jan. 2017), https://www.bls.gov/opub/mlr/2017/article/history-of-child-labor-in-the-united-states-part-2-the-reform-movement.htm; Margaret Murphy, *The Constitutionality of Minimum Wage: The Legal Battles of Elsie Parrish and Frances Perkins for a Fair Day's Pay*, 2021–22 PRINCETON HIST. REV. 34, 35.

77. *New York State*: Jill Lepore, *I.O.U.*, NEW YORKER (Apr. 6, 2009), https://www.newyorker.com/magazine/2009/04/13/i-o-u. *Georgia*: FELIX MORLEY, FREEDOM AND FEDERALISM 48 (1959).

78. James L. Buckley, *Restoring Federalism*, 11 CLAREMONT REV. BOOKS 35, 36 (2011).

79. National Pork Producers v. Ross, 143 S. Ct. 1142, 1150 (2023); Energy and Environment Legal Institute v. Epel, 793 F.3d 1169, 1170–71 (10th Cir. 2015).

80. Heather K. Gerken, *Federalism 3.0*, 105 CALIF. L. REV. 1695, 1710, 1716 (2017).

81. David F. Levi et al., *51 Imperfect Solutions: State and Federal Judges Consider the Role of State Constitutions in Rights Innovation*, 103 JUDICATURE 33, 40–41 (2019).

82. David F. Levi et al., *51 Imperfect Solutions: State and Federal Judges Consider the Role of State Constitutions in Rights Innovation*, 103 JUDICATURE 33, 44–45 (2019); Batson v. Kentucky, 476 U.S. 79, 92 (1986) (describing and overruling in part Swain v. Alabama, 380 U.S. 202 (1965)).

83. David F. Levi et al., *51 Imperfect Solutions: State and Federal Judges Consider the Role of State Constitutions in Rights Innovation*, 103 JUDICATURE 33, 44–45 (2019); *see also* Commonwealth v. Soares, 377 Mass. 461, 488 (1979); People v. Wheeler, 22 Cal.3d 258, 287 (1978).

84. Batson v. Kentucky, 476 U.S. 79, 100 (1986).

85. JEFFREY S. SUTTON, 51 IMPERFECT SOLUTIONS: STATES AND THE MAKING OF AMERICAN CONSTITUTIONAL LAW 108–114 (2018).

86. JEFFREY S. SUTTON, 51 IMPERFECT SOLUTIONS: STATES AND THE MAKING OF AMERICAN CONSTITUTIONAL LAW 85–91 (2018); *see also Eugenics: Its Origin and Development*, NATIONAL HUMAN GENOME RESEARCH INSTITUTE (Nov. 30, 2021), https://www.genome.gov/about-genomics/educational-resources/timelines/eugenics#:~:text=Discussions%20of%20eugenics%20began%20in,end%20of%20World%20War%20I.

87. Steven A. Farber, *U.S. Scientists' Role in the Eugenics Movement (1907–1939): A Contemporary Biologist's Perspective*, 5 ZEBRAFISH 243 (2008); *Eugenics: Its Origin and Development*, NATIONAL HUMAN GENOME RESEARCH INSTITUTE (Nov. 30, 2021) https://www.genome.gov/about-genomics/educational-resources/timelines/eugenics#:~:text=Discussions%20of%20eugenics%20began%20in,end%20of%20World%20War%20I.

88. Joseph Loconte, *One Hundred Years Ago, "Following the Science" Meant Supporting Eugenics*, NATIONAL REVIEW (July 17, 2022), https://www.nationalreview.com/2022/07/one-hundred-years-ago-following-the-science-meant-supporting-eugenics/.

89. Garland E. Allen, *Eugenics and American Social History, 1880–1950*, 31 GENOME 885, 886 (1989).

90. Adam S. Cohen, *Harvard's Eugenics Era*, HARVARD MAG. (Mar.–Apr. 2016), https://www.harvardmagazine.com/2016/03/harvards-eugenics-era.

91. JEFFREY S. SUTTON, 51 IMPERFECT SOLUTIONS: STATES AND THE MAKING OF AMERICAN CONSTITUTIONAL LAW 87 (2018).

92. Garland E. Allen, *Eugenics and American Social History, 1880–1950*, 31 GENOME 885, 885 (1989).

93. Adam S. Cohen, *Harvard's Eugenics Era*, HARVARD MAG. (Mar.–Apr. 2016), https://www.harvardmagazine.com/2016/03/harvards-eugenics-era.

94. Andrea DenHoed, *The Forgotten Lessons of the American Eugenics Movement*, NEW YORKER (Apr. 27, 2016), https://www.newyorker.com/books/page-turner/the-forgotten-lessons-of-the-american-eugenics-movement; Steven A. Farber, *U.S. Scientists' Role in the Eugenics Movement (1907–1939): A Contemporary Biologist's Perspective*, 5 ZEBRAFISH 243 (2008).

95. WILLIAM E. LEUCHTENBURG, THE SUPREME COURT REBORN: THE CONSTITUTIONAL REVOLUTION IN THE AGE OF ROOSEVELT 8 (1995) (quoting Albert S. Priddy, superintendent of the State Colony for Epileptics and Feeble-Minded in Lynchburg, Virginia).

96. JEFFREY S. SUTTON, 51 IMPERFECT SOLUTIONS: STATES AND THE MAKING OF AMERICAN CONSTITUTIONAL LAW 87 (2018); Nikita Stewart, *Planned Parenthood in N.Y. Disavows Margaret Sanger over Eugenics*, N.Y. TIMES (July 21, 2020), https://www.nytimes.com/2020/07/21/nyregion/planned-parenthood-margaret-sanger-eugenics.html.

97. G. K. CHESTERTON, EUGENICS AND OTHER EVILS 143 (1922); Joseph Loconte, *One Hundred Years Ago, "Following the Science" Meant Supporting Eugenics*, NATIONAL REVIEW (July 17, 2022), https://www.nationalreview.com/2022/07/one-hundred-years-ago-following-the-science-meant-supporting-eugenics/.

98. Russell Sparkes, *The Enemy of Eugenics*, 25 CHESTERTON REV. 117, 123 (1999); *see also* *G. K. Chesterton Publishes* Eugenics and Other Evils, EUGENICS ARCHIVES, https://eugenicsarchive.ca/discover/timeline/54fe2e1ecc8b722e04000006 (last visited July 19, 2022).

99. JEFFREY S. SUTTON, 51 IMPERFECT SOLUTIONS: STATES AND THE MAKING OF AMERICAN CONSTITUTIONAL LAW 91 (2018).

100. JEFFREY S. SUTTON, 51 IMPERFECT SOLUTIONS: STATES AND THE MAKING OF AMERICAN CONSTITUTIONAL LAW 96, 99 (2018).

101. Smith v. Board of Examiners of Feeble-Minded, 85 N.J.L. 46, 52–55 (N.J. 1913).

102. JEFFREY S. SUTTON, 51 IMPERFECT SOLUTIONS: STATES AND THE MAKING OF AMERICAN CONSTITUTIONAL LAW 100–07 (2018).

103. JEFFREY S. SUTTON, 51 IMPERFECT SOLUTIONS: STATES AND THE MAKING OF AMERICAN CONSTITUTIONAL LAW 107–08 (2018).

104. WILLIAM E. LEUCHTENBURG, THE SUPREME COURT REBORN: THE CONSTITUTIONAL REVOLUTION IN THE AGE OF ROOSEVELT 9 (1995).

105. WILLIAM E. LEUCHTENBURG, THE SUPREME COURT REBORN: THE CONSTITUTIONAL REVOLUTION IN THE AGE OF ROOSEVELT 9 (1995); JEFFREY S. SUTTON, 51 IMPERFECT SOLUTIONS: STATES AND THE MAKING OF AMERICAN CONSTITUTIONAL LAW 109–10 (2018).

106. JEFFREY S. SUTTON, 51 IMPERFECT SOLUTIONS: STATES AND THE MAKING OF AMERICAN CONSTITUTIONAL LAW 111–12 (2018) (quoting December 7, 1925, minutes of Board of the State Colony for Epileptics and Feeble-Minded) (emphasis added).

107. Buck v. Bell, 274 U.S. 200, 208 (1927).

108. Buck v. Bell, 274 U.S. 200, 205 (1927); CATHERINE DRINKER BOWEN, YANKEE FROM OLYMPUS: JUSTICE HOLMES AND HIS FAMILY (1945).

109. Buck v. Bell, 274 U.S. 200, 205–08 (1927).
110. Oliver Wendell Holmes, Jr., *Ideals and Doubts*, 10 ILL. L. REV. 1, 3 (1915).
111. Letter from Justice Oliver Wendell Holmes, Jr., to Dr. John Wu (July 21, 1925), in WILLIAM E. LEUCHTENBURG, THE SUPREME COURT REBORN: THE CONSTITUTIONAL REVOLUTION IN THE AGE OF ROOSEVELT 18–19 (1995).
112. Letter from Justice Oliver Wendell Holmes, Jr., to Lewis Einstein (May 19, 1927) in PAUL A. LOMBARDO, THREE GENERATIONS, NO IMBECILES: EUGENICS, THE SUPREME COURT, AND *BUCK V. BELL* 173 (2008).
113. JEFFREY S. SUTTON, 51 IMPERFECT SOLUTIONS: STATES AND THE MAKING OF AMERICAN CONSTITUTIONAL LAW 117, 130 (2018).
114. Adam S. Cohen, *Harvard's Eugenics Era*, HARVARD MAG. (Mar.–Apr. 2016), https://www.harvardmagazine.com/2016/03/harvards-eugenics-era.
115. JEFFREY S. SUTTON, 51 IMPERFECT SOLUTIONS: STATES AND THE MAKING OF AMERICAN CONSTITUTIONAL LAW 129–30 (2018).
116. Linda Villarosa, *The Long Shadow of Eugenics in America*, N.Y. TIMES (June 8, 2022), https://www.nytimes.com/2022/06/08/magazine/eugenics-movement-america.html.
117. WILLIAM E. LEUCHTENBURG, THE SUPREME COURT REBORN: THE CONSTITUTIONAL REVOLUTION IN THE AGE OF ROOSEVELT 23–24 (1995).
118. WILLIAM E. LEUCHTENBURG, THE SUPREME COURT REBORN: THE CONSTITUTIONAL REVOLUTION IN THE AGE OF ROOSEVELT 9–11, 24 (1995).
119. Karl Evers-Hillstrom, *State of Money in Politics: The Price of Victory Is Steep*, OPENSECRETS (Feb. 19, 2019), https://www.opensecrets.org/news/2019/02/state-of-money-in-politics-the-price-of-victory-is-steep/.
120. ADMINISTRATIVE CONFERENCE OF THE UNITED STATES & ADMINISTRATIVE LAW REVIEW, MASS AND FAKE COMMENTS IN AGENCY RULEMAKING 13 (Oct. 5, 2018).
121. JENNIFER L. LAWLESS, BECOMING A CANDIDATE: POLITICAL AMBITION AND THE DECISION TO RUN FOR OFFICE 2 (2012).
122. *Civilian Review Board*, OFFICE OF EQUITY AND CIVIL RIGHTS, https://civilrights.baltimorecity.gov/civilian-review-board (last visited June 12, 2023); *Historic Board*, BOROUGH OF COLLINGSWOOD, NEW JERSEY, http://www.collingswood.com/government/departments/historic_board.php (last visited June 12, 2023); *Youth Advisory Council (YAC)*, WINSTON-SALEM, NORTH CAROLINA, https://www.cityofws.org/630/Youth-Advisory-Council-YAC (last visited May 7, 2023).
123. 1 ALEXIS DE TOCQUEVILLE, DEMOCRACY IN AMERICA 73 (Henry Reeve trans., London: Saunders and Otley 3d ed. 1838) (1835).
124. John Gastil et al., *Civic Awakening in the Jury Room: A Test of the Connection Between Jury Deliberation and Political Participation*, 64 J. POL. 585, 593–94 (2002).
125. John Gastil et al., *From Group Member to Democratic Citizen: How Deliberating with Fellow Jurors Reshapes Civic Attitudes*, 34 HUM. COMMC'N RSCH. 137 (2008).
126. Brian Brown, *The Rise of Localist Politics*, NEW ATLANTIS (Spring 2011), https://www.thenewatlantis.com/publications/the-rise-of-localist-politics.
127. 2 ALEXIS DE TOCQUEVILLE, DEMOCRACY IN AMERICA 511 (J.P. Mayer ed., George Lawrence trans., Harper Perennial 2006) (1835).
128. 2 ALEXIS DE TOCQUEVILLE, DEMOCRACY IN AMERICA 511–12, 692 (J.P. Mayer ed., George Lawrence trans., Harper Perennial 2006) (1835).
129. 2 ALEXIS DE TOCQUEVILLE, DEMOCRACY IN AMERICA 124 (Francis Bowen ed., Henry Reeve trans., Cambridge: Sever and Francis 3d ed. 1863) (1835).
130. 2 ALEXIS DE TOCQUEVILLE, DEMOCRACY IN AMERICA 692 (J.P. Mayer ed., George Lawrence trans., Harper Perennial 2006) (1835).
131. Zoltan L. Hajnal, *Why Does No One Vote in Local Elections?*, N.Y. TIMES (Oct. 22, 2018), https://www.nytimes.com/2018/10/22/opinion/why-does-no-one-vote-in-local-elections.html.; Kriston Capps, *In the U.S., Almost No One Votes in Local Elections*, BLOOMBERG (Nov. 1, 2016), https://www.bloomberg.com/news/articles/2016-11-01/almost-no-one-votes-in-mayoral-elections-in-the-u-s.
132. Zoltan L. Hajnal, *Why Does No One Vote in Local Elections?*, N.Y. TIMES (Oct. 22, 2018), https://www.nytimes.com/2018/10/22/opinion/why-does-no-one-vote-in-local-elections.html.
133. Mike Maciag, *Voter Turnout Plummeting in Local Elections*, GOVERNING (Aug. 28, 2014), https://www.governing.com/archive/gov-voter-turnout-municipal-elections.html.

134. *New York City*: Brigid Bergin, *New York City Voter Turnout Hits Record Low for a May-oral Election*, GOTHAMIST (Dec. 1, 2021), https://gothamist.com/news/new-york-city-voter -turnout-hits-record-low-mayoral-election. *Philadelphia*: Daniel J. Hopkins, *Declining Turnout in Big-City Elections: A Growing Problem for Democratic Accountability* 3 MANHATTAN INSTITUTE (May 18, 2021), https://manhattan.institute/article/declining -turnout-in-big-city-elections-a-growing-problem-for-democratic-accountability.

135. Mike Maciag, *Voter Turnout Plummeting in Local Elections*, GOVERNING (Aug. 28, 2014), https://www.governing.com/archive/gov-voter-turnout-municipal-elections.html.

136. Zoltan L. Hajnal, *Why Does No One Vote in Local Elections?*, N.Y. TIMES (Oct. 22, 2018), https://www.nytimes.com/2018/10/22/opinion/why-does-no-one-vote-in-local -elections.html.

137. *Why Millennials Don't Vote for Mayor*, KNIGHT FOUNDATION, https://knightfoundation .org/features/votelocal/ (last visited June 23, 2022) (under obstacles, number 3).

138. Kriston Capps, *In the U.S., Almost No One Votes in Local Elections*, BLOOMBERG (Nov. 1, 2016), https://www.bloomberg.com/news/articles/2016-11-01/almost-no-one-votes -in-mayoral-elections-in-the-u-s.

139. *Partisan Polarization Surges in Bush, Obama Years*, 51 PEW RESEARCH CENTER (June 4, 2012), https://www.pewresearch.org/wp-content/uploads/sites/4/legacy-pdf /06-04-12-Values-Release.pdf.

140. 1 ALEXIS DE TOCQUEVILLE, DEMOCRACY IN AMERICA 64 (Harvey C. Mansfield & Delba Winthrop eds. & trans., University of Chicago Press 2000) (1835) (emphasis omitted).

141. 2 ALEXIS DE TOCQUEVILLE, DEMOCRACY IN AMERICA 513 (J.P. Mayer ed., George Lawrence trans., Harper Perennial 2006) (1835).

142. 1 ALEXIS DE TOCQUEVILLE, DEMOCRACY IN AMERICA 64 (Harvey C. Mansfield & Delba Winthrop eds. & trans., University of Chicago Press 2000) (1835).

143. Richard Weissbourd et al., *Loneliness in America: How the Pandemic Has Deepened an Epidemic of Loneliness and What We Can Do About It* 4, HARVARD GRADUATE SCHOOL OF EDUCATION (Feb. 8, 2021), https://static1.squarespace.com/static/5b 7c56e255b02c683659fe43/t/6021776bdd04957c4557c212/1612805995893 /Loneliness+in+America+2021_02_08_FINAL.pdf; Jena McGregor, *This Former Surgeon General Says There's a "Loneliness Epidemic" and Work Is Partly to Blame*, WASH. POST (Oct. 4, 2017), https://www.washingtonpost.com/news/on-leadership /wp/2017/10/04/this-former-surgeon-general-says-theres-a-loneliness-epidemic -and-work-is-partly-to-blame/.

CHAPTER 3: BUREAUCRACY UNBOUND

1. CHARLES DICKENS, LITTLE DORRIT 98 (1899) (1857).

2. *About Marty*, MARTY THE MAGICIAN, https://martythemagician.com/about (last visited Oct. 8, 2022); JN interview with Marty Hahne.

3. David A. Fahrenthold, *Watch Him Pull a USDA-Mandated Rabbit Disaster Plan Out of His Hat*, WASH. POST (July 16, 2013), https://www.washingtonpost.com /politics/watch-him-pull-a-usda-mandated-rabbit-disaster-plan-out-of-his-hat /2013/07/16/816f2f66-ed66-11e2-8163-2c7021381a75_story.html; Joe O'Connor, *Magician Ordered to Pull Rabbit Disaster Plan Out of His Hat After He Was Forced to Buy Special Bunny License*, NATIONAL POST (July 18, 2013), https://nationalpost .com/news/marty-the-magician-rabbit-disaster-plan; *see also* JN interview with Marty Hahne.

4. Animal Welfare Act of 1966, Pub. L. No. 89-544, 80 Stat. 350 (1966); *see also Animal Welfare Act Timeline*, USDA NATIONAL AGRICULTURAL LIBRARY, https://www.nal .usda.gov/collections/exhibits/awahistory/list (last visited Oct. 8, 2022).

5. 7 U.S.C. §§ 2132–34 (2005); *see also Animal Welfare Act Timeline*, USDA NATIONAL AGRICULTURAL LIBRARY, https://www.nal.usda.gov/collections/exhibits/awahistory /list (last visited Oct. 8, 2022).

6. 9 C.F.R. §§ 1.1, 2.1 (2005); David A. Fahrenthold, *Watch Him Pull a USDA-Mandated Rabbit Disaster Plan Out of His Hat*, WASH. POST (July 16, 2013), https://www .washingtonpost.com/politics/watch-him-pull-a-usda-mandated-rabbit-disaster -plan-out-of-his-hat/2013/07/16/816f2f66-ed66-11e2-8163-2c7021381a75_story.html.

7. 9 C.F.R. § 2.126 (2022); David A. Fahrenthold, *Watch Him Pull a USDA-Mandated Rabbit Disaster Plan Out of His Hat*, WASH. POST (July 16, 2013), https://www

.washingtonpost.com/politics/watch-him-pull-a-usda-mandated-rabbit-disaster
-plan-out-of-his-hat/2013/07/16/816f2f66-ed66-11e2-8163-2c7021381a75_story
.html; JN interview with Marty Hahne.

8.   Diane Katz, *Tales of the Red Tape #40: The USDA Rabbit Police*, DAILY SIGNAL
(July 2, 2013), https://www.dailysignal.com/2013/07/02/tales-of-the-red-tape-40
-the-usda-rabbit-police; JN interview with Marty Hahne.

9.   JN interview with Marty Hahne.

10. Handling of Animals; Contingency Plans, 73 Fed. Reg. 63085 (proposed Oct. 23,
2008); David A. Fahrenthold, *Watch Him Pull a USDA-Mandated Rabbit Disaster
Plan Out of His Hat*, WASH. POST (July 16, 2013), https://www.washingtonpost
.com/politics/watch-him-pull-a-usda-mandated-rabbit-disaster-plan-out-of-his
-hat/2013/07/16/816f2f66-ed66-11e2-8163-2c7021381a75_story.html.

11. Handling of Animals; Contingency Plans, 77 Fed. Reg. 76815, 76823 (Dec. 31,
2012; David A. Fahrenthold, *Watch Him Pull a USDA-Mandated Rabbit Disaster
Plan Out of His Hat*, WASH. POST (July 16, 2013), https://www.washingtonpost
.com/politics/watch-him-pull-a-usda-mandated-rabbit-disaster-plan-out-of-his
-hat/2013/07/16/816f2f66-ed66-11e2-8163-2c7021381a75_story.html.

12. David A. Fahrenthold, *Watch Him Pull a USDA-Mandated Rabbit Disaster Plan
Out of His Hat*, WASH. POST (July 16, 2013), https://www.washingtonpost.com
/politics/watch-him-pull-a-usda-mandated-rabbit-disaster-plan-out-of-his-hat
/2013/07/16/816f2f66-ed66-11e2-8163-2c7021381a75_story.html; JN interview with
Marty Hahne.

13. Joe O'Connor, *Magician Ordered to Pull Rabbit Disaster Plan Out of His Hat After
He Was Forced to Buy Special Bunny License*, NATIONAL POST (July 18, 2013), https://
nationalpost.com/news/marty-the-magician-rabbit-disaster-plan.

14. 7 U.S.C. § 2132(g) (2022); David A. Fahrenthold, *Watch Him Pull a USDA-Mandated
Rabbit Disaster Plan Out of His Hat*, WASH. POST (July 16, 2013), https://www
.washingtonpost.com/politics/watch-him-pull-a-usda-mandated-rabbit-disaster-plan
-out-of-his-hat/2013/07/16/816f2f66-ed66-11e2-8163-2c7021381a75_story.html.

15. David A. Fahrenthold, *Watch Him Pull a USDA-Mandated Rabbit Disaster Plan
Out of His Hat*, WASH. POST (July 16, 2013), https://www.washingtonpost.com
/politics/watch-him-pull-a-usda-mandated-rabbit-disaster-plan-out-of-his-hat
/2013/07/16/816f2f66-ed66-11e2-8163-2c7021381a75_story.html. After Marty's story
made national news and members of Congress intervened, the agency amended its regulations to exempt certain individuals and their animals from licensure and informed
Marty that he fell within the exemption. *See* 9 C.F.R. § 2.1(a)(3)(vii); JN interview
with Marty Hahne.

16. 907 Whitehead Street, Inc. v. Secretary of U.S. Department of Agriculture, 701 F.3d
1345, 1347 (11th Cir. 2012).

17. Lizette Alvarez, *Cats at Hemingway Museum Draw Tourists, and a Legal Battle*, N.Y.
TIMES (Dec. 22, 2012), https://www.nytimes.com/2012/12/23/us/cats-at-hemingway
-museum-draw-a-legal-battle.html; Noelle Talmon, *Ernest Hemingway's Home Is
Inhabited by Six-Toed Cats*, RIPLEY's (Feb. 16, 2021), https://www.ripleys.com/weird
-news/ernest-hemingways-cats/; *Purr-fect Ending to Battle over Hemingway's Cats*,
TODAY (Sep. 25, 2008), https://www.today.com/popculture/purr-fect-ending-battle
-over-hemingways-cats-1c9011097; *Our Cats*, THE ERNEST HEMINGWAY HOME AND
MUSEUM, https://www.hemingwayhome.com/our-cats (last visited March 23, 2023).

18. *Our Cats*, THE ERNEST HEMINGWAY HOME AND MUSEUM, https://www
.hemingwayhome.com/our-cats (last visited Mar. 27, 2023).

19. Lizette Alvarez, *Cats at Hemingway Museum Draw Tourists, and a Legal Battle*, N.Y.
TIMES (Dec. 22, 2012), https://www.nytimes.com/2012/12/23/us/cats-at-hemingway
-museum-draw-a-legal-battle.html; *Our Cats*, THE ERNEST HEMINGWAY HOME AND
MUSEUM, https://www.hemingwayhome.com/our-cats (last visited Mar. 27, 2023).

20. Lizette Alvarez, *Cats at Hemingway Museum Draw Tourists, and a Legal Battle*, N.Y.
TIMES (Dec. 22, 2012), https://www.nytimes.com/2012/12/23/us/cats-at-hemingway
-museum-draw-a-legal-battle.html; Keith Coffman, *Hemingway Museum and Six-
Toed Cats Ride Out Irma Unscathed*, REUTERS (Sep. 11, 2017), https://www.reuters
.com/article/uk-storm-irma-hemingway-idAFKCN1BM2UA; Gwen Filosa, *Hemingway
Cat "Jailed" After Tourist Complains of Bite Returns Home*, MIAMI HERALD (Aug. 20,

2016), https://www.miamiherald.com/news/local/community/florida-keys/article968 67412.html; *Our Cats*, THE ERNEST HEMINGWAY HOME AND MUSEUM (last visited Mar. 27, 2023), https://www.hemingwayhome.com/our-cats.

21. Lizette Alvarez, *Cats at Hemingway Museum Draw Tourists, and a Legal Battle*, N.Y. TIMES (Dec. 22, 2012), https://www.nytimes.com/2012/12/23/us/cats-at-hemingway -museum-draw-a-legal-battle.html; Laura Richardson, *Hemingway's Six-Toed Cats*, KEY WEST FLORIDA WEEKLY (July 16, 2020), https://keywest.floridaweekly.com/articles /hemingways-six-toed-cats/; *Our Cats*, THE ERNEST HEMINGWAY HOME AND MUSEUM https://www.hemingwayhome.com/our-cats (last visited Mar. 27, 2023).

22. Maggie Astor, *Hemingway's Six-Toed Cats Ride Out Hurricane Irma in Key West*, N.Y. TIMES (Sep. 11, 2017), https://www.nytimes.com/2017/09/11/us/hemingway -cats-irma.html.

23. Lizette Alvarez, *Cats at Hemingway Museum Draw Tourists, and a Legal Battle*, N.Y. TIMES (Dec. 22, 2012), https://www.nytimes.com/2012/12/23/us/cats-at -hemingway-museum-draw-a-legal-battle.html.

24. LEICESTER HEMINGWAY, MY BROTHER, ERNEST HEMINGWAY 278 (1996).

25. 907 Whitehead Street, Inc. v. Secretary of U.S. Department of Agriculture, 701 F.3d 1345, 1348 (11th Cir. 2012); 907 Whitehead Street, Inc. v. Vilsack, No. 09-10050-CIV, 2011 WL 13174696, at *3 (S.D. Fla. Aug. 12, 2011); 907 Whitehead Street, Inc. v. Vil- sack, No. 09-10050-CIV, 2010 WL 11505441, at *5 (S.D. Fla. Sep. 9, 2010) (agency arguing museum is like a "zoo" of cats).

26. 907 Whitehead Street, Inc. v. Secretary of U.S. Department of Agriculture, 701 F.3d 1345, 1347 (11th Cir. 2012); 907 Whitehead Street, Inc. v. Vilsack, No. 09-10050-CIV, 2010 WL 11505219, at *1 (S.D. Fla. Aug. 25, 2010); Complaint for Declaratory Judg- ment at 3–5, 907 Whitehead Street, Inc. v. Vilsack (S.D. Fla. Apr. 10, 2009) (No. 09-10050).

27. 907 Whitehead Street, Inc. v. Vilsack, No. 09-10050-CIV, 2010 WL 11505219, at *1 (S.D. Fla. Aug. 25, 2010); *see generally National Register of Historic Places*, U.S. GENERAL SERVICES ADMINISTRATION (May 4, 2018), https://www.gsa.gov/real-estate/historic -preservation/historic-building-stewardship/national-register-of-historic-places.

28. 907 Whitehead Street, Inc. v. Vilsack, No. 09-10050-CIV, 2010 WL 11505219, at *2 (S.D. Fla. Aug. 25, 2010); Complaint for Declaratory Judgment at 7, 907 Whitehead Street, Inc. v. Vilsack (S.D. Fla. Apr. 10, 2009) (No. 09-10050).

29. Sharyl Attkisson, *Giving Paws: Your Tax Dollars and the Hemingway Cats*, CBS NEWS (Oct. 19, 2007), https://www.cbsnews.com/news/giving-paws-your-tax-dollars-and -the-hemingway-cats/.

30. 907 Whitehead Street, Inc. v. Vilsack, No. 09-10050-CIV, 2010 WL 11505219, at *2 (S.D. Fla. Aug. 25, 2010); *Purr-fect Ending to Battle over Hemingway's Cats*, TODAY (Sep. 25, 2008), https://www.today.com/popculture/purr-fect-ending-battle-over -hemingways-cats-1c9011097.

31. 907 Whitehead Street, Inc. v. Vilsack, No. 09-10050-CIV, 2010 WL 11505219, at *2 (S.D. Fla. Aug. 25, 2010); Complaint for Declaratory Judgment at 8–10, 907 White- head Street, Inc. v. Vilsack (S.D. Fla. Apr. 10, 2009) (No. 09-10050).

32. Sharyl Attkisson, *A Federal Eye on Hemingway's Cats. Why?*, CBS NEWS (Oct. 19, 2007), https://www.cbsnews.com/news/a-federal-eye-on-hemingways-cats-why/.

33. Lizette Alvarez, *Cats at Hemingway Museum Draw Tourists, and a Legal Battle*, N.Y. TIMES (Dec. 22, 2012), https://www.nytimes.com/2012/12/23/us/cats-at-hemingway -museum-draw-a-legal-battle.html.

34. Lizette Alvarez, *Cats at Hemingway Museum Draw Tourists, and a Legal Battle*, N.Y. TIMES (Dec. 22, 2012), https://www.nytimes.com/2012/12/23/us/cats-at-hemingway -museum-draw-a-legal-battle.html; Kevin Underhill, *UPDATE: Battle over Cat Juris- diction Enters Fifth Year*, LOWERING THE BAR (Nov. 20, 2007), https://www.lower ingthebar.net/2007/11/update-battle-o.html.

35. Complaint for Declaratory Judgment at 10, 907 Whitehead Street, Inc. v. Vilsack (S.D. Fla. Apr. 10, 2009) (No. 09-10050).

36. Lizette Alvarez, *Cats at Hemingway Museum Draw Tourists, and a Legal Battle*, N.Y. TIMES (Dec. 22, 2012), https://www.nytimes.com/2012/12/23/us/cats-at-hemingway -museum-draw-a-legal-battle.html.

37. *Purr-fect Ending to Battle over Hemingway's Cats*, TODAY (Sep. 25, 2008), https://www
.today.com/popculture/purr-fect-ending-battle-over-hemingways-cats-1c9011097.

38. 907 Whitehead Street, Inc. v. Secretary of U.S. Department of Agriculture, 701 F.3d
1345, 1348–51 (11th Cir. 2012); Brief for Appellant at 13–17, 907 Whitehead Street,
Inc. v. Secretary of U.S. Department of Agriculture, 701 F.3d 1345 (11th Cir. 2012)
(No. 11-14217).

39. Sharyl Attkisson, *Giving Paws: Your Tax Dollars and the Hemingway Cats*, CBS NEWS
(Oct. 19, 2007), https://www.cbsnews.com/news/giving-paws-your-tax-dollars-and
-the-hemingway-cats/; Laura L. Myers, *Claws Out in Florida Keys over Hemingway
Cats*, REUTERS (July 18, 2007), https://www.reuters.com/article/us-usa-hemingway
-cats/claws-out-in-florida-keys-over-hemingway-cats-idUSN1719618820070717.

40. *Schoolhouse Rock!, I'm Just a Bill*, YOUTUBE (uploaded Aug. 13, 2012, originally
released Feb. 10, 1973), https://www.youtube.com/watch?v=GnfeodcX1Jo. We are
grateful to Professors Abbe R. Gluck and Anne Joseph O'Connell, and to Rosa Po,
for pointing out the disconnect between *Schoolhouse Rock!* and our present-day reality. See Abbe R. Gluck et al., *Unorthodox Lawmaking, Unorthodox Rulemaking*, 115
Colum. L. Rev. 1789, 1794 (2015).

41. Railroad Grade Crossings; Stopping Required, 49 C.F.R. § 392.10; *see also, e.g.,* Abbe
R. Gluck et al., *Unorthodox Lawmaking, Unorthodox Rulemaking*, 115 COLUM. L.
REV. 1789, 1794 (2015); Sam Brodey, *If Schoolhouse Rock Remade "I'm Just a Bill"
Today, It Would Be Depressing*, MINN. POST (Sep. 24, 2015), https://www.minnpost
.com/dc-dispatches/2015/09/if-schoolhouse-rock-remade-i-m-just-bill-today-it
-would-be-depressing/. Note that state laws often apply, too. *See, e.g.,* MASS. GEN.
LAWS ANN. ch. 90, § 15 (2023) ("Every person operating a school bus, or any motor
vehicle carrying explosive substances or flammable liquids as a cargo, or part of a
cargo, upon approaching a railroad crossing at grade, shall bring his vehicle to a full
stop not less than fifteen feet and not more than fifty feet from the nearest track of
said railroad, and shall not proceed to cross until it is safe to do so.").

42. *See* Aaron L. Nielson, *Deconstruction (Not Destruction)*, DÆDALUS, Summer 2021, at
143, 144 ("Nor are the stakes small. Many of the most controversial disputes in recent
years—including over immigration, national Internet policy, and greenhouse gases—
involve regulation, not legislation.").

43. *President Bush*: Exec. Order No. 13,435, 72 Fed. Reg. 34591 (June 20, 2007); *President
Discusses Stem Cell Research*, THE WHITE HOUSE (Aug. 9, 2001), https://georgewbush
-whitehouse.archives.gov/news/releases/2001/08/20010809-2.html; Judith A. Johnson
& Edward C. Liu, *Stem Cell Research: Science, Federal Research Funding, and Regulatory Oversight* 12, CONGRESSIONAL RESEARCH SERVICE (updated Jan. 10, 2013),
https://crsreports.congress.gov/product/pdf/RL/RL33540/48. *President Obama: Exercising Prosecutorial Discretion with Respect to Individuals Who Came to the United
States as Children*, U.S. DEPARTMENT OF HOMELAND SECURITY (June 15, 2012), https://
www.dhs.gov/xlibrary/assets/s1-exercising-prosecutorial-discretion-individuals-who
-came-to-us-as-children.pdf.

44. Neomi Rao, *The Hedgehog & the Fox in Administrative Law*, DÆDALUS, Summer
2021, at 220, 228–29.

45. Angela C. Erickson & Thomas Berry, *But Who Rules the Rulemakers?* 3, 35, PACIFIC
LEGAL FOUNDATION (2019), https://pacificlegal.org/wp-content/uploads/2021/09
/PLF-HHS-report_exec-summary_update_for-web.pdf.

46. *Federally Incurred Cost of Regulatory Changes and How Such Changes Are Made:
Hearing Before the S. Comm. on Homeland Sec. & Govt. Affs.*, 116th Cong. 37 (2019)
(statement of Thomas Berry, Pacific Legal Foundation).

47. Results of search for legislation passed by Congress during the 114th Congress
(2015–2016), which totaled 120 bills or joint resolutions in 2015 (5 of which were
vetoed without a successful override). *See* CONGRESS.GOV, https://www.congress.gov
/search?q=%7B%22source%22%3A%22legislation%22%2C%22bill-status%22%3
A%22law%22%2C%22congress%22%3A%22114%22%7D&pageSort=latestAction
%3Adesc&pageSize=100&page=1 (last visited Mar. 27, 2023).

48. *Reg Stats*, REGULATORY STUDIES CENTER, COLUMBIAN COLLEGE OF ARTS & SCIENCES,
GEORGE WASHINGTON UNIVERSITY, https://regulatorystudies.columbian.gwu.edu/reg

-stats (last visited Oct. 13, 2023); *see also* MAEVE P. CAREY, *Counting Regulations: An Overview of Rulemaking, Types of Federal Regulations, and Pages in the* Federal Register 29, CONGRESSIONAL RESEARCH SERVICE (2019), https://sgp.fas.org/crs/misc /R43056.pdf (3,410 final rule documents). The final rule documents figure captures the number of documents published in the final rules section of the Federal Register in a particular year. Of note, the number of final rule documents is not an exact measure of the number of final rules enacted because this figure counts actions such as rule modifications with temporary effects that never make it into the Code of Federal Regulations. Likewise for the proposed rule documents.

49. *Reg Stats*, REGULATORY STUDIES CENTER, COLUMBIAN COLLEGE OF ARTS & SCIENCES, GEORGE WASHINGTON UNIVERSITY, https://regulatorystudies.columbian.gwu.edu/reg -stats (last visited Oct. 13, 2023); *see also* MAEVE P. CAREY, *Counting Regulations: An Overview of Rulemaking, Types of Federal Regulations, and Pages in the* Federal Register 29, CONGRESSIONAL RESEARCH SERVICE (2019), https://sgp.fas.org/crs/misc /R43056.pdf (2,342 proposed rule documents).

50. PHILIP K. HOWARD, THE RULE OF NOBODY: SAVING AMERICA FROM DEAD LAWS AND SENSELESS BUREAUCRACY 107 (2014).

51. *Ketchup*: 21 C.F.R. § 155.194. *Peanut butter*: 21 C.F.R. § 164.150.

52. Modernization of the Labeling and Advertising Regulations for Wine, Distilled Spirits, and Malt Beverages, 85 Fed. Reg. 18704, 18716 (Apr. 2, 2020) (to be codified at 27 C.F.R. pt. 5); Mike Pomranz, *Vodka Can Finally Have a "Distinctive Character" Thanks to U.S. Regulations Change*, FOOD & WINE (May 5, 2020), https://www .foodandwine.com/news/vodka-definition-change-united-states.

53. *See* JAMES R. COPLAND, THE UNELECTED: HOW AN UNACCOUNTABLE ELITE IS GOVERNING AMERICA 22 (2020); *see also* Julian Davis Mortenson & Nicholas Bagley, *Delegation at the Founding*, 121 COLUM. L. REV. 277, 349–56 (2021); Ilan Wurman, *Nondelegation at the Founding*, 130 YALE L. J. 1490, 1506–12 (2021).

54. *A Big Day in the History of the United States Postal Service*, NATIONAL CONSTITUTION CENTER (Feb. 20, 2019), https://constitutioncenter.org/blog/a-big-day-in-the-history -of-the-united-states-postal-service.

55. *See* Julian Davis Mortenson & Nicholas Bagley, *Delegation at the Founding*, 121 COLUM. L. REV. 277, 350 (2021); Ilan Wurman, *Nondelegation at the Founding*, 130 YALE L. J. 1490, 1506 (2021).

56. *Cf.* An Act to Establish the Post-Office and Post Roads Within the United States, 2d Cong., Sess. I, Ch. 7, § 1 (Feb. 20, 1792).

57. *See* Ilan Wurman, *Nondelegation at the Founding*, 130 YALE L. J. 1490, 1506 (2021) (quoting 3 ANNALS OF CONGRESS 229 (1791)).

58. 3 ANNALS OF CONG. 238–39 (1791); *see* Ilan Wurman, *Nondelegation at the Founding*, 130 YALE L. J. 1490, 1506–07 (2021); *see id.* at 1507 ("James Madison, for his part, argued in opposition to Sedgwick's motion that 'there did not appear to be any necessity for *alienating* the powers of the House; and that if this should take place, it would be a violation of the Constitution.'") (quoting 3 ANNALS OF CONGRESS 238–39 (1791)).

59. 3 ANNALS OF CONGRESS 229–30 (1791) (statement of Rep. Livermore).

60. 3 ANNALS OF CONGRESS 233 (1791) (statement of Rep. Page); *see also* Ilan Wurman, *Nondelegation at the Founding*, 130 YALE L. J. 1490, 1507 (2021).

61. An Act to Establish the Post-Office and Post Roads Within the United States, 2d Cong., Sess. I, Ch. 7 (Feb. 20, 1792).

62. Wayman v. Southard, 23 U.S. (10 Wheat.) 1, 43 (1825); *see also* Gundy v. United States, 139 S. Ct. 2116, 2136 (2019) (Gorsuch, J., dissenting) (citing, e.g., Cargo of the Brig Aurora v. United States, 11 U.S. (7 Cranch) 382, 388 (1813); In re Kollock, 165 U.S. 526, 532 (1897)).

63. Marshall Field & Co. v. Clark, 143 U.S. 649, 692 (1892).

64. *See, e.g.*, 47 U.S.C. § 318 ("That the Commission if it shall find that the public interest, convenience, or necessity will be served thereby may waive or modify the foregoing provisions of this section for the operation of any station . . ."); Yakus v. United States, 321 U.S. 414, 423 (1944) ("In addition the prices established must be fair and equitable, and in fixing them the Administrator is directed to give due consideration, so far as practicable, to prevailing prices during the designated base period.").

65. 47 U.S.C. § 318; Yakus v. United States, 321 U.S. 414, 420, 423 (1944); 15 U.S.C. § 717d; *see also* FPC v. Hope Natural Gas Co., 320 U.S. 591, 600–01 (1944).

66. Gundy v. United States, 139 S. Ct. 2116, 2121–22 (2019) (citing 34 U.S.C. § 20913(d), enacted as part of the Sex Offender Registration and Notification Act).

67. WILLIAM O. DOUGLAS, GO EAST, YOUNG MAN: THE EARLY YEARS 217 (1974).

68. William J. Brennan, Jr., *Reason, Passion, and "The Progress of the Law,"* 42 REC. ASS'N B. CITY N.Y. 948, 970 (1987).

69. *See Annual Statistical Report on the Social Security Disability Insurance Program, 2020* 159–60, SOCIAL SECURITY ADMINISTRATION (2021), https://www.ssa.gov/policy /docs/statcomps/di_asr/2020/di_asr20.pdf; Julia Puaschunder & Martin Gelter, *The Law, Economics, and Governance of Generation Covid-19 Long-Haul,* 19 IND. HEALTH L. REV. 47, 96 (2022).

70. *See Fiscal Year 2022 Workload Data: Disability Decisions,* SOCIAL SECURITY ADMINISTRATION (Jan. 26, 2023), https://www.ssa.gov/foia/resources/proactivedisclosure/2023 /FY22%20Workload%20Data-Total.pdf.

71. Lisa Rein, *Judges Rebuke Social Security for Errors as Disability Denials Stack Up,* WASH. POST (May 25, 2023), https://www.washingtonpost.com/politics/2023/05/25 /social-security-disability-denials-court-remands/.

72. *The Administrative State: An Examination of Federal Rulemaking: Hearing Before the S. Comm. on Homeland Sec. & Governmental Affs.,* 114th Cong. 52 (2016) (statement of Jonathan Turley, Shapiro Professor of Public Interest Law, The George Washington University Law School); Jonathan Turley, *The Rise of the Fourth Branch of Government,* WASH. POST (May 24, 2013), https://www.washingtonpost.com/opinions/the-rise-of -the-fourth-branch-of-government/2013/05/24/c7faaad0-c2ed-11e2-9fe2-6ee52d 0eb7c1_story.html; *see also* Peggy Little, *Ray Lucia's Mythic Lift,* NEW CIVIL LIBERTIES ALLIANCE (June 19, 2020), https://nclalegal.org/2020/06/ray-lucias-mythic-lift/.

73. United States v. Arthrex, Inc., 141 S. Ct. 1970, 1993 (2021) (Gorsuch, J., concurring in part and dissenting in part).

74. *Cf.* 5 C.F.R. § 930.204(e)(2) (noting that agencies have control over ALJ promotions); *see, e.g.,* Jean Eaglesham, *SEC Wins with In-House Judges,* WALL ST. J. (May 6, 2015), https://www.wsj.com/articles/sec-wins-with-in-house-judges-1430965803 ("Lillian McEwen, who was an SEC judge from 1995 to 2007, said she came under fire from [the SEC's chief ALJ] for finding too often in favor of defendants.").

75. Jean Eaglesham, *SEC Wins with In-House Judges,* WALL ST. J. (May 6, 2015), https:// www.wsj.com/articles/sec-wins-with-in-house-judges-1430965803.

76. Oil States Energy v. Greene's Energy Group, 138 S. Ct. 1365, 1381 (2018) (Gorsuch, J., dissenting).

77. Bernard G. Segal, *The Administrative Law Judge—Thirty Years of Progress and the Road Ahead,* 62 A.B.A. J. 1424, 1426 (1976).

78. *See* PHILIP HAMBURGER, IS ADMINISTRATIVE LAW UNLAWFUL? 249 (2014); *see also* Biestek v. Berryhill, 139 S. Ct. 1148, 1152, 1154–55 (2019); Pellicano v. Office of Personnel Management, No. 21-1472, 2022 WL 621692, at *4 (3d Cir. Mar. 3, 2022) ("[T]he Federal Rules of Evidence generally do not apply in a strict sense to administrative proceedings . . ."); Malave v. Holder, 610 F.3d 483, 487 (7th Cir. 2010) ("Hearsay is regularly used in administrative adjudication . . ."); Evan D. Bernick, *Is Judicial Deference to Agency Fact-Finding Unlawful?,* 16 GEO. J. L. & PUB. POL'Y 27, 58 (2018) (citing Richardson v. Perales, 402 U.S. 389, 400 (1971)).

79. Biestek v. Berryhill, 139 S. Ct. 1148, 1158–59 (2019) (Gorsuch, J. dissenting); *see also* PHILIP HAMBURGER, IS ADMINISTRATIVE LAW UNLAWFUL? 249–50 (2014) (citing Hi-Tech Furnace Systems, Inc. v. FCC, 224 F.3d 781, 787–790 (D.C. Cir. 2000)); Evan D. Bernick, *Is Judicial Deference to Agency Fact-Finding Unlawful?,* 16 GEO. J. L. & PUB. POL'Y 27, 58 (2018).

80. PHILIP HAMBURGER, IS ADMINISTRATIVE LAW UNLAWFUL? 249 (2014).

81. Gideon Mark, *Response: SEC Enforcement Discretion,* 94 TEX. L. REV. 261, 262 (2016).

82. Jean Eaglesham, *Fairness of SEC Judges Is in Spotlight,* WALL ST. J. (Nov. 22, 2015), https://www.wsj.com/articles/fairness-of-sec-judges-is-in-spotlight-1448236970.

83. Joshua D. Wright, *Section 5 Revisited: Time for the FTC to Define the Scope of Its Unfair Methods of Competition Authority,* FEDERAL TRADE COMMISSION (Feb. 26, 2015),

https://www.ftc.gov/system/files/documents/public_statements/626811/150226bh_section_5_symposium.pdf (speech delivered as part of Symposium on Section 5 of the Federal Trade Commission Act).

84. CHARLES B. SWARTWOOD, III ET AL., REPORT AND RECOMMENDATION OF THE SPECIAL MASTER CONCERNING NOAA ENFORCEMENT ACTION OF CERTAIN DESIGNATED CASES 235 (2011).

85. Biestek v. Berryhill, 139 S. Ct. 1148, 1158–59, 1162–63 (2019) (Gorsuch, J., dissenting).

86. 1 ANNALS OF CONGRESS 518 (statement of Rep. Madison).

87. *President Franklin Delano Roosevelt and the New Deal*, LIBRARY OF CONGRESS, https://www.loc.gov/classroom-materials/united-states-history-primary-source-timeline/great-depression-and-world-war-ii-1929-1945/franklin-delano-roosevelt-and-the-new-deal/ (last visited Aug. 18, 2023); Gerhard Peters, *Presidential Election Margins of Victory*, THE AMERICAN PRESIDENCY PROJECT, https://www.presidency.ucsb.edu/node/323891 (last updated Nov. 7, 2020).

88. Marc Winerman, *The Origins of the FTC: Concentration, Cooperation, Control, and Competition*, 71 ANTITRUST L. J. 1, 2, 38 (2003) (discussing the beginnings of the FTC, including Wilson's involvement).

89. Federal Trade Commission Act, ch. 311, § 5, 38 Stat. 719 (1914) (current version at 15 U.S.C. § 45).

90. WILLIAM E. LEUCHTENBURG, THE SUPREME COURT REBORN 55–60, 76–77 (1995); William E. Leuchtenburg, *The Case of the Contentious Commissioner*, Humphrey's Executor v. U.S., in FREEDOM AND REFORM 278, 280 (Harold M. Hyman & Leonard W. Levy eds., 1967).

91. WILLIAM E. LEUCHTENBURG, THE SUPREME COURT REBORN 53–55, 57–62 (1995).

92. JOHN WHITECLAY CHAMBERS II, OSS TRAINING IN THE NATIONAL PARKS AND SERVICE ABROAD IN WORLD WAR II 8–10, 21 (2008); *see also OSS Records*, NATIONAL ARCHIVES, https://www.archives.gov/research/military/ww2/oss (last visited Sep. 30, 2023).

93. Brief for Samuel F. Rathbun, Executor at 6, 12–13, Humphrey's Executor v. United States, 295 U.S. 602 (1935) (No. 667); *cf.* WILLIAM E. LEUCHTENBURG, THE SUPREME COURT REBORN 58, 76 (1995).

94. Federal Trade Commission Act, ch. 311, § 1, 38 Stat. 719 (1914) (current version at 15 U.S.C. § 41).

95. WILLIAM E. LEUCHTENBURG, THE SUPREME COURT REBORN 62–64, 76 (1995).

96. Myers v. United States, 272 U.S. 52, 106–08, 131, 135 (1926); *see also* Jonathan L. Entin, *The Curious Case of the Pompous Postmaster:* Myers v. United States, 65 CASE W. RSRV. L. REV. 1059, 1065 (2015) ("Myers died in December 1924, but his widow continued the litigation in the name of his estate.").

97. Humphrey's Executor v. United States, 295 U.S. 602 (1935); *Solicitor General: Stanley Reed*, OFFICE OF THE SOLICITOR GENERAL, U.S. DEPARTMENT OF JUSTICE (Sep. 18, 2023), https://www.justice.gov/osg/bio/stanley-reed.

98. Humphrey's Executor v. United States, 295 U.S. 602, 624, 626–27, 630 (1935) (italics added).

99. WILLIAM E. LEUCHTENBURG, THE SUPREME COURT REBORN 75 (1995) (second quotation is quoting Edgar J. Goodrich, Former Member of the U.S. Board of Tax Appeals, in N.Y. TIMES (June 2, 1935)).

100. Samuel R. Olken, *Justice Sutherland Reconsidered*, 62 VAND. L. REV. 639, 643 (2009); William E. Leuchtenburg, *When Franklin Roosevelt Clashed with the Supreme Court—and Lost*, SMITHSONIAN MAG. (May 2005), https://www.smithsonianmag.com/history/when-franklin-roosevelt-clashed-with-the-supreme-court-and-lost-78497994/.

101. WILLIAM E. LEUCHTENBURG, THE SUPREME COURT REBORN 78–79 (1995) (quoting RAYMOND MOLEY, AFTER SEVEN YEARS 301 (1939)).

102. WILLIAM E. LEUCHTENBURG, THE SUPREME COURT REBORN 78–81 (1995).

103. George B. Shepherd, *Fierce Compromise: The Administrative Procedure Act Emerges from New Deal Politics*, 90 NW. U. L. REV. 1557, 1585 (1996) (citing Franklin D. Roosevelt, *Message from the President of the United States* (Jan. 12, 1937), in THE PRESIDENT'S COMMITTEE ON ADMINISTRATIVE MANAGEMENT, REPORT OF THE PRESIDENT'S COMMITTEE ON ADMINISTRATIVE MANAGEMENT iv (1937)).

104. WILLIAM E. LEUCHTENBURG, THE SUPREME COURT REBORN 80–81 (1995) (quoting JOSEPH ALSOP & TURNER CATLEDGE, THE 168 DAYS 13–14 (1938)).

105. DAVID GREENBERG, NIXON'S SHADOW: THE HISTORY OF AN IMAGE 307 (2003) (quoting HERBERT STEIN, PRESIDENTIAL ECONOMICS: THE MAKING OF ECONOMIC POLICY FROM ROOSEVELT TO REAGAN AND BEYOND 190 (2d rev. ed. 1988)); Gillian E. Metzger, *Foreword: 1930s Redux: The Administrative State Under Siege*, 131 HARV. L. REV. 1, 15 n.63 (2017) (citing JEFFERSON DECKER, THE OTHER RIGHTS REVOLUTION: CONSERVATIVE LAWYERS AND THE REMAKING OF AMERICAN GOVERNMENT 15, 20–22 (2016)).

106. E.J. Dionne, Jr., *Political Hacks v. Bureaucrats: Can't Public Servants Get Some Respect?*, BROOKINGS INSTITUTION (Mar. 1, 2001), https://www.brookings.edu/articles /political-hacks-v-bureaucrats-cant-public-servants-get-some-respect/.

107. Thomas Sowell, *Wake Up, Parents: Your Rights Are Being Eroded*, SOUTH FLORIDA SENTINEL (Aug. 19, 2000).

108. DAVID GRAEBER, THE UTOPIA OF RULES: ON TECHNOLOGY, STUPIDITY, AND THE SECRET JOYS OF BUREAUCRACY 82 (2015).

109. RICHARD P. NATHAN, THE ADMINISTRATIVE PRESIDENCY 2 (1986) (quoting Burt Schorr & Andy Pasztor, *Reaganites Make Sure That the Bureaucracy Toes the Line on Policy*, WALL ST. J. (Feb. 10, 1982)); RICHARD E. NEUSTADT, PRESIDENTIAL POWER AND THE MODERN PRESIDENTS: THE POLITICS OF LEADERSHIP FROM ROOSEVELT TO REAGAN 10 (1990); *see also* Elena Kagan, *Presidential Administration*, 114 HARV. L. REV. 2245, 2272 (2001) (discussing James Landis and his theories).

110. George B. Shepherd, *Fierce Compromise: The Administrative Procedure Act Emerges from New Deal Politics*, 90 NW. U. L. REV. 1557, 1565–69, 1595 (1996) (quoting Kenneth C. Davis & Walter Gellhorn, *Present at the Creation: Regulatory Reform Before 1946*, 38 ADMIN. L. REV. 511, 516 (1986)).

111. George B. Shepherd, *Fierce Compromise: The Administrative Procedure Act Emerges from New Deal Politics*, 90 NW. U. L. REV. 1557, 1590–91 (1996) (citing *Report of the Special Comm. on Administrative Law*, 63 ANN. REP. A.B.A. 331 (1938)).

112. *Report of the Special Comm. on Administrative Law*, 63 ANN. REP. A.B.A. 331, 342 (1938).

113. *Report of the Special Comm. on Administrative Law*, 63 ANN. REP. A.B.A. 331, 345 (1938) (quoting Mitchell Franklin, *Administrative Law in the United States*, 8 TULANE L. REV. 483, 484–85 (1934)).

114. *Report of the Special Comm. on Administrative Law*, 63 ANN. REP. A.B.A. 331, 359 (1938).

115. George B. Shepherd, *Fierce Compromise: The Administrative Procedure Act Emerges from New Deal Politics*, 90 NW. U. L. REV. 1557, 1576 (1996) (quoting *Proceedings of the Fifty-Eighth Annual Meeting of American Bar Association Los Angeles, California*, 58 ANN. REP. A.B.A. 57, 141 (1935) (statement of Chairman Louis G. Caldwell)).

116. Administrative Procedure Act (APA), Pub. L. 79-404, 60 Stat. 237 (1946); *see generally* George B. Shepherd, *Fierce Compromise: The Administrative Procedure Act Emerges from New Deal Politics*, 90 NW. U. L. REV. 1557 (1996).

117. *See* 5 U.S.C. §§ 553, 556–57.

118. Todd Garvey, *A Brief Overview of Rulemaking and Judicial Review* 3, CONGRESSIONAL RESEARCH SERVICE (updated March 27, 2017), https://crsreports.congress.gov /product/pdf/R/R41546/13.

119. 5 U.S.C. § 553; STEPHEN G. BREYER ET AL., ADMINISTRATIVE LAW AND REGULATORY POLICY 561 (9th ed. 2022) (noting that since the high-water mark of *Home Box Office, Inc. v. FCC*, 567 F.2d 9 (D.C. Cir. 1977), there have been "almost no decisions finding ex parte contacts in informal proceedings problematic").

120. 5 U.S.C. §§ 554, 556–57; *see also* Ben Harrington & Daniel J. Sheffner, *Informal Administrative Adjudication: An Overview* 2–4, CONGRESSIONAL RESEARCH SERVICE (October 1, 2021), https://crsreports.congress.gov/product/pdf/R/R46930.

121. 5 U.S.C. § 554, 556–57; Ben Harrington & Daniel J. Sheffner, *Informal Administrative Adjudication: An Overview* i, 6–7, CONGRESSIONAL RESEARCH SERVICE (October 1, 2021), https://crsreports.congress.gov/product/pdf/R/R46930.

122. Ben Harrington & Daniel J. Sheffner, *Informal Administrative Adjudication: An Overview* 5, CONGRESSIONAL RESEARCH SERVICE (October 1, 2021), https://crsreports .congress.gov/product/pdf/R/R46930.

123. Ben Harrington & Daniel J. Sheffner, *Informal Administrative Adjudication: An Overview* 8 n.72, CONGRESSIONAL RESEARCH SERVICE (October 1, 2021), https://

crsreports.congress.gov/product/pdf/R/R46930 (quoting Daniel J. Sheffner, *Access to Adjudication Materials on Federal Agency Websites*, 51 AKRON L. REV. 447, 450–51 (2017)).

124. Ben Harrington & Daniel J. Sheffner, *Informal Administrative Adjudication: An Overview* 9, CONGRESSIONAL RESEARCH SERVICE (October 1, 2021), https://crsreports .congress.gov/product/pdf/R/R46930; *see also* Kent H. Barnett & Russell Wheeler, *Non-ALJ Adjudicators in Federal Agencies: Status, Selection, Oversight, and Removal*, 53 GA. L. REV. 1, 8–11 (2018) (discussing the lessened protections for non-ALJs).

125. *See* 5 U.S.C. § 702.

126. *See* 5 U.S.C. § 706; George B. Shepherd, *Fierce Compromise: The Administrative Procedure Act Emerges from New Deal Politics*, 90 NW. U. L. REV. 1557, 1644–45 (1996) ("[I]n the bills that led directly to the APA, conservatives focused on procedural reform. The APA's provisions for judicial review were little more than an afterthought.").

127. 5 U.S.C. § 706(2).

128. Walter Gellhorn, *The Administrative Procedure Act: The Beginnings*, 72 VA. L. REV. 219, 232 (1986); George B. Shepherd, *Fierce Compromise: The Administrative Procedure Act Emerges from New Deal Politics*, 90 NW. U. L. REV. 1557, 1560 (1996).

129. *See* George B. Shepherd, *Fierce Compromise: The Administrative Procedure Act Emerges from New Deal Politics*, 90 NW. U. L. REV. 1557, 1559–61, 1674–83 (1996); *id.* at 1675 ("The bill passed both houses unanimously not because everyone was thrilled with the bill, but because private negotiations had permitted the parties to cobble together an agreement that all could at least tolerate.").

130. George B. Shepherd, *Fierce Compromise: The Administrative Procedure Act Emerges from New Deal Politics*, 90 NW. U. L. REV. 1557, 1671 (1996) (quoting 92 CONG. REC. 5646 (1946)).

131. *See* Aaron L. Nielson, *In Defense of Formal Rulemaking*, 75 OHIO ST. L. J. 237, 239 (2014) ("Although the APA provides for formal rulemaking, the Supreme Court largely put an end to it forty years ago in *United States v. Florida East Coast Railway Co.*"); Christopher J. Walker & Melissa F. Wasserman, *A New World of Agency Adjudication*, 107 CALIF. L. REV. 141, 143 (2019) ("The vast majority of agency adjudications today, however, do not look like APA formal adjudication.").

132. *See* 5 U.S.C. § 553(b)(3)(A); Nicholas R. Parrillo, *Federal Agency Guidance and the Power to Bind: An Empirical Study of Agencies and Industries*, 36 YALE J. ON REGUL. 165, 168–69 (2019).

133. Neomi Rao, *The Hedgehog & the Fox in Administrative Law*, DÆDALUS, Summer 2021, at 220, 228.

134. *See* 5 U.S.C. § 702.

135. Jonah B. Gelbach & David Marcus, *Rethinking Judicial Review of High Volume Agency Adjudication*, 96 TEX. L. REV. 1097, 1100 (2018).

136. *See* Economy Premier Assurance Co. v. Western National Mutual Insurance Co., 839 N.W.2d 749, 754 (Minn. Ct. App. 2013) (citing Bacon, Coke, Blackstone, and numerous nineteenth-century American cases); Folk Construction Co., Inc. v. United States, 2 Cl. Ct. 681, 688 (1983) ("Under the rule of *contra proferentem*, '[w]here the Government draws specifications which are fairly susceptible of a certain construction and the contractor actually and reasonably so construes them, justice and equity require that that construction be adopted'" (quoting Peter Kiewit Sons' Co. v. United States, 109 Ct. Cl. 390, 418 (1947))).

137. *See, e.g.*, Martin H. Redish & Lawrence C. Marshall, *Adjudicatory Independence and the Values of Procedural Due Process*, 95 YALE L. J. 455, 479–80 (1986).

138. Marbury v. Madison, 5 U.S. (1 Cranch) 137, 177 (1803).

139. Chevron U.S.A. Inc. v. Natural Resources Defense Council, Inc., 467 U.S. 837 (1984).

140. Buffington v. McDonough, 143 S. Ct. 14, 17–18 (2022) (Gorsuch, J., dissenting from the denial of certiorari).

141. 907 Whitehead Street, Inc. v. Secretary of U.S. Department of Agriculture, 701 F.3d 1345, 1350 (11th Cir. 2012).

142. *See* National Cable & Telecommunications Association v. Brand X Internet Services, 545 U.S. 967, 981–82 (2005).

143. Raymond M. Kethledge, *Hayek and the Rule of Law: Implications for Unenumerated Rights and the Administrative State*, 13 N.Y.U. J. L. & LIBERTY 193, 213 (2020).

144. *See, e.g.*, Ronald M. Levin, *The APA and the Assault on Deference*, 106 MINN. L. REV. 125, 183–90 (2021); Cass R. Sunstein, Chevron *as Law*, 107 GEO. L. J. 1613, 1641–57 (2019).
145. Kent Barnett & Christopher J. Walker, Chevron *in the Circuit Courts*, 116 MICH. L. REV. 1, 6 (2017).
146. 5 U.S.C. § 706(2)(E).
147. George B. Shepherd, *Fierce Compromise: The Administrative Procedure Act Emerges from New Deal Politics*, 90 NW. U. L. REV. 1557, 1602 (1996) ("However, other senators pointed out that courts had already imposed the substantial evidence rule; the bill merely codified existing common law." (citing Consolidated Edison Co. v. National Labor Relations Board, 305 U.S. 197, 229 (1938); National Labor Relations Board v. Montgomery Ward & Co., 133 F.2d 676, 685 (9th Cir. 1943))).
148. Consolidated Edison Co. v. National Labor Relations Board, 305 U.S. 197, 229 (1938); National Labor Relations Board v. Montgomery Ward & Co., 133 F.2d 676, 685–86 (9th Cir. 1943).
149. *See* Allentown Mack Sales and Service, Inc. v. National Labor Relations Board, 522 U.S. 359, 366–67 (1998).
150. George v. McDonough, 142 S. Ct. 1953, 1958 (2022); *id.* at 1965–66 (Gorsuch, J., dissenting).
151. George v. McDonough, 142 S. Ct. 1953, 1958 (2022) (citing 38 U.S.C. § 5109A).
152. George v. McDonough, 142 S. Ct. 1953, 1958–60 (2022); *id.* at 1966 (Gorsuch, J., dissenting); *see, e.g.*, George v. Wilkie, 30 Vet. App. 364, 373 (2019).
153. George v. McDonough, 142 S. Ct. 1953, 1957, 1960 (2022); *id.* at 1963 (Sotomayor, J., dissenting); *id.* at 1965 (Gorsuch, J., dissenting).
154. Patel v. Garland, 142 S. Ct. 1614, 1619 (2022); *id.* at 1628 (Gorsuch, J., dissenting).
155. Patel v. Garland, 142 S. Ct. 1614, 1628–29 (2022) (Gorsuch, J., dissenting) (quoting 8 U.S.C. §§ 1182(a)(6)(C)(ii)(I), 1255(i)(2)(A)).
156. Patel v. Garland, 142 S. Ct. 1614, 1620 (2022); *id.* at 1628–29 (Gorsuch, J., dissenting).
157. Patel v. Garland, 142 S. Ct. 1614, 1628 (2022) (Gorsuch, J., dissenting) (citing GA. COMP. R. & REGS. 375-3-1.02(3)(e), (7) (2022)).
158. Patel v. Garland, 142 S. Ct. 1614, 1619–21 (2022).
159. Patel v. Garland, 142 S. Ct. 1614, 1620–21 (2022); Patel v. U.S. Attorney General, 971 F.3d 1258, 1263–64, 1272–73 (11th Cir. 2020) (en banc); Patel v. U.S. Attorney General, 917 F.3d 1319, 1323, 1327 (11th Cir. 2019).
160. *See* Patel v. Garland, 142 S. Ct. 1614, 1618 (2022); *id.* at 1627 (Gorsuch, J., dissenting).
161. Yvette Borja, *The American Legal System Failed Pankajkumar Patel*, BALLS AND STRIKES (Dec. 3, 2021), https://ballsandstrikes.org/scotus/patel-v-garland-preview/.
162. *See, e.g.*, Brian R. Fry & Lloyd G. Nigro, *Five Great Issues in the Profession of Public Administration*, in HANDBOOK OF PUBLIC ADMINISTRATION 1164 (Jack Rabin et al. eds., 2d ed. 1998).
163. Woodrow Wilson, *The Study of Administration*, 2 POL. SCI. Q. 197–98, 201–03, 205–06 (1887).
164. *See, e.g.*, PHILIP HAMBURGER, IS ADMINISTRATIVE LAW UNLAWFUL? 458–59 (2014); Woodrow Wilson, *The Study of Administration*, 2 POL. SCI. Q. 197, 204 (1887).
165. Woodrow Wilson, *The Study of Administration*, 2 POL. SCI. Q. 197, 202, 204, 207 (1887).
166. WOODROW WILSON, CONGRESSIONAL GOVERNMENT: A STUDY IN AMERICAN POLITICS 285 (15th ed. 1913).
167. RONALD J. PESTRITTO, WOODROW WILSON AND THE ROOTS OF MODERN LIBERALISM 6 (2005).
168. Woodrow Wilson, *The Study of Administration*, 2 POL. SCI. Q. 197, 207–09 (1887).
169. *See* Cochran v. U.S. Securities and Exchange Commission, 20 F.4th 194, 216–17 (5th Cir. 2021) (en banc) (Oldham, J., concurring).
170. WOODROW WILSON, *Marginal Notes on John Richard Green*, in 1 THE PAPERS OF WOODROW WILSON 388 (Arthur S. Link ed., 1966); *see also* WOODROW WILSON, *Shorthand Diary*, in 1 THE PAPERS OF WOODROW WILSON 143 (Arthur S. Link ed., 1966); Cochran v. U.S. Securities and Exchange Commission, 20 F.4th 194, 216 (5th Cir. 2021) (en banc) (Oldham, J., concurring).
171. *See* Michael Kazin, *Woodrow Wilson Achieved a Lot. So Why Is He So Scorned?*, N.Y. TIMES (June 22, 2018), https://www.nytimes.com/2018/06/22/books/review/patricia-otoole-moralist-woodrow-wilson-biography.html; Jill Lepore, *Why Woodrow*

Wilson Makes a Good Bad Guy, N.Y. TIMES (May 22, 2013), https://www.nytimes
.com/roomfordebate/2010/10/10/hating-woodrow-wilson/why-woodrow-wilson
-makes-a-good-bad-guy.

172. WOODROW WILSON, *Notes for Lectures at Johns Hopkins*, in 7 THE PAPERS OF WOODROW WILSON 121–22 (Arthur S. Link ed., 1966); *see also* PHILIP HAMBURGER, IS ADMINISTRATIVE LAW UNLAWFUL? 464 (2014).

173. RONALD J. PESTRITTO, WOODROW WILSON AND THE ROOTS OF MODERN LIBERALISM 127–28, 165 (2005); *see also* Cochran v. U.S. Securities and Exchange Commission, 20 F.4th 194, 218–19 (5th Cir. 2021) (en banc) (Oldham, J., concurring).

174. JAMES M. LANDIS, THE ADMINISTRATIVE PROCESS 1 (1938).

175. *See* Marc Winerman, *The Origins of the FTC: Concentration, Cooperation, Control, and Competition*, 71 ANTITRUST L. J. 1, 2, 38 (2003) (discussing the beginnings of the FTC).

176. *See, e.g., The Federalist* No. 51 (James Madison), in THE FEDERALIST PAPERS 320–25 (Clinton Rossiter ed., 1961).

177. Philip Ball, *"Wisdom of the Crowd": The Myths and Realities*, BBC (July 7, 2014), https://www.bbc.com/future/article/20140708-when-crowd-wisdom-goes-wrong.

178. See e.g., JAMES SUROWIECKI, THE WISDOM OF CROWDS (2005).

179. *See, e.g., The Federalist* No. 70 (Alexander Hamilton), in THE FEDERALIST PAPERS 426–27 (Clinton Rossiter ed., 1961).

180. *The Federalist* No. 62 (probably James Madison), in THE FEDERALIST PAPERS 382 (Clinton Rossiter ed., 1961).

181. Elena Kagan, *Presidential Administration*, 114 HARV. L. REV. 2245, 2261 (2001).

182. *See The Federalist* No. 51 (James Madison), in THE FEDERALIST PAPERS 321–22 (Clinton Rossiter ed., 1961) ("But the great security against a gradual concentration of the several powers in the same department, consists in giving to those who administer each department the necessary constitutional means and personal motives to resist encroachments of the others. The provision for defense must in this, as in all other cases, be made commensurate to the danger of attack. Ambition must be made to counteract ambition.").

183. Friedrich A. Hayek, *The Use of Knowledge in Society*, 35 AM. ECON. REV. 519, 520–22 (1945).

184. Barack Obama, *Address Before a Joint Session of the Congress on the State of the Union* 8–9, GOVINFO (Jan. 25, 2011), https://www.govinfo.gov/content/pkg/DCPD
-201100047/pdf/DCPD-201100047.pdf; *see also* Angie Drobnic Holan, *Obama Says the One Department Regulates Salmon in Freshwater and Another Regulates Them in Saltwater*, POLITIFACT (Jan. 26, 2011), https://www.politifact.com
/factchecks/2011/jan/26/barack-obama/obama-says-one-department-regulates
-salmon-freshwa/; *Obama Takes Aim at Government Bureaucracy*, CBS NEWS (Jan. 13, 2012), https://www.cbsnews.com/news/obama-takes-aim-at-government
-bureaucracy/.

185. Angie Drobnic Holan, *Obama Says the One Department Regulates Salmon in Freshwater and Another Regulates Them in Saltwater*, POLITIFACT (Jan. 26, 2011), https://www.politifact.com/factchecks/2011/jan/26/barack-obama/obama-says-one
-department-regulates-salmon-freshwa/.

186. Angie Drobnic Holan, *Obama Says the One Department Regulates Salmon in Freshwater and Another Regulates Them in Saltwater*, POLITIFACT (Jan. 26, 2011), https://www.politifact.com/factchecks/2011/jan/26/barack-obama/obama-says-one
-department-regulates-salmon-freshwa/.

187. Nicole Hallett, *"Dysfunctional" Doesn't Begin to Describe Our Immigration Bureaucracy*, THE HILL (Aug. 12, 2021), https://thehill.com/opinion/immigration/567493
-dysfunctional-doesnt-begin-to-describe-our-immigration-bureaucracy/.

188. DAVID GRAEBER, THE UTOPIA OF RULES: ON TECHNOLOGY, STUPIDITY, AND THE SECRET JOYS OF BUREAUCRACY 48–49 (2015).

189. EDWIN J. FEULNER, JR., *Foreword* to FRIEDRICH A. HAYEK, THE ROAD TO SERFDOM WITH THE INTELLECTUALS AND SOCIALISM 20 (2005) (1945).

190. LEARNED HAND, THE BILL OF RIGHTS 73 (4th prtg. 1958).

191. HANNAH ARENDT, CRISES OF THE REPUBLIC 178 (1972).

CHAPTER 4: THE SWORD OF DAMOCLES

1. Arnett v. Kennedy, 416 U.S. 134, 231 (1974) (Marshall, J., dissenting).

2. United States v. Unser, 165 F.3d 755, 757 (10th Cir. 1999); *San Juan National Forest*, U.S. FOREST SERVICE, https://www.fs.usda.gov/sanjuan (last visited Feb. 4, 2024).

3. Richard Goldstein, *Bobby Unser, Racing Clan's Three-Time Indy 500 Winner, Dies at 87*, N.Y. TIMES (May 3, 2021), https://www.nytimes.com/2021/05/03/sports/autoracing/bobby-unser-dead.html; *Al Unser, a Four-Time Winner of the Indianapolis 500, Dies at 82*, PBS NEWS (Dec. 10, 2021), https://www.pbs.org/newshour/nation/al-unser-a-four-time-winner-of-indianapolis-500-dies-at-82; *Bobby Unser Papers*, HENRY FORD MUSEUM, https://www.thehenryford.org/collections-and-research/digital-collections/archival-collections/364291/#:~:text=and%20Bobby%20Unser's%20father%20Jerry,races%20and%20Formula%201%20races (last visited Feb. 4, 2024).

4. Curt Cavin, *Trip Down Victory Lane: Bobby Unser's House of Fame*, INDYSTAR (Mar. 24, 2016), https://www.indystar.com/story/sports/motor/2016/03/24/trip-down-victory-lane-bobby-unser-and-his-house-fame/82128752/; *History of Pikes Peak International Hill Climb*, PIKES PEAK INTERNATIONAL HILL CLIMB, https://ppihc.org/history/ (last visited Feb. 4, 2024); *see also* Marc Wiley, *The Pikes Peak Hill Climb Is More than Just Another Race*, MOTORBISCUIT (July 1, 2023), https://www.motorbiscuit.com/pikes-peak-hill-climb-more-just-another-race/.

5. Richard Goldstein, *Bobby Unser, Racing Clan's Three-Time Indy 500 Winner, Dies at 87*, N.Y. TIMES (May 3, 2021), https://www.nytimes.com/2021/05/03/sports/autoracing/bobby-unser-dead.html; *Bobby Unser Papers*, HENRY FORD MUSEUM, https://www.thehenryford.org/collections-and-research/digital-collections/archival-collections/364291/ (last visited Feb. 4, 2024).

6. Mike Hembree, *Inside Unserville: A Unique Visit with Racing Legend Bobby Unser at His Home in Albuquerque*, AUTOWEEK (Sep. 12, 2017), https://www.autoweek.com/racing/indycar/a1830221/inside-unserville-visit-racing-legend-bobby-unser-his-home-albuquerque/.

7. Irv Moss, *Colorado Classics: Bobby Unser "King" of Pikes Peak Hill Climb*, The Denver Post, May 9, 2011, https://www.denverpost.com/2011/05/09/colorado-classics-bobby-unser-king-of-pikes-peak-hill-climb/; *Bobby Unser Celebrating with Champagne*, https://www.gettyimages.com/detail/news-photo/manitou-springs-colo-with-his-son-bobby-r-at-his-side-bobby-news-photo/515175644 (last visited March 14, 2024).

8. United States v. Unser, 165 F.3d 755, 757 (10th Cir. 1999); *Bobby Unser, Friend Survive Wilderness Ordeal—Lost in Mountains, Racing Legend Walks 14 Miles to Safety*, SEATTLE TIMES (Dec. 23, 1996), https://archive.seattletimes.com/archive/?date=19961223&slug=2366545; *Administrative Crimes: Excerpts of Testimony and Questioning of Bobby Unser*, 3 ENV. LAW AND PROP. RIGHTS PRAC. GROUP NEWSL. 1 (1999).

9. United States v. Unser, 165 F.3d 755, 757 (10th Cir. 1999); *Reining In Overcriminalization: Assessing the Problem, Proposing Solutions: Hearing Before the Subcomm. on Crime, Terrorism, and Homeland Sec. of the H. Comm. on the Judiciary*, 111th Cong. 13 (2010) (testimony of Bobby Unser); *Administrative Crimes: Excerpts of Testimony and Questioning of Bobby Unser*, 3 ENV. LAW & PROP. RIGHTS PRAC. GROUP NEWSL. 1 (1999).

10. Rio Grande Foundation, *Bobby Unser Accidental Criminal*, YOUTUBE (May 19, 2016), https://www.youtube.com/watch?v=7dlj9HbIxxU; *see also Implementation of Wilderness Act: Oversight Hearing Before the H. Subcomm. on National Parks and Public Lands and the Subcomm. on Forest and Forest Health*, 105th Cong. 14 (1997) (statement of Bobby Unser).

11. United States v. Unser, 165 F.3d 755, 757 (10th Cir. 1999); *Reining In Overcriminalization: Assessing the Problem, Proposing Solutions: Hearing Before the Subcomm. on Crime, Terrorism, and Homeland Sec. of the H. Comm. on the Judiciary*, 111th Cong. 13 (2010) (testimony of Bobby Unser).

12. *Implementation of Wilderness Act: Oversight Hearing Before the H. Subcomm. on National Parks and Public Lands and the Subcomm. on Forest and Forest Health*, 105th Cong. 14 (1997) (statement of Bobby Unser); *Bobby Unser Survives Snowmobiling*

Ordeal, N.Y. TIMES (Dec. 23, 1996); United States v. Unser, 165 F.3d 755, 757 (10th Cir. 1999).

13. United States v. Unser, 165 F.3d 755, 758 (10th Cir. 1999); *Implementation of Wilderness Act: Oversight Hearing Before the H. Subcomm. on National Parks and Public Lands and the Subcomm. on Forest and Forest Health*, 105th Cong. 14 (1997) (statement of Bobby Unser); *Reining In Overcriminalization: Assessing the Problem, Proposing Solutions: Hearing Before the Subcomm. on Crime, Terrorism, and Homeland Sec. of the H. Comm. on the Judiciary*, 111th Cong. 14 (2010) (testimony of Bobby Unser).

14. United States v. Unser, 165 F.3d 755, 758–59 (10th Cir. 1999); *Implementation of Wilderness Act: Oversight Hearing Before the H. Subcomm. on National Parks and Public Lands and the Subcomm. on Forest and Forest Health*, 105th Cong. 15 (1997) (statement of Bobby Unser).

15. David Wallis, *Bobby Unser, Race Car Champion as Scofflaw*, SALON (June 6, 1997), https://www.salon.com/1997/06/06/news_322/.

16. The Heritage Foundation, *Indy 500 Winner Bobby Unser vs. the U.S. Government*, YOUTUBE (Mar. 11, 2011), https://www.youtube.com/watch?v=UfR4PLNdr_c.

17. United States v. Unser, 165 F.3d 755, 759 (10th Cir. 1999).

18. Wilderness Act, Pub. L. No. 88-577, 78 Stat. 890 (1964); United States v. Unser, 165 F.3d 755, 759 (10th Cir. 1999); *South San Juan Wilderness: San Juan*, U.S. FOREST SERVICE, https://www.fs.usda.gov/recarea/sanjuan/recarea/?recid=81038 (last visited Feb. 4, 2024).

19. *Reining In Overcriminalization: Assessing the Problem, Proposing Solutions: Hearing Before the Subcomm. on Crime, Terrorism, and Homeland Sec. of the H. Comm. on the Judiciary*, 111th Cong. 15 (2010) (testimony of Bobby Unser); *Unser Furious after Being Cited in Snowmobiling Incident*, AP NEWS (Jan. 9, 1997).

20. United States v. Unser, 165 F.3d 755, 757–58, 760–61 (10th Cir. 1999); *Reining In Overcriminalization: Assessing the Problem, Proposing Solutions: Hearing Before the Subcomm. on Crime, Terrorism, and Homeland Sec. of the H. Comm. on the Judiciary*, 111th Cong. 15 (2010) (testimony of Bobby Unser); JN interview with William Pendley.

21. United States v. Unser, 165 F.3d 755, 757, 761, 767 (10th Cir. 1999); Richard Goldstein, *Bobby Unser, Racing Clan's Three-Time Indy 500 Winner, Dies at 87*, N.Y. TIMES (May 3, 2021).

22. The Heritage Foundation, *Indy 500 Winner Bobby Unser vs. the U.S. Government*, YOUTUBE (Mar. 11, 2011), https://www.youtube.com/watch?v=UfR4PLNdr_c.

23. Richard Goldstein, *Bobby Unser, Racing Clan's Three-Time Indy 500 Winner, Dies at 87*, N.Y. TIMES (May 3, 2021), https://www.nytimes.com/2021/05/03/sports /autoracing/bobby-unser-dead.html.

24. Francis A. Allen, *The Morality of Means: Three Problems in Criminal Sanctions*, 42 U. PITT. L. REV. 737, 738 (1981).

25. Herbert Wechsler, *The Challenge of a Model Penal Code*, 65 HARV. L. REV. 1097, 1098 (1952).

26. Henry M. Hart, Jr., *The Aims of the Criminal Law*, 23 L. & CONTEMP. PROBS. 401, 405 (Summer 1958); *see also, e.g.*, Paul Rosenzweig, *The Over-criminalization of Social and Economic Conduct*, THE HERITAGE FOUNDATION (Apr. 17, 2003), https:// www.heritage.org/crime-and-justice/report/the-over-criminalization-social-and -economic-conduct.

27. *Home siding*: James R. Copland & Rafael A. Mangual, *Overcriminalizing America: An Overview and Model Legislation for the States* 5, MANHATTAN INSTITUTE (Aug. 2018), https://media4.manhattan-institute.org/sites/default/files/R-JC-0818.pdf (citing Madeleine Morgenstern, *Minnesota Man Thrown in Jail for . . . Failing to Put Up Siding on His Home*, BLAZE MEDIA (Mar. 21, 2012), https://www.theblaze.com /news/2012/03/21/minnesota-man-thrown-in-jail-for-failing-to-put-up-siding-on -his-home); *Subway arrest*: *Girl Arrested for Eating in Subway*, ABC NEWS (Nov. 16, 2000), https://abcnews.go.com/US/story?id=94999&page=1. *Feeding homeless*: Fort Lauderdale Food Not Bombs v. City of Fort Lauderdale, 11 F.4th 1266, 1274 (2021); Lindsey Bever, *Fort Lauderdale Cracks Down on Feeding Homeless in Public, Arrests 90-Year-Old Man Who Did It Anyway*, WASH. POST (Nov. 5, 2014), https://www

.washingtonpost.com/news/morning-mix/wp/2014/11/05/fort-lauderdale-cracks
-down-on-feeding-homeless-in-public-arrests-90-year-old-man/; *Court Finds Fort
Lauderdale Park Rule Violated Demonstrators' First Amendment Rights, Assigns
Damages in Food Sharing Case*, SOUTHERN LEGAL COUNSEL (Dec. 17, 2021), https://
www.southernlegal.org/news/court-finds-fort-lauderdale-park-rule-violated
-demonstrators-first-amendment-rights-assigns-damages-food-sharing-case.

28. A.M. ex. rel. F.M. v. Holmes, 830 F.3d 1123, 1140 (10th Cir. 2016); *see also* NM Stat §
30-20-13(D) (2018).

29. Henry K. Lee, *San Mateo Pays Family of Boy Pepper-Sprayed by Cop*, SFGATE (Dec. 8,
2011), https://www.sfgate.com/bayarea/article/San-Mateo-pays-family-of-boy-pepper
-sprayed-by-cop-2384518.php; Sara Rimer, *Unruly Students Facing Arrest, Not Detention*, N.Y. TIMES (Jan. 4, 2004), https://www.nytimes.com/2004/01/04/us/unruly
-students-facing-arrest-not-detention.html.

30. DOUGLAS HUSAK, OVERCRIMINALIZATION: THE LIMITS OF THE CRIMINAL LAW 24 (2009).

31. Harvey Silverglate, THREE FELONIES A DAY: HOW THE FEDS TARGET THE INNOCENT
(2009); *see also* L. Gordon Crovitz, *You Commit Three Felonies a Day*, WALL ST. J.
(Sep. 27, 2009), https://www.wsj.com/articles/SB10001424052748704471504574
38900830760842.

32. Crimes Act of 1790, Ch. 9, 1 Stat. 113 (1790); *see also* Gary Fields & John R. Emshwiller,
As Criminal Laws Proliferate, More Are Ensnared, WALL ST. J. (July 23, 2011), https://
www.wsj.com/articles/SB10001424052748703749504576172714184601654.

33. J.A. STRAZZELLA, FEDERALIZATION OF CRIMINAL LAW 7 (1998) (italics removed).

34. This figure derives from a study of laws enacted between 2000 and 2007. John S.
Baker, Jr., *Revisiting the Explosive Growth of Federal Crimes 1*, HERITAGE FOUN-
DATION (June 16, 2008), https://www.heritage.org/report/revisiting-the-explosive
-growth-federal-crimes; *see also Over-criminalization of Conduct/Over-federalization
of Criminal Law: Hearing Before the Subcomm. on Crime, Terrorism, and Homeland
Sec. of the H. Comm. on the Judiciary*, 111th Cong. 3 (2009) (statement of Rep. Louie
Gohmert, Ranking Member); J. Richard Broughton, *Congressional Inquiry and the
Federal Criminal Law*, 46 U. RICH. L. REV. 457, 459–60 (2012).

35. 16 U.S.C. § 551; 36 C.F.R. § 261.16(a) (1999); *see also* 36 C.F.R. § 261.18(a) (2005).

36. John S. Baker, Jr., *Measuring the Explosive Growth of Federal Crime Legislation*, 25
FEDERALIST SOC'Y REV. 2 (2004).

37. Kathleen F. Brickey, *Criminal Mischief: The Federalization of American Criminal
Law*, 46 HASTINGS L. J. 1135, 1146 (1995).

38. Joe Luppino-Esposito, *Criminal Justice Reform Through a Focus on Federalism* in
THE ENFORCEMENT MAZE: OVER-CRIMINALIZING AMERICAN ENTERPRISE 75, U.S.
CHAMBER INSTITUTE FOR LEGAL REFORM & NATIONAL ASSOCIATION OF CRIMINAL
DEFENSE LAWYERS (2018); *see also* William L. Anderson, *Federal Crimes and the De-
struction of Law*, REGULATION, Winter 2009–2010, at 10, 11.

39. *Historical Population Change Date (1910–2020)*, U.S. CENSUS BUREAU (Apr. 26,
2021), https://www.census.gov/data/tables/time-series/dec/popchange-data-text
.html.

40. *"Overcriminalization" Making Us a Nation of Felons?*, CHRISTIAN BROADCASTING
NETWORK (Mar. 29, 2012), https://www1.cbn.com/content/overcriminalization
-making-us-nation-felons (around minute 5); *see also, e.g., Criminal Enforcement
Overview*, U.S. ENVIRONMENTAL PROTECTION AGENCY (July 28, 2023), https://www
.epa.gov/enforcement/criminal-enforcement-overview.

41. *An Overview of the U.S. Department of Education*, U.S. DEPARTMENT OF EDUCATION,
https://www2.ed.gov/about/overview/focus/what.html (last visited Nov. 10, 2022);
Investigation Services, U.S. DEPARTMENT OF EDUCATION, https://www2.ed.gov
/about/offices/list/oig/investpage.html (last visited Nov. 15, 2022).

42. Brian A. Reaves, *Federal Law Enforcement Officers, 2008* 14, U.S. DEPARTMENT OF
JUSTICE (June 2012), https://bjs.ojp.gov/content/pub/pdf/fleo08.pdf.

43. JED S. RAKOFF, WHY THE INNOCENT PLEAD GUILTY AND THE GUILTY GO FREE: AND
OTHER PARADOXES OF OUR BROKEN LEGAL SYSTEM 13 (2021).

44. *Too Many Laws, Too Many Prisoners*, THE ECONOMIST (July 22, 2010), https://
www.economist.com/briefing/2010/07/22/too-many-laws-too-many-prisoners.

45. *A Matter of Time: The Causes and Consequences of Rising Time Served in America's*

Prisons 5, 7, URBAN INSTITUTE (2017), https://apps.urban.org/features/long-prison -terms/intro.html.

46. *Too Many Laws, Too Many Prisoners*, THE ECONOMIST (July 22, 2010), https:// www.economist.com/briefing/2010/07/22/too-many-laws-too-many-prisoners; *No End in Sight: America's Enduring Reliance on Life Imprisonment* 4, 13, 20, THE SENTENCING PROJECT (2021), https://www.sentencingproject.org/publications /no-end-in-sight-americas-enduring-reliance-on-life-imprisonment/; *see also* Marta Nelson, Samuel Feineh, & Maris Mapolski, *A New Paradigm for Sentencing in the United States* 8, VERA INSTITUTE OF JUSTICE (Feb. 2023), https://www.vera.org/down loads/publications/Vera-Sentencing-Report-2023.pdf.

47. HELEN FAIR & ROY WALMSLEY, WORLD PRISON POPULATION LIST (5th ed. 2021).

48. Walter Pavlo, *Statistics Show Federal Bureau of Prisons Unable to Implement Key Policies During Crisis*, FORBES (Feb. 7, 2022), https://www.forbes.com/sites /walterpavlo/2022/02/07/statistics-show-federal-bureau-of-prisons-unable-to -implement-key-policies-during-crisis/?sh=379ca78d7585; Emily Widra, *Since You Asked: Just How Overcrowded Were Prisons Before the Pandemic, and at This Time of Social Distancing, How Overcrowded Are They Now?*, PRISON POLICY INITIATIVE (2020), https://www.prisonpolicy.org/blog/2020/12/21/overcrowding/.

49. *See What Are Collateral Consequences?*, NATIONAL INVENTORY OF COLLATERAL CON- SEQUENCES OF CONVICTION, https://niccc.nationalreentryresourcecenter.org/ (last visited Feb. 4, 2024).

50. David Cole, *As Freedom Advances: The Paradox of Severity in American Criminal Justice*, 3 U. PA. J. CONST. L. 455, 457–58 (2001).

51. E. Ann Carson, *Prisoners in 2021—Statistical Tables* 1, U.S. DEPARTMENT OF JUS- TICE, BUREAU OF JUSTICE STATISTICS (Dec. 2022), https://bjs.ojp.gov/sites/g/files /xyckuh236/files/media/document/p21st.pdf; Rich Kluckow & Zhen Zeng, *Correc- tional Populations in the United States, 2020—Statistical Tables* 1, U.S. DEPARTMENT OF JUSTICE, BUREAU OF JUSTICE STATISTICS (Mar. 2022), https://bjs.ojp.gov/content /pub/pdf/cpus20st.pdf.

52. Rich Kluckow & Zhen Zeng, *Correctional Populations in the United States, 2020— Statistical Tables* 1, U.S. DEPARTMENT OF JUSTICE, BUREAU OF JUSTICE STATISTICS (Mar. 2022), https://bjs.ojp.gov/content/pub/pdf/cpus20st.pdf.

53. TASK FORCE ON THE ADMINISTRATION OF JUSTICE OF THE PRESIDENT'S COMMISSION ON LAW ENFORCEMENT AND ADMINISTRATION OF JUSTICE, TASK FORCE REPORT: THE COURTS 106 (1967).

54. WILLIAM J. STUNTZ, THE COLLAPSE OF AMERICAN CRIMINAL JUSTICE 3 (2011).

55. Michael Tracey, *Police Charged Thousands of People for Petty COVID Violations*, BROWNSTONE INSTITUTE (Nov. 9, 2021), https://brownstone.org/articles/police -charged-thousands-of-people-for-petty-covid-violations/.

56. Arizona v. Mayorkas, 143 S. Ct. 1312, 1314 (2023) (Gorsuch, J., statement).

57. Melissa Chan, *"It's Unenforceable." The Problem with Trying to Police COVID-19 Restrictions*, TIME (Dec. 21, 2020), https://time.com/5921863/police-enforce-covid -restrictions/.

58. TRENT ENGLAND, ANDREW M. GROSSMAN, & ERICA A. LITTLE, *The Unlikely Orchid Smuggler*, in ONE NATION UNDER ARREST: HOW CRAZY LAWS, ROGUE PROSECUTORS, AND ACTIVIST JUDGES THREATEN YOUR LIBERTY 61–65 (Paul Rosenzweig & Brian W. Walsh eds., 2010).

59. *Over-criminalization of Conduct/Over-federalization of Criminal Law: Hearing Before the Subcomm. on Crime, Terrorism, and Homeland Sec. of the H. Comm. on the Judiciary*, 111th Cong. 33–34 (2009) (testimony of Kathy Norris); *Too Many Laws, Too Many Prisoners*, THE ECONOMIST (July 22, 2010), https://www.economist.com /briefing/2010/07/22/too-many-laws-too-many-prisoners.

60. TRENT ENGLAND, ANDREW M. GROSSMAN, & ERICA A. LITTLE, *The Unlikely Orchid Smuggler*, in ONE NATION UNDER ARREST: HOW CRAZY LAWS, ROGUE PROSECUTORS, AND ACTIVIST JUDGES THREATEN YOUR LIBERTY 73–75 (Paul Rosenzweig & Brian W. Walsh eds., 2010).

61. *Over-criminalization of Conduct/Over-federalization of Criminal Law: Hearing Be- fore the Subcomm. on Crime, Terrorism, and Homeland Sec. of the H. Comm. on the Judiciary*, 111th Cong. 35 (2009) (testimony of Kathy Norris).

62. TRENT ENGLAND, ANDREW M. GROSSMAN, & ERICA A. LITTLE, *The Unlikely Orchid Smuggler*, in ONE NATION UNDER ARREST: HOW CRAZY LAWS, ROGUE PROSECU-TORS, AND ACTIVIST JUDGES THREATEN YOUR LIBERTY 61, 76–77 (Paul Rosenzweig & Brian W. Walsh eds., 2010); *Over-criminalization of Conduct/Over-federalization of Criminal Law: Hearing Before the Subcomm. on Crime, Terrorism, and Homeland Sec. of the H. Comm. on the Judiciary*, 111th Cong. 74 (2009) (testimony of Kathy Norris).

63. Morissette v. United States, 342 U.S. 246, 247 (1952); Petition for Writ of Certiorari at 2, Morissette v. United States, 342 U.S. 246 (1952) (No. 593-12); HENRY A. SILVER-GLATE, *Federal Criminal Law: Punishing Benign Intentions—A Betrayal of Professor Hart's Admonition to Prosecute Only the Blameworthy*, in IN THE NAME OF JUSTICE: LEADING EXPERTS REEXAMINE THE CLASSIC ARTICLE "THE AIMS OF THE CRIMINAL LAW" 69–70 (Timothy Lynch ed., 2009).

64. Morissette v. United States, 342 U.S. 246, 247 (1952); Brief in Opposition at 4, Morissette v. United States, 342 U.S. 246 (1952) (No. 593-12); *CPI Inflation Calcula-tor*, BUREAU OF LABOR STATISTICS, https://data.bls.gov/cgi-bin/cpicalc.pl.

65. Morissette v. United States, 342 U.S. 246, 248–63, 275–76 (1952); Petition for Writ of Certiorari at 2, Morissette v. United States, 342 U.S. 246 (1952) (No. 593-12).

66. O.W. HOLMES, JR., THE COMMON LAW 3 (1881).

67. Herbert Wechsler, *American Law Institute. II. A Thoughtful Code of Substantive Law*, 45 J. CRIM. L., CRIMINOLOGY, & POL. SCI. 524, 528 (1955).

68. MODEL PENAL CODE § 2.02 (1962); John C. Coffee, Jr., *Does "Unlawful" Mean "Crim-inal"?: Reflections on the Disappearing Tort/Crime Distinction in American Law*, 71 B. U. L. REV. 193, 210 (1991); *see also* MODEL PENAL CODE § 2.05 (1962).

69. MODEL PENAL CODE §§ 2.02, 2.05 (1962); *see generally* Paul H. Robinson & Markus D. Dubber, *The American Model Penal Code: A Brief Overview*, 10 NEW CRIM. L. REV. 319, 334–36 (2007); Scott England, *Default Culpability Requirements: The Model Penal Code and Beyond*, 99 OR. L. REV. 43, 50 (2020).

70. Francis Bowes Sayre, *Public Welfare Offenses*, 33 COLUM. L. REV. 55, 72 (1933).

71. John C. Coffee, Jr., *Does "Unlawful" Mean "Criminal"?: Reflections on the Disappear-ing Tort/Crime Distinction in American Law*, 71 B.U. L. REV. 193, 198, 216–17 (1991).

72. J. Richard Broughton, *Congressional Inquiry and the Federal Criminal Law*, 46 U. RICH. L. REV. 457, 476 (2012); Brian W. Walsh & Tiffany M. Joslyn, *Without Intent: How Congress Is Eroding the Criminal Intent Requirement in Federal Law* 11, 22, THE HERITAGE FOUNDATION & NATIONAL ASSOCIATION OF CRIMINAL DEFENSE LAWYERS (2010), http://s3.amazonaws.com/thf_media/2010/pdf/WithoutIntent_lo-res.pdf.

73. John C. Coffee, Jr., *Does "Unlawful" Mean "Criminal"?: Reflections on the Disappear-ing Tort/Crime Distinction in American Law*, 71 B.U. L. REV. 193, 198 (1991).

74. Sessions v. Dimaya, 138 S. Ct. 1204, 1224–25 (2018) (Gorsuch, J., concurring in part and concurring in the judgment).

75. FCC v. Fox Television Stations, Inc., 567 U.S. 239, 253 (2012).

76. United States v. Standard Oil Co., 384 U.S. 224, 236 (1966) (Harlan, J., dissenting).

77. *See, e.g.*, Johnson v. United States, 576 U.S. 591, 595–96 (2015).

78. Ronald L. Gainer, *Federal Criminal Code Reform: Past and Future*, 2 BUFF. CRIM. L. REV. 45, 57 (1998).

79. *See, e.g.*, Julie R. O'Sullivan, *The Federal Criminal "Code" Is a Disgrace: Obstruction Statutes as Case Study*, 96 J. CRIM. L. & CRIMINOLOGY 643 (2006).

80. United States v. Wilson, 159 F. 3d 280, 283–84, 288–89 (7th Cir. 1998); *Over-criminalization of Conduct/Over-federalization of Criminal Law: Hearing Before the Subcomm. on Crime, Terrorism, and Homeland Sec. of the H. Comm. on the Judiciary*, 111th Cong. 20-21 (2009) (testimony of Timothy Lynch, Cato Institute).

81. *Over-criminalization of Conduct/Over-federalization of Criminal Law: Hearing Be-fore the Subcomm. on Crime, Terrorism, and Homeland Sec. of the H. Comm. on the Judiciary*, 111th Cong. 21 (2009) (testimony of Timothy Lynch, Cato Institute).

82. Albert B. Crenshaw, *IRS Giving Wrong Answers on 1 Out of 3 Phone Questions*, WASH. POST (Mar. 11, 1989), https://www.washingtonpost.com/archive/business/1989/03/11/irs-giving-wrong-answers-on-1-out-of-3-phone-questions/bd780f24-9772-4e24-8a5e-b8078eb814e2/.

83. *Telephone Performance Measures Do Not Provide an Accurate Assessment of Service to*

Taxpayers 2, fig. 2, TREASURY INSPECTOR GENERAL FOR TAX ADMINISTRATION (June 2, 2019), https://www.tigta.gov/sites/default/files/reports/2022-02/201940041fr.pdf; *Spotlighting IRS Customer Service Challenges: Hearing Before the Comm. on Finance United States Senate*, 117th Cong. 6 (2022) (statement of Erin M. Collins, National Taxpayer Advocate).

84. 18 U.S.C. §§ 1341 & 1346.
85. *See, e.g.*, Sorich v. United States, 555 U.S. 1204, 1206 (2009) (Scalia, J., dissenting from the denial of certiorari) (collecting cases); United States v. Rybicki, 354 F.3d 124, 162–63 (2d Cir. 2003) (Jacobs, J., dissenting) (collecting cases).
86. Transcript of Oral Argument at 30, Black v. United States, 561 U.S. 465 (2010) (No. 08-876); CATO INSTITUTE, CATO HANDBOOK FOR POLICYMAKERS 194 (8th ed. 2017).
87. Black v. United States, 561 U.S. 465 (2010); Skilling v. United States, 561 U.S. 358 (2010).
88. *See* Percoco v. United States, 143 S. Ct. 1130, 1141 (2023) (Gorsuch, J., concurring in the judgment).
89. Dubin v. United States, 143 S. Ct. 1557, 1574 (2023) (Gorsuch, J., concurring in the judgment).
90. Henry M. Hart, Jr., *The Aims of the Criminal Law*, 23 L. & CONTEMP. PROBS. 401, 413–14 (1958).
91. Henry M. Hart, Jr., *The Aims of the Criminal Law*, 23 L. & CONTEMP. PROBS. 401, 419, 423 (1958).
92. *See, e.g.*, United States v. Sheldon, 15 U.S. 119, 121 (1817) (Washington, J.) ("[T]his affords no good reason for construing a penal law by equity, so as to extend it to cases not within the correct and ordinary meaning of the expressions of the law."); United States v. Mann, 26 F. Cas. 1153, 1157 (C.C.D.N.H. 1812) (Story, J.) ("It is a principle grown hoary in age and wisdom, that penal statutes are to be construed strictly, and criminal statutes to be examined with a favorable regard to the accused."); *see also* Amy Coney Barrett, *Substantive Canons and Faithful Agency*, 90 B.U. L. REV. 109, 129–30 nn.90–92 (2010) (collecting cases).
93. Amy Coney Barrett, *Substantive Canons and Faithful Agency*, 90 B.U. L. REV. 109, 128 (2010); David S. Romantz, *Reconstructing the Rule of Lenity*, 40 CARDOZO L. REV. 523, 525, 538 (2018).
94. United States v. Wiltberger, 18 U.S. 76, 77, 93–96, 105 (1820); Robert D. Peltz & Lawrence W. Kaye, *The Long Reach of U.S. Law over Crimes Occurring on the High Seas*, 20 U.S.F. MAR. L. J. 199, 214 (2008) ("Jurisdiction was found not to exist for crimes occurring on a ship in China's Tigris River thirty-five miles from the river's mouth." (citing United States v. Wiltberger, 18 U.S. 76 (1820))).
95. *See, e.g.*, United States v. Wiltberger, 18 U.S. 76, 95–96, 105 (1820); Wooden v. United States, 142 S. Ct. 1063, 1084–85 (2022) (Gorsuch, J., concurring).
96. Muscarello v. United States, 524 U.S. 125, 126 (1998) (emphasis added) (quoting 18 U.S.C. § 924(c)(1)).
97. Muscarello v. United States, 524 U.S. 125, 127–28, 130–31, 138–39 (1998).
98. David Amsden, *The Brilliant Life and Tragic Death of Aaron Swartz*, ROLLING STONE (Feb. 15, 2013), https://www.rollingstone.com/culture/culture-news/the-brilliant-life-and-tragic-death-of-aaron-swartz-177191/; Elizabeth Day, *Aaron Swartz: Hacker, Genius . . . Martyr?*, GUARDIAN (June 1, 2013), https://www.theguardian.com/technology/2013/jun/02/aaron-swartz-hacker-genius-martyr-girlfriend-interview.
99. David Amsden, *The Brilliant Life and Tragic Death of Aaron Swartz*, ROLLING STONE (Feb. 15, 2013), https://www.rollingstone.com/culture/culture-news/the-brilliant-life-and-tragic-death-of-aaron-swartz-177191/; John Schwartz, *An Effort to Upgrade a Court Archive System to Free and Easy*, N.Y. TIMES (Feb. 12, 2009), https://www.nytimes.com/2009/02/13/us/13records.html.
100. *JSTOR Evidence in United States vs. Aaron Swartz, Summary of Events*, JSTOR (July 30, 2013), https://docs.jstor.org/summary.html; David Amsden, *The Brilliant Life and Tragic Death of Aaron Swartz*, ROLLING STONE (Feb. 15, 2013), https://www.rollingstone.com/culture/culture-news/the-brilliant-life-and-tragic-death-of-aaron-swartz-177191/.
101. Marcella Bombardieri, *The Inside Story of MIT and Aaron Swartz*, BOSTON GLOBE (Mar. 30, 2014), https://www3.bostonglobe.com/metro/2014/03/29/the-inside-story-mit-and-aaron-swartz/YvJZ5P6VHaPJusReuaN7SI/story.html?arc404=true.

102. Marcella Bombardieri, *The Inside Story of MIT and Aaron Swartz*, BOSTON GLOBE (Mar. 30, 2014), https://www3.bostonglobe.com/metro/2014/03/29/the-inside-story -mit-and-aaron-swartz/YvJZ5P6VHaPJusReuaN7SI/story.html?arc404=true; Elizabeth Day, *Aaron Swartz: Hacker, Genius . . . Martyr?*, GUARDIAN (June 1, 2013), https://www .theguardian.com/technology/2013/jun/02/aaron-swartz-hacker-genius-martyr-girl friend-interview.

103. *JSTOR Evidence in United States vs. Aaron Swartz, Summary of Events*, JSTOR (July 30, 2013), https://docs.jstor.org/summary.html.

104. Indictment of Aaron Swartz at ¶¶ 34–37, United States v. Swartz, No. 11-CR-10260-NMG (D. Mass. July 14, 2011). The state filed its own charges but later dropped them. *State Drops Charges Against Swartz; Federal Charges Remain*, THE TECH (Mar. 16, 2012), https://thetech.com/2012/03/16/swartz-v132-n12.

105. Larissa MacFarquhar, *Requiem for a Dream*, NEW YORKER (Mar. 3, 2013), https:// www.newyorker.com/magazine/2013/03/11/requiem-for-a-dream; Letter from Elliot R. Peters to Robin C. Ashton, *Re: United States v. Aaron Swartz* (Jan. 28, 2013) (on file with the authors).

106. David Amsden, *The Brilliant Life and Tragic Death of Aaron Swartz*, ROLLING STONE (Feb. 15, 2013), https://www.rollingstone.com/culture/culture-news/the-brilliant-life -and-tragic-death-of-aaron-swartz-177191/.

107. Michael Daly, *Aaron Swartz's Unbending Prosecutors Insisted on Prison Time*, DAILY BEAST (July 12, 2017), https://www.thedailybeast.com/aaron-swartzs-unbending -prosecutors-insisted-on-prison-time; Elizabeth Day, *Aaron Swartz: Hacker, Genius . . . Martyr?*, GUARDIAN (June 1, 2013), https://www.theguardian.com/technology/2013 /jun/02/aaron-swartz-hacker-genius-martyr-girlfriend-interview.

108. *Superseding Indictment of Aaron Swartz*, WIRED (Sep. 12, 2012), https://www.wired .com/images_blogs/threatlevel/2012/09/swartzsuperseding.pdf; Noam Cohen, *A Data Crusader, a Defendant and Now, a Cause*, N.Y. TIMES (Jan 13, 2013), https:// www.nytimes.com/2013/01/14/technology/aaron-swartz-a-data-crusader-and -now-a-cause.html.

109. Larissa MacFarquhar, *Requiem for a Dream*, NEW YORKER (Mar. 3, 2013), https:// www.newyorker.com/magazine/2013/03/11/requiem-for-a-dream.

110. Elizabeth Day, *Aaron Swartz: Hacker, Genius . . . Martyr?*, GUARDIAN (June 1, 2013), https://www.theguardian.com/technology/2013/jun/02/aaron-swartz-hacker -genius-martyr-girlfriend-interview.

111. Owen Thomas, *Family of Aaron Swartz Blames MIT, Prosecutors for His Death*, INSIDER (Jan. 12, 2013), https://www.businessinsider.com/statement-family-aaron -swartz-2013-1.

112. *Prosecutor Ortiz Defends Charges Against Swartz*, WBUR (Jan. 16, 2013), https:// www.wbur.org/news/2013/01/16/ortiz-aaron-swartz-statement.

113. Lawrence Lessig, *Prosecutor as Bully*, LESSIG BLOG, https://lessig.tumblr.com /post/40347463044/prosecutor-as-bully (last visited Feb. 12, 2023).

114. Clare Garvie, Alvaro M. Bedoya, & Jonathan Frankle, *The Perpetual Line-up: Unregulated Police Face Recognition in America* 2, GEORGETOWN LAW CENTER ON PRIVACY AND TECHNOLOGY (Oct. 18, 2016), https://www.perpetuallineup.org/sites/default /files/2016-12/The%20Perpetual%20Line-Up%20-%20Center%20on%20Privacy %20and%20Technology%20at%20Georgetown%20Law%20-%20121616.pdf.

115. *Curbside trash*: California v. Greenwood, 486 U.S. 35, 37 (1988). *Bank records, medical records, DNA*: *See, e.g.*, Carpenter v. United States, 138 S. Ct. 2206, 2262 (2018) (Gorsuch, J., dissenting); Ferguson v. City of Charleston, 532 U.S. 67, 78 n.13 (2001) (declining to decide whether the Fourth Amendment protects "circumstances in which state hospital employees, like other citizens, may have a duty to provide law enforcement officials with evidence of criminal conduct acquired in the course of routine treatment"); United States v. Miller, 425 U.S. 435, 437 (1976) (bank records); Maryland v. King, 569 U.S. 435, 440 (2013) (DNA). Post-*Carpenter*, several lower courts have found that there is no reasonable expectation of privacy in some, though perhaps not all, medical records. *See, e.g.*, United States Department of Justice v. Ricco Jonas, 24 F.4th 718, 734–40 (1st Cir. 2022) (finding that there is no reasonable expectation of privacy in one's prescription drug records); United States v. Motley, 443 F. Supp. 3d 1203, 1210–15 (D. Nev. 2020)

(same); United States v. Grant, No. 18-cr-00391-EMC-1, 2020 U.S. Dist. LEXIS 27270, at *7–11 (N.D. Cal. Feb. 18, 2020) (finding that there is no reasonable expectation of privacy in VA medical records). *Backyard helicopter*: Florida v. Riley, 488 U.S. 445, 448 (1989).

116. Carpenter v. United States, 138 S. Ct. 2206, 2262 (2018) (Gorsuch, J., dissenting) (citing Katz v. United States, 389 U. S. 347, 361 (1967) (Harlan, J., concurring)).

117. UNITED STATES SENTENCING COMMISSION, 2022 ANNUAL REPORT AND SOURCEBOOK OF FEDERAL SENTENCING STATISTICS 56 (2023) (federal); SEAN ROSENMERKEL, MATTHEW DUROSE, & DONALD FAROLE, JR., *Felony Sentences in State Courts, 2006—Statistical Tables* 1, BUREAU OF JUSTICE STATISTICS, https://bjs.ojp.gov /content/pub/pdf/fssc06st.pdf (last updated Nov. 2010) (state); *see also* Susan R. Klein, Aleza S. Remis, & Donna Lee Elm, *Waiving the Criminal Justice System: An Empirical and Constitutional Analysis*, 52 AM. CRIM. L. REV. 73, 75 (2015); Anna Offit, *Prosecuting in the Shadow of the Jury*, 113 NW. U. L. REV. 1071, 1075 (2019) (citing VICTOR E. FLANGO & THOMAS M. CLARKE, REIMAGINING COURTS: A DESIGN FOR THE TWENTY-FIRST CENTURY 68 tbl.4a1, 69 tbl.4a2 (2015) (survey of fifteen state jurisdictions revealing that only 1.1 percent of criminal cases were resolved by trial in 2009)).

118. Albert Alschuler, *Plea Bargaining and Its History*, 79 COLUM. L. REV. 1, 4–6 (1979).

119. Ronald F. Wright, *Trial Distortion and the End of Innocence in Federal Criminal Justice*, 154 U. PA. L. REV. 79, 84 (2005).

120. NATIONAL ASSOCIATION OF CRIMINAL DEFENSE LAWYERS, THE TRIAL PENALTY: THE SIXTH AMENDMENT RIGHT TO TRIAL ON THE VERGE OF EXTINCTION AND HOW TO SAVE IT 20 (2018).

121. Statement of Reasons, United States v. Kupa, 976 F. Supp. 2d 417, 420 (E.D.N.Y. 2013); *see also An Offer You Can't Refuse*, HUMAN RIGHTS WATCH (Dec. 5, 2013), https://www.hrw.org/report/2013/12/05/offer-you-cant-refuse/how-us-federal -prosecutors-force-drug-defendants-plead.

122. *See, e.g.*, Tim Lynch, *The Devil's Bargain: How Plea Agreements, Never Contemplated by the Framers, Undermine Justice*, CATO INSTITUTE (June 24, 2011), https://www .cato.org/commentary/devils-bargain-how-plea-agreements-never-contemplated -framers-undermine-justice ("From the government's perspective, plea bargaining has two advantages. First, it's less expensive and time-consuming than jury trials, which means prosecutors can haul more people into court and legislators can add more offenses to the criminal code. Second, by cutting the jury out of the picture, prosecutors and judges acquire more influence over case outcomes.").

123. Bordenkircher v. Hayes, 434 U.S. 357, 358–59, 359 & n.3, 361–62 (1978) (internal citation omitted).

124. WILLIAM J. STUNTZ, THE COLLAPSE OF AMERICAN CRIMINAL JUSTICE 260 (2011).

125. *Letter from Thomas Jefferson to Thomas Paine, 11 July 1789*, NATIONAL ARCHIVES, https://founders.archives.gov/documents/Jefferson/01-15-02-0259.

126. *Crown v. John Peter Zenger, 1735*, HISTORICAL SOCIETY OF THE NEW YORK COURTS, https://history.nycourts.gov/case/crown-v-zenger/ (last visited Feb. 4, 2024); Walker Lewis, *The Right to Complain: The Trial of John Peter Zenger*, 46 AM. BAR ASS'N J. 27, 28 (1960); Arthur E. Sutherland, *A Brief Narrative of the Case and Trial of John Peter Zenger*, 77 HARV. L. REV. 787 (1964); John R. Vile, *John Peter Zenger*, THE FIRST AMENDMENT ENCYCLOPEDIA, https://www.mtsu.edu/first-amendment/article/1235 /john-peter-zenger (last visited Sep. 19, 2023).

127. *Crown v. John Peter Zenger, 1735*, HISTORICAL SOCIETY OF THE NEW YORK COURTS, https://history.nycourts.gov/case/crown-v-zenger/ (last visited Feb. 4, 2024); Walker Lewis, *The Right to Complain: The Trial of John Peter Zenger*, 46 AM. BAR ASS'N J. 27, 28 (1960); Jon P. McClanahan, *The "True" Right to Trial by Jury: The Founders' Formulation and Its Demise*, 111 W. VA. L. REV. 791, 800 (2009); Arthur E. Sutherland, *A Brief Narrative of the Case and Trial of John Peter Zenger*, 77 HARV. L. REV. 787 (1964).

128. *Crown v. John Peter Zenger, 1735*, HISTORICAL SOCIETY OF THE NEW YORK COURTS, https://history.nycourts.gov/case/crown-v-zenger/ (last visited Feb. 4, 2024); Jon P. McClanahan, *The "True" Right to Trial by Jury: The Founders' Formulation and Its Demise*, 111 W. VA. L. REV. 791, 800 (2009); Arthur E. Sutherland, *A Brief Narrative of the Case and Trial of John Peter Zenger by James Alexander*, 77 HARV. L. REV. 787

(1964); *see also* Walker Lewis, *The Right to Complain: The Trial of John Peter Zenger*, 46 AM. BAR ASS'N J. 27, 30 (1960).

129. *Crown v. John Peter Zenger, 1735*, HISTORICAL SOCIETY OF THE NEW YORK COURTS, https://history.nycourts.gov/case/crown-v-zenger/ (last visited Feb. 4, 2024).

130. *Crown v. John Peter Zenger, 1735*, HISTORICAL SOCIETY OF THE NEW YORK COURTS, https://history.nycourts.gov/case/crown-v-zenger/ (last visited Feb. 4, 2024); Arthur E. Sutherland, *A Brief Narrative of the Case and Trial of John Peter Zenger by James Alexander*, 77 HARV. L. REV. 787, 788 (1964).

131. Olmstead v. United States, 277 U.S. 438, 479 (1928) (Brandeis, J., dissenting), *overruled by* Katz v. United States, 389 U.S. 347 (1967).

CHAPTER 5: THE FORGOTTEN AMERICANS

1. JEAN PIAGET, THE MORAL JUDGMENT OF THE CHILD 189 (1932).
2. STEVEN M. NOLT, A HISTORY OF THE AMISH 56, 63 (3d ed. 2015).
3. MENNONITE FAMILY HISTORY 6 (2019); *see also* JOHN A. HOSTETLER, AMISH SOCIETY 60–61 (4th ed. 1993); STEVEN M. NOLT, A HISTORY OF THE AMISH 56 (3d ed. 2015).
4. STEVEN M. NOLT, A HISTORY OF THE AMISH 56 (3d ed. 2015).
5. PENNSYLVANIA CHARTER OF PRIVILEGES art I. (1701); STEVEN M. NOLT, A HISTORY OF THE AMISH 63–64 (3d ed. 2015).
6. STEVEN M. NOLT, A HISTORY OF THE AMISH 9–12, 40–42, chapter 3 (3d ed. 2015).
7. DONALD B. KRAYBILL, KAREN M. JOHNSON-WEINER, & STEVEN M. NOLT, THE AMISH 24–35 (2013).
8. DONALD B. KRAYBILL, KAREN M. JOHNSON-WEINER, & STEVEN M. NOLT, THE AMISH 356–57 (2013); STEVEN M. NOLT, A HISTORY OF THE AMISH 289–92 (3d ed. 2015).
9. Wisconsin v. Yoder, 406 U.S. 205, 223–24 (1972).
10. Mast v. Fillmore County, 141 S. Ct. 2430, 2430–31 (2021) (Gorsuch, J., concurring in the decision to grant, vacate, and remand).
11. Mast v. Fillmore County, 141 S. Ct. 2430, 2431 (2021) (Gorsuch, J., concurring in the decision to grant, vacate, and remand); DONALD B. KRAYBILL, KAREN M. JOHNSON-WEINER, & STEVEN M. NOLT, THE AMISH 146–47 (2013).
12. STEVEN M. NOLT, A HISTORY OF THE AMISH 267 (3d ed. 2015).
13. Findings of Fact, Conclusions of Law, Order for Judgment, and Judgment at 25, Mast v. County of Fillmore, No. 23-CV-17-351 (Minn. Dist. Ct. Apr. 22, 2019) (No. 23-CV-17-351); DONALD B. KRAYBILL, KAREN M. JOHNSON-WEINER, & STEVEN M. NOLT, THE AMISH 282–83 (2013); Karen M. Johnson-Weiner, *Technological Diversity and Cultural Change Among Contemporary Amish Groups*, 88 MENNONITE Q. REV. 5–8, 12–13 (2014).
14. Karen M. Johnson-Weiner, *Technological Diversity and Cultural Change Among Contemporary Amish Groups*, 88 MENNONITE Q. REV. 5, 8 (2014).
15. Findings and Order for Temporary Injunction at 2, County of Fillmore v. Mast (Minn. Dist. Ct. Nov. 29, 2016) (No. 23-CV-16-658); Defendant's Memorandum of Law in Opposition to Plaintiff's Motion for Temporary Restraining Order at 2, 7, County of Fillmore v. Mast (Minn. Dist. Ct. Oct. 28, 2016) (No. 23-CV-16-658).
16. Mast v. Fillmore County, 141 S. Ct. 2430, 2431 (2021) (Gorsuch, J., concurring in the decision to grant, vacate, and remand); Stipulation and Order at 2, County of Fillmore v. Mast (Minn. Dist. Ct. Sep. 20, 2017) (No. 23-CV-16-658); Findings and Order for Temporary Injunction at 2, County of Fillmore v. Mast (Minn. Dist. Ct. Nov. 29, 2016) (No. 23-CV-16-658); Complaint, County of Fillmore v. Mast (Minn. Dist. Ct. Sep. 29, 2016) (No. 23-CV-16-658).
17. Mast v. Fillmore County, 141 S. Ct. 2430, 2431 (2021) (Gorsuch, J., concurring in the decision to grant, vacate, and remand); Appellant's Brief and Addendum at 11–12, Mast v. County of Fillmore (Minn. Ct. App. Dec. 20, 2019) (No. A19-1375).
18. MINN. R. 7080.1500, subp. 2 (2013); Mast v. Fillmore County, 141 S. Ct. 2430, 2432 (2021) (Gorsuch, J., concurring in the decision to grant, vacate, and remand); *see also* Plaintiffs' Proposed Amended and Additional Findings and Conclusions, and Memorandum in Support of Motion for New Trial at 2–3, Mast v. County of Fillmore (Minn. Dist. Ct. May 21, 2019) (No. 23-CV-17-351).
19. Exhibit G, Letter from Michael P. Frauenkron, Fillmore County Feedlot Officer (June 24, 2015), attached to Complaint, County of Fillmore v. Mast (Minn. Dist. Ct. Sep. 29,

2016) (No. 23-CV-16-658); Exhibit L, Letter from Brett A. Corson, Fillmore County Attorney, to Amos Mast and Mattie Mast at 1 (Sep. 22, 2016), attached to Amended Complaint, County of Fillmore v. Mast (Minn. Dist. Ct. July 19, 2017) (No. 23-CV-16-658); Complaint at 5–10, County of Fillmore v. Mast (Minn. Dist. Ct. Sep. 29, 2016) (No. 23-CV-16-658).

20. Defendant's Memorandum of Law in Opposition to Plaintiff's Motion for Temporary Restraining Order at 2–4, 7, County of Fillmore v. Mast (Minn. Dist. Ct. Oct. 28, 2016) (No. 23-CV-16-658); Complaint at 8, County of Fillmore v. Mast (Minn. Dist. Ct. Sep. 29, 2016) (No. 23-CV-16-658).

21. Petition for Writ of Certiorari at 9–11, Mast v. Fillmore County, 141 S. Ct. 2430 (2021) (No. 20-7028).

22. Mast v. Fillmore County, 141 S. Ct. 2430, 2431 (2021) (Gorsuch, J., concurring in the decision to grant, vacate, and remand); Answer and Counterclaim at 5–11, Swartzentruber v. Minnesota Pollution Control Agency (Minn. Dist. Ct. Apr. 27, 2017) (No. 62-CV-17-2033).

23. Petition for Writ of Certiorari at 11, Mast v. Fillmore County, 141 S. Ct. 2430 (2021) (No. 20-7028); Findings of Fact, Conclusions of Law, Order for Judgment, and Judgment at 25–27, 33–34, Mast v. Fillmore County (Minn. Dist. Ct. Apr. 23, 2019) (No. 23-CV-17-351).

24. Mast v. Fillmore County, 141 S. Ct. 2430, 2431 (2021) (Gorsuch, J., concurring in the decision to grant, vacate, and remand); Trial Court Transcript of Nov. 26, 2018 Hearing on Petitioner's Motion for Amended Findings and for a New Trial at 178, Mast v. Fillmore County (Minn. Dist. Ct. Nov. 26, 2018) (No. 23-CV-17-351).

25. Mast v. Fillmore County, 141 S. Ct. 2430, 2430 (2021) (remanding to the Minnesota Court of Appeals); Order, Mast v. Fillmore County (Minn. Ct. App. Aug. 21, 2021) (No. 23-CV-17-351) (remanding to state district court); Findings of Fact, Conclusions of Law, Order for Judgment, and Judgment at 1, 5, Mast v. Fillmore County (Minn. Dist. Ct. Sep. 7, 2022) (No. 23-CV-17-351); Opinion, Mast v. Fillmore County, State of Minnesota Court of Appeals (Minn. Ct. App. July 10, 2023) (No. 23-CV-17-351).

26. JAY COST, JAMES MADISON: AMERICA'S FIRST POLITICIAN 17–19, 24 (2021).

27. JAY COST, JAMES MADISON: AMERICA'S FIRST POLITICIAN 1, 17, 26–27, 75–86, 172, 344 (2021); JOSEPH NATHAN KANE, FACTS ABOUT THE PRESIDENTS: A COMPILATION OF BIOGRAPHICAL AND HISTORICAL INFORMATION 344 (6th ed. 1993); *see also Virginia Plan (1787)*, NATIONAL ARCHIVES, https://www.archives.gov/milestone-documents/virginia-plan (last visited May 10, 2022).

28. *See* EDWARD J. LARSON & MICHAEL P. WINSHIP, THE CONSTITUTIONAL CONVENTION: A NARRATIVE HISTORY FROM THE NOTES OF JAMES MADISON 9–10 (2005).

29. RON CHERNOW, WASHINGTON: A LIFE 566 (2010); JAY COST, JAMES MADISON: AMERICA'S FIRST POLITICIAN 178 (2021).

30. *Vices of the Political System of the United States, April 1787*, NATIONAL ARCHIVES, https://founders.archives.gov/documents/Madison/01-09-02-0187 (last visited June 16, 2022).

31. *The Federalist* No. 62 (probably James Madison), in THE FEDERALIST PAPERS 382 (Clinton Rossiter ed., 1961).

32. OFFICE OF MANAGEMENT AND BUDGET, INFORMATION COLLECTION BUDGET OF THE UNITED STATES GOVERNMENT 2 (2016); Cass R. Sunstein, *Sludge and Ordeals*, 68 DUKE L. J. 1843, 1847 (2019).

33. Cass R. Sunstein, *Sludge and Ordeals*, 68 DUKE L. J. 1843, 1848–50, 1859 (2019).

34. *See, e.g.*, BRUCE CANNON GIBNEY, THE NONSENSE FACTORY: THE MAKING AND BREAKING OF THE AMERICAN LEGAL SYSTEM 126 (2019) (citing John D. Graham & James W. Broughel, *Stealth Regulation: Addressing Agency Evasion of OIRA and the Administrative Procedure Act*, 1 HARV. J. L. & PUB. POL'Y: FEDERALIST EDITION 30, 39–40 (2014)); Nicholas R. Parrillo, *Federal Agency Guidance and the Power to Bind: An Empirical Study of Agencies and Industries*, 36 YALE J. ON REGUL. 165, 174 (2019).

35. De Niz Robles v. Lynch, 803 F.3d 1165 (10th Cir. 2015); In re Robles, No. A074 577 772, 2014 WL 3889484 at *1 (B.I.A. July 11, 2014).

36. Padilla–Caldera v. Gonzales, 426 F.3d 1294, 1300–01 (10th Cir.2005), *amended and superseded on reh'g*, 453 F.3d 1237, 1244 (10th Cir.2006); *see also* De Niz Robles v. Lynch, 803 F.3d 1165, 1167 (10th Cir. 2015).

37. De Niz Robles v. Lynch, 803 F.3d 1165, 1167, 1178 (10th Cir. 2015); In re Robles, No. A074 577 772, 2014 WL 3889484 at *1–2, *4 (B.I.A. July 11, 2014).
38. Jill Lepore, *The History Test: How Should the Courts Use History?*, NEW YORKER (Mar. 20, 2017), https://www.newyorker.com/magazine/2017/03/27/weaponizing-the-past.
39. De Niz Robles v. Lynch, 803 F.3d 1165 (10th Cir. 2015); *see also* In re Robles, No. A074 577 772, 2016 WL 1722529 at *1 (B.I.A. Mar. 31, 2016) (remanding to the immigration judge for entry of a new decision).
40. Jill Lepore, *The History Test: How Should the Courts Use History?*, NEW YORKER (Mar. 20, 2017), https://www.newyorker.com/magazine/2017/03/27/weaponizing-the-past.
41. Steve Eder, *When Picking Apples on a Farm with 5,000 Rules, Watch Out for the Ladders*, N.Y. TIMES (Dec. 27, 2017), https://www.nytimes.com/2017/12/27/business/picking-apples-on-a-farm-with-5000-rules-watch-out-for-the-ladders.html; see also PHILIP K. HOWARD, TRY COMMON SENSE: REPLACING THE FAILED IDEOLOGIES OF RIGHT AND LEFT 20 (2019).
42. CHARLES B. SWARTWOOD, III, REPORT AND RECOMMENDATION OF THE SPECIAL MASTER CONCERNING NOAA ENFORCEMENT ACTION OF CERTAIN DESIGNATED CASES 232 (Apr. 2011).
43. U.S. DEPARTMENT OF COMMERCE, NATIONAL OCEANIC AND ATMOSPHERIC ADMINISTRATION, 2010 FINAL REPORT ON THE PERFORMANCE OF THE NORTHEAST MULTISPECIES (GROUNDFISH) FISHERY (MAY 2010–APRIL 2011) viii, 26–27, 30 (2011); U.S. DEPARTMENT OF COMMERCE, OFFICE OF THE INSPECTOR GENERAL, NATIONAL OCEANIC AND ATMOSPHERIC ADMINISTRATION, REVIEW OF NOAA FISHERIES ENFORCEMENT PROGRAMS AND OPERATIONS 9 (2010); Anne H. Beaudreau et al., *Thirty Years of Change and the Future of Alaskan Fisheries: Shifts in Fishing Participation and Diversification in Response to Environmental, Regulatory and Economic Pressures*, 20 FISH & FISHERIES 608 (2019); Claire Kelloway, *Catch Shares Lead to Consolidation of Alaskan Fisheries*, FERN (May 28, 2019), https://thefern.org/ag_insider/catch-shares-lead-to-consolidation-of-alaskan-fisheries/.
44. Susanne Rust, *System Turns US Fishing Rights into Commodity, Squeezes Small Fishermen*, REVEAL NEWS (Mar. 12, 2013), https://revealnews.org/article/system-turns-us-fishing-rights-into-commodity-squeezes-small-fishermen/; *see also* Pacific Coast Federation of Fishermen's Associations v. Blank, 693 F.3d 1084, 1086 (9th Cir. 2012) (featuring fishermen's associations arguing that new regulations disadvantage them).
45. *Expediting Economic Growth: How Streamlining Federal Permitting Can Cut Red Tape for Small Businesses: Hearing Before the H. Comm. on Small Business*, 115th Cong. 5 (Sep. 6, 2017) (statement of Philip K. Howard, Chair, Common Good); NICOLE V. CRAIN & W. MARK CRAIN, THE IMPACT OF REGULATORY COSTS ON SMALL FIRMS iv (2010).
46. *See, e.g.*, W. MARK CRAIN & NICOLE V. CRAIN, THE COST OF FEDERAL REGULATION TO THE U.S. ECONOMY, MANUFACTURING AND SMALL BUSINESS 1 (2014); Chris Edwards, *Entrepreneurs and Regulations: Removing State and Local Barriers to New Businesses* 7–10, CATO INSTITUTE (May 5, 2021), https://www.cato.org/sites/cato.org/files/2021-05/pa-916.pdf; Michael Hendrix, *Regulations Impact Small Business and the Heart of America's Economy*, U.S. CHAMBER OF COMMERCE FOUNDATION (Mar. 14, 2017).
47. *2017 NSBA Small Business Regulations Survey* 14, NATIONAL SMALL BUSINESS ASSOCIATION (2017), https://docs.house.gov/meetings/SM/SM00/20170215/105571/HHRG-115-SM00-Bio-ReynoldsT-20170215.pdf.
48. James Kwak, *The End of Small Business*, WASH. POST (July 9, 2020), https://www.washingtonpost.com/outlook/2020/07/09/after-covid-19-giant-corporations-chains-may-be-only-ones-left/; *see also* Gustavo Grullon et al., *Are US Industries Becoming More Concentrated?*, 23 REV. FIN. 697, 698 (2019) (finding, among other things, that "the market share of the four largest [U.S.] public and private firms has grown significantly for most industries, and both the average and median sizes of public firms, that is, the largest players in the economy, have tripled in real terms").
49. OFFICE OF MANAGEMENT AND BUDGET, OFFICE OF INFORMATION AND REGULATORY AFFAIRS, 2018, 2019, AND 2020 REPORT TO CONGRESS ON THE BENEFITS AND COSTS OF FEDERAL REGULATIONS AND AGENCY COMPLIANCE WITH THE UNFUNDED MANDATES REFORM ACT 23 (2021).

50. Nora Esposito, *Small Business Facts: Spotlight on Minority-Owned Employer Businesses*, U.S. SMALL BUSINESS ADMINISTRATION, OFFICE OF ADVOCACY (May 23, 2019), https://advocacy.sba.gov/2019/05/23/small-business-facts-spotlight-on-minority-owned-employer-businesses/; Camilo Mondragón-Vélez, *How Does Middle-Class Financial Health Affect Entrepreneurship in America?*, CENTER FOR AMERICAN PROGRESS (May 21, 2015), https://www.americanprogress.org/wp-content/uploads/sites/2/2015/05/MiddleClassEntrepreneurs-5.7.pdf.

51. Mike Lee, *Fighting Regulatory Capture in the 21st Century*, THE REGULATORY REVIEW (June 16, 2016), https://www.theregreview.org/2016/06/16/lee-fighting-regulatory-capture-in-the-21st-century.

52. George J. Stigler, *The Theory of Economic Regulation*, 2 BELL J. ECON. & MGMT. SCI. 3, 10–13 (1971); *see also* Susan E. Dudley, *Let's Not Forget George Stigler's Lessons About Regulatory Capture*, PROMARKET (May 20, 2021), https://www.promarket.org/2021/05/20/george-stiglers-lesson-regulatory-capture-rent-seeking.

53. *See, e.g.*, Steven M. Teles, *Kludgeocracy in America*, NATIONAL AFFAIRS (Fall 2013), https://www.nationalaffairs.com/publications/detail/kludgeocracy-in-america.

54. Douglas Ginsburg, *A New Economic Theory of Regulation: Rent Extraction Rather than Rent Creation*, 97 MICH. L. REV. 1771, 1772–73 (1999).

55. St. Joseph Abbey v. Castille, 712 F.3d 215, 217–18 (5th Cir. 2013); Jennifer Levitz, *Coffins Made with Brotherly Love Have Undertakers Throwing Dirt*, WALL ST. J. (Aug. 25, 2010), https://www.wsj.com/articles/SB10001424052748703846604575448083489852328; JN interview with Abbot Justin Brown and Deacon Mark Coudrain.

56. LOUISIANA STATE BOARD OF EMBALMERS & FUNERAL DIRECTORS, https://www.lsbefd.state.la.us (last visited Mar. 15, 2023).

57. Jennifer Levitz, *Coffins Made with Brotherly Love Have Undertakers Throwing Dirt*, WALL ST. J. (Aug. 25, 2010), https://www.wsj.com/articles/SB10001424052748703846604575448083489852328; JN interview with Scott Bullock.

58. St. Joseph Abbey v. Castille, 712 F.3d 215, 218 (5th Cir. 2013); Jennifer Levitz, *Coffins Made with Brotherly Love Have Undertakers Throwing Dirt*, WALL ST. J. (Aug. 25, 2010), https://www.wsj.com/articles/SB10001424052748703846604575448083489852328; Letter from Michael H. Rasch, General Counsel, Louisiana State Board of Embalmers and Funeral Directors, to Justin Brown, Abbott, St. Joseph Abbey, and Mark Coudrain, Deacon, St. Joseph Abbey (Dec. 11, 2007) (on file with authors); JN interview with Abbot Justin Brown and Deacon Mark Coudrain.

59. Jennifer Levitz, *Coffins Made with Brotherly Love Have Undertakers Throwing Dirt*, WALL ST. J. (Aug. 25, 2010), https://www.wsj.com/articles/SB10001424052748703846604575448083489852328.

60. St. Joseph Abbey v. Castille, 712 F.3d 215, 219 (5th Cir. 2013); Brief of Appellees at 14, St. Joseph Abbey v. Castille, 712 F.3d 215 (5th Cir. 2013) (No. 11–30756); Jennifer Levitz, *Coffins Made with Brotherly Love Have Undertakers Throwing Dirt*, WALL ST. J. (Aug. 25, 2010), https://www.wsj.com/articles/SB10001424052748703846604575448083489852328; JN interview with Abbot Justin Brown and Deacon Mark Coudrain.

61. Jennifer Levitz, *Coffins Made with Brotherly Love Have Undertakers Throwing Dirt*, WALL ST. J. (Aug. 25, 2010), https://www.wsj.com/articles/SB10001424052748703846604575448083489852328; JN interview with Abbot Justin Brown and Deacon Mark Coudrain.

62. St. Joseph Abbey v. Castille, 712 F.3d 215, 227 (5th Cir. 2013).

63. KANSAS BAR ASSOCIATION, A FLASH REPORT ON THE 2017 ECONOMICS OF LAW PRACTICE SURVEY IN KANSAS 16 (2017); Roy Strom, *Big Law Rates Topping $2,000 Leave Value "In Eye of Beholder,"* BLOOMBERG LAW (June 9, 2022), https://news.bloomberglaw.com/business-and-practice/big-law-rates-topping-2-000-leave-value-in-eye-of-beholder.

64. Paula Hannaford-Agor, *Measuring the Cost of Civil Litigation: Findings from a Survey of Trial Lawyers*, VOIR DIRE, Spring 2013, at 22, 26 fig. 3; *Income in the United States: 2021*, U.S. CENSUS BUREAU (Sep. 13, 2022), https://www.census.gov/library/publications/2022/demo/p60-276.html#:~:text=Real%20median%20household%20income%20was,and%20Table%20A%2D1).

65. *United States District Courts—National Judicial Caseload Profile*, U.S. COURTS

(Mar. 31, 2022), https://www.uscourts.gov/sites/default/files/fcms_na_distprofile03 31.2022.pdf (showing a median of 32.6 months from civil filing to trial); *As Workloads Rise in Federal Courts, Judge Counts Remain Flat*, SYRACUSE UNIVERSITY (Oct. 14, 2014), https://trac.syr.edu/tracreports/judge/364/ (showing a median of 16 months from civil filing to trial in FY 1993).

66. *Civil Justice, United States*, WORLD JUSTICE PROJECT, https://worldjusticeproject .org/rule-of-law-index/factors/2021/United%20States/Civil%20Justice/ (last visited June 18, 2022).

67. Zachariah DeMeola, *IAALS' Comment to the California Task Force on Legal Regulation and Enhancing the Provision of Legal Services*, INSTITUTE FOR THE ADVANCEMENT OF THE AMERICAN LEGAL SYSTEM (Oct. 4, 2019), https://iaals.du.edu/blog /iaals-comment-california-task-force-legal-regulation-and-enhancing-provision -legal-services.

68. Mitchell Levy, *Empirical Patterns of Pro Se Litigation in Federal District Courts*, 85 U. CHI. L. REV. 1819, 1843–44 (2018) ("[A]cross essentially all of those lawsuits, pro se litigants fare dramatically worse than their represented counterparts.").

69. HAGUE INSTITUTE FOR INNOVATION OF LAW (HIIL) & INSTITUTE FOR THE ADVANCEMENT OF THE AMERICAN LEGAL SYSTEM (IAALS), JUSTICE NEEDS AND SATISFACTION IN THE UNITED STATES OF AMERICA 8, 76 (2021).

70. *See, e.g., Living Trust Overview*, LEGALZOOM, https://www.legalzoom.com/personal /estate-planning/living-trust-overview.html (last visited June 18, 2022); Eric Kroh, *DOJ, FTC Say Legal Documents Software Helps Consumers*, LAW360 (June 13, 2016), https://www.law360.com/articles/806288/doj-ftc-say-legal-documents-software -helps-consumers; Caroline Shipman, *Unauthorized Practice of Law Claims Against LegalZoom—Who Do These Lawsuits Protect, and Is the Rule Outdated?*, 32 GEO. J. LEGAL ETHICS 939, 941–43 (2019).

71. Robert Ambrogi, *Latest Legal Victory Has LegalZoom Poised for Growth*, ABA J. (Aug. 1, 2014), https://www.abajournal.com/magazine/article/latest_legal_victory_has_legal zoom_poised_for_growth/; Caroline Shipman, *Unauthorized Practice of Law Claims Against LegalZoom—Who Do These Lawsuits Protect, and Is the Rule Outdated?*, 32 GEO. J. LEGAL ETHICS 939, 945–50 (2019). For the lawsuits themselves, *see, e.g.*, Legal Zoom.com Inc. v. North Carolina State Bar, No. 11 CVS 15111, 2015 WL 6441853 (N.C. Super. Ct. Oct. 22, 2015); Janson v. LegalZoom.com, Inc., 802 F. Supp. 2d 1053 (W.D. Mo. 2011); Report on Findings of Facts and Recommendation to Approve the Settlement Agreement, Medlock v. LegalZoom.Com, Inc., No. 2012-208067, 2013 S.C. LEXIS 362 (S.C. Oct. 18, 2013).

72. AMERICAN BAR ASSOCIATION, MODEL RULES OF PROFESSIONAL CONDUCT, R. 5.5(b) (2019); Caroline Shipman, *Unauthorized Practice of Law Claims Against LegalZoom—Who Do These Lawsuits Protect, and Is the Rule Outdated?*, 32 GEO. J. LEGAL ETHICS 939, 943–44 (2019). States have adopted Model Rule 5.5 to varying degrees. *See* Emily McClure, *LegalZoom and Online Legal Service Providers: Is the Development and Sale of Interactive Questionnaires That Generate Legal Documents the Unauthorized Practice of Law?*, 105 KY. L. J. 563, 566 (2017).

73. Gillian K. Hadfield, *Higher Demand, Lower Supply? A Comparative Assessment of the Legal Resource Landscape for Ordinary Americans*, 37 FORDHAM URB. L. J. 129, 154 (2010); Caroline Shipman, *Unauthorized Practice of Law Claims Against LegalZoom—Who Do These Lawsuits Protect, and Is the Rule Outdated?*, 32 GEO. J. LEGAL ETHICS 939, 945–50 (2019).

74. *See* AMERICAN BAR ASSOCIATION, MODEL RULES OF PROFESSIONAL CONDUCT, R. 5.4 & 5.4 cmt. 1 (2020).

75. Jason Solomon, Deborah Rhose, & Annie Wanless, *How Reforming Rule 5.4 Would Benefit Lawyers and Consumers, Promote Innovation, and Increase Access to Justice* 2, STANFORD CENTER ON THE LEGAL PROFESSION (Apr. 2020), https://law.stanford .edu/wp-content/uploads/2020/04/Rule_5.4_Whitepaper_-_Final.pdf.

76. Neil M. Gorsuch, *Access to Affordable Justice*, 100 JUDICATURE 46, 49–50 (2016).

77. *Cf.* Neil M. Gorsuch, *Access to Affordable Justice*, 100 JUDICATURE 46, 51–52 (2016); *Domestic Legal Education*, NATIONAL CONFERENCE ON BAR EXAMINERS, https:// reports.ncbex.org/comp-guide/charts/chart-3/ (last visited June 9, 2023).

78. ANTHONY P. CARNEVALE, ARTEM GULISH, & KATHRYN PELTIER CAMPBELL, IF NOT NOW,

WHEN? THE URGENT NEED FOR AN ALL-ONE-SYSTEM APPROACH TO YOUTH POLICY 24 (2021), https://cewgeorgetown.wpenginepowered.com/wp-content/uploads/cew-all _one_system-fr.pdf; *Cost of Attendance*, LAW SCHOOL TRANSPARENCY, https://www .lawschooltransparency.com/trends/costs/tuition (last visited Mar. 15, 2023).

79. *See, e.g., How Much Does Law School Cost?*, PENN STATE UNIVERSITY, https://dus.psu .edu/pre-law/how-much-does-law-school-cost (last visited June 18, 2022).

80. Melanie Hanson, *Average Law School Debt*, EDUCATION DATA INITIATIVE (June 15, 2023), https://educationdata.org/average-law-school-debt.

81. Neil M. Gorsuch, *Access to Affordable Justice*, 100 JUDICATURE 46, 52 (2016).

82. Jennifer S. Bard & Larry Cunningham, *The Legal Profession Is Failing Low-Income and Middle-Class People. Let's Fix That*, WASH. POST (June 5, 2017), https://www .washingtonpost.com/opinions/the-legal-profession-is-failing-low-income-and -middle-class-people-lets-fix-that/2017/06/02/e266200a-246b-11e7-bb9d-8cd6118e 1409_story.html.

83. Neil M. Gorsuch, *Access to Affordable Justice*, 100 JUDICATURE 46, 52 (2016).

84. CHARLES DICKENS, BLEAK HOUSE 621 (1996); Joseph Tartakovsky, *Dickens v. Lawyers*, N.Y. TIMES (Feb. 5, 2012), https://www.nytimes.com/2012/02/06/opinion/dickens-v -lawyers.html.

85. Rebecca L. Haffajee & Michelle M. Mello, *Thinking Globally, Acting Locally—The U.S. Response to Covid-19*, NEW ENGLAND J. OF MEDICINE (May 28, 2020), https:// www.nejm.org/doi/full/10.1056/nejmp2006740.

86. *See, e.g.*, Desrosiers v. Governor, 158 N.E.3d 827, 837–39 (Mass. 2020).

87. *See, e.g., Coronavirus Executive Order 14*, OFFICE OF GOVERNOR GREG ABBOTT (Mar. 31, 2020), https://gov.texas.gov/uploads/files/press/EO-GA-14_Statewide _Essential_Service_and_Activity_COVID-19_IMAGE_03-31-2020.pdf; *Executive Order No. 20-91*, OFFICE OF GOVERNOR RON DESANTIS (Apr. 1, 2020), https://www .flgov.com/wp-content/uploads/orders/2020/EO_20-91.pdf.

88. *See, e.g., COVID-19 Executive Order No. 16*, OFFICE OF GOVERNOR J.B. PRITZKER (Apr. 1, 2020), https://www.illinois.gov/government/executive-orders/executive -order.executive-order-number-18.2020.html (extending the initial stay-at-home order); *Executive Order No. 2020-42*, OFFICE OF GOVERNOR GRETCHEN WHITMER (Apr. 9, 2020), https://www.michigan.gov/whitmer/news/state-orders-and-directives /2020/04/09/executive-order-2020-42 (extending the initial stay-at-home order); *Executive Order No. 202.18*, OFFICE OF GOVERNOR ANDREW CUOMO (Apr. 16, 2020), https://www.governor.ny.gov/sites/default/files/atoms/files/EO_202.18.pdf (extend- ing the initial stay-at-home order).

89. *States' COVID-19 Public Health Emergency Declarations*, NATIONAL ACADEMY FOR STATE HEALTH POLICY, https://nashp.org/states-covid-19-public-health-emergency -declarations/ (last updated June 13, 2023).

90. Joint Resolution of Apr. 10, 2023, Pub. L. No. 118–3, 137 Stat. 6 (2023); *COVID-19 Public Health Emergency (PHE)*, U.S. DEPARTMENT OF HEALTH AND HUMAN SERVICES, https://www.hhs.gov/coronavirus/covid-19-public-health-emergency/index.html (last updated May 16, 2023).

91. *See, e.g.*, Temporary Halt in Residential Evictions to Prevent the Further Spread of COVID-19, 85 Fed. Reg. 55292 (Sep. 4, 2020) (initial CDC eviction moratorium) ("In the event that this Order qualifies as a rule under the APA, notice and com- ment and a delay in effective date are not required because there is good cause to dispense with prior public notice and comment and the opportunity to comment on this Order and the delay in effective date."); Biden v. Missouri, 142 S. Ct. 647, 651 (2022) (discussing the HHS vaccine mandate, which was promulgated without notice and comment).

92. Alabama Association of Realtors v. U.S. Department of Health and Human Services, 141 S. Ct. 2485, 2486–88 (2021).

93. National Federation of Independent Business v. Department of Labor, Occupational Safety and Health Administration, 142 S. Ct. 661, 663–64, 666 (2022).

94. *See, e.g., COVID-19 Resources for State Leaders: 2022 Executive Orders*, COUNCIL OF STATE GOVERNMENTS, https://web.csg.org/covid19/2022-state-executive-orders/ (last visited June 12, 2023); *COVID-19 Resources for State Leaders: 2020–2021 Executive Orders*, COUNCIL OF STATE GOVERNMENTS, https://web.csg.org/covid19

/executive-orders/ (last visited June 12, 2023); *see also Executive Order No. 202.3*, OFFICE OF GOVERNOR ANDREW CUOMO (Mar. 16, 2020), https://www.governor .ny.gov/sites/default/files/atoms/files/EO_202.3.pdf (limiting gatherings and closing businesses); *COVID-19 Executive Order No. 3*, OFFICE OF GOVERNOR J.B. PRITZKER (Mar. 13, 2020), https://www2.illinois.gov/Documents/ExecOrders/2020/Executive Order-2020-05.pdf (closing schools); *Executive Order No. 20-52*, OFFICE OF GOVERNOR LAURA KELLY (July 2, 2020), https://governor.kansas.gov/wp-content /uploads/2020/07/20200702093130003.pdf (mandating masks); *Seventh Modification: Declaration of a State of Emergency*, OFFICE OF GOVERNOR JOHN CARNEY (Mar. 29, 2020), https://governor.delaware.gov/health-soe/seventh-state-of-emergency/ (restricting travel).

95. *See, e.g.*, Matt Gray, *Keep Kids off Playgrounds. They're Closed to Stop Coronavirus Spreading, Towns Say*, NJ.COM (Mar. 18, 2020), https://www.nj.com/coronavirus /2020/03/some-nj-towns-closing-playgrounds-over-coronavirus-concerns.html; Kirsti Marohn, *Some Playgrounds Remain Open, Despite Coronavirus Worries. But Are They Safe?*, MPR NEWS (Apr. 2, 2020), https://www.mprnews.org/story/2020 /04/02/some-playgrounds-remain-open-despite-coronavirus-worries-are-they-safe.

96. Hannah Fry, *Paddle Boarder Chased by Boat, Arrested in Malibu After Flouting Coronavirus Closures*, L.A. TIMES (Apr. 3, 2020) https://www.latimes.com/california /story/2020-04-03/paddle-boarder-arrested-in-malibu-after-flouting-coronavirus -closures; Jared Leone, *Coronavirus: City Fills Skatepark with 37 Tons of Sand to Deter Skaters*, KIRO7 (Apr. 18, 2020), https://www.kiro7.com/news/trending /coronavirus-city-fills-skatepark-with-37-tons-sand-deter-skaters/P36K2J3RLBB CZB3RVJC3G2X5HY/.

97. *See, e.g.*, Alexandra Kerr, *A Historical Timeline of COVID-19 in New York City*, INVESTO-PEDIA, https://www.investopedia.com/historical-timeline-of-covid-19-in-new-york -city-5071986 (last updated Apr. 5, 2021); *A Year of COVID-19 in Pennsylvania*, ABC27, https://www.abc27.com/timeline-of-a-year-of-covid-19-in-pennsylvania/ (last visited June 14, 2023).

98. Nick Paumgarten, *How Restaurants Survive the Long Pandemic Winter*, NEW YORKER (Feb. 22, 2021), https://www.newyorker.com/magazine/2021/03/01/how -restaurants-survive-the-long-pandemic-winter.

99. Shannon Bond, *Facebook Widens Ban on COVID-19 Vaccine Misinformation in Push to Boost Confidence*, NPR (Feb. 8, 2021), https://www.npr.org/2021/02/08/965390755 /facebook-widens-ban-on-covid-19-vaccine-misinformation-in-push-to-boost -confiden; Kari Paul, *Facebook Bans Misinformation About All Vaccines After Years of Controversy*, GUARDIAN (Feb. 8, 2021), https://www.theguardian.com/technology /2021/feb/08/facebook-bans-vaccine-misinformation; Kim Lyons, *Facebook Suspends Anti-mask Group for Spreading COVID-19 Misinformation*, THE VERGE (July 20, 2020), https://www.theverge.com/2020/7/20/21331060/anti-mask-groups-facebook -misinformation; *see also* Michelle Crouch, *12 Things You Can't Post About the Coronavirus on Facebook*, AARP (Feb. 24, 2021), https://www.aarp.org/health/conditions -treatments/info-2021/facebook-blocks-coronavirus-misinformation.html.

100. *Cf.* Jon Cohen, *Scientists "Strongly Condemn" Rumors and Conspiracy Theories About Origin of Coronavirus Outbreak*, SCIENCE (Feb. 19, 2020), https://www .science.org/content/article/scientists-strongly-condemn-rumors-and-conspiracy -theories-about-origin-coronavirus; Elizabeth Dwoskin, *Facebook Reverses Policy, Will Not Ban Posts That Say Covid Was Man-made*, WASH. POST (May 28, 2021), https://www.washingtonpost.com/technology/2021/05/27/facebook-covid-man -made/; Olafimihan Oshin, *Washington Post Issues Correction on 2020 Report on Tom Cotton, Lab-Leak Theory*, THE HILL (June 1, 2021), https://thehill.com/home news/media/556418-washington-post-issues-correction-on-2020-report-on-tom -cotton-lab-leak-theory; Alexandra Stevenson, *Senator Tom Cotton Repeats Fringe Theory of Coronavirus Origins*, N.Y. TIMES (Feb. 18, 2020), https://www.nytimes .com/2020/02/17/business/media/coronavirus-tom-cotton-china.html.

101. *About LinkedIn*, LINKEDIN, https://about.linkedin.com/ (last visited Oct. 8, 2023); *LinkedIn Censors Harvard Epidemiologist Martin Kulldorff*, BROWNSTONE INSTITUTE (Aug. 13, 2021), https://brownstone.org/articles/linkedin-censors-harvard -epidemiologist-martin-kulldorff/.

102. Daniel Victor, *YouTube Suspends Rand Paul over Video Disputing Mask Benefits*, N.Y. TIMES (Aug. 11, 2021), https://www.nytimes.com/2021/08/11/business/youtube -rand-paul-covid-masks.html.

103. Ron Johnson, *YouTube Cancels the U.S. Senate*, WALL ST. J. (Feb. 2, 2021), https:// www.wsj.com/articles/youtube-cancels-the-u-s-senate-11612288061.

104. David Kihara, *Twitter Blocks—and Then Restores—Covid-19 Vaccination Post from Florida's Surgeon General*, POLITICO (Oct. 9, 2022), https://www.politico.com /news/2022/10/09/twitter-covid-vaccination-florida-surgeon-general-joe -ladapo-00061074.

105. Calvary Chapel Dayton Valley v. Sisolak, 140 S. Ct. 2603, 2604–06 (2020) (Alito, J., dissenting from denial of application for injunctive relief); *id.* at 2609 (Gorsuch, J., dissenting from denial of application for injunctive relief); Emergency Application for an Injunction Pending Appellate Review at 6–8, Calvary Chapel Dayton Valley v. Sisolak, 140 S. Ct. 2603 (2020) (No. 20-639).

106. South Bay United Pentecostal Church v. Newsom, 141 S. Ct. 716, 717–20 (2021) (statement of Gorsuch, J.).

107. Roman Catholic Diocese of Brooklyn v. Cuomo, 141 S. Ct. 63, 65–67 (2020); *id.* at 69 (Gorsuch, J., concurring).

108. James Kwak, *The End of Small Business*, WASH. POST (July 9, 2020), https://www .washingtonpost.com/outlook/2020/07/09/after-covid-19-giant-corporations -chains-may-be-only-ones-left/.

109. Leland D. Crane et al., *Business Exit During the COVID-19 Pandemic: Non-traditional Measures in Historical Context* 4, FEDERAL RESERVE BOARD (2021), https://www .federalreserve.gov/econres/feds/files/2020089r1pap.pdf; Ruth Simon, *Covid-19's Toll on U.S. Business? 200,000 Extra Closures in Pandemic's First Year*, WALL ST. J. (Apr. 16, 2021), https://www.wsj.com/articles/covid-19s-toll-on-u-s-business-200 -000-extra-closures-in-pandemics-first-year-11618580619.

110. Lucas Misera, *An Uphill Battle: COVID-19's Outsized Toll on Minority-Owned Firms*, FEDERAL RESERVE BANK OF CLEVELAND (Oct. 8, 2020), https://www.clevelandfed .org/newsroom-and-events/publications/community-development-briefs/db -20201008-misera-report.aspx.

111. David Zweig, *$25,000 Pod Schools: How Well-to-Do Children Will Weather the Pandemic*, N.Y. TIMES (July 30, 2020), https://www.nytimes.com/2020/07/30/nyregion /pod-schools-hastings-on-hudson.html.

112. Brian Baxter, *Amazon Legal Chief's Pay Topped $17 Million During Busy Year*, BLOOMBERG LAW (Apr. 16, 2021), https://news.bloomberglaw.com/business-and -practice/amazon-legal-chiefs-pay-topped-17-million-during-restive-year.

113. Chuck Collins, *U.S. Billionaire Wealth Surged by 70 Percent, or $2.1 Trillion, During Pandemic*, INSTITUTE FOR POLICY STUDIES (Oct. 18, 2021), https:// ips-dc.org/u-s-billionaire-wealth-surged-by-70-percent-or-2-1-trillion-during -pandemic-theyre-now-worth-a-combined-5-trillion/; CREDIT SUISSE, RESEARCH INSTITUTE, *Global Wealth Report 2021* 15, 17, 20 (2021); Adam Barnes, *U.S. Billionaire Wealth Skyrockets During Pandemic*, THE HILL (Oct. 18, 2021), https:// thehill.com/changing-america/respect/equality/577204-us-billionaire-wealth -skyrockets-during-pandemic; Kalyeena Makortoff, *World Gained 5.2m Millionaires Last Year in Covid Crisis—Report*, GUARDIAN (June 22, 2021), https://www .theguardian.com/news/2021/jun/22/world-has-gained-52m-new-millionaires -in-covid-crisis-report.

114. *The Federalist* No. 62 (probably James Madison), in THE FEDERALIST PAPERS 381 (Clinton Rossiter ed., 1961).

CHAPTER 6: THREE FREEDOMS

1. ALDOUS HUXLEY, BRAVE NEW WORLD 91 (Harper & Row 1989) (1932).

2. JOHN LOCKE, TWO TREATISES OF GOVERNMENT 306 (Peter Laslett ed., 1988) (1690) (italics removed).

3. *See* Attorney General John Ashcroft, *Prepared Remarks at the Federalist Society National Convention, Saturday, November 15, 2003*, U.S. DEPARTMENT OF JUSTICE, https://www.justice.gov/archive/ag/speeches/2003/111503ag.htm.

4. RANDY E. BARNETT, THE STRUCTURE OF LIBERTY: JUSTICE AND THE RULE OF LAW 2

(2d ed. 2014); Ryan Ori & Jemal R. Brinson, *Willis Tower Getting New Elevators: Here Are the Ups and Downs*, CHI. TRIB. (May 4, 2018), https://www.chicagotribune .com/business/ct-biz-willis-tower-elevators-numbers-htmlstory.html (over 100 stories); *see also Remarks of Attorney General John Ashcroft, Eighth Circuit Judges Conference, Duluth, Minnesota, August 7, 2002*, U.S. DEPARTMENT OF JUSTICE, https://www.justice.gov/archive/ag/speeches/2002/080702eighthcircuitjudge sagremarks.htm.

5. Whitney v. California, 274 U.S. 357, 395 (1927) (Brandeis, J., concurring), *overruled by* Brandenburg v. Ohio, 395 U.S. 444 (1969).

6. JOHN STUART MILL, ON LIBERTY 26 (2d ed. 1859).

7. JOHN STUART MILL, ON LIBERTY 27 (2d ed. 1859).

8. West Virginia State Board of Education v. Barnette, 319 U.S. 624, 640–41 (1943).

9. 303 Creative LLC v. Elenis, 143 S. Ct. 2298, 2310 (2023) (quoting Boy Scouts of America v. Dale, 530 U.S. 640, 660–661 (2000)) (first quote); *id.* (quoting Whitney v. California, 247 U.S. 357, 375 (1927) (Brandeis, J., concurring)) (second quote).

10. 303 Creative LLC v. Elenis, 143 S. Ct. 2298, 2311 (2023).

11. West Virginia State Board of Education v. Barnette, 319 U.S. 624, 641 (1943).

12. George Orwell, *The Freedom of the Press*, TIMES LITERARY SUPPLEMENT, 1039 (Sep. 1972).

13. Kennedy v. Bremerton School District, 142 S. Ct. 2407, 2421, 2426 (2022).

14. Capitol Square Review and Advisory Board v. Pinette, 515 U.S. 753, 760 (1995).

15. Joint Appendix at 39–41, 65, Fulton v. City of Philadelphia, 141 S. Ct. 1868 (2021) (No. 19-123).

16. Becket, *Fostering Love, Sharonell Fulton's Story*, at 0:20, YOUTUBE (Sep. 10, 2019), https://www.youtube.com/watch?v=l-cNdoK2JSk.

17. Joint Appendix at 59, 60, 63, Fulton v. City of Philadelphia, 141 S. Ct. 1868 (2021) (No. 19-123).

18. Kathryn Jean Lopez, *O, Cecilia!*, NATIONAL REVIEW (Nov. 5, 2018), https://www .nationalreview.com/2018/11/national-adoption-month-cecilia-paul-generous-life/.

19. Becket, *Free to Foster: Protecting the Oldest Foster Agency in Philadelphia*, at 2:29, 2:37, YOUTUBE (Sep. 23, 2020), https://www.youtube.com/watch?v=Y_HV6oWztbM.

20. Brief of Petitioner at 3, Fulton v. City of Philadelphia, 141 S. Ct. 1868 (2021) (No. 19-123); Joint Appendix at 51, 58, 61–62, 65–66, Fulton v. City of Philadelphia, 141 S. Ct. 1868 (2021) (No. 19-123); The History of Catholic Social Services, https:// cssphiladelphia.org/about/history/ (last visited March 24, 2024).

21. The History of Catholic Social Services, https://cssphiladelphia.org/about/history/ (last visited March 24, 2024); Brief of Nebraska, Arizona, and Ohio as Amici Curiae Supporting Petitioners at 9, Fulton v. City of Philadelphia, 141 S. Ct. 1868 (2021) (No. 19-123); see also Brief of Petitioner at 4, Fulton v. City of Philadelphia, 141 S. Ct. 1868 (2021) (No. 19-123).

22. Brief for the United States as Amicus Curiae Supporting Petitioners at 3, Fulton v. City of Philadelphia, 141 S. Ct. 1868 (2021) (No. 19-123) (quoting Appendix of Petitioner at 12a).

23. Brief of Nebraska, Arizona, and Ohio as Amici Curiae Supporting Petitioners at 27, Fulton v. City of Philadelphia, 141 S. Ct. 1868 (2021) (No. 19-123) (quoting Appendix of Petitioner at 254a); Brief for the United States as Amicus Curiae Supporting Petitioners at 3, Fulton v. City of Philadelphia, 141 S. Ct. 1868 (2021) (No. 19-123); *see also* Fulton v. City of Philadelphia, 141 S. Ct. 1868, 1885 (2021) (Alito, J., concurring in the judgment) ("[i]nto the early twentieth century, the care of orphaned and abandoned children in the United States remained largely in the hands of private charitable and religious organizations.") (quoting Brief for Annie E. Casey Foundation et al. as Amici Curiae 4–5).

24. Appendix of Petitioner at 158a, 254a, Fulton v. City of Philadelphia, 141 S. Ct. 1868 (2021) (No. 19-123); Brief of Nebraska, Arizona, and Ohio as Amici Curiae Supporting Petitioners at 9–10, Fulton v. City of Philadelphia, 141 S. Ct. 1868 (2021) (No. 19-123).

25. Brief of Nebraska, Arizona, and Ohio as Amici Curiae Supporting Petitioners at 10, Fulton v. City of Philadelphia, 141 S. Ct. 1868 (2021) (No. 19-123) (quoting Appendix of Petitioner at 255a for first quotation).

26. 23 PA. STAT. § 6362(a); PHILA. CODE § 21-1801; Fulton v. City of Philadelphia, 141 S.

Ct. 1868, 1875 (2021); Brief of Petitioner at 4–5, Fulton v. City of Philadelphia, 141 S. Ct. 1868 (2021) (No. 19-123); Brief for the United States as Amicus Curiae Supporting Petitioners at 1–2, Fulton v. City of Philadelphia, 141 S. Ct. 1868 (2021) (No. 19-123) (citing Appendix of Petitioner at 13a).

27. Brief for the United States as Amicus Curiae Supporting Petitioners at 1, Fulton v. City of Philadelphia, 141 S. Ct. 1868 (2021) (No. 19-123) ("The City of Philadelphia has protective custody of over 5000 children who have been abused or neglected." (citing Appendix of Petitioner at 194a)); *Become a Foster Parent*, CITY OF PHILADELPHIA, https://www .phila.gov/services/birth-marriage-life-events/birth-adoption-and-parenting /become-a-foster-parent/ (last visited Feb. 4, 2024) ("Roughly 3,400 children and youth are in foster care at any given time in this city."); Kathleen Creamer, *Testimony on Philadelphia DHS and Improving Outcomes for Children (IOC)*, COMMUNITY LEGAL SERVICES OF PHILADELPHIA (June 14, 2016), https://clsphila.org/family/dhs-ioc-testimony/ ("In 2012 . . . there were just over 4,100 children in [Philadelphia] DHS custody. Today [in 2016], there are 6,100 children in DHS custody."); Steve Volk, *For Families Involved in Philly's Child Welfare System, This Program Is Building a Safety Net*, KENSINGTON VOICE (Nov. 12, 2020), https://www.kensingtonvoice.com/en/child-welfare-system -philadelphia-social-work-community-legal-services/ (reporting in 2020 that there were 4,900 children in foster care in Philadelphia).

28. Brief of Petitioner at 7, Fulton v. City of Philadelphia, 141 S. Ct. 1868 (2021) (No. 19-123) (citing Appendix of Petitioner at 13a); Brief for the United States as Amicus Curiae Supporting Petitioners at 2, Fulton v. City of Philadelphia, 141 S. Ct. 1868 (2021) (No. 19-123).

29. Brief for the United States as Amicus Curiae Supporting Petitioners at 2, Fulton v. City of Philadelphia, 141 S. Ct. 1868 (2021) (No. 19-123) (quoting Appendix of Petitioner at 197a).

30. Fulton v. City of Philadelphia, 141 S. Ct. 1868, 1875 (2021); Brief for the United States as Amicus Curiae Supporting Petitioners at 2, Fulton v. City of Philadelphia, 141 S. Ct. 1868 (2021) (No. 19-123).

31. 55 PA. CODE § 3700.64; *see also* Brief for the United States as Amicus Curiae Supporting Petitioners at 2, Fulton v. City of Philadelphia, 141 S. Ct. 1868 (2021) (No. 19-123).

32. Fulton v. City of Philadelphia, 141 S. Ct. 1868, 1875 (2021) (quoting 55 Pa. Code §3700.69 (2020)).

33. Joint Appendix at 105–06, 292 Fulton v. City of Philadelphia, 141 S. Ct. 1868 (2021) (No. 19-123).

34. Brief of Respondent at 1, Fulton v. City of Philadelphia, 141 S. Ct. 1868 (2021) (No. 19-123).

35. Joint Appendix at 49, 54, 292 Fulton v. City of Philadelphia, 141 S. Ct. 1868 (2021) (No. 19-123).

36. Joint Appendix at 52, 292 Fulton v. City of Philadelphia, 141 S. Ct. 1868 (2021) (No. 19-123).

37. Brief for Former Foster Children and Foster/Adoptive Parents and the Catholic Association Foundation as Amici Curiae Supporting Petitioners at 3, 12, Fulton v. City of Philadelphia, 141 S. Ct. 1868 (2021) (No. 19-123); Brief of Petitioner at 5, Fulton v. City of Philadelphia, 141 S. Ct. 1868 (2021) (No. 19-123).

38. John DeGarmo, *America's Foster Care Crisis: The Shortage of Foster Parents for Children in Crisis*, MEDIUM (Jan. 31, 2022), https://drjohndegarmo.medium.com/foster -care-crisis-in-2022-americas-shortage-of-foster-parents-a95ed2929579; Scott Simon, *There's a Nationwide Shortage of Foster Care Families*, NPR (July 15, 2023), https:// www.npr.org/2023/07/15/1187929875/theres-a-nationwide-shortage-of-foster-care -families; *see also Foster Care Parents Shortage in Philadelphia*, CSS PHILADELPHIA, https://cssphiladelphia.org/foster-care-parents-shortage-in-philadelphia/ (last visited Feb. 4, 2024).

39. *Every Kid Needs a Family* 5, THE ANNIE E. CASEY FOUNDATION (2015), https:// assets.aecf.org/m/resourcedoc/aecf-EveryKidNeedsAFamily-2015.pdf; Emily Wax-Thibodeaux, *"We Are Just Destroying These Kids": The Foster Children Growing Up Inside Detention Centers*, WASH. POST (Dec. 30, 2019), https://www.washingtonpost .com/national/we-are-just-destroying-these-kids-the-foster-children-growing-up

-inside-detention-centers/2019/12/30/97f65f3a-eaa2-11e9-9c6d-436a0df4f31d
_story.html; *see also A National Look at the Use of Congregate Care in Child Welfare*
2, U.S. DEPARTMENT OF HEALTH AND HUMAN SERVICES, ADMINISTRATION FOR CHIL-
DREN AND FAMILIES, CHILDREN'S BUREAU (May 13, 2015), https://www.acf.hhs.gov
/sites/default/files/documents/cb/cbcongregatecare_brief.pdf.

40. John DeGarmo, *America's Foster Care Crisis: The Shortage of Foster Parents for
     Children in Crisis*, MEDIUM (Jan. 31, 2022), https://drjohndegarmo.medium.com
     /foster-care-crisis-in-2022-americas-shortage-of-foster-parents-a95ed2929579;
     Jessica Harrington, *Fresno Social Workers Call for Change as Children Sleep on
     Floors, Desks While Waiting for a Home*, ABC30 ACTION NEWS (Oct. 15, 2021), https://
     abc30.com/fresno-county-cps-social-workers/11126229/.

41. Allegra Abramo & Susanna Ray, *Crisis in Foster Care System Leaves Kids Rootless,
     Vulnerable*, INVESTIGATE WEST (Sep. 20, 2016), https://www.invw.org/2016/09/20
     /crises-in-foster-care-system-leaves-kids-rootless-vulnerable/.

42. *Every Kid Needs a Family* 5, THE ANNIE E. CASEY FOUNDATION (2015), https://assets
     .aecf.org/m/resourcedoc/aecf-EveryKidNeedsAFamily-2015; Emily Wax-Thibodeaux,
     *"We Are Just Destroying These Kids": The Foster Children Growing Up Inside De-
     tention Centers*, WASH. POST (Dec. 30, 2019), https://www.washingtonpost.com
     /national/we-are-just-destroying-these-kids-the-foster-children-growing-up-inside
     -detention-centers/2019/12/30/97f65f3a-eaa2-11e9-9c6d-436a0df4f31d_story.html.

43. Emily Wax-Thibodeaux, *"We Are Just Destroying These Kids": The Foster Children
     Growing Up Inside Detention Centers*, WASH. POST (Dec. 30, 2019), https://www
     .washingtonpost.com/national/we-are-just-destroying-these-kids-the-foster-children
     -growing-up-inside-detention-centers/2019/12/30/97f65f3a-eaa2-11e9-9c6d-436a0d
     f4f31d_story.html.

44. Julia Terruso, *Philly Puts Out "Urgent" Call—300 Families Needed for Fostering*,
     PHILA. INQUIRER (Mar. 18, 2018), https://www.inquirer.com/philly/news/foster
     -parents-dhs-philly-child-welfare-adoptions-20180308.html; *see also Foster Care
     Parents Shortage in Philadelphia*, CSS PHILADELPHIA, https://cssphiladelphia.org
     /foster-care-parents-shortage-in-philadelphia/ (last visited Feb. 4, 2024).

45. Brief of Petitioner at 12, Fulton v. City of Philadelphia, 141 S. Ct. 1868 (2021) (No. 19-
     123); Brief for the United States as Amicus Curiae Supporting Petitioners at 4, Fulton
     v. City of Philadelphia, 141 S. Ct. 1868 (2021) (No. 19-123).

46. Fulton v. City of Philadelphia, 141 S. Ct. 1868, 1875 (2021); Appendix of Petitioner at
     258a, Fulton v. City of Philadelphia, 141 S. Ct. 1868 (2021) (No. 19-123).

47. Fulton v. City of Philadelphia, 141 S. Ct. 1868, 1875 (2021); Brief of Petitioner at 8,
     Fulton v. City of Philadelphia, 141 S. Ct. 1868 (2021) (No. 19-123).

48. Appendix of Petitioner at 147a, Fulton v. City of Philadelphia, 141 S. Ct. 1868 (2021)
     (No. 19-123); Brief for the United States as Amicus Curiae Supporting Petitioners at
     4, Fulton v. City of Philadelphia, 141 S. Ct. 1868 (2021) (No. 19-123).

49. Brief for the United States as Amicus Curiae Supporting Petitioners at 4–6, Fulton
     v. City of Philadelphia, 141 S. Ct. 1868 (2021) (No. 19-123); Joint Appendix at 183,
     Fulton v. City of Philadelphia, 141 S. Ct. 1868 (2021) (No. 19-123).

50. Christine Rousselle, *City of Philadelphia to Pay $2 Million to Catholic Foster Care
     Agency in Settlement*, CATHOLIC NEWS AGENCY (Nov. 23, 2021), https://www.catholic
     newsagency.com/news/249688/city-of-philadelphia-to-pay-2-dollars-million-to
     -catholic-foster-care-agency-in-settlement.

51. Brief for the United States as Amicus Curiae Supporting Petitioners at 3, Fulton v.
     City of Philadelphia, 141 S. Ct. 1868 (2021) (No. 19-123) (quoting Appendix of Peti-
     tioner at 12a); *see also* Fulton v. City of Philadelphia, 141 S. Ct. 1868, 1884–85 (2021)
     (Alito, J., concurring in the judgment).

52. Supplemental Appendix at 4–5, Fulton v. City of Philadelphia, 141 S. Ct. 1868 (2021)
     (No. 19-123); Joint Appendix at 17, 442–43 Fulton v. City of Philadelphia, 141 S. Ct.
     1868 (2021) (No. 19-123).

53. Brief of Petitioner at 11, Fulton v. City of Philadelphia, 141 S. Ct. 1868 (2021) (No. 19-
     123) (citing Appendix of Petitioner at 141a–142a).

54. Joint Appendix at 59, 63, Fulton v. City of Philadelphia, 141 S. Ct. 1868 (2021) (No.
     19-123).

55. Becket, *Free to Foster: Protecting the Oldest Foster Agency in Philadelphia*, at 0:47, YOUTUBE (Sep. 23, 2020), https://www.youtube.com/watch?v=Y_HV6oWztbM.

56. Joint Appendix at 63, Fulton v. City of Philadelphia, 141 S. Ct. 1868 (2021) (No. 19-123) (Paul's statement); *id.* at 66, 68–69 (Fulton's statement); *id.* at 54 (Simms-Busch's statement).

57. Appendix of Petitioner at 18a, Fulton v. City of Philadelphia, 141 S. Ct. 1868 (2021) (No. 19-123); Brief of Respondent at 8, Fulton v. City of Philadelphia, 141 S. Ct. 1868 (2021) (No. 19-123).

58. Brief of Respondent at 8, Fulton v. City of Philadelphia, 141 S. Ct. 1868 (2021) (No. 19-123); Joint Appendix at 482, Fulton v. City of Philadelphia, 141 S. Ct. 1868 (2021) (No. 19-123); Ruth Graham, *Major Evangelical Adoption Agency Will Now Serve Gay Parents Nationwide*, N.Y. TIMES (Mar. 1, 2021), https://www.nytimes.com/2021/03/01/us/bethany-adoption-agency-lgbtq.html.

59. Chris Palusky, *Giving Up? Not on Vulnerable Children*, BETHANY, https://bethany.org/resources/giving-up-not-on-vulnerable-children (last visited Feb. 4, 2024).

60. *See, e.g.*, Brief of Petitioner at 2, Fulton v. City of Philadelphia, 141 S. Ct. 1868 (2021) (No. 19-123).

61. Joint Appendix at 445, Fulton v. City of Philadelphia, 141 S. Ct. 1868 (2021) (No. 19-123).

62. Fulton v. City of Philadelphia, 141 S. Ct. 1868, 1876 (2021).

63. Arthur M. Schlesinger, *Biography of a Nation of Joiners*, 50 AM. HIST. REV. 1 (1944).

64. Mary D. McConaghy et al., *Penn in the 18th Century*, UNIVERSITY OF. PENNSYL-VANIA, UNIVERSITY ARCHIVES & RECORDS CENTER (2004), https://archives.upenn.edu/exhibits/penn-history/18th-century/; Arthur M. Schlesinger, *Biography of a Nation of Joiners*, 50 AM. HIST. REV. 1, 3 (1944); *"At the Instance of Benjamin Franklin": A Brief History of the Library Company of Philadelphia* 5, 116 LIBRARY COMPANY of PHILADELPHIA (2015), https://www.librarycompany.org/about/Atthe Instance2015_98709140764695.pdf.

65. Arthur M. Schlesinger, *Biography of a Nation of Joiners*, 50 AM. HIST. REV. 1 (1944).

66. 1 ANNALS OF CONGRESS 759–60 (1789) (Joseph Gales ed., 1834); *see also* Michael W. McConnell, *Keynote Address: Freedom of Association: Campus Religious Groups*, 97 WASH. U. L. REV. 1641, 1641–42 (2020).

67. Connie Cass, *Poll: Americans Don't Trust One Another*, USA TODAY (Nov. 30, 2013), https://www.usatoday.com/story/news/nation/2013/11/30/poll-americans-dont-trust-one-another/3792179/; Kevin Vallier, *Why Are Americans So Distrustful of Each Other?*, WALL ST. J. (Dec. 17, 2020), https://www.wsj.com/articles/why-are-americans-so-distrustful-of-each-other-11608217988; *see also* Lee Rainie, Scott Keeter, & Andrew Perrin, *Trust and Distrust in America*, PEW RESEARCH CENTER (July 22, 2019), https://www.pewresearch.org/politics/2019/07/22/trust-and-distrust-in-america/.

68. ROBERT D. PUTNAM, BOWLING ALONE: THE COLLAPSE AND REVIVAL OF AMERICAN COMMUNITY 137 (2000).

69. Robert D. Putnam, *Bowling Alone: America's Declining Social Capital*, 6 J. DEMOC-RACY 65, 65 (1995).

70. Erica Hernandez, *Elderly Floresville Couple Shares Heartbreaking Moment Through Nursing Home Window*, KSAT (Mar. 15, 2020), https://www.ksat.com/news/local/2020/03/15/elderly-floresville-couple-share-heartbreaking-moment-through-nursing-home-window/.

71. Bill Hutchinson, *Recovering Addicts Say Coronavirus Creates New Challenge to Stay Sober*, ABC NEWS (Apr. 2, 2020), https://abcnews.go.com/Health/lot-struggles-recovering-addicts-coronavirus-creates-challenge-stay/story?id=69914643.

72. Bill Hutchinson, *Recovering Addicts Say Coronavirus Creates New Challenge to Stay Sober*, ABC NEWS (Apr. 2, 2020), https://abcnews.go.com/Health/lot-struggles-recovering-addicts-coronavirus-creates-challenge-stay/story?id=69914643.

73. Carter Sherman, *Coronavirus Is Forcing AA Meetings to Close, and People Are Worried About Relapse*, VICE (Mar. 17, 2020), https://www.vice.com/en/article/qjdmdb/coronavirus-is-forcing-aa-meetings-to-close-and-people-are-worried-about-relapse.

74. Jayne O'Donnell, *"The Only Thing Missing Are the Hugs": How People Fight Addic-*

tion amid Coronavirus Social Distancing, USA TODAY (Mar. 13, 2020), https://www
.usatoday.com/story/news/health/2020/03/13/coronavirus-social-distancing-hard
-aa-groups-sobriety-recovery/5015169002/.

75. Martha Bebinger, *Opioid Addiction Is "a Disease of Isolation," So Pandemic Puts
Recovery at Risk*, NPR (Mar. 27, 2020), https://www.npr.org/sections/health-shots
/2020/03/27/820806440/opioid-addiction-is-a-disease-of-isolation-so-pandemic
-puts-recovery-at-risk.

76. Emma Goldberg, *"Relapsing Left and Right": Trying to Overcome Addiction in
a Pandemic*, N.Y. TIMES (Jan. 4, 2021), https://www.nytimes.com/2021/01/04
/nyregion/addiction-treatment-coronavirus-new-york-new-jersey.html.

77. *See, e.g.*, Irina Ivanova & Thom Craver, *Closed Due to Coronavirus: List of Activities
and State Shutdowns over COVID-19 Outbreak Concerns*, CBS NEWS (Mar. 18, 2020),
https://www.cbsnews.com/news/closed-due-to-coronavirus-list-of-activities-and
-state-shutdowns-over-covid-19-outbreak-concerns/.

78. Editorial Board, *Nursing Home Patients Are Dying of Loneliness*, N.Y. TIMES
(Dec. 29, 2020), https://www.nytimes.com/2020/12/29/opinion/coronavirus-nursing
-homes.html.

79. *See, e.g.*, U.S. DEPARTMENT OF HEALTH AND HUMAN SERVICES, CENTERS FOR DIS-
EASE CONTROL AND PREVENTION, CDC ACTIVITIES AND INITIATIVES SUPPORTING THE
COVID-19 RESPONSE AND THE PRESIDENT'S PLAN FOR OPENING AMERICA UP AGAIN:
MAY 2020 42 (2020); Angela Couloumbis & Cynthia Fernandez, *Gov. Tom Wolf
Orders Pennsylvania Schools Closed Through Rest of Academic Year*, SPOTLIGHT PA
(Apr. 9, 2020), https://www.spotlightpa.org/news/2020/04/pennsylvania-coronavirus
-schools-closed-tom-wolf/; Laura Meckler & Rachel Weiner, *CDC Guidelines, Released
at Last, Offer Low-Key Guide to Reopening*, WASH. POST (May 19, 2020), https://www
.washingtonpost.com/local/education/cdc-guidelines-released-at-last-offer-low-key
-guide-to-reopening/2020/05/19/c99eb63a-99f8-11ea-a282-386f56d579e6_story
.html ("The CDC recommends that schools remain closed in step one, which it does
not define.").

80. *See, e.g.*, Madeline Holcombe & Stephanie Gallman, *Here's a Look at What States
Are Exempting Religious Gatherings from Stay at Home Orders*, CNN (Apr. 2, 2020),
https://www.cnn.com/2020/04/02/us/stay-at-home-order-religious-exemptions
-states-coronavirus/index.html (reporting that as of April 2020, twenty-seven of the
thirty-nine states that had implemented stay-at-home orders had not exempted religious services); Tom Gjelten, *States Consider Whether Religious Services Qualify
as "Essential,"* NPR (Apr. 1, 2020), https://www.npr.org/sections/coronavirus-live
-updates/2020/04/01/825667542/states-consider-whether-religious-services-qualify
-as-essential ("Many churches and other houses of worship have been forced to close in
response to government bans on public gatherings of more than ten people.").

81. *See, e.g.*, *Telemedicine During COVID-19: Video vs. Phone Visits and the Digital
Divide*, NEW YORK UNIVERSITY (Nov. 15, 2021), https://www.nyu.edu/about/news
-publications/news/2021/november/telemedicine-during-covid-19.html ("Telemedicine
visits accounted for more than 60 percent of patient care at New York community
health centers during the peak of the COVID-19 pandemic in spring 2020."); Ji Eun
Chang et al., *Telephone vs. Video Visits During COVID-19: Safety-Net Provider Per-
spectives*, 34 J. AM. BD. FAM. MED. 1103, 1106 (2021); Nina Keck, *Elderly Couple Uses
FaceTime to Stay Connected During Coronavirus Pandemic*, NPR (Mar. 21, 2020),
https://www.npr.org/2020/03/21/818947938/elderly-couple-uses-facetime-to-stay
-connected-during-coronavirus-pandemic.

82. Michael Martin, *Computer and Internet Use in the United States, 2018*, U.S. CEN-
SUS BUREAU (Apr. 21, 2021), https://www.census.gov/content/dam/Census/library
/publications/2021/acs/acs-49.pdf.

83. CALIFORNIA DEPARTMENT OF PUBLIC HEALTH, GUIDANCE FOR THE PREVENTION OF
COVID-19 TRANSMISSION FOR GATHERINGS (Nov. 13, 2020), in Emergency Application
Appendix at App. 190–94, Tandon v. Newsom, 141 S. Ct. 1294 (2021) (No. 20A151)
("For any gatherings permitted under this guidance, the space must be large enough
so that everyone at a gathering can maintain at least a 6-foot physical distance from
others (not including their own household) at all times."); *see also* Tandon v. Newsom,
992 F.3d 916, 918 (9th Cir. 2021), rev'd, 141 S. Ct. 1294 (2021).

84. *Executive Order No. 67 2–3*, OFFICE OF GOVERNOR CHARLES D. BAKER (Apr. 29, 2021), https://www.mass.gov/doc/covid-19-order-67/download.

85. *Vaccine and Mask Requirements to Mitigate the Spread of COVID-19 in Head Start Programs*, 86 Fed. Reg. 68052 (Nov. 30, 2021) (imposing the requirement); Mitigating the Spread of COVID-19 in Head Start Programs, 88 Fed. Reg. 993 (Jan. 6, 2023) (lifting the requirement).

86. *See, e.g.*, CALIFORNIA DEPARTMENT OF PUBLIC HEALTH, GUIDANCE FOR THE PREVENTION OF COVID-19 TRANSMISSION FOR GATHERINGS (Nov. 13, 2020), in Emergency Application Appendix at App. 190–94, Tandon v. Newsom, 141 S. Ct. 1294 (2021) (No. 20A151); *see also* Tandon v. Newsom, 992 F.3d 916, 918 (9th Cir. 2021), rev'd, 141 S. Ct. 1294 (2021); *Guidance for the Use of Face Coverings*, CALIFORNIA DEPARTMENT OF PUBLIC HEALTH (June 18, 2020), https://www.cdph.ca.gov/Programs/CID/DCDC /Pages/COVID-19/guidance-for-face-coverings_06-18-2020.aspx; Hailey Branson-Potts, *Angry Parents Won't Let Officials Slide over Closed Playgrounds, Packed Malls*, L.A. TIMES (Dec. 3, 2020), https://www.latimes.com/california/story/2020-12-03 /covid-19-la-parents-anger-closed-playgrounds.

87. Declaration by Jeremy Wong (Oct. 19, 2020), in Emergency Application Appendix at App. 196-97, Tandon v. Newsom, 141 S. Ct. 1294 (2021) (No. 20A151); Fiona Kelliher, *"Never in My Wildest Thoughts": Supreme Court Strikes Rules Barring California Home Worship*, MERCURY NEWS (Apr. 10, 2021), https://www.mercury news.com/2021/04/10/never-in-my-wildest-thoughts-supreme-court-strikes-rules -barring-home-worship.

88. *See, e.g.*, CALIFORNIA DEPARTMENT OF PUBLIC HEALTH, GUIDANCE FOR THE PREVENTION OF COVID-19 TRANSMISSION FOR GATHERINGS (Nov. 13, 2020), in Emergency Application Appendix at App. 190–94, Tandon v. Newsom, 141 S. Ct. 1294 (2021) (No. 20A151); *see also* Declaration by Jeremy Wong (Oct. 19, 2020), in Emergency Application Appendix at App. 196–97, Tandon v. Newsom, 141 S. Ct. 1294 (2021) (No. 20A151).

89. CALIFORNIA DEPARTMENT OF PUBLIC HEALTH, BLUEPRINT FOR A SAFER ECONOMY: ACTIVITY AND BUSINESS TIERS (Mar. 11, 2021), in Emergency Application Appendix at App. 183–89, Tandon v. Newsom, 141 S. Ct. 1294 (2021) (No. 20A151); *see also* Tandon v. Newsom, 992 F.3d 916, 918 n.1 (9th Cir. 2021), rev'd, 141 S. Ct. 1294 (2021).

90. CALIFORNIA DEPARTMENT OF PUBLIC HEALTH, GUIDANCE FOR THE PREVENTION OF COVID-19 TRANSMISSION FOR GATHERINGS (Nov. 13, 2020), in Emergency Application Appendix at App. 191–92, Tandon v. Newsom, 141 S. Ct. 1294 (2021) (No. 20A151); *see also* Tandon v. Newsom, 992 F.3d 916, 917–18 (9th Cir. 2021), rev'd, 141 S. Ct. 1294 (2021).

91. Tandon v. Newsom, 992 F.3d 916, 933–34 (9th Cir. 2021) (Bumatay, J., dissenting in part), rev'd, 141 S. Ct. 1294 (2021); *COVID-19 Industry Guidance: Hair Salons and Barbershops 3*, CALIFORNIA DEPARTMENT OF PUBLIC HEALTH (Oct. 20, 2020), https://files.covid19.ca.gov/pdf/guidance-hair-salons--en.pdf; *COVID-19 Industry Guidance: Expanded Personal Care Services 11*, CALIFORNIA DEPARTMENT OF PUBLIC HEALTH (Oct. 20, 2020), https://files.covid19.ca.gov/pdf/guidance-expanded-personal-care-services--en.pdf ("Electrologists should wear a face shield for eye protection (with a face covering) when they are providing clients treatment on facial or neck areas *that do not enable the client to wear a face covering*" (emphasis added)); *see also* CALIFORNIA DEPARTMENT OF PUBLIC HEALTH, BLUEPRINT FOR A SAFER ECONOMY: ACTIVITY AND BUSINESS TIERS (Mar. 11, 2021), in Emergency Application Appendix at App. 184, Tandon v. Newsom, 141 S. Ct. 1294 (2021) (No. 20A151) (listing "personal care services" as "open indoors with modifications" in all tiers).

92. Tandon v. Newsom, 992 F.3d 916, 934 (9th Cir. 2021) (Bumatay, J., dissenting in part), rev'd, 141 S. Ct. 1294 (2021).

93. Declaration by Jeremy Wong (Oct. 19, 2020), in Emergency Application Appendix at App. 197, Tandon v. Newsom, 141 S. Ct. 1294 (2021) (No. 20A151).

94. Fiona Kelliher, *"Never in My Wildest Thoughts": Supreme Court Strikes Rules Barring California Home Worship*, MERCURY NEWS (Apr. 10, 2021), https://www.mercury news.com/2021/04/10/never-in-my-wildest-thoughts-supreme-court-strikes-rules -barring-home-worship/.

95. Jay Bhattacharya, *A Conversation with Lord Sumption*, COLLATERAL GLOBAL (July 17,

2021), https://collateralglobal.org/article/a-conversation-with-lord-sumption/.

96. DEPARTMENT OF HEALTH AND HUMAN SERVICES, OFFICE OF THE U.S. SURGEON GENERAL, OUR EPIDEMIC OF LONELINESS AND ISOLATION: THE U.S. SURGEON GENERAL'S ADVISORY ON THE HEALING EFFECTS OF SOCIAL CONNECTION AND COMMUNITY 8 (2023); *see also* Lisa Jarvis, *The Epidemic of Isolation Is as Harmful as Smoking*, WASH. POST (May 8, 2023), https://www.washingtonpost.com/business/2023/05/08/this-epidemic-of-isolation-is-as-harmful-as-smoking/3f2d683a-eda5-11ed-b67d-a219ec5dfd30_story.html.

97. DEPARTMENT OF HEALTH AND HUMAN SERVICES, OFFICE OF THE U.S. SURGEON GENERAL, OUR EPIDEMIC OF LONELINESS AND ISOLATION: THE U.S. SURGEON GENERAL'S ADVISORY ON THE HEALING EFFECTS OF SOCIAL CONNECTION AND COMMUNITY 4, 8, 28 (2023).

98. *Loneliness and Social Isolation Linked to Serious Health Conditions*, CDC (Apr. 29, 2021), https://www.cdc.gov/aging/publications/features/lonely-older-adults.html.

99. *See, e.g.*, Benedict Carey, *For Some Teens, It's Been a Year of Anxiety and Trips to the E.R.*, N.Y. TIMES (Oct. 5, 2021), https://www.nytimes.com/2021/02/23/health/coronavirus-mental-health-teens.html; Christina Caron, *8-Year-Olds in Despair: The Mental Health Crisis Is Getting Younger*, N.Y. TIMES (July 28, 2021), https://www.nytimes.com/2021/06/28/well/mind/mental-health-kids-suicide.html; Matt Richtel, *Surgeon General Warns of Youth Mental Health Crisis*, N.Y. TIMES (Dec. 7, 2021), https://www.nytimes.com/2021/12/07/science/pandemic-adolescents-depression-anxiety.html.

100. *See, e.g.*, Todd Gregory, *Surveys Suggest Violence Against Women Has Intensified During the Pandemic, a U.N. Report Says*, N.Y. TIMES (Nov. 24, 2021), https://www.nytimes.com/2021/11/24/world/americas/violence-against-women-covid.html (describing a rise in domestic violence internationally); Jeffrey Kluger, *Domestic Violence Is a Pandemic Within the Covid-19 Pandemic*, TIME (Feb. 3, 2021), https://time.com/5928539/domestic-violence-covid-19/ (documenting domestic violence in the United States); Liz Mineo, *"Shadow Pandemic" of Domestic Violence*, HARVARD GAZETTE (June 29, 2022), https://news.harvard.edu/gazette/story/2022/06/shadow-pandemic-of-domestic-violence/ ("The National Commission on COVID-19 and Criminal Justice [the source incorrectly failed to capitalize Criminal Justice] shows an increase [in domestic violence] in the U.S. by a little over 8 percent, following the imposition of lockdown orders during 2020."); Alex R. Piquero et al., *Domestic Violence During the Covid-19 Pandemic—Evidence from a Systematic Review and Meta-analysis*, 74 J. CRIM. JUST. 1, 5 (2021) ("Incidents of domestic violence increased in response to stay-at-home/lockdown orders, a finding that is based on several studies from different cities, states, and several countries around the world.").

101. Sarah Mervosh, *The Pandemic Erased Two Decades of Progress in Math and Reading*, N.Y. TIMES (Sep. 1, 2022), https://www.nytimes.com/2022/09/01/us/national-test-scores-math-reading-pandemic.html.

102. Natalie Grover, *Children Born During Pandemic Have Lower IQs, US Study Finds*, GUARDIAN (Aug. 12, 2021), https://www.theguardian.com/world/2021/aug/12/children-born-during-pandemic-have-lower-iqs-us-study-finds; *see also* Sean C.L. Deoni et al., *The Covid-19 Pandemic and Early Child Cognitive Development: A Comparison of Development in Children Born During the Pandemic and Historical References* (PubMed preprint, Aug. 16, 2022), https://pubmed.ncbi.nlm.nih.gov/34401887/.

103. Editorial Board, *Nursing Home Patients Are Dying of Loneliness*, N.Y. TIMES (Dec. 29, 2020), https://www.nytimes.com/2020/12/29/opinion/coronavirus-nursing-homes.html; Emily Paulin, *Is Extended Isolation Killing Older Adults in Long-Term Care?*, AARP (Sep. 3, 2020), https://www.aarp.org/caregiving/health/info-2020/covid-isolation-killing-nursing-home-residents.html.

104. Emily Paulin, *Is Extended Isolation Killing Older Adults in Long-Term Care?*, AARP (Sep. 3, 2020), https://www.aarp.org/caregiving/health/info-2020/covid-isolation-killing-nursing-home-residents.html.

105. Alexiss Jeffers et al., *Impact of Social Isolation during the COVID-19 Pandemic on Mental Health, Substance Use, and Homelessness: Qualitative Interviews with Behavioral Health Providers*, 19 INT'L J. ENV'T RSCH. & PUB. HEALTH 1, 13 (2022).

106. *Drug Overdose Deaths in the U.S. Top 100,000 Annually*, CENTERS FOR DISEASE CONTROL AND PREVENTION (Nov. 17, 2021), https://www.cdc.gov/nchs/pressroom/nchs

_press_releases/2021/20211117.htm; Roni Caryn Rabin, *Overdose Deaths Reached Record High as the Pandemic Spread*, N.Y. TIMES (Nov. 17, 2021), https://www.nytimes.com/2021/11/17/health/drug-overdoses-fentanyl-deaths.html.

107. Roni Caryn Rabin, *Overdose Deaths Reached Record High as the Pandemic Spread*, N.Y. TIMES (Nov. 17, 2021), https://www.nytimes.com/2021/11/17/health/drug-overdoses-fentanyl-deaths.html.

108. Lauren J. Tanz et al., *A Qualitative Assessment of Circumstances Surrounding Drug Overdose Deaths During the Early Stages of the COVID-19 Pandemic* 1, CDC (Aug. 2022), https://www.cdc.gov/drugoverdose/pdf/sudors-covid-databrief-22.pdf; *see also U.S. Overdose Deaths in 2021 Increased Half as Much as in 2020—but Are Still Up 15%*, CDC (May 11, 2022), https://www.cdc.gov/nchs/pressroom/nchs_press_releases/2022/202205.htm.

109. *See* Arizona v. Mayorkas, 143 S. Ct. 1312 (2023) (Gorsuch, J., statement) (this and next paragraph).

110. Tish Harrison Warren, *I Miss Singing at Church*, N.Y. TIMES (Apr. 5, 2020), https://www.nytimes.com/2020/04/05/opinion/coronavirus-church-religion.html.

111. 1 ALEXIS DE TOCQUEVILLE, DEMOCRACY IN AMERICA 243 (J.P. Mayer ed., George Lawrence trans., Harper Perennial 2006) (1835).

112. Complaint for Declaratory and Injunctive Relief at 4, ¶11, Brantley v. Kuntz, 98 F. Supp. 3d 884 (W.D. Tex. 2015) (No. 1:13-cv-00872-SS); Tashara Parker, *Rooted: Meet the Woman Who Fought State of Texas over Natural Hair Braiding and Won*, WFAA (Apr. 23, 2021), https://www.wfaa.com/article/news/community/rooted/rooted-isis-brantley-shares-her-hair-story-natural/287-2fdbef65-62e4-4d8f-9fcb-b0940eaefd80.

113. John L. Hanson, Jr., *A Conversation with Isis Brantley*, at 1:16, KUT 90.5 (Aug. 18, 2021), https://www.kut.org/life-arts/2021-08-18/a-conversation-with-isis-brantley.

114. Complaint for Declaratory and Injunctive Relief at 4–5, ¶12, Brantley v. Kuntz, 98 F. Supp. 3d 884 (W.D. Tex. 2015) (No. 1:13-cv-00872-SS).

115. Angela C. Erickson, *Barriers to Braiding: How Job-Killing Licensing Laws Tangle Natural Hair Care in Needless Red Tape* 1, 3, INSTITUTE FOR JUSTICE (July 2016), https://ij.org/wp-content/uploads/2016/07/Barriers_To_Braiding-2.pdf.

116. Sahaar Turner, *Healing Through Hair: Isis Brantley Is an Icon for Natural Beauty and Empowerment*, NUBIAN IMPULSE (July 25, 2018), https://www.nubianimpulse.com/post/healing-through-hair-isis-brantley-is-an-icon-for-natural-beauty-and-empowerment-1.

117. *Isis Brantley*, INSTITUTE FOR JUSTICE (Mar. 13, 2015), https://ij.org/client/isis-brantley/; Tashara Parker, *Rooted: Meet the Woman Who Fought State of Texas over Natural Hair Braiding and Won*, WFAA (Apr. 23, 2021), https://www.wfaa.com/article/news/community/rooted/rooted-isis-brantley-shares-her-hair-story-natural/287-2fdbef65-62e4-4d8f-9fcb-b0940eaefd80.

118. *The Isis Brantley Story*, NATURALLY ISIS, https://www.naturallyisis.com/about (last visited Oct. 28, 2023); *see also* JN interview with Arif Panju.

119. Sahaar Turner, *Healing Through Hair: Isis Brantley Is an Icon for Natural Beauty and Empowerment*, NUBIAN IMPULSE (July 25, 2018), https://www.nubianimpulse.com/post/healing-through-hair-isis-brantley-is-an-icon-for-natural-beauty-and-empowerment-1.

120. Complaint for Declaratory and Injunctive Relief at 9, ¶37, Brantley v. Kuntz, 98 F. Supp. 3d 884 (W.D. Tex. 2015) (No. 1:13-cv-00872-SS).

121. John L. Hanson, Jr., *A Conversation with Isis Brantley*, at 3:59, KUT 90.5 (Aug. 18, 2021), https://www.kut.org/life-arts/2021-08-18/a-conversation-with-isis-brantley; Prachi Gupta, *This Woman Fought for 20 Years to Change the Rules for Hair Braiding in Texas. This Week She Scored a Major Victory*, COSMOPOLITAN (June 10, 2015), https://www.cosmopolitan.com/style-beauty/news/a41742/isis-brantley-hair-braiding-texas/; JN interview with Arif Panju.

122. Wesley Hottot, *Bureaucratic Barbed Wire: How Occupational Licensing Fences Out Texas Entrepreneurs*, INSTITUTE FOR JUSTICE 21 (Oct. 2009), https://ij.org/wp-content/uploads/2015/03/txstudyv3.pdf; Prachi Gupta, *This Woman Fought for 20 Years to Change the Rules for Hair Braiding in Texas. This Week She Scored a*

Major Victory, COSMOPOLITAN (June 10, 2015), https://www.cosmopolitan.com /style-beauty/news/a41742/isis-brantley-hair-braiding-texas/; JN interview with Arif Panju.

123. *Hair Braider Salaries,* GLASSDOOR, https://www.glassdoor.com/Salaries/hair -braider-salary-SRCH_KO0,12.htm (last updated Oct. 15, 2023); *see also Barbers, Hairstylists, and Cosmetologists,* BUREAU OF LABOR STATISTICS, https://www.bls.gov /ooh/personal-care-and-service/barbers-hairstylists-and-cosmetologists.htm (last visited Feb. 4, 2024) (listing 2022 median pay of barbers, hairstylists, and cosmetologists at $33,400 per year); Edward J. Timmons & Catherine Konieczny, *Untangling Hair Braider Deregulation in Virginia* fig. 5, CATO J. (Fall 2018), https://www.cato .org/cato-journal/fall-2018/untangling-hair-braider-deregulation-virginia.

124. Wesley Hottot, *Bureaucratic Barbed Wire: How Occupational Licensing Fences Out Texas Entrepreneurs* 21, INSTITUTE FOR JUSTICE (Oct. 2009), https://ij.org /wp-content/uploads/2015/03/txstudyv3.pdf; Prachi Gupta, *This Woman Fought for 20 Years to Change the Rules for Hair Braiding in Texas. This Week She Scored a Major Victory,* COSMOPOLITAN (June 10, 2015), https://www.cosmopolitan.com /style-beauty/news/a41742/isis-brantley-hair-braiding-texas/; *see also* Peter Coy, *Why Does a Hair Braider Need a License?,* N.Y. TIMES (Apr. 8, 2022), https://www.nytimes .com/2022/04/08/opinion/professional-licensing.html ("Braiding does not involve harsh chemicals or sharp objects, so even if it's done badly, nobody gets injured.").

125. Tashara Parker, *Rooted: Meet the Woman Who Fought State of Texas over Natural Hair Braiding and Won,* WFAA (Apr. 23, 2021), https://www.wfaa.com/article/news /community/rooted/rooted-isis-brantley-shares-her-hair-story-natural/287-2fdbef65 -62e4-4d8f-9fcb-b0940eaefd80.

126. *Hanging by a Thread: Texas Eyebrow Threaders Fight Irrational Licensing,* IN-STITUTE FOR JUSTICE, https://ij.org/case/patel-v-tx-department-of-licensing-and -regulation/ (last visited Nov. 11, 2023); Katya Kazakina, *An Age-Old Way to Arch Your Brows,* N.Y. TIMES (Nov. 24, 2002), https://www.nytimes.com/2002/11/24 /style/noticed-an-age-old-way-to-arch-your-brows.html; Anthony Sanders & Nick Sibilla, *Don't Thread on Me,* FEDERALIST SOCIETY (July 13, 2016), https://fedsoc.org /commentary/fedsoc-blog/don-t-thread-on-me#_ftnref4; Patel v. Texas Department of Licensing and Regulation, 469 S.W.3d 69, 73 (Tex. 2015).

127. *What Is the Average Eyebrow Threading Salary by State,* ZIPRECRUITER, https:// www.ziprecruiter.com/Salaries/What-Is-the-Average-Eyebrow-Threading-Salary -by-State (last visited Nov. 11, 2023).

128. Original Petition, Application for Injunctive Relief, and Request for Disclosure at 10, ¶ 46, Patel v. Texas Department of Licensing and Regulation, 2011 WL 766171 (No. D-1-GN-09-004118); *Hanging by a Thread: Texas Eyebrow Threaders Fight Irratio-nal Licensing,* INSTITUTE FOR JUSTICE, https://ij.org/case/patel-v-tx-department-of -licensing-and-regulation/ (last visited Nov. 11, 2023); *see also, e.g.,* Paradise Afshar, *Eyebrow Threading Holds Cultural Significance for South Asians, Middle Easterners,* ATLANTA J.-CONST. (Oct. 27, 2021), https://www.ajc.com/news/eyebrow-threading -holds-cultural-significance-for-south-asians-middle-easterners/5Q627KYPYJAVJ MCSTKOBWOAGFA/ (reporting that the founder of an eyebrow salon in Georgia "taught herself how to thread when she was 14").

129. Original Petition, Application for Injunctive Relief, and Request for Disclosure at 5-6, 15, ¶¶ 20-25, 27, 84, Patel v. Texas Department of Licensing and Regulation, 2011 WL 766171 (No. D-1-GN-09-004118); *Hanging by a Thread: Texas Eyebrow Threaders Fight Irrational Licensing,* INSTITUTE FOR JUSTICE, https://ij.org/case /patel-v-tx-department-of-licensing-and-regulation/ (last visited Nov. 11, 2023); In-stitute for Justice, *Five Things You Need to Know About the Texas Supreme Court Ruling Protecting Economic Liberty,* at 2:28, YOUTUBE (Aug. 19, 2015), https://www .youtube.com/watch?v=Cf4MdTqgSuA.

130. Patel v. Texas Department of Licensing and Regulation, 469 S.W.3d 69, 73. 88 n.5 (Tex. 2015) (quoting Act of Apr. 25, 1935, 44th Leg., R.S., ch. 116, 1935 TEX. GEN. LAWS 304, 304-11); State Response Brief on the Merits at 11, Patel v. Texas Depart-ment of Licensing and Regulation, 469 S.W.3d 69 (Tex. 2015) (No. 12-0657).

131. State Response Brief on the Merits at 11, Patel v. Texas Department of Licensing and

Regulation, 469 S.W.3d 69 (Tex. 2015) (No. 12-0657); Original Petition, Application for Injunctive Relief, and Request for Disclosure 14, ¶ 77, Patel v. Tex. Dep't of Licensing and Regulation, 2011 WL 766171 (No. D-1-GN-09-004118).

132. Patel v. Texas Department of Licensing and Regulation, 469 S.W.3d 69, 88, 90 (Tex. 2015).

133. Stephanie Nicola, *What Is Color Psychology?*, WEBMD (Apr. 27, 2022), https://www .webmd.com/mental-health/what-is-color-psychology.

134. Patel v. Texas Department of Licensing and Regulation, 469 S.W.3d 69, 88 (Tex. 2015).

135. Original Petition, Application for Injunctive Relief, and Request for Disclosure at 5–6, ¶ 24, Patel v. Texas Department of Licensing and Regulation, 2011 WL 766171 (No. D-1-GN-09-004118) (Tahereh Rokhti); Anthony Sanders & Nick Sibilla, *Don't Thread on Me*, FEDERALIST SOCIETY (July 13, 2016), https://fedsoc.org/commentary /fedsoc-blog/don-t-thread-on-me#_ftnref4 (Vijay Yogi).

136. Alana Rocha, *Eyebrow Threading Regulations to Go Before High Court*, TEX. TRIB. (Feb. 25, 2014), https://www.texastribune.org/2014/02/25/texas-eyebrow -threading-industry-under-microscope/; Anthony Sanders & Nick Sibilla, *Don't Thread on Me*, FEDERALIST SOCIETY (July 13, 2016), https://fedsoc.org/commentary /fedsoc-blog/don-t-thread-on-me#_ftnref4.

137. Suman Guha Mozumder, *Indian-American Jobs at Stake over Texas Eyebrow Threading Rule*, REDIFF BUSINESS (Feb. 7, 2014), https://www.rediff.com/money/slide-show /slide-show-1-indian-american-jobs-at-stake-over-texas-eyebrow-threading-rule /20140207.htm.

138. Patel v. Texas Department of Licensing and Regulation, 469 S.W.3d 69, 102 (Tex. 2015) (Willett, J., concurring); Wesley Hottot, *Bureaucratic Barbed Wire: How Occupational Licensing Fences Out Texas Entrepreneurs* 2, INSTITUTE FOR JUSTICE (Oct. 2009), https://ij.org/wp-content/uploads/2015/03/txstudyv3.pdf; see also *82d Tex. H. Comm. on Gov't Efficiency & Reform, Interim Report to the 83rd Tex. Leg.* 57 (Jan. 2013), http://www.house.state.tx.us/_media/pdf/committees/reports/82interim/House -Committee-on-Goverement-Efficiency-and-Refrom-Interim-Report.pdf; *Texas State Board of Medical Examiners Records: An Inventory of State Board of Medical Examiners Records at the Texas State Archives, 1901–1975, 1978–1985, Bulk 1901–1975*, TEXAS ARCHIVAL RESOURCES ONLINE, https://txarchives.org/tslac/finding_aids/20135.xml (last visited Feb. 4, 2024) ("Initial licensing of medical practitioners in Texas began in 1837 with the creation of the Board of Medical Censors by the 2nd Congress of the Republic of Texas."); *Texas State Board of Dental Examiners Records: An Inventory of the State Board of Dental Examiners Records at the Texas State Archives, 1961–2005, 2018–2021*, TEXAS ARCHIVAL RESOURCES ONLINE, https://txarchives.org/tslac/find ing_aids/30132.xml (last visited Feb. 4, 2024) ("For well over a century, the State of Texas has provided for examining boards to safeguard the dental health of Texans by licensing qualified dental professionals, and by sanctioning violators of laws and rules regulating dentistry. The earliest legislation regulating dentistry in Texas was in 1889.").

139. Kevin C. Smith, Comment, *Unspooling the Furrowed Brow: How Eyebrow Threaders Will Protect Economic Freedom in Texas*, 48 TEX. TECH L. REV. ONLINE 71, 74 (2015).

140. *See, e.g.*, 16 TEX. ADMIN. CODE § 59.80(a)–(e) (2023) (laying out provider application fee, provider renewal application fee, course-approval fee per occupation, revised /duplicate license/certificate/permit/registration fee, and record fee for continuing education requirements imposed on various occupations pursuant to 16 TEX. ADMIN. CODE § 59.3); 22 TEX. ADMIN. CODE § 223.1(a) (2023) (laying out various fees associated with a nursing license).

141. Wesley Hottot, *Bureaucratic Barbed Wire: How Occupational Licensing Fences Out Texas Entrepreneurs* 32, INSTITUTE FOR JUSTICE (Oct. 2009), https://ij.org/wp -content/uploads/2015/03/txstudyv3.pdf; COUNCIL FOR INTERIOR DESIGN QUALIFI- CATION, NCIDQ CANDIDATE HANDBOOK 6, 13 (2023).

142. Wesley Hottot, *Bureaucratic Barbed Wire: How Occupational Licensing Fences Out Texas Entrepreneurs* 17, INSTITUTE FOR JUSTICE (Oct. 2009), https://ij.org/wp -content/uploads/2015/03/txstudyv3.pdf; TEXAS COMMISSION ON LAW ENFORCEMENT,

SUNSET ADVISORY COMMISSION STAFF REPORT, 88TH LEGISLATURE 16 (2022) ("The 87th Legislature increased the required number of training hours for peace officers from 696 to 720 by adding additional hours to existing topics . . .").

143. Noah Trudeau & Edward Timmons, *2023 State Occupational Licensing Index* 11, ARCHBRIDGE INSTITUTE (2023), https://www.archbridgeinstitute.org/wp-content /uploads/2023/03/2023-State-Occupational-Licensing-Index.pdf; *see also Ranking Burdens by State*, INSTITUTE FOR JUSTICE, https://ij.org/report/license-to-work-3 /report/results/ranking-burdens-by-state/#table6 (last visited Nov. 14, 2023).

144. ANNAPOLIS CODE § 7.24.010 (2023), https://library.municode.com/md/annapolis /codes/code_of_ordinances?nodeId=TIT7BULITARE_CH7.24FO (last visited Nov. 14, 2023); *Forms*, ANNAPOLIS, MARYLAND, https://www.annapolis.gov/416/Forms (last visited Nov. 14, 2023); ANNAPOLIS CODE § 7.24.010 (2023), https://library .municode.com/md/annapolis/codes/code_of_ordinances?nodeId=TIT7BULI TARE_CH7.24FO.

145. LA. STAT. ANN. § 3:3807(B)(2)–(3) (2023); *Licensing and Permits*, DEPARTMENT OF AGRICULTURE AND FORESTRY, https://www.ldaf.la.gov/licensing-permits (last visited Nov. 14, 2023); Elizabeth Crisp, *Effort to End Florist Licensing in Louisiana Nipped in the Bud with Senate Panel's Rejection*, THE ADVOCATE (May 1, 2018), https://www.theadvocate.com/baton_rouge/news/politics/legislature/effort-to -end-florist-licensing-in-louisiana-nipped-in-the-bud-with-senate-panels-rejection /article_4058ed8e-4d59-11e8-aced-a3f61ef63b1c.html; Adam B. Summers, *Occupational Licensing: Ranking States and Exploring Alternatives* 28, REASON FOUNDATION (Aug. 2007), https://reason.org/wp-content/uploads/files/762c8fe96431b6fa5e27 ca64eaa1818b.pdf. For the makeup of the Louisiana Horticulture Commission, see LA. STAT. ANN. § 3:3801(A) (2023).

146. DEPARTMENT OF THE TREASURY OFFICE OF ECONOMIC POLICY, COUNCIL OF ECONOMIC ADVISERS, & DEPARTMENT OF LABOR, OCCUPATIONAL LICENSING: A FRAMEWORK FOR POLICYMAKERS 4–5, 36 (2015); *see also Barriers to Work: Improving Access to Licensed Occupations for Immigrants with Work Authorization*, NATIONAL CONFERENCE OF STATE LEGISLATURES (Aug. 7, 2023), https://www.ncsl.org/labor-and-employment /barriers-to-work-improving-access-to-licensed-occupations-for-immigrants-with -work-authorization.

147. MILTON FRIEDMAN & ROSE FRIEDMAN, CAPITALISM AND FREEDOM 137 (4th ann. ed. 2002).

148. Prachi Gupta, *This Woman Fought for 20 Years to Change the Rules for Hair Braiding in Texas. This Week She Scored a Major Victory*, COSMOPOLITAN (June 10, 2015), https:// www.cosmopolitan.com/style-beauty/news/a41742/isis-brantley-hair-braiding-texas/.

149. John L. Hanson, Jr., *A Conversation with Isis Brantley*, at 22:00, KUT 90.5 (Aug. 18, 2021), https://www.kut.org/life-arts/2021-08-18/a-conversation-with-isis-brantley; JN interview with Arif Panju.

150. Complaint for Declaratory and Injunctive Relief at 8–9, ¶32–33, 35, Brantley v. Kuntz, 98 F. Supp. 3d 884 (W.D. Tex. 2015) (No. 1:13-cv-00872-SS); JN interview with Arif Panju.

151. Prachi Gupta, *This Woman Fought for 20 Years to Change the Rules for Hair Braiding in Texas. This Week She Scored a Major Victory*, COSMOPOLITAN (June 10, 2015), https://www.cosmopolitan.com/style-beauty/news/a41742/isis-brantley-hair-braiding -texas/.

152. Brantley v. Kuntz, 98 F. Supp. 3d 884, 886, 888 (W.D. Tex. 2015); JN interview with Arif Panju.

153. Complaint for Declaratory and Injunctive Relief at 12, ¶52–53, Brantley v. Kuntz, 98 F. Supp. 3d 884 (W.D. Tex. 2015) (No. 1:13-cv-00872-SS); Amy Martyn, *Natural Hair Guru Isis Brantley Is Suing Texas for the Right to Teach Hair-Braiding*, DALLAS OBSERVER (Oct. 2, 2013), https://www.dallasobserver.com/news/natural-hair-guru -isis-brantley-is-suing-texas-for-the-right-to-teach-hair-braiding-7141765.

154. Amy Martyn, *Natural Hair Guru Isis Brantley Is Suing Texas for the Right to Teach Hair-Braiding*, DALLAS OBSERVER (Oct. 2, 2013), https://www.dallasobserver.com /news/natural-hair-guru-isis-brantley-is-suing-texas-for-the-right-to-teach-hair -braiding-7141765.

155. *Texas Hair Braiding Instruction,* INSTITUTE FOR JUSTICE, https://ij.org/case/txbraiding/ (last visited Nov. 14, 2023) ("In January 2015, a federal court declared the three barber school requirements unconstitutional as applied to hair braiding schools. . . . In the wake of our victory in federal court, IJ and Isis Brantley worked in the Texas Legislature to completely deregulate the practice of natural hair braiding. Those efforts proved successful. HB 2717 was passed unanimously by both the Texas House and Texas Senate. On June 10, 2015, the bill was signed into law and the practice of natural hair braiding was fully deregulated in the Lone Star State.").

156. Texas Tribune, *Texas Repeals Regulations on Hair Braiding,* RAW STORY (June 9, 2015), https://www.rawstory.com/2015/06/texas-repeals-regulations-on-hair-braiding/.

157. Prachi Gupta, *This Woman Fought for 20 Years to Change the Rules for Hair Braiding in Texas. This Week She Scored a Major Victory,* COSMOPOLITAN (June 10, 2015), https://www.cosmopolitan.com/style-beauty/news/a41742/isis-brantley-hair-braiding-texas/.

158. *Braider Opportunity and Freedom Act,* INSTITUTE FOR JUSTICE, https://ij.org/legislation/braider-opportunity-and-freedom-act/ (last visited Nov. 14, 2023).

159. Patel v. Texas Department of Licensing and Regulation, 469 S.W.3d 69, 74, 90 (Tex. 2015).

160. J. Justin Wilson, *Texas Supreme Court Strikes Down Useless Eyebrow Threading License,* INSTITUTE FOR JUSTICE (June 26, 2015), https://ij.org/press-release/texas-supreme-court-strikes-down-useless-eyebrow-threading-license/.

CHAPTER 7: THE SPIRIT OF LIBERTY

1. 2 ALEXIS DE TOCQUEVILLE, DEMOCRACY IN AMERICA 516 (Harvey C. Mansfield & Delba Winthrop eds. & trans., University of Chicago Press 2000) (1835).

2. *James M. Landis Found Dead in Swimming Pool at His Home; Advisor to Three Presidents and Ex-Dean of Harvard Law School Was 64,* N.Y. TIMES, July 31, 1964, at 1.

3. THOMAS K. MCCRAW, PROPHETS OF REGULATION 153 (1984).

4. *James M. Landis Found Dead in Swimming Pool at His Home; Advisor to Three Presidents and Ex-Dean of Harvard Law School was 64,* N.Y. TIMES, July 31, 1964, at 1.

5. THOMAS K. MCCRAW, PROPHETS OF REGULATION 155 (1984).

6. DONALD A. RITCHIE, JAMES M. LANDIS: DEAN OF THE REGULATORS 13–14, 17–18 (1980).

7. JUSTIN O'BRIEN, THE TRIUMPH, TRAGEDY, AND LOST LEGACY OF JAMES M. LANDIS: A LIFE ON FIRE 8 (2014).

8. DONALD A. RITCHIE, JAMES M. LANDIS: DEAN OF THE REGULATORS 24 (1980).

9. Myers v. United States, 272 U.S. 52 (1926).

10. DONALD A. RITCHIE, JAMES M. LANDIS: DEAN OF THE REGULATORS 25, 28, 39–40 (1980).

11. THOMAS K. MCCRAW, PROPHETS OF REGULATION 159 (1984); DONALD A. RITCHIE, JAMES M. LANDIS: DEAN OF THE REGULATORS 40 (1980).

12. DONALD A. RITCHIE, JAMES M. LANDIS: DEAN OF THE REGULATORS 43, 50, 53–54, 59–60, 65 (1980).

13. THOMAS K. MCCRAW, PROPHETS OF REGULATION 178 (1984).

14. DONALD A. RITCHIE, JAMES M. LANDIS: DEAN OF THE REGULATORS 75, 85–86 (1980); Michael R. Bechloss, *Review: The Life of James Landis,* 95 HARV. L. REV. 1179, 1182 (1982).

15. Elena Kagan, *Presidential Administration,* 114 HARV. L. REV. 2245, 2261 (2001).

16. JAMES M. LANDIS, THE ADMINISTRATIVE PROCESS 1 (1938); *see also* THOMAS K. MCCRAW, PROPHETS OF REGULATION 213 (1984).

17. THOMAS K. MCCRAW, PROPHETS OF REGULATION 204 (1984); DONALD A. RITCHIE, JAMES M. LANDIS: DEAN OF THE REGULATORS 86–87 (1980).

18. DONALD A. RITCHIE, JAMES M. LANDIS: DEAN OF THE REGULATORS 116–18, 136–41, 153–54 (1980); Michael R. Bechloss, *Review: The Life of James Landis,* 95 HARV. L. REV. 1179, 1184 (1982).

19. DONALD A. RITCHIE, JAMES M. LANDIS: DEAN OF THE REGULATORS 159–60 (1980); *The Rise and Fall of SEC Pioneer James Landis,* NPR (Dec. 11, 2004), https://www.npr.org/templates/story/story.php?storyId=4223423.

20. DONALD A. RITCHIE, JAMES M. LANDIS: DEAN OF THE REGULATORS 160, 162, 170, 174, 176–77 (1980).

21. JUSTIN O'BRIEN, THE TRIUMPH, TRAGEDY, AND LOST LEGACY OF JAMES M. LANDIS: A LIFE ON FIRE 139 (2014).

22. THOMAS K. MCCRAW, PROPHETS OF REGULATION 206 (1984).

23. James M. Landis, *Report on Regulatory Agencies to the President-Elect* 4, 13, 16, SEC HISTORICAL SOCIETY (Dec. 21, 1960), https://www.sechistorical.org/collection/papers /1960/1960_1221_Landis_report.pdf.

24. THOMAS K. MCCRAW, PROPHETS OF REGULATION 207 (1984); DONALD A. RITCHIE, JAMES M. LANDIS: DEAN OF THE REGULATORS 178, 186–87 (1980).

25. DONALD A. RITCHIE, JAMES M. LANDIS: DEAN OF THE REGULATORS 187–88 (1980).

26. THOMAS K. MCCRAW, PROPHETS OF REGULATION 207–08 (1984); *see also* DONALD A. RITCHIE, JAMES M. LANDIS: DEAN OF THE REGULATORS 193–95 (1980).

27. THOMAS K. MCCRAW, PROPHETS OF REGULATION 208 (1984); *James M. Landis Found Dead in Swimming Pool at His Home; Advisor to Three Presidents and Ex-Dean of Harvard Law School Was 64*, N.Y. TIMES (July 31, 1964), at 1.

28. THOMAS K. MCCRAW, PROPHETS OF REGULATION 204 (1984).

29. THOMAS K. MCCRAW, PROPHETS OF REGULATION 208 (1984); *James M. Landis Found Dead in Swimming Pool at His Home; Advisor to Three Presidents and Ex-Dean of Harvard Law School was 64*, N.Y. TIMES, July 31, 1964, at 1.

30. JUSTIN O'BRIEN, THE TRIUMPH, TRAGEDY, AND LOST LEGACY OF JAMES M. LANDIS: A LIFE ON FIRE 4, 161 (2014).

31. DONALD A. RITCHIE, JAMES M. LANDIS: DEAN OF THE REGULATORS 195, 202 (1980); *CPI Inflation Calculator*, BUREAU OF LABOR STATISTICS, https://data.bls.gov/cgi-bin /cpicalc.pl.

32. DONALD A. RITCHIE, JAMES M. LANDIS: DEAN OF THE REGULATORS 195, 202 (1980).

33. JUSTIN O'BRIEN, THE TRIUMPH, TRAGEDY, AND LOST LEGACY OF JAMES M. LANDIS: A LIFE ON FIRE 152 (2014).

34. 2 MAX WEBER, ECONOMY AND SOCIETY 987 (Guenther Roth & Claus Wittich eds., 1978).

35. THEODORE DALRYMPLE, NOT WITH A BANG BUT A WHIMPER: THE POLITICS AND CULTURE OF DECLINE 217 (2008).

36. New State Ice Co. v. Liebmann, 285 U.S. 262, 311 (1932).

37. *Gov. Snyder Signs Bills Eliminating Outdated Laws on Dueling, Cursing and Trampling Blackberry Bushes*, MICHIGAN.GOV (Dec. 15, 2015), https://www.michigan .gov/formergovernors/recent/snyder/press-releases/2015/12/15/gov-snyder-signs -bills-eliminating-outdated-laws-on-dueling-cursing-and-trampling-blackberry -bushes.

38. N.J. STAT. Ann. § 1:12A-1 to -9 (West 2023); N.Y. Legis. Law § Ch. 32, art. 4-A (Mc-Kinney 2024); Michael Waters, *Hundreds of Wacky, Obsolete Laws Still Exist. Why Don't More States Remove Them?*, VOX (Dec. 6, 2019), https://www.vox.com/the -highlight/2019/11/18/20963411/weird-old-laws-historical-obsolete-laws.

39. *Gov. Snyder Signs Bills Eliminating Outdated Laws on Dueling, Cursing and Trampling Blackberry Bushes*, MICHIGAN.GOV (Dec. 15, 2015), https://www.michigan.gov /formergovernors/recent/snyder/press-releases/2015/12/15/gov-snyder-signs-bills -eliminating-outdated-laws-on-dueling-cursing-and-trampling-blackberry-bushes; Rick Pluta, *Legislature Launches Project to Repeal Outdated Laws*, WMUK (Mar. 24, 2015), https://www.wmuk.org/sw-michigan/2015-03-24/legislature-launches -project-to-repeal-outdated-laws; Michael Waters, *Hundreds of Wacky, Obsolete Laws Still Exist. Why Don't More States Remove Them?*, VOX (Dec. 6, 2019), https://www .vox.com/the-highlight/2019/11/18/20963411/weird-old-laws-historical-obsolete -laws.

40. Brad Little, *How Idaho Ushered in the Largest Regulatory Cuts in State History*, OFFICE OF THE GOVERNOR OF IDAHO (June 19, 2019), https://gov.idaho.gov/press release/opinion-how-idaho-ushered-in-the-largest-regulatory-cuts-in-state-history/; Rich Ehisen, *Occupational Licensing Reform Gains Steam in Statehouses*, STATE NET CAPITOL J. (Feb. 5, 2021).

41. *Governor Raimondo Announces Largest Successful Regulatory Reform Effort in State History*, RI.GOV (Oct. 15, 2018), https://www.ri.gov/press/view/34428; Timothy Sandefur & Jon Riches, *Confronting the Administrative State*, GOLDWATER INSTITUTE (Apr. 29, 2020), https://goldwaterinstitute.org/administrative-state-blueprint/.

42. TEXAS SUNSET ADVISORY COMMISSION, SUNSET IN TEXAS 1 (2023); *Impact of Sunset Reviews*, TEXAS SUNSET ADVISORY COMMISSION, https://www.sunset.texas.gov/how-sunset-works/impact-sunset-reviews (last visited Feb. 4, 2024); *Frequently Asked Questions*, TEXAS SUNSET ADVISORY COMMISSION, https://www.sunset.texas.gov/about-us/frequently-asked-questions (last visited Feb. 4, 2024).

43. *See, e.g.*, VT. STAT. ANN. tit. 3, § 268 (repealed 2017) (West 2023).

44. J.D. Tuccille, *It's Becoming Easier to Get Permission to Work, but Not by Enough*, REASON (July 25, 2022), https://reason.com/2022/07/25/its-becoming-easier-to-get-permission-to-work-but-not-by-enough/.

45. ARIZ. REV. STAT. ANN. § 32-4302 (2024); *Arizona Is Now the First State to Recognize Occupational Licenses from Other States*, GOLDWATER INSTITUTE (Apr. 10, 2019), https://www.goldwaterinstitute.org/arizona-is-now-the-first-state-to-recognize-occupational-licenses-from-other-states/.

46. Marc Joffe, *Two States Embrace Occupational Licensing Reform*, CATO INSTITUTE (Jan. 17, 2023), https://www.cato.org/blog/two-states-embrace-occupational-licensing-reform.

47. H.B. 1193, 2020 Leg., Reg. Sess. (Fla. 2020); H.B. 442, 133rd Gen. Assemb., Reg. Sess. (Ohio 2021); Rich Ehisen, *Occupational Licensing Reform Gains Steam in Statehouses*, STATE NET CAPITOL J. (Feb. 5, 2021).

48. *What We Do*, UTAH OFFICE OF LEGAL SERVICES INNOVATION, https://utahinnovation office.org/about/what-we-do/ (last visited Feb. 17, 2024); *Information for Interested Applicants*, UTAH OFFICE OF LEGAL SERVICES INNOVATION, https://utahinnovation office.org/info-for-interested-applicants/ (last visited Feb. 17, 2024); Logan Cornett & Zachariah DeMeola, *Data from Utah's Sandbox Shows Extraordinary Promise, Refutes Fears of Harm*, INSTITUTE FOR THE ADVANCEMENT OF THE AMERICAN LEGAL SYSTEM (Sep. 15, 2021), https://iaals.du.edu/blog/data-utahs-sandbox-shows-extraordinary-promise-refutes-fears-harm.

49. ARIZ. R. CIV. P. 26.1 (f)(1); Neil M. Gorsuch, *Access to Affordable Justice*, 100 JU-DICATURE 47, 49, 51 (2016); *see also* CAL. BUS. & PROF. CODE §§ 6400–15 (2020); *Understanding Unauthorized Practice of Law Issues*, COLORADO SUPREME COURT (DEC. 15, 2014), https://coloradosupremecourt.com/PDF/UPL/Understanding%20 Practice%20of%20Law%20Issues.pdf.

50. DONALD A. RITCHIE, JAMES M. LANDIS: DEAN OF THE REGULATORS 140–41, 160 (1980); David R. Henderson, *The Unpredictability of Deregulation: The Case of Airlines*, HOOVER INSTITUTION (Dec. 19, 2018), https://www.hoover.org/research /unpredictability-deregulation-case-airlines.

51. Michael A. Katz, *The American Experience Under the Airline Deregulation Act of 1978—An Airline Perspective*, 6 HOFSTRA LAB. & EMP. L. J. 87, 88 (1988).

52. David R. Henderson, *The Unpredictability of Deregulation: The Case of Air-lines*, HOOVER INSTITUTION (Dec. 19, 2018), https://www.hoover.org/research /unpredictability-deregulation-case-airlines.

53. *Justice Breyer on Airline Deregulation*, at 11:00, C-SPAN (Feb. 28, 1999), https://www .c-span.org/video/?c4663910/user-clip-justice-stephen-breyer-airline-deregulation.

54. David R. Henderson, *The Unpredictability of Deregulation: The Case of Air-lines*, HOOVER INSTITUTION (Dec. 19, 2018), https://www.hoover.org/research /unpredictability-deregulation-case-airlines; *see also* Matt Welch & Alexis Garcia, *When Democrats Loved Deregulation*, REASON (Dec. 12, 2018), https://reason .com/2018/12/12/when-democrats-loved-deregulation/.

55. Airline Deregulation Act of 1978, Pub. L. No. 95-504, 92 Stat. 1705 (1978); *see also Air-line Deregulation: When Everything Changed*, NATIONAL AIR AND SPACE MUSEUM (Dec. 17, 2021), https://airandspace.si.edu/stories/editorial/airline-deregulation-when-everything-changed.

56. Michael A. Katz, *The American Experience Under the Airline Deregulation Act of 1978—An Airline Perspective*, 6 HOFSTRA LAB. & EMP. L. J. 87, 88, 93 (1988).

57. *See e.g., Justice Breyer on Airline Deregulation*, at 25:00, C-SPAN (Feb. 28, 1999), https://www.c-span.org/video/?c4663910/user-clip-justice-stephen-breyer-airline -deregulation; Alfred E. Kahn, *I Would Do It Again*, 12 REGULATION 22, 23–24 (1988); Michael A. Katz, *The American Experience Under the Airline Deregulation Act of 1978—An Airline Perspective*, 6 HOFSTRA LAB. & EMP. L. J. 87, 93–94 (1988).

58. Mark J. Perry, *Even with Baggage Fees, the "Miracle of Flight" Remains a Real Bargain; Average 2011 Airfare Was 40% Below 1980 Average*, AMERICAN ENTERPRISE INSTITUTE (Oct. 6, 2012), https://www.aei.org/carpe-diem/even-with-baggage-fees -the-miracle-of-flight-remains-a-real-bargain-average-2011-airfare-was-40-below -1980-average/; *see also* Derek Thompson, *How Airline Ticket Prices Fell 50 Percent in 30 Years (And Why Nobody Noticed)*, ATLANTIC (Feb. 28, 2013), https://www .theatlantic.com/business/archive/2013/02/how-airline-ticket-prices-fell-50-in-30 -years-and-why-nobody-noticed/273506/.

59. *Justice Breyer on Airline Deregulation*, at 1:30, C-SPAN (Feb. 28, 1999), https://www .c-span.org/video/?c4663910/user-clip-justice-stephen-breyer-airline-deregulation.

60. Exec. Order No. 13,771, 82 Fed. Reg. 9339 (Jan. 30, 2017); Lydia Wheeler & Lisa Hagen, *Trump Signs "2-for-1" Order to Reduce Regulation*, THE HILL (Jan. 30, 2017), https://thehill.com/homenews/administration/316839-trump-to-sign-order -reducing-regulations/.

61. Exec. Order No. 13,563, 76 Fed. Reg. 3821 (Jan. 18, 2011); *President Obama's State of the Union Address*, N.Y. TIMES (Jan. 24, 2012), https://www.nytimes.com/2012/01/25 /us/politics/state-of-the-union-2012-transcript.html.

62. Ike Brannon, *Fixing Regulatory Overreach*, CATO INSTITUTE (June 6, 2016), https:// www.cato.org/commentary/fixing-regulatory-overreach.

63. *President Obama's State of the Union Address*, N.Y. TIMES (Jan. 24, 2012), https:// www.nytimes.com/2012/01/25/us/politics/state-of-the-union-2012-transcript.html.

64. Ike Brannon, *Fixing Regulatory Overreach*, CATO INSTITUTE (June 6, 2016), https:// www.cato.org/commentary/fixing-regulatory-overreach; *President Obama's State of the Union Address*, N.Y. TIMES (Jan. 24, 2012), https://www.nytimes.com/2012/01/25 /us/politics/state-of-the-union-2012-transcript.html.

65. Learned Hand, *The Spirit of Liberty*, 33 N.Y. ST. B. J. 415 (1961).

66. Letter from *Thomas Jefferson to William Charles Jarvis, 28 September 1820*, NATIONAL ARCHIVES, https://founders.archives.gov/documents/Jefferson/03-16-02-0234.

67. Olivia Waxman, *Citizenship Day Used to Be Called "I Am an American Day." Here's How It Came to Be—and Why It Changed*, TIME (Sep. 17, 2019), https://time.com /5677862/citizenship-day-history/.

68. Joint Resolution of May 3, 1940, Pub. Res. 76-67, 54 Stat. 178 (1940).

69. Joint Resolution of Feb. 29, 1952, Pub. L. No. 82-261, 66 Stat. 9 (1952); Olivia Waxman, *Citizenship Day Used to Be Called "I Am an American Day." Here's How It Came to Be—and Why It Changed*, TIME (Sep. 17, 2019), https://time.com/5677862 /citizenship-day-history/.

70. Consolidated Appropriations Act, 2005, Pub. L. No. 108-447, Div. J, tit. I, § 111(c) (1), 118 Stat. 2809, 3344–45 (2004); Joint Resolution of Feb. 29, 1952, Pub. L. No. 82-261, 66 Stat. 9 (1952); Olivia Waxman, *Citizenship Day Used to Be Called "I Am an American Day." Here's How It Came to Be—and Why It Changed*, TIME (Sep. 17, 2019), https://time.com/5677862/citizenship-day-history/.

71. Liz Atwood, *Lack of Funds Cancels "I Am An American Day,"* BALTIMORE SUN (Sep. 13, 1995), https://www.baltimoresun.com/1995/09/13/lack-of-funds-cancels-i-am-an-american-day-parade-for-95/ (quote); Clayton Knowles, *BALTIMORE GIVES MUSKIE BIG HELLO; Democrat Rides in Parade – Crowd Put at 500,000*, N.Y. TIMES (Sep. 16, 1968), https://www.nytimes.com/1968/09/16/archives/baltimore -gives-muskie-big-hello-democrat-rides-in-parade-crowd-put.html (500,000); Eli Pousson, *I Am an American Day Parade*, BALTIMORE HERITAGE, https://explore .baltimoreheritage.org/items/show/663 (last visited Feb. 22, 2023) (300,000).

72. *Remarks of Representative John F. Kennedy at an "I Am An American Day" Program, Mineola, New York, May 18, 1947*, JOHN F. KENNEDY PRESIDENTIAL LIBRARY AND MUSEUM, https://www.jfklibrary.org/archives/other-resources/john-f-kennedy -speeches/mineola-ny-19470518; Eli Pousson, *I Am An American Day Parade*, BALTIMORE HERITAGE, HTTPS://EXPLORE.BALTIMOREHERITAGE.ORG/ITEMS/SHOW/663 (last visited Feb. 22, 2023) (Hollywood stars).

73. *"I'm an American," Script No. 8*, NBC, June 22, 1940; *see also* Olivia Waxman, *Citizenship Day Used to Be Called "I Am an American Day." Here's How It Came to Be—and Why It Changed*, TIME (Sep. 17, 2019), https://time.com/5677862/citizenship-day -history.

74. *Remarks of Representative John F. Kennedy at an "I Am An American Day" Program, Mineola, New York, May 18, 1947*, JOHN F. KENNEDY PRESIDENTIAL LIBRARY AND MUSEUM, https://www.jfklibrary.org/archives/other-resources/john-f-kennedy -speeches/mineola-ny-19470518.

75. Shawn Healy, *How States Can Strengthen K–12 Civics Education*, EDNOTE (July 22, 2022), https://ednote.ecs.org/how-states-can-strengthen-k-12-civics-education/; *see also Current State Policies*, CIVXNOW, https://civxnow.org/our-work/state-policy / (last visited Nov. 25, 2023).

76. *Americans' Civics Knowledge Drops on First Amendment and Branches of Government*, ANNENBERG PUBLIC POLICY CENTER, UNIVERSITY OF PENNSYLVANIA (Sep. 13, 2022), https://www.annenbergpublicpolicycenter.org/americans-civics-knowledge -drops-on-first-amendment-and-branches-of-government/.

77. Catherine Rampell, *Are Americans Fed Up with Democracy?*, MILWAUKEE J. SENTINEL (Aug. 17, 2016), https://www.jsonline.com/story/opinion/columnists/2016/08/17 /rampell-americans-fed-up-democracy/88894808/.

78. Allyson Escobar, *Most of Us Would Fail the U.S. Citizenship Test, Survey Finds*, NBC NEWS (Oct. 12, 2018), https://www.nbcnews.com/news/latino/most-us-would-fail -u-s-citizenship-test-survey-finds-n918961.

79. Sarah Maslin Nir, *A Fourth of July Symbol of Unity That May No Longer Unite*, N.Y. TIMES (July 3, 2021), https://www.nytimes.com/2021/07/03/nyregion/american -flag-politics-polarization.html.

80. Adam Liptak, *"We the People" Loses Appeal with People Around the World*, N.Y. TIMES (Feb. 6, 2012), https://www.nytimes.com/2012/02/07/us/we-the-people-loses-appeal -with-people-around-the-world.html.

81. *Letter from Thomas Jefferson to Charles Yancey, January 6, 1816*, LIBRARY OF CONGRESS, http://www.loc.gov/resource/mtj1.048_0731_0734.

82. Shawn Healy, *Momentum Grows for Stronger Civic Education Across States*, AMERICAN BAR ASSOCIATION (Jan. 4, 2022), https://www.americanbar.org/groups/crsj /publications/human_rights_magazine_home/the-state-of-civic-education-in -america/momentum-grows-for-stronger-civic-education-across-states/.

83. *Mission & History*, NATIONAL CONSTITUTION CENTER, https://constitutioncenter .org/about/mission-history (last visited Nov. 19, 2023).

84. *The United States Constitution*, NATIONAL CONSTITUTION CENTER, https://constitu tioncenter.org/the-constitution (last visited Nov. 19, 2023).

85. *Interpretation & Debate, The Fourth Amendment*, NATIONAL CONSTITUTION CENTER, https://constitutioncenter.org/the-constitution/amendments/amendment-iv/ interpretations/121#:~:text=According%20to%20the%20Fourth%20Amendment ,their%20property%2C%20and%20their%20homes (last visited Nov. 19, 2023).

86. JN interview with Jeffrey Rosen; JN email with Lauren Sylling.

87. *The Drafting Table*, NATIONAL CONSTITUTION CENTER, https://constitutioncenter .org/the-constitution/drafting-table (last visited Nov. 19, 2023).

88. JN interview with Jeffrey Rosen.

89. *See, e.g., Letter to Bernard Moore (ca. 1773)*, NATIONAL CONSTITUTION CENTER, https://constitutioncenter.org/the-constitution/historic-document-library/detail /thomas-jeffersonletter-to-bernard-moore-ca-1773 (last visited Nov. 19, 2023); JN interview with Jeffrey Rosen.

90. James Madison, *Notes on Ancient and Modern Confederacies* (1786), in 9 THE PAPERS OF JAMES MADISON 3, 4 (Robert A. Rutland & William M.E. Rachal eds., 1975); Derek A. Webb, *The Original Meaning of Civility: Democratic Deliberation at the Philadelphia Constitutional Convention*, 64 S.C. L. REV. 183, 208 (2012).

91. Joan Biskupic, *As She Faces Dementia, Sandra Day O'Connor Is a Pioneer Again*, CNN (Oct. 23, 2018), https://www.cnn.com/2018/10/23/politics/sandra-day-oconnor -alzheimers-dementia-cancer/index.html.

92. Jay O'Connor & Scott O'Connor, *Our Mom, Sandra Day O'Connor, Knew Something About Politics That America Forgot*, USA TODAY (May 12, 2022), https://www.azcentral .com/story/opinion/op-ed/2022/05/12/sandra-day-oconnor-knew-politics-common -ground-civics/9724714002/.

93. Letter from Sandra Day O'Connor, Oct. 23, 2018, SANDRA DAY O'CONNOR INSTITUTE

FOR AMERICAN DEMOCRACY, https://oconnorinstitute.org/wp-content/uploads/Public
-Letter-from-Sandra-Day-OConnor-10-23-16.pdf.

94. JN interview with Louise Dube; *see also* Letter from Sandra Day O'Connor, Oct. 23, 2018, SANDRA DAY O'CONNOR INSTITUTE FOR AMERICAN DEMOCRACY, https://oconnor institute.org/wp-content/uploads/Public-Letter-from-Sandra-Day-OConnor -10-23-16.pdf.

95. Shawn Healy, *Momentum Grows for Stronger Civic Education Across States*, AMER-ICAN BAR ASSOCIATION (Jan. 4, 2022), https://www.americanbar.org/groups/crsj /publications/human_rights_magazine_home/the-state-of-civic-education-in -america/momentum-grows-for-stronger-civic-education-across-states/; Kimberly Adams, *What Federal Funding for Civics Reveals About American Political Discourse*, MARKETPLACE (Nov. 6, 2019), https://www.marketplace.org/2019/11/06 /what-federal-funding-for-civics-reveals-about-american-political-discourse/.

96. 3 WILLIAM WALLER HENING, THE STATUTES AT LARGE: BEING A COLLECTION OF ALL THE LAWS OF VIRGINIA FROM THE FIRST SESSION OF THE LEGISLATURE, IN THE YEAR 1619 197, 419–32 (1823); *see also* Kate Egner Gruber, *The History of Williamsburg*, AMERICAN BATTLEFIELD TRUST, https://www.battlefields.org/learn/articles/history -williamsburg (last visited Feb. 4, 2024).

97. Kate Egner Gruber, *The History of Williamsburg*, AMERICAN BATTLEFIELD TRUST, https://www.battlefields.org/learn/articles/history-williamsburg (last visited Feb. 4, 2024); *History*, CITY OF WILLIAMSBURG, https://www.williamsburgva.gov/488/History (last visited Feb. 4, 2024); *see also* Charles E. Hatch, *The "Affair Near James Island"* (or, *"The Battle of Green Spring"*), 53 VA. MAG. OF HIST. & BIOGRAPHY 172 (1945); *About Colonial Williamsburg*, COLONIAL WILLIAMSBURG, https://www.colonial williamsburg.org/learn/about-colonial-williamsburg/ (last visited Nov. 19, 2023).

98. *Our Organization*, COLONIAL WILLIAMSBURG, https://www.colonialwilliamsburg.org /learn/about-colonial-williamsburg/our-organization/ (last visited Nov. 19, 2023).

99. *See Know Before You Go*, COLONIAL WILLIAMSBURG, https://www.colonialwilliams burg.org/visit/know-before-you-go/?from=home (last visited Nov. 19, 2023); *Meet Our Nation Builders*, COLONIAL WILLIAMSBURG, https://www.colonialwilliamsburg.org /explore/nation-builders/ (last visited Nov. 19, 2023); *History of Colonial Williamsburg*, COLONIAL WILLIAMSBURG, https://www.colonialwilliamsburg.org/learn/about -colonial-williamsburg/history/?from=navabout (last visited Nov. 19, 2023); *James Armistead Lafayette*, COLONIAL WILLIAMSBURG, https://www.colonialwilliamsburg .org/explore/nation-builders/james-armistead-lafayette/ (last visited Nov. 19, 2023); *Historic Trade: Cabinetmaker & Harpsichord Maker*, COLONIAL WILLIAMSBURG, https://www.colonialwilliamsburg.org/locations/cabinetmaker-harpsichord-maker / (last visited Nov. 19, 2023); *Historic Trade: Blacksmith*, COLONIAL WILLIAMSBURG, https://www.colonialwilliamsburg.org/locations/anderson-blacksmith-shop-and -public-armoury/ (last visited Feb. 4, 2024); *Historic Trade: Weaver*, COLONIAL WILLIAMSBURG, https://www.colonialwilliamsburg.org/locations/weaver/ (last visited Feb. 4, 2024).

100. *Bray-Diggs House, Original Home of the 18th Century Williamsburg Bray School, Moves from William & Mary to Colonial Williamsburg Historic Area*, COLONIAL WILLIAMSBURG, https://media.colonialwilliamsburg.org/media/documents/01182023 _Press_Release_BraySchoolMove.pdf (last visited Nov. 19, 2023); *Williamsburg Bray School*, COLONIAL WILLIAMSBURG, https://www.colonialwilliamsburg.org/learn /research-and-education/architectural-research/williamsburg-bray-school-initiative / (last visited Nov. 19, 2023).

101. JN interview with Mia Nagawiecki.

102. *See, e.g.*, George Washington, *Eighth Annual Message to the United States Senate and House of Representatives (Dec. 7, 1796)* in THE PAPERS OF GEORGE WASHINGTON 321 (Jennifer E. Steenshorne, ed., 2020).

103. *The Constitution Drafting Project*, NATIONAL CONSTITUTION CENTER, https:// constitutioncenter.org/news-debate/special-projects/constitution-drafting-project (last visited Nov. 19, 2023); *Introduction to the Progressive Constitution*, NA-TIONAL CONSTITUTION CENTER, https://constitutioncenter.org/news-debate/special -projects/constitution-drafting-project/the-progressive-constitution/introduction

-to-the-progressive-constitution (last visited Nov. 19, 2023); JN interview with Jeffrey Rosen.

104. *Jared Sparks to James Madison, 30 March 1831*, NATIONAL ARCHIVES, https://founders .archives.gov/documents/Madison/99-02-02-2315; *see also* Thomas B. Griffith, *Civic Charity and the Constitution*, 43 HARV. J. L. & PUB. POL'Y. 633, 635 (2020); Derek A. Webb, *The Original Meaning of Civility: Democratic Deliberation at the Philadelphia Constitutional Convention*, 64 S.C. L. REV. 183, 197 (2012).

105. Derek A. Webb, *The Original Meaning of Civility: Democratic Deliberation at the Philadelphia Constitutional Convention*, 64 S.C. L. REV. 183, 196 (2012).

106. DANIEL WEBSTER, AN ANNIVERSARY ADDRESS, DELIVERED BEFORE THE FEDERAL GENTLEMEN OF CONCORD AND ITS VICINITY 2 (1806).

107. Derek A. Webb, *The Original Meaning of Civility: Democratic Deliberation at the Philadelphia Constitutional Convention*, 64 S.C. L. REV. 183, 190, 192 (2012).

108. JOHN P. KAMINSKI, SECRECY AND THE CONSTITUTIONAL CONVENTION 7 (2005).

109. RETURN OF THE WHOLE NUMBER OF PERSONS WITHIN THE SEVERAL DISTRICTS OF THE UNITED STATES 3 (1793); 1 THE RECORDS OF THE FEDERAL CONVENTION OF 1787 10–11 n.* (Max Farrand ed., 1911); Derek A. Webb, *The Original Meaning of Civility: Democratic Deliberation at the Philadelphia Constitutional Convention*, 64 S.C. L. REV. 183, 194 (2012).

110. STEPHEN L. CARTER, CIVILITY: MANNERS, MORALS, AND THE ETIQUETTE OF DEMOC-RACY 23, 132 (1998).

111. Charles Homans & Alyce McFadden, *Today's Politics Divide Parties, and Friends and Families, Too*, N.Y. TIMES (Oct. 18, 2022), https://www.nytimes.com/2022/10/18/us /politics/political-division-friends-family.html.

112. *Cross-Tabs for October 2022 Times/Siena Poll of Registered Voters*, N.Y. TIMES (Oct. 18, 2022), https://www.nytimes.com/interactive/2022/10/18/upshot/times-siena-poll -registered-voters-crosstabs.html.

113. David Brooks, *The Retreat to Tribalism*, N.Y. TIMES (Jan. 1, 2018), https://www.ny times.com/2018/01/01/opinion/the-retreat-to-tribalism.html; *As Partisan Hostility Grows, Signs of Frustration with the Two-Party System*, PEW RESEARCH CENTER (Aug. 9, 2022), https://www.pewresearch.org/politics/2022/08/09/as-partisan -hostility-grows-signs-of-frustration-with-the-two-party-system/.

114. *As Partisan Hostility Grows, Signs of Frustration with the Two-Party System*, PEW RESEARCH CENTER (Aug. 9, 2022), https://www.pewresearch.org/politics/2022/08 /09/as-partisan-hostility-grows-signs-of-frustration-with-the-two-party-system/.

115. John Villasenor, *Views Among College Students Regarding the First Amendment: Results from a New Survey*, BROOKINGS INSTITUTION (Sep. 18, 2017), https:// www.brookings.edu/articles/views-among-college-students-regarding-the-first -amendment-results-from-a-new-survey/.

116. Christopher St. Aubin & Jacob Liedke, *Most Americans Favor Restrictions on False Information, Violent Content Online*, PEW RESEARCH CENTER (July 20, 2023), https://www.pewresearch.org/short-reads/2023/07/20/most-americans-favor -restrictions-on-false-information-violent-content-online/.

117. John F. Kennedy, *Remarks on the 20th Anniversary of the Voice of America, 26 February 1962*, JOHN F. KENNEDY PRESIDENTIAL LIBRARY AND MUSEUM, https://www .jfklibrary.org/asset-viewer/archives/JFKWHA/1962/JFKWHA-075-005/JFK WHA-075-005.

118. David Brooks, *The Retreat to Tribalism*, N.Y. TIMES (Jan. 1, 2018), https://www .nytimes.com/2018/01/01/opinion/the-retreat-to-tribalism.html; *see generally, e.g.,* STEPHEN L. CARTER, CIVILITY: MANNERS, MORALS, AND THE ETIQUETTE OF DEMOC-RACY (1998).

119. George Packer, *A New Report Offers Insights into Tribalism in the Age of Trump*, NEW YORKER (Oct. 12, 2018), https://www.newyorker.com/news/daily-comment/a-new -report-offers-insights-into-tribalism-in-the-age-of-trump.

120. STEPHEN L. CARTER, CIVILITY: MANNERS, MORALS, AND THE ETIQUETTE OF DEMOC-RACY 13-14 (1998).

121. *The Stand No. VII [21 April 1798]*, NATIONAL ARCHIVES, https://founders.archives. gov/documents/Hamilton/01-21-02-0242; *Letter from Thomas Jefferson to George Washington, 9 September 1792*, NATIONAL ARCHIVES, https://founders.archives.gov

/documents/Jefferson/01-24-02-0330; *see also* Mary Kay Linge, *How Hatred Between Hamilton and Jefferson Gave Rise to a Polarized US*, N.Y. POST (July 3, 2021), https://nypost.com/2021/07/03/how-hamilton-and-jeffersons-hatred-gave-rise-to-a-polarized-us/.

122. STEPHEN L. CARTER, CIVILITY: MANNERS, MORALS, AND THE ETIQUETTE OF DEMOCRACY 14 (1998) (canings); Becky Little, *Violence in Congress Before the Civil War: From Canings and Stabbings to Murder*, HISTORY (July 24, 2019), https://www.history.com/news/charles-sumner-caning-cilley-duel-congressional-violence; *see also generally* JOANNE B. FREEMAN, THE FIELD OF BLOOD: VIOLENCE IN CONGRESS AND THE ROAD TO CIVIL WAR (2018).

123. Sedition Act, ch. 74, 1 Stat. 596 (1798) (expired 1801).

124. Michael Kent Curtis, *The Fraying Fabric of Freedom: Crisis and Criminal Law in Struggles for Democracy and Freedom of Expression*, 44 TEX. TECH L. REV. 89, 96–97 (2011); Ronald G. Shafer, *The Thin-Skinned President Who Made It Illegal to Criticize His Office*, WASH. POST (Sep. 8, 2018), https://www.washingtonpost.com/news/retropolis/wp/2018/09/08/the-thin-skinned-president-who-made-it-illegal-to-criticize-his-office/.

125. Arthur C. Brooks, *Our Culture of Contempt*, N.Y. TIMES (Mar. 2, 2019), https://www.nytimes.com/2019/03/02/opinion/sunday/political-polarization.html.

126. JN interview with Jeffrey Rosen.

127. Jeffrey Rosen & Sal Khan, *How Ideological Foes United on Ideas for Amending the Constitution*, WASH. POST (Feb. 1, 2023), https://www.washingtonpost.com/opinions/2023/02/01/ideological-foes-amendment-constitution.

128. *See* DECLARATION OF INDEPENDENCE OF THE DEMOCRATIC REPUBLIC OF VIETNAM (Sep. 2, 1945); DECLARATION OF INDEPENDENCE OF THE CZECHOSLOVAK NATION (Oct. 28, 1918).

129. Abraham Lincoln, *Peoria Speech, October 16, 1854*, NATIONAL PARK SERVICE, https://www.nps.gov/liho/learn/historyculture/peoriaspeech.htm; *see also* Abraham Lincoln, *The Gettysburg Address, November 19, 1863*, LIBRARY OF CONGRESS, https://www.abrahamlincolnonline.org/lincoln/speeches/gettysburg.htm.

130. *Seneca Falls Declaration (1848)*, NATIONAL CONSTITUTION CENTER, https://constitutioncenter.org/the-constitution/historic-document-library/detail/seneca-falls-declaration-1848 (emphasis added).

131. *Read Martin Luther King Jr.'s "I Have a Dream" Speech in Its Entirety*, NPR (Jan. 16, 2023), https://www.npr.org/2010/01/18/122701268/i-have-a-dream-speech-in-its-entirety.

132. George P. Fletcher, *Ambivalence About Treason*, 82 N.C. L. REV. 1611, 1614 (2004); Lee Habeeb, *A Letter to the University of Virginia's President on Jefferson's Legacy*, NEWSWEEK (Sep. 7, 2022), https://www.newsweek.com/letter-university-virginias-president-jeffersons-legacy-1740700.

133. *Founding Fathers on the Declaration of Independence*, NATIONAL PARK SERVICE, https://www.nps.gov/inde/learn/historyculture/resources-declaration-quotes.htm (last visited Feb 4, 2024).

134. NATIONAL PARK SERVICE, SIGNERS OF THE DECLARATION: HISTORIC PLACES COMMEMORATING THE SIGNING OF THE DECLARATION 31 (Robert G. Ferris ed., 1973).

135. NATIONAL PARK SERVICE, SIGNERS OF THE DECLARATION: HISTORIC PLACES COMMEMORATING THE SIGNING OF THE DECLARATION 48, 151 (Robert G. Ferris ed., 1973); *see also* Nathaniel Dwight, SKETCHES OF THE LIVES OF THE SIGNERS OF THE DECLARATION OF INDEPENDENCE 146 (1830); B.J. LOSSING, BIOGRAPHICAL SKETCHES OF THE SIGNERS OF THE DECLARATION OF AMERICAN INDEPENDENCE 91–92 n.* (1856).

136. NATIONAL PARK SERVICE, SIGNERS OF THE DECLARATION: HISTORIC PLACES COMMEMORATING THE SIGNING OF THE DECLARATION 31 (Robert G. Ferris ed., 1973).

137. NATIONAL PARK SERVICE, SIGNERS OF THE DECLARATION: HISTORIC PLACES COMMEMORATING THE SIGNING OF THE DECLARATION 31, 94–95 (Robert G. Ferris ed., 1973); NATHANIEL DWIGHT, SKETCHES OF THE LIVES OF THE SIGNERS OF THE DECLARATION OF INDEPENDENCE 112 (1830); CHARLES A. GOODRICH, LIVES OF THE SIGNERS OF THE DECLARATION OF INDEPENDENCE 196 (8th ed. 1840); B.J. LOSSING, BIOGRAPHICAL SKETCHES OF THE SIGNERS OF THE DECLARATION OF AMERICAN INDEPENDENCE 73 (1856).

138. NATHANIEL DWIGHT, SKETCHES OF THE LIVES OF THE SIGNERS OF THE DECLARATION OF INDEPENDENCE 142 (1830); B.J. LOSSING, BIOGRAPHICAL SKETCHES OF THE SIGNERS OF THE DECLARATION OF AMERICAN INDEPENDENCE 88–89 & n.† (1856).

139. NATIONAL PARK SERVICE, SIGNERS OF THE DECLARATION: HISTORIC PLACES COMMEMORATING THE SIGNING OF THE DECLARATION 112 (Robert G. Ferris ed., 1973); NATHANIEL DWIGHT, SKETCHES OF THE LIVES OF THE SIGNERS OF THE DECLARATION OF INDEPENDENCE 317 (1830); B.J. LOSSING, BIOGRAPHICAL SKETCHES OF THE SIGNERS OF THE DECLARATION OF AMERICAN INDEPENDENCE 192–93 & n.‡ (1856).

140. *Survey of Historic Sites and Buildings: Nelson House (Colonial National Historical Park)*, NATIONAL PARK SERVICE (July 4, 2004), https://www.nps.gov/parkhistory/online_books/declaration/site52.htm; NATIONAL PARK SERVICE, SIGNERS OF THE DECLARATION: HISTORIC PLACES COMMEMORATING THE SIGNING OF THE DECLARATION 248 (Robert G. Ferris ed., 1973).

141. *Brigadier General Thomas Nelson Jr.*, NATIONAL PARK SERVICE (Feb. 26, 2015), https://www.nps.gov/york/learn/historyculture/nelsonjrbio.htm; *see also* NATIONAL PARK SERVICE, SIGNERS OF THE DECLARATION: HISTORIC PLACES COMMEMORATING THE SIGNING OF THE DECLARATION 112 (Robert G. Ferris ed., 1973).

142. NATIONAL PARK SERVICE, SIGNERS OF THE DECLARATION: HISTORIC PLACES COMMEMORATING THE SIGNING OF THE DECLARATION 31 (Robert G. Ferris ed., 1973); Marvin L. Simner, *Why Did the Signers of the Declaration Engage in This Treasonous Act?*, J. OF THE AMERICAN REVOLUTION (Aug. 25, 2021), https://allthingsliberty.com/2021/08/did-the-signers-of-the-declaration-of-independence-engage-in-a-treasonous-act/ (quoting ANONYMOUS, AMERICAN'S OWN BOOK 12 (1857)). We are not the first to remark on the courage and personal sacrifices of those who signed the Declaration of Independence. Not all accounts of the signatories' stories have been accurate in their recounting of the facts. See, e.g., Ella Lee, *Fact Check: Decades-Old Essay About Declaration of Independence Signatories Is Partly False*, USA Today (July 12, 2021), https://www.usatoday.com/story/news/factcheck/2021/07/12/fact-check-declaration-independence-post-signers-partly-false/7926316002/. We remain grateful, nevertheless, for those individuals—whose identities are now unknown—who first so poignantly remarked on our founders' courage and fates.

143. GEORGE WASHINGTON, WASHINGTON'S RULES OF CIVILITY AND DECENT BEHAVIOR IN COMPANY AND CONVERSATION, LIBRARY OF CONGRESS (1888), https://www.loc.gov/resource/gdclccn.09030979/?st=gallery; *see also* Charles R. Kesler, *Civility and Citizenship in Washington's America and Ours*, 29 IMPRIMIS (2000), https://imprimis.hillsdale.edu/civility-and-citizenship-in-washingtons-america-and-ours/.

144. Plessy v. Ferguson, 163 U.S. 537, 559 (1896) (Harlan, J., dissenting), *overruled by* Brown v. Board of Education, 347 U.S. 483 (1954).

145. Brown v. Board of Education, 347 U.S. 483 (1954).

146. JN interview with Sandra Yates.

EPILOGUE

1.   ALEXANDER SOLZHENITSYN, WARNING TO THE WEST 53 (1976).

INFORMATION ON IMAGES

CHAPTER 1: AN INTRODUCTION TO LAW'S EMPIRE

Page 10: © Thomas Bender, USA TODAY NETWORK
Page 12: Sandra Yates
Page 17: Reg Stats, Regulatory Studies Center, The George Washington University

CHAPTER 2: FAR FROM HOME

Page 34: Photographer Samuel Hamilton, in HARRY C. FREEMAN, A BRIEF HISTORY OF BUTTE, MONTANA: THE WORLD'S GREATEST MINING CAMP 71 (1900)
Page 36: Image 941-880, Montana Historical Society Research Center Photograph Archives, Helena, MT
Page 36: Library of Congress, Prints & Photographs Division, Harris & Ewing Collection, https://loc.gov/pictures/resource/hec.14962/
Page 37: Photographer Samuel Hamilton, in HARRY C. FREEMAN, A BRIEF HISTORY OF BUTTE, MONTANA: THE WORLD'S GREATEST MINING CAMP 90 (1900)
Page 40: Photo by Arthur Rothstein, 1939. Library of Congress, Prints & Photographs Division, Farm Security Administration/Office of War Information Collection, https://www.loc.gov/item/2017777816/
Page 46: Data from the White House Office of Management and Budget
Page 51: Ca'Jon Martin, Digital Media Marketing Manager, The Kalamazoo Promise
Page 58: Arthur Estabrook Papers, M.E. Grenander Special Collections & Archives, University at Albany, SUNY
Page 59: Library of Congress, Prints & Photographs Division, National Photo Company Collection, www.loc.gov/item/2016849747/

CHAPTER 3: BUREAUCRACY UNBOUND

Page 67: Marty Hahne
Page 70: Ernest Hemingway Photographs Collection, John F. Kennedy Presidential Library and Museum, Boston, MA

CHAPTER 4: THE SWORD OF DAMOCLES

Page 102: © Bettmann/Getty Images
Page 107: The Heritage Foundation, *Count the Code: Quantifying Federalization of Criminal Statutes*
Page 124: Sage Ross/Creative Commons Attribution—Sharealike 2.0
Page 130: Illustration in *History of the City of New York*, by Martha J. Lamb and Mrs. Burton Harrison, 1877. Library of Congress, Prints & Photographs Division, National Photo Company Collection, https://www.loc.gov/resource/cph.3a49841

CHAPTER 5: THE FORGOTTEN AMERICANS

Page 142: Photo Courtesy of American Farmland Trust
Page 146: Saint Joseph Abbey
Page 154: Hartford Courant

CHAPTER 6: THREE FREEDOMS

Page 162: Becket Fund for Religious Liberty
Page 174: Priscilla Sekula
Page 178: Institute for Justice

CHAPTER 7: THE SPIRIT OF LIBERTY

Page 186: Photo by the Office of Emergency Management, 1941–1943. Library of Congress, Prints & Photographs Division, Farm Security Administration/Office of War Information Collection, https://www.loc.gov/resource/fsa.8b01552/

Page 196: © CQ Archive/Getty Images

Page 205: National Park Service

INDEX

Italicized page numbers refer to photographs and charts.

actus reus, criminal law and, 115
Adams, John, 209, 211
addiction recovery, effect of covid-19
  restrictions on, 170–71, 174–75
administrative law judges (ALJs), 79–80, 87
Administrative Procedure Act (APA),
  86–93, 190
Administrative Process, The (Landis), 188
administrative state. *See* agencies; ordered
  liberty
agencies, 66–100
  Administrative Procedure Act and
    lack of judicial review, 86–93,
    190
  appeals to and administrative law
    judges, 77–80
  concerns about "fourth branch"
    of government and, 84–85,
    193, 210
  consequences to individual liberty,
    97–100
  Constitution and presidential
    oversight of, 80–84
  criminal law and, 108–9
  guidance documents and, 17–18,
    88, 139, 148
  Landis and administrative state,
    185–92
  legislative power transferred away
    from elected representatives
    to, 84–85, 95
  licensing examples, 66–73
  list of recently created federal
    agencies, 44–45
  quasi-legislative and quasi-judicial
    powers of, 73–74, 83–87
  Wilson and "public
    administration," 81, 93–97
  see also ordered liberty
airline deregulation, 195–98
Airline Deregulation Act (1978), 197
Alschuler, Albert, 126
Amazon, 156
American Bar Association (ABA), 19, 21,
  78, 85–86, 107

Amish families, septic systems and
  application of laws, 132–36
apple orchard, compliance costs of
  regulations and, 142–43
Arendt, Hannah, 15, 28, 100
Arizona, 194
Articles of Confederation, 46
assembly. *See* freedom of assembly
Atlantic Richfield Company, 39–41

Baker, Thomas, 18
Baltimore Sun, The, 199
Barnett, Randy, 158–59
Ben Franklin's World podcast, 203
Beria, Lavrentiy, 22–23
Best and the Brightest, The (Halberstam),
  49–50
Bethany Christian Services, 166
Bezos, Jeff, 156
Biestek, Michael, 79–80, 88, 90–91
Bill of Rights. *See* freedom of assembly;
  freedom of speech
Bleak House (Dickens), 151
Board of Immigration Appeals (BIA), 92,
  140, 141
Bowling Alone (Putnam), 24, 168–69
Brandeis, Louis, 1–2, 17–18, 47, 131, 159, 187
Brantley, Isis, 177–79, *178*, 183–84
Bray School, 203
Brennan, William J., Jr., 77
Breyer, Stephen, 91, 118, 195–98, *196*, 201
Brown, Abbot Justin, *146*
Brown v. Board of Education, 54, 61, 213
Buck, Carrie, 54–61, *58*
Buck v. Bell, 57–59, 61
Buckley, James L., 53
Bush, George W., 73–74
Butte, MT, Superfund cleanup and federal
  versus state authority, 33–42, *37*, *40*, 61

California
  covid-19 pandemic and, 153, 155, 172
  eugenics and, 56
  foster care and, 164
  licensing and, 195

cancer. *See* Butte, MT
Caring Hearts, 2–3
Carter, Stephen, 206, 208
caskets, regulatory capture and, 144–47, *146*
Catholic Social Services (CSS), in
　　Philadelphia, 162–67
cats. *See* Hemingway, Ernest
Census Bureau, 171
Centers for Disease Control (CDC),
　　covid-19 restrictions and, 152, 171,
　　174–75
chain of dependence, of Madison, 81, 83
Chesterton, G. K., 55–56
*Chevron v. Natural Resources Defense
　　Council*, 89, 90, 140
Citizenship Day, 199
civic education, importance to liberty,
　　198–204
civic life, laws and decline in trust, 23–25,
　　31–32, 168–69, 215
Civil Aeronautics Board (CAB)
　　　　federal regulatory reforms and,
　　　　195–98, 201
　　　　Landis and, 188–89, 190
civil dialogue
　　　　contemporary challenges of,
　　　　207–10
　　　　drafters of Constitution and,
　　　　204–7
Civil Rights Act (1964), 16
Clark, William A., 35, *36*, 61
Code of Federal Regulations, 17, *17*, 73,
　　108, 139
Cole, David, 110
*Collapse of American Criminal Justice,
　　The* (Stuntz), 128
Colonial Williamsburg Foundation, 203
compliance costs, of following laws and
　　regulations, 141–44
Computer Fraud and Abuse Act (1986), 123
Connecticut, *154*
Consolidated Appropriations Act (2021), 16
Constitution, of U.S.
　　　　Article I and legislative powers, 76
　　　　Article II and executive power,
　　　　80–84
　　　　Article III and jury trials, 126
　　　　balance of state and federal powers
　　　　in, 46–50
　　　　civic education and, 198–204
　　　　Constitution Convention and civil
　　　　dialogue, 204–7, *205*
　　　　First Amendment freedoms, 159,
　　　　160–67, 207–8
　　　　Fourth Amendment and searches,
　　　　125
　　　　law-making as focus of, 15–16,
　　　　25–29, 96
　　　　Madison and, 6, 26–28, 137–38

mediation of freedom and rule of
　　law in, 192–93
Nineteenth Amendment and
　　women's suffrage, 52
Seventeenth Amendment and
　　election of senators, 35
Sixth Amendment and jury trials,
　　126
Wilson and administrative state,
　　94–97
Constitution Day, 199
contra proferentem, courts and, 89
Cooney, Frank and Vickie, 33–34, 41–42
copper. *See* Butte, MT
Cosby, William, 129
Coudrain, Mark, *146*
Council of Economic Advisors, 182–83
covid-19 pandemic
　　　　changing rules and regulations
　　　　regarding, 151–55, *154*
　　　　economic consequences of
　　　　response to, 155–57
　　　　federal authorities and, 48, 111
　　　　restrictions on freedom of
　　　　assembly and, 159, 167–77
Credit Suisse, 156
criminal law
　　　　fair notice demand and, 117–20
　　　　increase in number of federal
　　　　crimes, 105–9, *107*
　　　　increase in punishments and
　　　　prison terms, 109–13
　　　　mens rea requirements and, 115–17
　　　　rule of lenity and, 120–21
　　　　shift from individual to collective
　　　　interests and, 114–17
　　　　trend to plea agreements and away
　　　　from jury trials, 122–31
　　　　Unser and, 101–5, *102*, 108, 116–17,
　　　　125, 126
Cummings, Homer, 82

Daly, Marcus, 35–36, *36*
De Niz Robles, Alfonzo, 139–41
Declaration of Independence, 15, 25, *96*, 159
　　　　courage of contemporary
　　　　defenders of rights, 212–14
　　　　courage of signers in defense of
　　　　rights, 210–12
　　　　250th anniversary of, 210
deference doctrines, agencies and, 72, 90,
　　99, 140–41
Department of Agriculture, 67
Department of Commerce, 143
Department of Defense, 43
Department of Education, 23, 109
Department of Health and Human
　　Services, 74
Department of Justice, 21, 92, 110, 118

Department of the Treasury, 182–83
Department of Transportation, 73
Department of Veterans Affairs, 91
Dickens, Charles, 151
Donovan, William "Wild Bill," 82–83
Douglas, William O., 25, 77
du Brissac, Bronislava, 199

Economist, The, 109
Einstein, Alfred, 200
Engineering and Mining Journal, 36–37
England, Trent, 111
Environmental Protection Agency (EPA),
39–41, 118
e pluribus unum, Constitution Convention
and civil dialogue, 204–7
equality under the law, increase in number
of laws and, 132–57
Amish families and septic system
laws, 132–36
compliance costs and apple
orchards, 141–44
covid-19 pandemic regulations
and, 151–57
De Niz Robles and immigration,
139–41
difficulty for individuals to find
relevant statutes, 138–41
Madison's concerns about too
much law, 136–38
need for lawyers and, 147–51
regulatory capture and caskets,
144–47
eugenics, state versus federal governments
and, 54–61
Eugenics and Other Evils (Chesterton),
55–56
executive orders, 1–2
covid-19 pandemic and, 152–55,
175–76
eyebrow threading, licensing and
restrictions on, 179–84

Facebook, 153
fair notice demand, criminal law and, 117–20
Federal Register, 2, 17–19
Federal Reserve, 156
Federal Trade Commission (FTC), 79,
81–82, 84, 95, 96, 187
federalism
Butte, MT, and federal versus state
authority, 33–42
Carrie Buck, eugenics, and federal
versus state authority, 54–61
Constitution and balance of state
and federal powers, 26, 46–50
importance of individual's
participation in state and local
government, 61–65

states as laboratories of democracy,
47, 50–54, 192–95
transfer of authority from states to
federal government, 42–45, *46*
Federalist No. 62, 138
Ferguson, Niall, 24
Feulner, Edwin J., Jr., 99
51 Imperfect Solutions (Sutton), 54
firearms, rule of lenity and, 121
First Amendment. *See* freedom of
assembly; freedom of speech
fishing
administrative law judges and, 79
compliance costs of regulations
and, 143
Sarbanes-Oxley Act and, 9–14, 16,
23, 29–31
Florida, 154, 194
Food and Drug Administration (FDA), 74
Forbes, 19
Fortune, 191
foster care, freedom of religious speech
and, 159, 160–67
"fourth branch" of government. *See*
agencies
Frankfurter, Felix, 187
Franklin, Benjamin, 75, 167
freedom of assembly, covid-19 restrictions
on, 159, 167–77
freedom of speech
foster care and religious principles,
159, 160–67
growing contemporary intolerance
of, 207, 208
Friedman, Milton, 183
Fulton, Sharonell, 161, *162*, 163–64, 166

Galton, Francis, 55, 95
Gayton, Robert, 102–3
George, Kevin, 91, 93, 99
Gerken, Heather, 53
Germany, Nazi era and eugenics in, 59–60
Gerry, Elbridge, 211
Ginsburg, Douglas, 145
Ginsburg, Ruth Bader, 80
Glasscock, C. B., 34
Gonzales, Jimmy, *174*
Graeger, David, 85
Grossman, Andrew M., 111
guidance documents, to rules and
regulations, 17–18, 88, 139, 148

Hahne, Marty, 66–69, *67,* 73–74
hair braiding, licensing and restrictions on,
177–80
Halberstam, David, 49–50
Hamburger, Philip, 78–79
Hamilton, Alexander, 208–9
Hamilton, Andrew, 129–30

Hand, Learned, *95–96, 99,* 198–99, 208
Harlan, John Marshall II, 117, 212–13
Harrison, Benjamin, 211
Hart, Henry M., Jr., 105, 119–20
Hart, John, 211–12
Harvard Magazine, 55
Havel, Vaclav, 3–4, 6–7
Hayek, Friedrich, 32, 97, 99
Hayes, Paul, 128
hazardous waste. *See* Butte, MT
Hearst, William Randolph, 199
Hemingway, Ernest, 69–73, *70,* 89
Hill, The, 98
Hip Pocket Incident, 1–2
Holmes, Oliver Wendell, Jr., 57–59, *59,* 115
Holt, Charles, 209
Hoolahan, Shaun, 33–34, 39, 41–42
Howard, Philip K., 20, 144
Hughes, Charles Evans, 2
Humphrey, William, 81–84
Husak, Douglas, 106

"I Am An American Day," 199, 200, 208
"I Miss Singing at Church" (*New York Times*), 176–77
iCivics, 202
Idaho, 193, 194
identity theft, fair notice demand and, 119
Independence Hall, in Philadelphia, *205*
Institute for the Advancement of the American Legal System, 195
Internal Revenue Service (IRS), 118, 133, 191–92
International Conference of Funeral Service Examining Boards, 146–47

Jackson, Robert H., 84, 115, 160
Jefferson, Thomas, 129, 137, 199, 201, 202, 208
Johnson, Lyndon, 49–50
JSTOR, 122–23
judicial review, APA and lack of, 86–93
jury trials, criminal justice trends and, 125–31

Kagan, Elena, 96, 188
Kahn, Alfred, 197
Kalamazoo Promise, 50–51, *51,* 61
Kennedy, Edward, 195–98, *196*
Kennedy, John F., 189–91, 193, 200, 208
Kennedy, Joseph, Sr., 189
Kennedy, Robert F., 191
Kethledge, Raymond, 90
Khan, Sal, 210
King, Martin Luther, Jr., 211

Lafayette, James Armistead, 203
Landis, James M., *95, 186,* 193
    administrative state and career of, 81, 185–92, *196*

laws, generally
    ambiguity and, 73–77, 89, 121
    consequences of too many, to trust and civic bonds, 23–25, 31–32, 168–69, 215
    increase in length and number of laws, 4–6, 16–23
    increase in state and local as well as federal laws, 18–19
    judicial decisions and, 18
    necessary for ordered liberty, 158–59
    see also criminal law; equality under the law; licensing laws
lawyers
    regulations and citizens' need for, 147–51
    states and regulatory reform and, 194–95
Legal Zoom, 149
"Legend of Landis, The" (*Fortune*), 191
lenity, rule of, 120–21
Lessig, Lawrence, 122, 124–25
liberty. *See* ordered liberty
licensing laws
    Hahne and rabbit, 66–69
    hair braiding and eyebrow threading and, 177–84
    Hemingway's cats and, 69–73
    monks and burial caskets, 106
    states and reform of, 194
Lincoln, Abraham, 210–11
LinkedIn, 153–54
Little, Erica A., 111
Liu, Goodwin, 53–54
Locke, John, 158
loneliness
    covid-19 restrictions and, 170–77
    epidemic of, 65
    see also freedom of assembly
Louisiana, 144–47, 182

MacArthur, Douglas, 199
Madison, James, 75, 202
    chain of dependence of, 81, 83
    civil dialogue and, 206
    Constitution and, 6, 26–28, 75, 206, 210
    on effects of too many laws, 137–38
    federalism and, 47, 48
Malone, Michael P., 34
Marshall, John, 76, 89, 120–21
Maryland, 182
Massachusetts, 18–19, 155, 172
Massachusetts Institute of Technology (MIT), 122–23, 125
Mast, Amos and Mattie, 134–36
McCraw, Thomas K., 185
McNeil, C. B., 38

meden agan ("nothing in excess"), 32
mens rea, criminal law and, 115–17, 127, 131
Mill, John Stuart, 159–60
mining. *See* Butte, MT
Minnesota, 134–36
Miss Katie (Yateses' boat), 11–12, *12*
Missionary Sisters of the Blessed Trinity, 162–63
Momin, Nazira, 180
More in Common, 209
Morissette, Joseph, 114–17, 138
Morris, Gouverneur, 28
Muscarello v. United States, 121
Myers, Serge, 40, 42
Myers v. United States, 82–84, 187

Nader, Ralph, 197
National Association of Criminal Defense Lawyers, 108–9
National Constitution Center, 201–2, 204, 209–10
National Oceanic and Atmospheric Administration, 109
Nelson, Ben, 46
Nelson, K. Ray, 60
Nelson, Thomas, J., 212
nemo judex in causa sua, courts and, 89
Nevada, 154–55
New City City, 19, 64
New Jersey, 56, 193
New York State, 155, 193
New York Times, 19, 51, 72, 122, 142–43, 171, 175–76
New Yorker, 153
New-York Weekly Journal, 129–30
Nivola, Pietro, 42–43
Nixon, Richard M., 85
No Child Left Behind Act (2001), 16
Norris, George, 111–13, 126
nursing homes, covid-19 restrictions on freedom of assembly and, 171, *174*, 175
Nyman, Rose, 34, 41–42

Obama, Barack, 74, 97–98, 198
O'Brien, Justin, 185
Occupational Safety and Health Administration, 48, 152
O'Connor, Sandra Day, 202
Office of Management and Budget, 74
Ohio, 194
orchids, federal laws and, 111–13
ordered liberty, 185–214
    administrative state and, 185–92
    CAB and federal deregulation, 195–98
    civic education's importance to, 198–204
    civil dialogue's importance to, 204–10

courage of citizens in defense of rights, 210–14
freedom of assembly and covid-19 restrictions, 159, 167–77
freedom of religious speech and foster care, 159, 160–67
laws impact on, 158–59
pursuit of happiness and cosmetology licensing, 159, 177–84
states as laboratories of democracy, 47, 50–54, 192–95
Orwell, George, 160

Pacific Legal Foundation, 74
Packer, George, 208
Page, John, 168
Paine, Thomas, 15
Parkinson, C. Northcote, 20
Patel, Ashish, *178*, 180, 181, 184
Patel, Pankajkumar, 91–93
Patient Protection and Affordable Care Act, 16
Paul, Cecilia, 161–62, 166
Paul, Thomas, 162, 163
People for the Ethical Treatment of Animals (PETA), 72
Pestritto, Ronald J., 94, 95
Pew Research Center, 64, 207–8
Philadelphia, PA
    election turnout in, 64
    foster care system and religious speech, 161–67
Philadelphia Inquirer, 164–65
Pius XI, Pope, 48
plea agreements, criminal law and trend toward, 122–31
"Plea Bargaining and Its History" (Alschuler), 126
Plessy v. Ferguson, 53–54, 213
Postal Act (1792), 75–76
Pound, Roscoe, 85, 187
prison terms, effects of increase in federal laws on, 109–13
Prussia, Wilson and, 93–94
Public Access to Court Electronic Records (PACER), 122
public administration, Wilson and, 93–97
Punke, Michael, 34
"pursuit of happiness," right of, 159
    licensing for hair braiding and eyebrow threading and, 177–84
Putnam, Robert, 24, 168–69

quasi-legislative and quasi-judicial powers, of agencies, 73–74, 83–87

rabbits. *See* Hahne, Marty
Rajabali, Nasim, 180

Rakoff, Jed, 109
Rao, Neomi, 74
Rayburn, Sam, 50
Raz, Joseph, 28
Reed, Chris, 169–70, 195
Reed, Stanley, 82–83
regulatory capture, 53, 197
　　caskets and, 144–47, *146*
　　lawyers and, 147–51
religious speech, foster care and freedom
　　of, 159, 160–67
Rhode Island, 193
Ritchie, Donald A., 185
Rockefeller, John D., 55
Rokhti, Tahereh, 180, 181
Roman Catholic Church
　　foster care and, 159, 190–97
　　"subsidiarity" and, 48
Roosevelt, Franklin D., 20, 81–84, 95,
　　96, 187
Roosevelt, Theodore, 55
Rosen, Jeffrey, 210
rule of law
　　deference documents and, 90
　　liberty and, 31, 136, 192–93
　　Madison and Constitution, 27–29
　　"too much law" and, 111
rule of lenity, 89, 120–21
*Rules of Civility and Decent Behavior
　　in Company and Conversation*
　　(Washington), 212
Rush, Benjamin, 211

Saint Joseph Abbey, 144–47
Sanger, Margaret, 55
Sarbanes-Oxley Act, fishing and, 9–14,
　　16, 23, 29–31
Sayre, Francis Bowes, 116
Schlesinger, Arthur, 167–68
Schoolhouse Rock! videos, 73
Science, 55
Scientific American, 55
Securities and Exchange Commission
　　(SEC), 78–79, 95, 187
Sedgwick, Theodore, 75, 168
Sedition Act, 209
Seneca Falls Convention (1848), 211
septic systems, and application of laws,
　　132–36
Silverglate, Harvey, 106
Simms-Busch, Toni, 161, 162, 163, 166
skateboard parks, covid-19 pandemic
　　and, 153, *154*
Small Business Administration, 144
Smith, Alice, 56
Social Security Administration, 20,
　　77–78, 80
Solzhenitsyn , Aleksandr, 215
Sotomayor, Sonia, 80, 91

*Sourcebook of United States Executive
　　Agencies*, 19
Sowell, Thomas, 85
speech. *See* freedom of speech
states, as laboratories for democracy, 47,
　　50–54, 192–95. *See also individual
　　states*
sterilization. *See* eugenics
Stigler, George, 197
Stuntz, William, 111, 128
suffrage
　　states and, 52
　　Wilson and, 94–95
Sumption, Jonathan, 173
Sunstein, Cass, 138–39
Superfund site. *See* Butte, MT
Supreme Court, of U.S.
　　Brown v. Board of Education, 54,
　　　61, 213
　　Buck v. Bell, 57–59, 61
　　Butte, MT clean up and, 41
　　case law library of, 202
　　*Chevron v. Natural Resources
　　　Defense Council*, 89, 90
　　Congress and legislative power, 76
　　eugenics and, 57–59
　　foster care and, 167
　　George and, 91, 93
　　Hayes and, 128
　　manslaughter on high seas and,
　　　120–21
　　Morissette and, 115
　　Muscarello v. United States, 121
　　Myers v. United States, 82–84, 187
　　Pankajkumar and, 92–93
　　Plessy v. Ferguson, 53–54, 213
　　Sarbanes-Oxley Act and fishing,
　　　14, 29
　　*West Virginia State Board of
　　　Education v. Barnette*, 160
Sutherland, George, 83–84
Sutton, Jeffery, 54, 56
Swartz, Aaron, 122–25, *124*, 126, 127
Swartzentruber Amish, 134–36

Taft, William Howard, 83, 187
Ten Eyck family, 142–43
Ten Eyck, Peter II, *142*
Texas
　　licensing for hair braiding and
　　　eyebrow threading, 177–84
　　"sunset" for agencies in, 193–94
Time magazine, 111, 199
Tocqueville, Alexis de, 23–24, 47, 62–65,
　　169, 177, 215
toto coelo, criminal law and, 120
Trollope, Frances, 208
Truman, Harry S., 85, 189, 190
Trump, Donald J., 198

Turley, Jonathan, 78
Twain, Mark, 35

United Kingdom, 150, 151
University of Northern Colorado, 63
Unser, Bobby, 101–5, *102*, 108, 116–17, 125, 126
U.S. Chamber Institute for Legal Reform, 109
U.S. Code, 16, 21, 117, 139
Utah, 194–95

Villasenor, John, 207
Virginia, 18, 206

Wall Street Journal, 78, 79
Washington, George, 137, 158, 212
Washington Post, The, 20, 38, 67, 144, 164, 209
Washington State, 164
Webb, Derek, 206
Weber, Max, 192

Webster, Daniel, 29, 205
Wechsler, Herbert, 105, 115
West Virginia State Board of Education v. Barnette, 160
Wilderness Act (1964), 104
Wilson, Carlton, 117–18, 119
Wilson, Woodrow
    eugenics and, 56
    public administration and, 81, 93–97
    suffrage and, 94–95
Wisconsin, 45
"wisdom of crowds," 95–96
Wong, Jeremy, 172–73
Works Progress Administration (WPA), 20
Wyoming, 52

Yates, John and Sandra, 9–14, *10*, 16, 23, 29–31, 109, 138, 143, 177, 213–14
Yogi, Vijay Lakshmi, 180, 181
YouTube, 154

Zenger, John, 129–31, *130*

ABOUT THE AUTHORS

NEIL GORSUCH is an Associate Justice of the United States Supreme Court. His most recent book, *A Republic, If You Can Keep It,* was a *New York Times* bestseller and won the 2022 Burton Award for Book of the Year in Law.

JANIE NITZE most recently served as a Senate-confirmed board member of the Privacy and Civil Liberties Oversight Board. Previously, she was a fellow at Harvard Law School, where her areas of scholarly interest focused on separation of powers and national security, and was an attorney with the Office of Legal Counsel in the Department of Justice. Janie received her B.A. in physics and her M.A. in statistics from Harvard University and her J.D. from Harvard Law School. She has clerked for Justices Sonia Sotomayor and Neil Gorsuch of the U.S. Supreme Court.